Computing Fundamentals
DIGITAL LITERACY EDITION

Faithe Wempen

Rosie Hattersley, Richard Millett, and Kate Shoup

WILEY

This edition first published 2014

Registered office

John Wiley & Sons Ltd, The Atrium, Southern Gate, Chichester, West Sussex, PO19 8SQ, United Kingdom

For details of our global editorial offices, for customer services and for information about how to apply for permission to reuse the copyright material in this book please see our website at www.wiley.com.

A catalogue record for this book is available from the British Library.

ISBN 978-1-118-97474-2 (paperback); 978-1-118-97472-8 (ePDF)

Set in 10 pt. ITC GalliardStd by TCS/SPS

Printed in the United Kingdom by Bell & Bain

To Margaret.

Publisher's Acknowledgements

Some of the people who helped bring this book to market include the following:

Editorial and Production
VP Consumer and Technology Publishing Director: Michelle Leete
Associate Director–Book Content Management: Martin Tribe
Associate Publisher: Chris Webb
Associate Commissioning Editor: Ellie Scott
Senior Project Editor: Sara Shlaer
Project Editor: Tom Dinse
Copy Editor: Debbye Butler
Technical Editors: Richard Millett, Nick Vandome
Editorial Manager: Rev Mengle
Editorial Assistant: Claire Johnson

Marketing
Marketing Manager: Lorna Mein
Associate Marketing Manager: Carrie Sherrill
Assistant Marketing Manager: Dave Allen

About the Author

Faithe Wempen, M.A., is a Microsoft Office Master Instructor, an A+ Certified PC technician, and an adjunct instructor of Computer Information Technology at Indiana University/Purdue University at Indianapolis. She is the author of more than 140 books on computer hardware and software, and her online courses have educated more than a quarter of a million students for corporate clients, including Hewlett Packard and Sony.

About the Contributors

Rosemary Hattersley is a U.K.-based tech journalist with extensive experience writing for *PC Advisor, Computeractive,* and *Macworld* as well as a number of other technology and business websites and publications. She is the author of *Hudl For Dummies* and co-author of Wiley's *iPad For the Older and Wiser,* 3rd Edition, both from Wiley.

Richard Millet is a lead instructor working for Firebrand Training. He has over 30 years of experience in the computer industry and has worked with all versions of Windows since its inception. He is responsible for producing training material for companies, specializing in computer security. He also delivers technical training on a wide variety of subjects to all age groups from college students upwards. He currently lives in Berkshire, England, with his wife Shelagh and Merlin the cat.

Kate Shoup has authored more than 30 books and has edited scores more. Kate has also co-written a feature-length screenplay (and starred in the ensuing film) and worked as the sports editor for *NUVO Newsweekly.* When not writing, Kate, an Indy Car fanatic, loves to ski, read, and ride her motorcycle. She lives in Indianapolis, Indiana, with her fiancé, her daughter, and their dog.

Acknowledgments

Thank you to my wonderful editing team at Wiley, including Chris Webb, Ellie Scott, Sara Shlaer, Tom Dinse, Richard Millett, Nick Vandome, and Debbye Butler, for keeping me on track and making my writing as good as it can be. Your professionalism and good humor made this a pleasant project, and your editing skills made it a quality product.

Contents at a Glance

Contents

Introduction

Welcome to *Computing Fundamentals Digital Literacy Edition!* This book is designed to prepare you for success in a modern world full of computers—not only the traditional computers such as desktop and notebook PCs, but also computers that you interact with in other places too, like your bank's ATM or your employer's computerized cash register. In this book, you will learn about the technologies that drive our computerized society, including the Internet and local area networks (LANs).

What You Will Learn

This book will help you become a digitally literate person—that is, someone who understands how computer technology fits into our modern society and knows how to navigate a variety of computing environments. The topics covered include the following:

- *Operating systems:* You'll compare major operating systems and learn what types of devices each operating system is designed to run on. You'll learn how to navigate in Windows 7 too, including how to run applications and manage files.
- *Computer hardware and concepts:* You'll learn about the physical parts of computers, including input, processing, output, and storage.
- *Computer software and concepts:* You will find out about the main types of application software and what each type is useful for. You'll learn how to choose, install, update, use, and remove applications in Windows 7.
- *Browsers:* You will learn how to use a web browser to find information on the Internet.
- *Networking concepts:* You will find out how computer networks work, including the hardware and software required for them.
- *Digital communication:* You will learn how to communicate online in a variety of ways, including email, instant messaging, video chat, and web conferencing.
- *Digital citizenship:* You will learn the etiquette standards and customs of the online world, and the legal and ethical issues involved in worldwide online computing.
- *Safe computing:* You'll find out what the dangers are in using the Internet and other networks and learn methods of protecting your privacy and safeguarding your computer and its data.

Chapter Features

Each chapter provides many different ways of helping you learn, not only in the printed book, but also in the online resource supplements. Here is a quick summary of the aids you will find in this book:

- **Learning Objectives:** Each chapter starts out with a list of learning objectives, giving you a practical look at what you will learn.

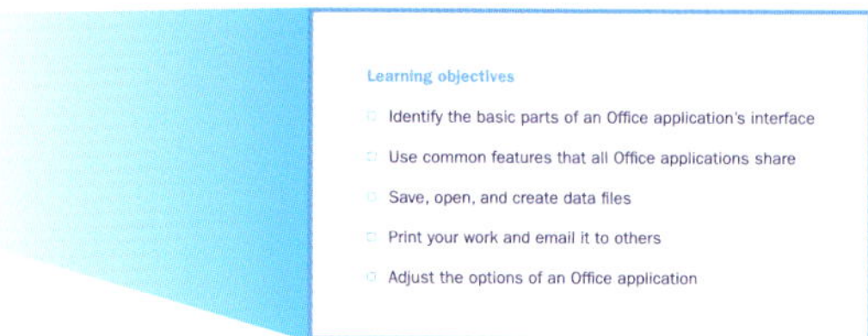

Learning objectives

- Identify the basic parts of an Office application's interface
- Use common features that all Office applications share
- Save, open, and create data files
- Print your work and email it to others
- Adjust the options of an Office application

- **Definitions:** Key terms appear in color in the text, and their definitions appear in the margin for easy lookup. The key terms are also compiled into a glossary in the back of the book.

Scrolling the display does not move the insertion point. To move the insertion point, click where you want it to go, or use the directional arrow keys on your keyboard to move it. In Excel, there is no insertion point, but a thick outline around the active cell shows the cell in which content will be entered.

insertion point The flashing vertical line that indicates where typed text will appear.

- **Notes, Tips, and Cautions:** These special-purpose notes appear in the text whenever there is extra information you should know.

Ctrl+S is the keyboard shortcut for the Save command; Ctrl+N is the shortcut for the New command (to start a new file); and Ctrl+O is the shortcut for the Open command to open an existing file). TIP

- **Careers in IT:** In these features, you will learn about some careers that relate to the topics you are studying.

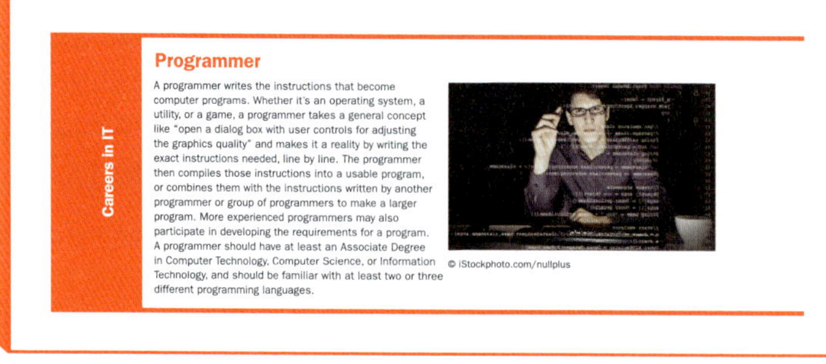

Careers in IT

Programmer

A programmer writes the instructions that become computer programs. Whether it's an operating system, a utility, or a game, a programmer takes a general concept like "open a dialog box with user controls for adjusting the graphics quality" and makes it a reality by writing the exact instructions needed, line by line. The programmer then compiles those instructions into a usable program, or combines them with the instructions written by another programmer or group of programmers to make a larger program. More experienced programmers may also participate in developing the requirements for a program. A programmer should have at least an Associate Degree in Computer Technology, Computer Science, or Information Technology, and should be familiar with at least two or three different programming languages.

© iStockphoto.com/nullplus

- **Put It to Work:** These features explain practical uses for the topics you are learning about, and in some cases suggest activities you can try to put the information to immediate use.

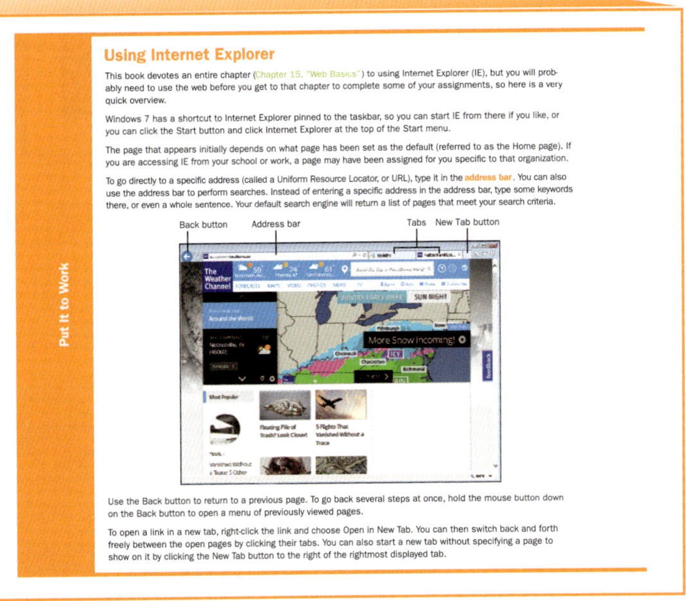

Put It to Work

Using Internet Explorer

This book devotes an entire chapter (Chapter 15, "Web Basics") to using Internet Explorer (IE), but you will probably need to use the web before you get to that chapter to complete some of your assignments, so here is a very quick overview.

Windows 7 has a shortcut to Internet Explorer pinned to the taskbar, so you can start IE from there if you like, or you can click the Start button and click Internet Explorer at the top of the Start menu.

The page that appears initially depends on what page has been set as the default (referred to as the Home page). If you are accessing IE from your school or work, a page may have been assigned for you specific to that organization.

To go directly to a specific address (called a Uniform Resource Locator, or URL), type it in the **address bar**. You can also use the address bar to perform searches. Instead of entering a specific address in the address bar, type some keywords there, or even a whole sentence. Your default search engine will return a list of pages that meet your search criteria.

Use the Back button to return to a previous page. To go back several steps at once, hold the mouse button down on the Back button to open a menu of previously viewed pages.

To open a link in a new tab, right-click the link and choose Open in New Tab. You can then switch back and forth freely between the open pages by clicking their tabs. You can also start a new tab without specifying a page to show on it by clicking the New Tab button to the right of the rightmost displayed tab.

- **Privacy and Security:** These features spotlight information that may be useful in keeping you safe from privacy and security violations, such as security features in an application or a type of hardware or software that enhances security.

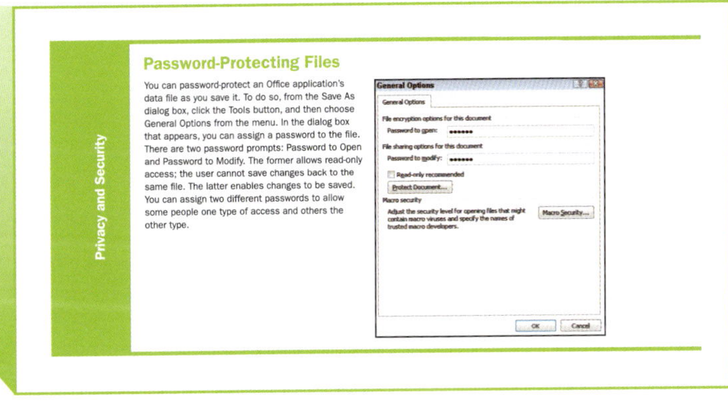

Privacy and Security

Password-Protecting Files

You can password-protect an Office application's data file as you save it. To do so, from the Save As dialog box, click the Tools button, and then choose General Options from the menu. In the dialog box that appears, you can assign a password to the file. There are two password prompts: Password to Open and Password to Modify. The former allows read-only access; the user cannot save changes back to the same file. The latter enables changes to be saved. You can assign two different passwords to allow some people one type of access and others the other type.

Troubleshooting

Restarting Helps!

If you talk to any computer professional about a problem you are having with your computer, the first thing he or she will probably ask you is: *Have you tried restarting?* That's because restarting Windows can cure a variety of one-time or occasional problems that may occur. For example, suppose your mouse pointer starts jumping around wildly as you move the mouse. That's a problem with the display adapter, and it can almost always be cured by restarting the PC. Another common problem that restarting usually fixes is a keyboard that suddenly starts sending the wrong characters to the PC as you type.

- **Troubleshooting:** These features provide information about solving common problems with the technology you are learning about.

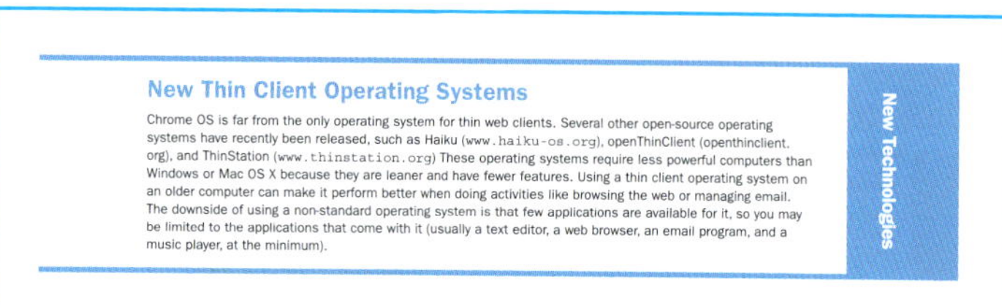

New Thin Client Operating Systems

Chrome OS is far from the only operating system for thin web clients. Several other open-source operating systems have recently been released, such as Haiku (`www.haiku-os.org`), openThinClient (openthinclient.org), and ThinStation (`www.thinstation.org`) These operating systems require less powerful computers than Windows or Mac OS X because they are leaner and have fewer features. Using a thin client operating system on an older computer can make it perform better when doing activities like browsing the web or managing email. The downside of using a non-standard operating system is that few applications are available for it, so you may be limited to the applications that come with it (usually a text editor, a web browser, an email program, and a music player, at the minimum).

New Technologies

- **New Technology:** In these features, you will learn about up-and-coming tools and technologies to watch for in the next few years, or recently developed innovations that are improving people's lives right now.

- **Step by Step:** Where it is useful to have exact step-by-step instructions for performing a task, a special Step by Step box appears listing the steps to follow.

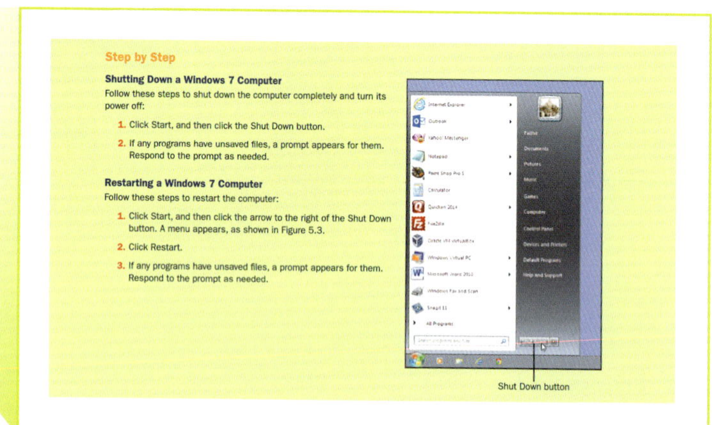

Step by Step

Shutting Down a Windows 7 Computer

Follow these steps to shut down the computer completely and turn its power off:

1. Click Start, and then click the Shut Down button.
2. If any programs have unsaved files, a prompt appears for them. Respond to the prompt as needed.

Restarting a Windows 7 Computer

Follow these steps to restart the computer:

1. Click Start, and then click the arrow to the right of the Shut Down button. A menu appears, as shown in Figure 5.3.
2. Click Restart.
3. If any programs have unsaved files, a prompt appears for them. Respond to the prompt as needed.

- **Quick Review:** At the end of each major section of a chapter are several review questions that you can use to test your understanding of the material. If you can't easily answer these questions, you should re-read the section.

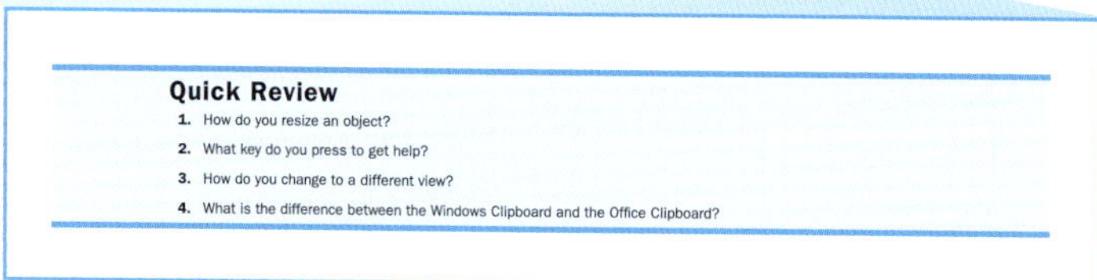

Quick Review

1. How do you resize an object?
2. What key do you press to get help?
3. How do you change to a different view?
4. What is the difference between the Windows Clipboard and the Office Clipboard?

End-of-Chapter Features

At the end of each chapter, you will find special features that will help you review the key points of the chapter and to test and demonstrate your learning.

- **Summary:** A section-by-section summary briefly reviews the main points of the chapter, with the key terms you should know highlighted.

Summary

Understanding System Software

System software includes the BIOS, the operating system, and utility programs that perform system maintenance and protection.

A computer's **platform** is its type of hardware. Only certain operating systems can run on certain platforms. The **Intel platform**, also called IBM-compatible, is the most popular platform; this platform's most popular operating system is Windows. The 32-bit Intel platform is called **x86**, and the 64-bit version is called **x64**.

Most operating systems use a **graphical user interface (GUI)**, but some operating systems, especially those designed for use on servers, use a **command-line interface**. UNIX is an example.

There are many types of **utility software** for performing various system maintenance tasks. **Antivirus**, **firewall**, and **anti-spyware** programs protect from outside attacks and malicious software (**malware**). **Anti-spam** programs cut down on the amount of junk email you receive. A **disk checking program** can find and fix file system errors, and a **registry cleanup program** can find and fix inconsistent or unneeded entries in the **registry**. **Backup software** can automate the process of backing up important files.

Comparing the Major Operating Systems

Mac OS X is the operating system on most Apple desktop and notebook computers. Its latest version is OS X 10.9, code named **Mavericks**. Its main competitor is **Microsoft Windows**, which is the most popular operating system in the world, used on more than 90% of all desktop and notebook PCs.

Linux is an open-source operating system based on UNIX. The basic version is free, but you can purchase a packaged collection of add-ons and utility programs with it called a distribution (**distro**). A distro typically includes a GUI, as an alternative to Linux's native command-line interface.

You can run multiple operating systems on a single computer by setting it up to **multi-boot**, or to use a **virtual machine** to run the secondary operating system within the first one.

A **thin client** operating system such as Chrome OS is designed for small portable notebook computers that are used primarily for going online.

A **server** is a computer that serves an entire network rather than an individual user. The most popular server operating systems are **Linux**, **UNIX**, and **Windows Server**.

Tablets and smartphones have an operating system that is preinstalled on a chip (**system-on-chip**, or **SoC**). Users can download **apps**, which are add-on applications that extend the device's capabilities. The popular SoC operating systems are **iOS**, **Android**, **Windows RT**, and **Windows Phone**.

Understanding Device Drivers

A **device driver** translates between the operating system and a hardware device. You can update a device driver to solve some performance problems you may have with the device, and **roll back** the driver if the new driver doesn't work as well as the previous one.

When you install a new piece of hardware, Windows uses a technology called Plug and Play to identify the device and locate a driver for it if possible.

- **Key Terms:** A list of the vocabulary words from the chapter appears, so you can make sure you know each one. If a word on this list doesn't sound familiar, page back through the chapter to review its definition.

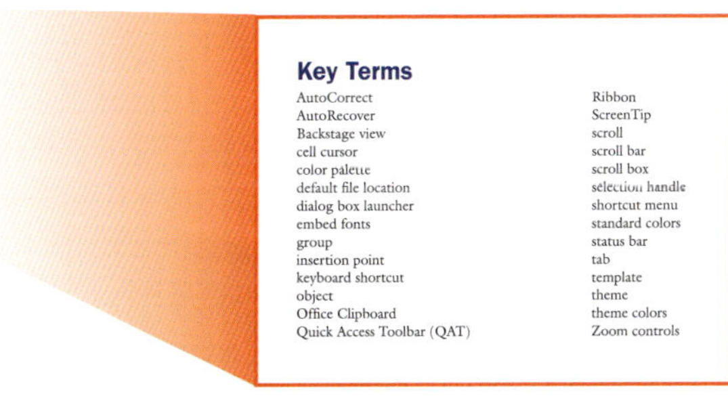

Key Terms

AutoCorrect
AutoRecover
Backstage view
cell cursor
color palette
default file location
dialog box launcher
embed fonts
group
insertion point
keyboard shortcut
object
Office Clipboard
Quick Access Toolbar (QAT)
Ribbon
ScreenTip
scroll
scroll bar
scroll box
selection handle
shortcut menu
standard colors
status bar
tab
template
theme
theme colors
Zoom controls

- **Test Yourself:** A variety of exercises help you demonstrate your knowledge, including:

Test Yourself

Fact Check

1. Which of these is NOT a type of system software?
   a. word processing software
   b. backup software
   c. BIOS
   d. operating system
2. Which operating system has a command-line interface by default?
   a. iOS
   b. UNIX
   c. Android
   d. Windows RT
3. Which of these is a thin client OS?
   a. Windows Server
   b. Chrome OS
   c. Mac OS X
   d. UNIX
4. In a _____, users employ a keyboard to type commands at a prompt.
   a. command-line interface
   b. graphical user interface
   c. utility interface
   d. compressed interface
5. What file system is the default for Windows 7 system volumes?
   a. NTFS
   b. FAT32
   c. HFS+
   d. UDF
6. A volume letter is followed by what symbol?
   a. ; (semi-colon)
   b. % (percent sign)
   c. : (colon)
   d. & (ampersand)
7. Where in Windows Explorer does a file's path appear?
   a. address bar
   b. ribbon
   c. title bar
   d. navigation pane

Fact Check

1. Which of these is NOT a type of system software?
   a. word processing software
   b. backup software
   c. BIOS
   d. operating system
2. Which operating system has a command-line interface by default?
   a. iOS
   b. UNIX
   c. Android
   d. Windows RT

- Fact Check: A short multiple-choice quiz.

- Matching: An exercise in which you match terms to their meanings.

Matching

Match the term to its description.

a. x86
b. GUI
c. Linux
d. shell
e. SoC
f. UDF
g. root directory

1. _______The 32-bit version of the Intel platform
2. _______A user interface that uses pictures and a pointing device to issue commands
3. _______An open-source operating system used on a variety of platforms
4. _______An operating system's user interface
5. _______The file system used on DVDs
6. _______An operating system that comes preinstalled on a chip on a portable device
7. _______The top-level folder on a volume

Sum It Up

1. List three types of system software.
2. What is the difference between an OS and a platform?
3. List five types of utility programs.
4. List three operating systems that would run on an IBM-compatible desktop PC.
5. Name three operating systems used on smartphones.
6. Explain the purpose of Plug and Play technology.
7. Explain the purpose of partitioning a drive.
8. Give an example of a complete path to a file, and explain the parts of the path.

- Sum It Up: A variety of open-ended questions that guide you to put your newly acquired knowledge into your own words.

- Explore More: These activity suggestions provide ideas for going further with several of the topics you learned about in the chapter.

Explore More

Linux Distros

Suppose you want to put Linux on an older desktop PC and give it to a relative who wants to use the Internet. But that person doesn't know much about computers, so you must find a Linux distro that is very easy to use, even for a beginner. Do a web search on the terms ***Linux distro beginner***. Based on the information you find, choose two Linux distros you think would meet your needs, and explain why you chose the ones you did.

Examining File Associations

Windows 7 has default extension associations for various file types. For example, when you double-click on a file with a txt extension, Windows 7 opens it in Notepad because Notepad is the default application for the txt extension.

When you have more than one application that is capable of opening a certain type of file, you may want to change Windows's default setting for that extension. For example, if you have both Microsoft Word and WordPad, you might prefer one over the other for opening files with an rtf extension.

Think It Over

NTFS Compression and Encryption

NTFS compression and encryption both make files slightly slower to access. In addition, using encryption introduces another level of responsibility into file management because you must back up the encryption key so you can get your files back in the event of a system disaster that causes the hard drive to be inaccessible via the operating system. Given those drawbacks, do you think either of those features would be worth it to you, personally?

Backup Scheduling

Suppose you were designing your own backup schedule for your computer. Which folders or files would you back up? Regarding the files you did not choose to back up, why did you exclude them? How often would you perform a full backup? How often would you perform a differential or incremental backup—and which would it be? Think about your answers, and give a reason for each one.

- Think It Over: These philosophical and practical discussion questions can be springboards to personal writing assignments or used as in-class or small group discussion starters.

Online Features

You can enhance your understanding of the material by exploring the book's companion website at `www.wiley.com/go/computingfundamentalsdigitallit`. On the website, you'll find additional Fact Check questions and answers for each chapter.

Part I

Computer Basics and Hardware

11
12
13
14
15
16
17
1
2
3
4
5
6
7
8
9
10
11
12
1X
11X

Chapter 1

Computer Basics

Learning objectives

- Understand the purpose and elements of information systems
- Recognize the different types of computers
- Distinguish the main software types
- Identify the components of a computer system
- Understand how computers communicate

Welcome to *Computing Fundamentals: Digital Literacy Edition!* This book helps prepare you for success in a world that is filled with computers. At work, at school, at home, in stores, and as you travel, computers help make things run more smoothly.

Think about the average day in your life—all the places you go and all the things you do. How many of them involve a computer of some type? Probably quite a few. For example, you might wake up in the morning to the sound of a digital alarm clock. As you eat breakfast, you might browse the day's news on your home computer or a tablet PC. The vehicle you ride in to work or school probably has at least one computerized component in it, and perhaps as you travel you talk to a friend on your cell phone. When you get to work or school, your supervisor or teacher might use a computer to assign work to you, or to teach a lesson. On the way home, you might stop at a restaurant where a cashier inputs your order into a computer-based ordering system that then relays your order to the kitchen staff. Before you go to bed, you might watch a DVD movie using a DVD player and a digital TV, both with computers in them.

In this chapter, you will learn the basics that most computer systems have in common, whether it's a desktop PC, a smartphone, or the software in your car that tells you it's time for an oil change. You'll find out how computers represent, encode, and process data, and how they communicate with one another. Many of the topics that this chapter covers in overview form are explored in greater detail later in the book.

Understanding Information Systems

information system An interconnected environment for managing and processing data using a computer.

An information system is a complete interconnected environment in which raw data—quantifiable facts and figures—is turned into useful information. An information system includes the following parts: people, hardware, software, procedures, and data (see Figure 1.1).

- **People:** If you think about it, the only reason computers exist is to help people accomplish their goals. Therefore when planning an information system, it's critical to understand what the people hope to get out of it. Do they need certain information? Do they need for the computer to activate a device that performs a task? Are they looking to be entertained or educated? The first step in planning an information system is to analyze the requirements of the people.
- **Hardware:** When most people think of computers, they immediately think of hardware, the physical parts of the computer system. The hardware includes circuit boards with silicon chips and transistors mounted on them, input devices like the keyboard and mouse, and output devices like printers and monitors.
- **Software:** Computer hardware just sits there idle unless it has software, which is a program that tells the hardware what to do. There are many different levels of software, including the operating system (like Windows or Mac OS) and applications (like a word processing or accounting program).
- **Procedures:** The software doesn't run itself (usually). People must interact with the computer to tell it what software to run. For example, before you can write checks with your accounting software, you must start up the software, open the file that stores the data for the business, and issue the command that opens the checking account register. You can learn procedures from the online Help system in the application, from a printed user manual, from a training class, or by trial and error.
- **Data:** Computer programs operate upon the data they receive. For example, in your accounting software, you enter data about the checks you are writing—the date, the amount, the recipient—and the program stores that data so you can recall it later.

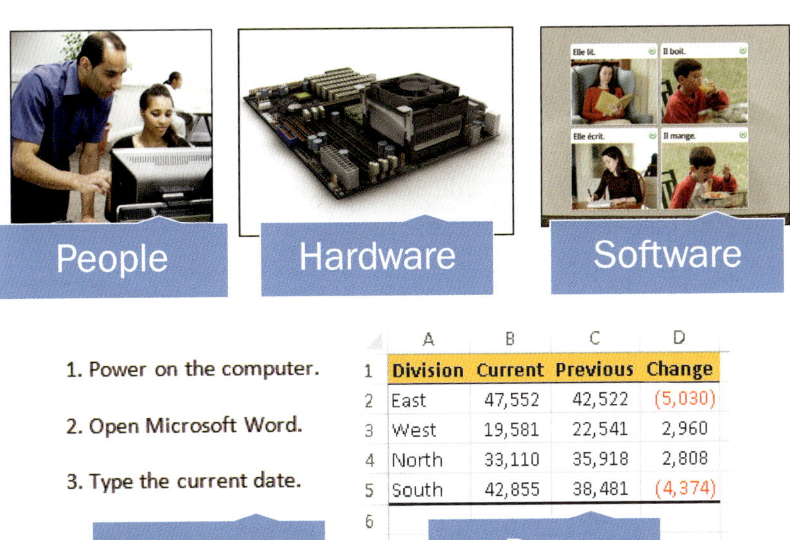

	A	B	C	D
1	Division	Current	Previous	Change
2	East	47,552	42,522	(5,030)
3	West	19,581	22,541	2,960
4	North	33,110	35,918	2,808
5	South	42,855	38,481	(4,374)
6				
7				

Figure 1.1 An information system involves these five components.

Careers in IT

Information Systems Manager

An Information Systems (IS) manager looks at the "big picture" of a company's computer systems. As you discover in this chapter, an information system consists of people, procedures, software, hardware, and data. The IS manager is the person who brings them all together to get results. An IS manager might oversee an initiative to satisfy an information need, such as for production managers to receive daily reports. This initiative might include assembling a team of programmers, identifying the required hardware and software, developing procedures for handling the information request, and delivering the data to the managers in an easy-to-use format.

Quick Review

1. What are the five parts of an information system?
2. What is the difference between hardware and software?
3. What is the difference between software and data?

Identifying Computer Types

As you learned in the preceding section, **hardware** is the physical part of the computer system. Hardware consists of components inside a computer as well as the external devices that interact with it, such as printers, cables, and monitors.

hardware The physical parts of the computer system.

personal computer A computer designed to be used by only one person at a time.

Personal Computers

When most people think about computers, they picture a **personal computer**, or PC. This type of computer is called *personal* because it is designed for only one person to use at a time. Personal computers fall into several categories that are differentiated from one another by their sizes. The most common sizes are:

desktop PC A computer designed to be set up at a desk and not often moved, with input and output devices separate from the system unit.

system unit The main part of the computer, containing the essential components.

- **Desktop PC:** A computer designed to be used at a desk, and seldom moved. This type of computer consists of a large metal box called a **system unit** that contains most of the essential components, with a separate monitor, keyboard, and mouse that all plug into the system unit (see Figure 1.2).

© iStockphoto.com/Viktorus

Figure 1.2 A desktop PC contains a separate system unit, monitor, keyboard, and mouse.

notebook PC A portable PC where the screen and keyboard fold up against one another for storage and transport; also known as a laptop.

pointing device An input device such as a mouse or touchpad that enables users to move an onscreen pointer to select content and issue commands.

netbook A small notebook PC designed primarily for accessing the Internet.

- **Notebook PC:** A portable computer designed to fold up like a notebook for carrying, as shown in Figure 1.3. The cover opens up to reveal a built-in screen, keyboard, and **pointing device**, which substitutes for a mouse. This type of computer is sometimes called a laptop. A smaller version of a notebook PC is sometimes referred to as a **netbook** (which is short for *Internet book*, implying that this type of computer is primarily for accessing the Internet rather than running applications).

© iStockphoto.com/daboost

Figure 1.3 A notebook PC has a built-in monitor, keyboard, and pointing device, such as a touchpad.

tablet PC A lightweight slate-style computer with a touch screen, designed for easy portability.

- **Tablet PC:** A portable computer that consists of a touch-sensitive display screen mounted on a tablet-size plastic frame with a small computer inside, as in Figure 1.4. There is no built-in keyboard or pointing device; a software-based keyboard pops up onscreen when needed, and your finger sliding on the screen serves as a pointing device.

© iStockphoto.com/UmbertoPantalone

Figure 1.4 A tablet computer is a touch-sensitive slate.

- **Smartphone:** A mobile phone that can run computer applications and has Internet access capability (see Figure 1.5). Smartphones usually have a touch-sensitive screen, and provide voice calls, text messaging, and Internet access. Many have a variety of location-aware applications, such as a **global positioning system (GPS)** and mapping program and a local business guide.

Figure 1.5 A smartphone combines the capabilities of a cell phone with a small touch-sensitive tablet screen.

smartphone A cellular phone that includes computer applications and Internet access capability.

global positioning system (GPS) A device that determines your current position by communicating with an orbiting satellite and provides maps and driving directions.

Multi-User Computers

Multi-user computers are designed to serve groups of people, from a small office to a huge international enterprise. Here are some common types of multi-user computers:

- **Server:** A computer dedicated to serving and supporting a network, a group of network users, and/or their information needs. Many networks employ servers to provide a centrally accessible storage space for data, and share common devices like printers and scanners. A small network server may look similar to a desktop PC, but may have a different operating system, such as Windows Server or Linux. A large server that manages a wide-ranging network may look similar to a mainframe. A group of servers located together in a single room or facility is called a **server farm**, or server cluster. Large Internet service provider (ISP) companies maintain extensive server farms.
- **Mainframe:** A large and powerful computer capable of processing and storing large amounts of business data. For example, a mainframe might collect all the sales data from hundreds of cash registers in a large department store and make it available to executives. The modern mainframe unit itself is a large cabinet, or a series of cabinets, each about the size of a refrigerator (see Figure 1.6). A mainframe may be stored in its own air-conditioned room in a business or school, and may have multiple employees monitoring and maintaining it. In earlier decades, smaller and less expensive multi-user computers called minicomputers were employed in many businesses, but minicomputers are no longer widely used.

server A computer that is dedicated to performing network tasks such as managing files, printers, or email for multiple users.

server farm A group of servers located in the same physical area.

mainframe A large and powerful computer capable of serving many users and processing large amounts of data at once.

Figure 1.6 A mainframe is a powerful business computer system that can receive and process data from many sources at once.

supercomputer The largest and most powerful type of computer, surpassing the capability of a mainframe, typically used in research and academics.

- **Supercomputer:** A supercomputer is the largest and most powerful type of computer available, occupying large rooms and even entire floors of a building. Supercomputers are often employed in fields such as cryptanalysis (code breaking), molecular modeling, weather forecasting, and climate mapping. Supercomputers typically are used in high-tech academic, governmental, and scientific research facilities. Figure 1.7 shows a supercomputer.

Figure 1.7 This IBM Blue Gene/P supercomputer is located at the Argonne National Laboratory in Lemont, Illinois, USA.

Put It to Work

Mapping the Human Genome

Supercomputers played a critical role in the Human Genome Project (HGP), a multi-national research project that sought to define the unique genetic sequences that comprise the 23 chromosome pairs of human DNA. The project began in the 1980s, and by April 2003, 99% of the human genome had been mapped with 99.99% accuracy. Work continues on genomes today, with thousands of human genomes completely sequenced and many more mapped at a more basic level. The power of a supercomputer was essential for processing the enormous amount of data. The data that this project collected may help researchers develop cures for diseases like cancer, as well as promote advances in biotechnology and molecular medicine.

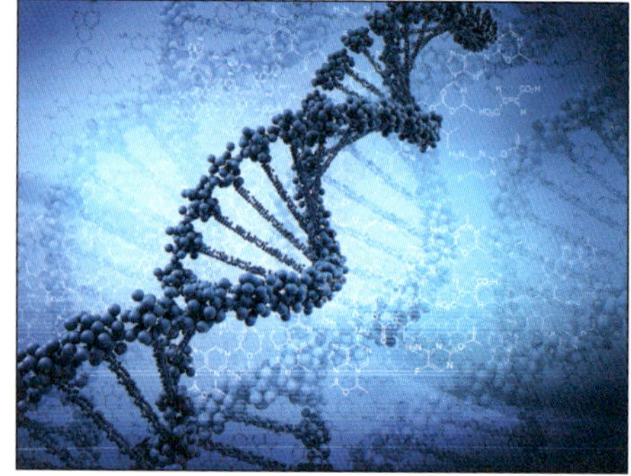

Quick Review

1. What is a brief definition of "personal computer"?
2. What key characteristics of a desktop PC distinguish it from a notebook PC?
3. What are the differences between a server, a mainframe, and a supercomputer?

Understanding Software Types

Software tells the hardware what to do, but different kinds of software accomplish that at different levels. The following sections provide an overview of the types of software a computer might include.

software The programs that tell the computer what to do.

BIOS

The most basic software is the Basic Input Output System (BIOS). This software is stored on a read-only chip on the motherboard so that it doesn't accidentally get changed or corrupted. This important software helps the computer start up and performs some basic testing on the hardware.

BIOS The software that initializes and tests the system at startup.

Operating Systems

The operating system (OS) manages all the computer's activities after startup. The operating system serves several purposes:

operating system Software that maintains the computer's interface, manages files, runs applications, and communicates with hardware.

- **It provides the user interface** that humans use to communicate commands and receive feedback.
- **It runs applications,** and enables humans to interact with them.
- **It controls and manages the file storage system.**
- **It communicates with the hardware,** instructing it to take action to accomplish tasks. For example, the OS tells the printer to print a document, and tells the monitor what image to display.

Microsoft Windows is the most popular operating system; Figure 1.8 shows the Windows 7 interface. Other operating systems include Mac OS and Linux for desktop and notebook PCs, UNIX for mainframes and servers, and Android for tablets and smartphones. Special versions of Windows and Mac OS also power tablets and smartphones. Each operating system has its own unique set of features, benefits, and drawbacks, so it pays to learn as much as you can about the operating systems available and choose a computer that will run the operating system that best fits your needs. You will learn much more about operating systems in general in Chapter 4, "Operating System Basics," and more about the Windows 7 interface in Chapter 5, "Introduction to Windows 7."

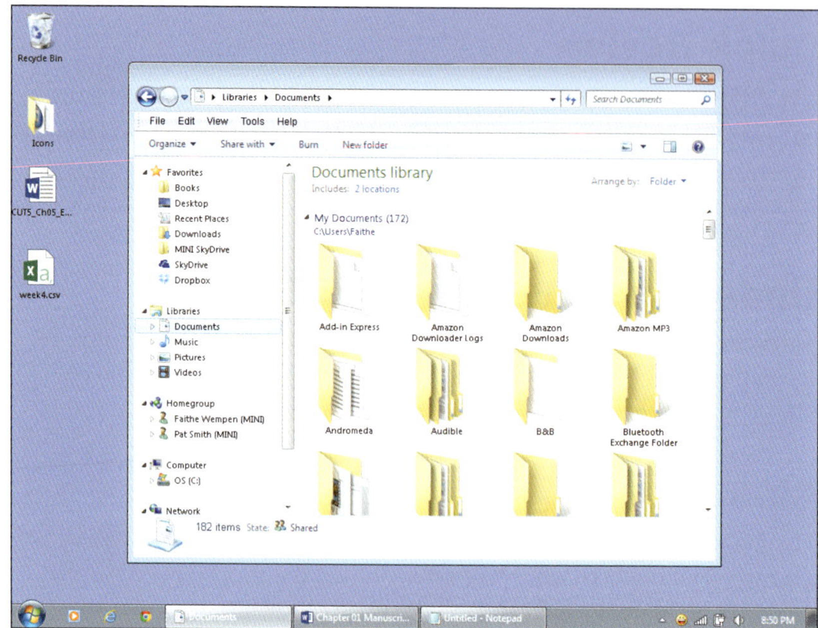

Figure 1.8 The Windows 7 interface.

Step by Step

Identifying Your Windows Version

Each version of Microsoft Windows is available in various editions; Windows 7 comes in several editions, including Home Basic, Professional, and Enterprise, for example. Use this procedure to determine what version and edition of Windows you have on your computer:

1. Click the Start button. Right-click Computer, and choose Properties. (Right-click means to press only the right side of your mouse.) An information page appears.
2. Look under the Windows Edition heading. The version and edition of your Windows operating system appear there. If a service pack is installed, that information also appears.

This book uses Windows 7 for all its examples.

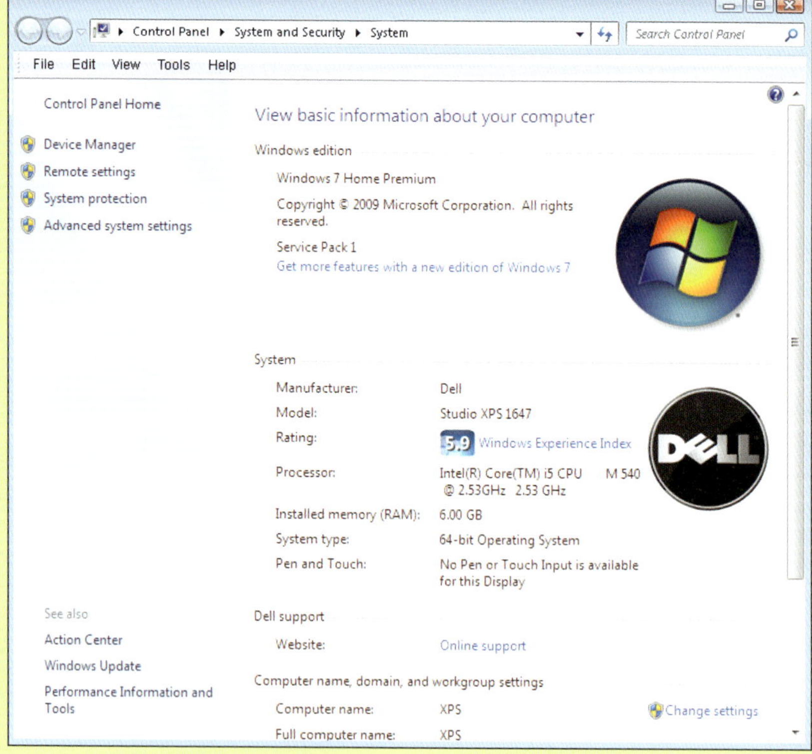

Utilities

In addition to the main components of an operating system, utility software may also be available, either provided free with the OS or added on. Utility programs assist with a wide range of system maintenance and security functions, such as checking storage disks for errors, blocking security and privacy threats, and backing up important files.

utility software Software that performs some useful service to the operating system, such as optimizing or correcting the file storage system, backing up files, or ensuring security or privacy.

Application Software

Application software is software that is designed to do something productive or fun, something of interest to a human user. The OS keeps the computer running, but the applications give people a reason to use the computer.

application software Software that helps a human perform a useful task for work or play.

Most computers come with some application software already installed. You can purchase additional software, and many applications are available for free. The software may be provided on a CD or DVD disc, or may be downloaded and installed via the Internet.

Productivity software helps you accomplish practical tasks such as managing your money, charting numeric data, writing documents, storing data, and sending email. Perhaps the best known example in this software category is Microsoft Office, a suite of applications that includes a word processor, a spreadsheet application, a database application, an application for creating business presentations, and an email and contact management system. A suite is a group of applications that are designed to work well together and that share some common interface characteristics. Notice in Figure 1.9 that each of the three applications has a similar toolbar across the top.

productivity software Software that helps a human perform one or more business or personal enrichment tasks.

Microsoft Office A productivity suite of applications commonly used in businesses for word processing, spreadsheets, databases, presentation, and email.

suite A group of applications designed to complement each other's capabilities and work together closely, often with a consistent interface between the applications.

Figure 1.9 These Microsoft Office applications—Word, Excel, and PowerPoint—share a common interface.

In addition to general suites like Office, dozens of other types of productivity software perform functions specific to certain professions, like accounting, customer relationship management (CRM), and appointment scheduling. On the technical side, software is available to help engineers and technicians create technical drawings and blueprints, develop new computer software, operate manufacturing and testing machinery, and much more.

Software as a Service (SaaS) A model of software sales that leases access to the software rather than selling a copy outright to the user.

Using Online Apps

Using Online Apps

Did you know that you can also use some software without installing it on your computer? **Software as a Service (SaaS)** is a new way of thinking about accessing and paying for software. Rather than buying a software product once, installing it on your computer and "owning" it forever, with the SaaS model you pay a usage fee for the software, which remains the property of the company. The software and any associated data are stored online. The company provides free updates for as long as you keep renewing your usage. Microsoft Office can optionally be rented this way through the Office 365 program, and many other applications are also being offered as services. SaaS has many benefits. The cost is typically lower than for buying the software outright, and updates and new versions are free and automatically provided.

Applications can also assist in education and training. For example, applications can train employees to perform new tasks or to use new productivity software, and can test their understanding of the training by administering and auto-scoring quizzes. In schools, applications can be used to simulate laboratory experiments and experiences, to assist with note-taking and review, and to help instructors create multimedia learning materials that students can use at their own pace. Some classes are even delivered entirely online through web-based software.

Applications can also entertain. You can find a wide variety of applications related to virtually any interest—cooking, sports and fitness, photography, science, and thousands more topics. Thousands of games are designed for every age group and interest, from simple matching and memory games to epic fantasy adventures to realistic first-person shooting games.

Quick Review

1. What are the four key functions of an operating system?
2. How is application software different from an operating system?
3. What is productivity software? Name the widely used productivity suite available from Microsoft.

Computer System Components

Every computer system is made up of multiple electronic components. These components fall into four broad categories that serve different purposes in the **information processing cycle**, shown in Figure 1.10. You will learn more about the information processing cycle in Chapter 2, "The System Unit."

information processing cycle The four-step process that data moves through as it is processed by a computer. Consists of input, processing, output, and storage.

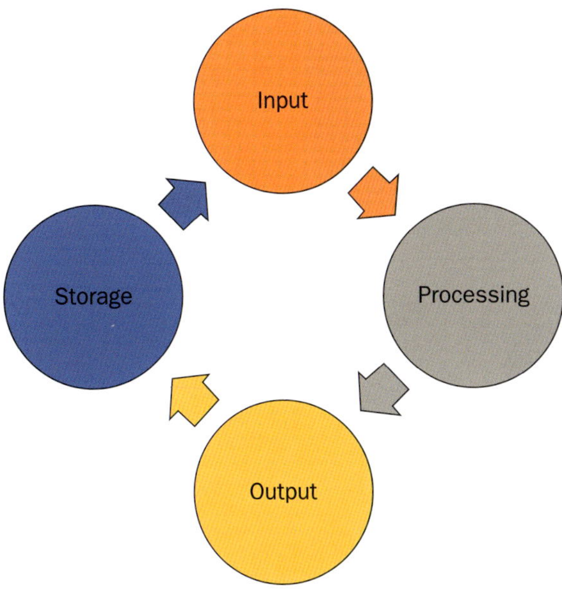

Figure 1.10 The information processing cycle.

- **Input:** Components that help humans put data into the computer. Examples include a keyboard, mouse, and touch screen.
- **Processing:** Components that move and process the data inside the computer. The motherboard and its processor and memory chips fall into this category.
- **Output:** Components that provide the results of the processing to humans. The monitor is the primary output device; other examples include printers and speakers.
- **Storage:** Components that store software and data until it is needed. Storage components include hard drives, USB flash drives, and DVDs.

As you learned earlier in this chapter, the system unit is the main box that constitutes the computer. Some devices are external—that is, they are outside the system unit—and some are internal. On a desktop PC, most input and output devices are external; on a notebook, tablet, or smartphone, they are an integral part of the device but external devices can be added. Figure 1.11 shows the computer's main components and their roles in information processing.

Figure 1.11 Components of a typical desktop computer system.

How Data Is Represented on a Computer

bit A single binary digit, with a value of either 1 (on) or 0 (off).

byte An 8-digit binary number, composed of eight bits.

The smallest unit of data in a computer is a bit. A **bit** is a single binary digit, with either a 1 (on) or 0 (off) value. Eight bits can combine to make a **byte**, which is an 8-digit binary number, as shown in Figure 1.12.

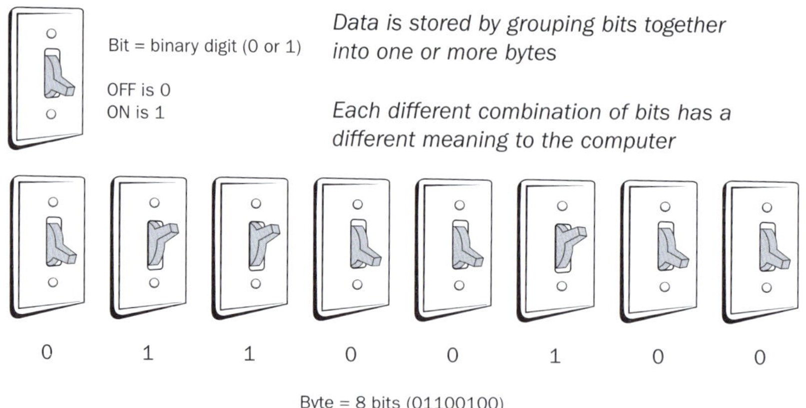

Figure 1.12 Computers combine eight binary digits (bits) to make a byte.

Modern systems work with thousands, millions, and even billions of bytes at a time. Table 1.1 lists the names for certain multiples of bytes.

Table 1.1 Common Quantities of Bytes

Term	*Number of Bytes*
Kilobyte (KB)	1024 (approximately one thousand)
Megabyte (MB)	1,048,576 (approximately one million)
Gigabyte (GB)	1,073,741,824 (approximately one billion)
Terabyte (TB)	1,099,411,627,776 (approximately one trillion)
Petabyte (PB)	1,125,899,906,842,624 (approximately one quadrillion)

NOTE

Both memory and storage capacities are measured in bytes. For example, a computer might have 8GB RAM (memory) and a 500GB hard drive.

Input Devices

An input device provides a way to get data into the computer. The oldest and most common input device is a keyboard. A desktop PC has an external keyboard, while a notebook PC has a built-in keyboard. Tablets and smartphones have a software-based keyboard that pops up onscreen when needed.

keyboard An input device that allows users to type data into a computer using a standard set of typing keys.

Computers that use a graphical interface usually employ a pointing device. The pointing device moves an onscreen pointer (usually an arrow) to align with objects onscreen, and then the user presses a button on the pointing device to do something to the pointed-at object. A mouse is the most common pointing device, but there are many other types too, such as trackballs, touchpads, and touch-sensitive screens. You will learn more about input devices in Chapter 3, "Input, Output, and Storage."

Processing Devices

The motherboard is the large circuit board inside the computer that everything else plugs into. The key components located on the motherboard are the processor (also called the Central Processing Unit, or CPU) and the memory (also called Random Access Memory, or RAM). To support these components, the motherboard has electrically conductive pathways called buses that carry the data from place to place, and a chipset, which is a controller that directs the bus traffic. Figure 1.13 shows a motherboard removed from the computer case so you can see it more clearly.

motherboard A large circuit board inside a computer that controls the operations of all other components.

processor The chip in the computer that performs math calculations, processing data. Also called the Central Processing Unit (CPU).

memory Temporary electronic storage that holds the values of data bits using transistors.

bus A conductive pathway built into a circuit board, used to move data.

chipset The controller chip on a circuit board.

Chapter 2 covers these components in more detail and explains how they work together.

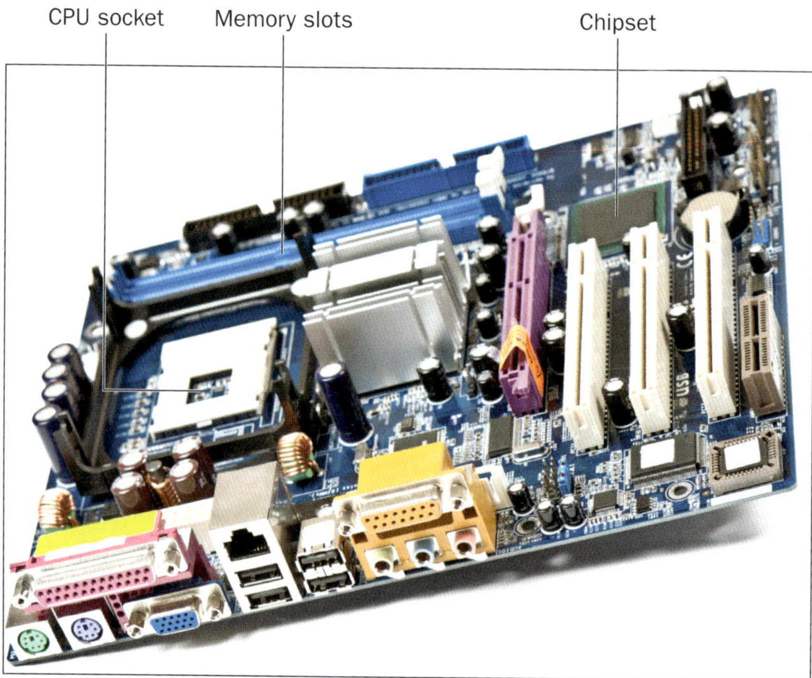

© iStockphoto.com/kirstypargeter

Figure 1.13 A motherboard. The CPU is under the tall tower, which is a cooling fan. The slots to the left of the CPU will hold the small circuit boards containing memory.

Output Devices

monitor A display screen on which a computer's output appears.

Information comes out of a computer through an output device such as a **monitor**. When you move the mouse or type a character on a keyboard, you see the results instantly on the monitor. The monitor helps you communicate with the operating system; without the monitor, you wouldn't know if the OS had received and understood your instructions or if the application had accepted the data you input. Besides monitors, other output devices include printers (for producing hard-copy output) and speakers (for providing audio feedback).

Storage Devices

Storage devices enable software and data to be preserved and reused. Storage can be either removable or non-removable. (Non-removable storage is actually removable too if you have the right tools and knowledge, but in this case the distinction refers to being *easily* removable or not.)

hard drive A sealed metal box that stores computer data using either mechanical or solid-state technology.

The most common type of storage is an internal **hard drive**, which is a sealed metal box inside the system unit. Hard drives are usually internal, making them non-removable. Some hard drives are removable, though; external hard drives easily connect to and disconnect from a port on the outside of the system unit. Other removable storage devices include USB flash drives and optical discs (CDs and DVDs). Chapter 3 covers storage devices in more detail, and explains the technologies behind them.

Quick Review

1. Name at least two devices from each of these categories: input, processing, output, and storage.
2. What is the purpose of the motherboard?

How Computers Communicate

Early computers did not communicate easily with one another. Data was typically carried between computers on floppy disks and other low-capacity removable disks, or using slow dial-up modems. Network connections were difficult to set up and transferred data very slowly. Nowadays, however, communication technology has advanced greatly, and there are many choices for making computers connect to one another.

Ethernet Networking

Most computers today are part of one or more networks. A **network** is a group of computers that share resources (such as printers or Internet service) and/or data (such as files). The most common network standard is **Ethernet**. Ethernet networks can be either wired or wireless (or a combination of the two), but the term Ethernet is most often applied to the wired kind of connection. Figure 1.14 shows an Ethernet port on the side of a notebook PC. Most PCs have a **network adapter**, which provides network connectivity services and a port into which you can plug an Ethernet cable.

network Two or more computers connected to share data and resources.

Ethernet The current dominant standard for local area networking devices.

network adapter A hardware component that enables a computer to connect to a network.

Figure 1.14 Ethernet is the most common type of network connection. Most computers have an Ethernet port.

Wireless Ethernet is more often called **Wi-Fi**, or 802.11. Most portable devices such as tablets and phones use wireless connections and do not have the capability for wired networking. Chapter 8, "Networking and Internet Basics," explains networking technology in more detail.

Wi-Fi Wireless Ethernet. A means of connecting computers and other devices wirelessly. Another name for it is IEEE 802.11, its technical standard.

In a small network, such as in a home or small business, one end of an Ethernet cable plugs into the computer, and the other end plugs into a controller box called a **router** that manages the network traffic between the connected devices. If you have **broadband** (always on) Internet access, the device that brings that service into your home or business is frequently called the router, and then the router shares the Internet connection among all the computers.

router A connection box for Ethernet networks that physically joins the devices in the network (wired) or provides wireless connectivity (wireless), and enables a connection to an outside network such as the Internet.

broadband A fast, always-on network connection.

If you have a Wi-Fi wireless router and a wireless network adapter in the computer, the computer can connect to the router via radio frequency (RF) waves, so no cables are required.

Bluetooth Networking

Bluetooth is a short-range wireless alternative to wireless Ethernet (Wi-Fi), used primarily to connect wireless devices directly to specific computers. For example, you might have a Bluetooth wireless headset for your cell phone, or a Bluetooth speaker for your MP3 player. Bluetooth's limited range (10 meters) makes it impractical as a replacement for Wi-Fi, but it provides an easy and economical way for one device to connect with another within a limited space without Ethernet hardware.

The Internet

The Internet is the world's largest network. When you use the Internet, your computer becomes a member of this giant network, and you can communicate with any other computer on the Internet, to the extent that its owner has chosen to make it available. For example, you can exchange email messages, download files, and view web pages stored anywhere in the world.

Internet service provider (ISP) A company that maintains a direct connection to the Internet and leases access to it to individuals and companies.

Individual computers don't connect directly to the Internet, however; they go through an **Internet service provider (ISP)**, a company that provides a connection to the Internet for a fee. Your ISP may be your local phone or cable TV company, or at work or school it may be a service that your employer or school partners with. An ISP provides a device (a modem or terminal adapter) that translates your computer's requests into Internet-compatible data.

Privacy and Security

Wireless Router Security

A wired router is fairly secure by nature because you have to have physical access to it to plug a cable into it. A wireless router, however, is not secure because anyone within transmission range can connect to it. Wireless routers come with optional security features you can enable that will assign a code (like a password) that is required for a computer to connect to it. The first time that computer connects to the router, a prompt appears for the code; after the first successful connection, the code is stored and the computer can connect to the router automatically.

If you do not enable security on your wireless router, you should make sure that you do not have file sharing enabled on any of your computers. Otherwise an unknown person could not only use your Internet connection without permission, but could also view, change, copy, and even delete your important data files. An intruder might also be able to gather enough information about you from your data files to steal your identity.

Quick Review

1. What is the most common standard for wired networking?
2. What types of connections are most suitable for Bluetooth networking?

Summary

Understanding Information Systems

An **information system** is a complete interconnected environment in which raw data—quantifiable facts and figures—is turned into useful information. An information system includes the following parts: people, hardware, software, procedures, and data.

Identifying Computer Types

A **personal computer (PC)** is a computer designed for only one person to use at a time. Examples include **desktop PCs**, **notebook PCs**, **tablet PCs**, and **smartphones**. Other computers support multiple users at once, including **servers**, **mainframes**, and **supercomputers**.

Understanding Software Types

Software tells the hardware what to do. The **operating system** (**OS**) manages the computer's activities. An operating system provides a user interface, runs applications, manages files, and communicates with hardware.

Application software is software that is designed to do something productive or fun. **Productivity software** helps you accomplish practical tasks; one example is the **Microsoft Office** suite. A **suite** is a group of applications designed to work together. Software may be bought on CD or DVD, downloaded and installed, or may be leased as **Software as a Service** (**SaaS**).

Computer System Components

The **information processing cycle** consists of these four parts: input, processing, output, and storage. Each component in a computer contributes to one or more parts of that cycle.

Input devices move data into a computer. Examples include a **keyboard** and **mouse**. A mouse is a type of **pointing device**; pointing devices move the onscreen pointer and select objects onscreen.

Processing components manipulate the data inside the PC, and include the **motherboard** and its **processor**, **memory**, **chipset**, and **buses**.

Output devices deliver the results of the processing to the user. The **monitor** (display screen) is the most common output device; others include speakers and printers.

How Computers Communicate

Most computers are part of one or more **networks**. The most common network standard is **Ethernet**, which can be wired or wireless. Wireless Ethernet is called **Wi-Fi**. To connect to a network, the computer needs a network adapter (wired or wireless). A home network uses a **router** to connect the computers to one another and to connect to a shared **broadband** Internet connection if available.

Bluetooth is a short-range wireless alternative to Wi-Fi, used primarily to connect wireless devices directly to specific computers.

The **Internet** is a huge worldwide network. To participate in the Internet, individuals and companies must contract with an **Internet service provider** (**ISP**) for access.

Key Terms

application software
BIOS
bit
broadband
buses
byte
chipset
desktop PC
Ethernet
global positioning system (GPS)
hard drive
hardware
information processing cycle
information system
Internet service provider (ISP)
keyboard
mainframe
memory
Microsoft Office
monitor
motherboard
netbook
network
network adapter
notebook PC
operating system (OS)
personal computer (PC)
pointing device
processor
productivity software
router
server
server farm
smartphone
software
Software as a Service (SaaS)
suite
supercomputer
system unit
tablet PC
utility programs
Wi-Fi

Test Yourself

Fact Check

1. Which of these is NOT one of the five parts of an information system?
    a. data
    b. procedures
    c. people
    d. networks
2. Which of these is a personal computer?
    a. server
    b. tablet PC
    c. mainframe
    d. supercomputer
3. On a desktop PC, the motherboard, processor, and memory are contained in the
    a. system unit
    b. monitor
    c. tablet
    d. pointing device

4. Which of these is NOT one of the functions of an operating system?

   a. Run applications

   b. Provide a user interface

   c. Communicate with hardware

   d. Send and receive email

5. Windows 7 and UNIX are examples of a(n) ________ __________ (two words).

6. True or false: Games are a type of application software.

   a. True

   b. False

7. The information processing cycle consists of four phases: input, _______, output, and storage.

8. True or false: A trackball is a type of output device.

   a. True

   b. False

9. Which of the following is NOT located on the motherboard?

   a. processor

   b. chipset

   c. buses

   d. touchpad

10. True or false: Wi-Fi is a synonym for Bluetooth.

   a. True

   b. False

Matching

Match the computer type to its description.

a. desktop

b. mainframe

c. notebook

d. supercomputer

e. tablet

1. _______Personal computer with input and output devices separate from the system unit

2. _______Touchscreen computer with no separate keyboard and mouse

3. _______Portable PC that folds for transport, containing a built-in keyboard and built-in display screen

4. _______A large, powerful, cabinet-sized computer designed to process large amounts of input and output

5. _______A powerful, room-sized computer for scientific research

Sum It Up

1. What are the five parts of an information system?
2. What is the difference between a server and a mainframe?
3. What distinguishes an operating system from an application?
4. What are the four parts of the information processing cycle?
5. What is Wi-Fi and what equipment does it require?

Think It Over

Software as a Service

Suppose you had the chance to buy a productivity suite like Microsoft Office for a certain price and keep that version indefinitely, or to subscribe to a service that enabled you to use Office for as long as you continued paying the subscription fee. Suppose that the subscription cost was 1/30th per month of the cost to buy it outright. Which would be a better value for you, and why?

What if it were a game that you could either buy or subscribe to? Would you rather buy it outright and be able to play it forever, or would you rather subscribe to it?

Shopping for Tablet PCs

Suppose you are shopping for a tablet PC for use in your classes. Using the Internet, research at least one model of iPad, one tablet that has the Windows OS, and one model that uses the Android OS. Then answer the following questions:

- Which tablet has the fastest processor and the most memory?
- Which tablet OS has the most apps available for it?
- Which model has the longest battery life?
- Which tablets have the capability of attaching external keyboards?
- Which tablet has the largest screen size and the highest resolution?
- What features do you personally find most important, and which model would serve those needs best?

Sharing Wi-Fi

Suppose your family pays for broadband Internet service, and you have a wireless router that allows everyone in the family to share the Internet connection. The wireless router has security on it, so that a code is required to connect to it. This prevents your neighbors from using your Internet connection without permission. A neighbor asks for the code so he and his family can use your Internet connection. What do you say? Explain how you came to your decision.

- No, it would be unfair to the ISP for you to use the Internet without paying for it. You must pay for your own separate connection.
- Yes, you can use it, but you must pay me for part of the expense of the service.
- Yes, you can use it for free. Here is the code.
- Some other answer (explain).

Chapter 2

The System Unit

Learning objectives

- Recognize how data is processed
- Understand processors
- Understand memory types and functions
- Identify and use ports and buses

The heart of any computer is its system unit. As you learned in Chapter 1, "Computer Basics," the system unit is the main body of the computer, containing the essential components it needs to function.

If you have ever shopped for a computer, you probably noticed that some models cost much more than others—many times more. The quality and features of the components inside the system unit are the primary reason why cost varies so widely. Two computers can look identical from the outside but be very different in their capabilities and performance levels.

In this chapter, you will learn what happens inside the system unit, and what role each key component plays in making the computer fast and efficient at performing the tasks you ask of it. When you understand these things, you will be able to decipher a computer's technical specifications with confidence and select the models that have the best balance of cost and features for your situation.

Careers in IT

Bench Repair Technician

A bench repair technician is like a mechanic for computers. As the word *bench* implies, this technician works primarily at a workbench in a repair shop, although mobile repair technician positions are also available. Bench repair technicians can diagnose system problems with computers that customers bring in for repairs, including both hardware problems like defective parts and software problems like virus infections. This position requires either a two-year degree in Computer Technology or a professional certification such as CompTIA's A+ certification. It is a good job for someone who prefers working mostly with the computers themselves rather than with their users.

Understanding CPUs

central processing unit (CPU) The main processor in a computer.

Every computer has at least one processor, also called a central processing unit (CPU). The CPU contains millions of tiny transistors and pathways that take in data and instructions, process (calculate) the data according to the instructions, and output the results of the calculations. A computer may also have smaller processors used in specific subsystems, such as a graphics processor.

Every CPU includes the following components:

- The **control unit** manages the flow of data through the CPU. It directs data to and from the other components within the CPU.
- The **arithmetic logic unit (ALU)** component does the actual processing. It receives data and instructions and delivers a result. For example, if it received the numbers 3 and 5, and the instruction *Sum,* it would return 8.
- **Registers** are holding areas for both data and instructions. There are many different registers, each with its own special purpose. For example, there are registers that hold data, registers that hold instructions, registers that store logical states (yes/no), temporary values that serve as increment counters, and so on.

Physical Composition of a CPU

semiconductor Material that is electricity-neutral, neither a good conductor nor a flow preventer.

Physically, a CPU is a very small and thin sheet of semiconductor material (usually silicon) with a complex array of tiny transistors and buses stamped into it with a die. Semiconductor material is used for CPUs because it does not affect the flow of electricity one way or another: The semiconductor neither conducts nor impedes the electrical flow. The components inside the CPU are so small that you need a microscope to see them.

The CPU is fragile, so it is protected by a sturdy ceramic and metal casing; some models are mounted on miniature square circuit boards. The underside of this casing contains either tiny pins or tiny metal dots, precisely spaced, that align with connectors on the CPU socket on the motherboard. Each pin or dot is a separate communication line, carrying a different piece of data. Figure 2.1 shows both sides of a CPU designed for a desktop PC, for example. CPUs come in different sizes and have to match the socket type on the corresponding motherboard.

© iStockphoto.com/scanrail

Figure 2.1 A typical CPU, back and front.

Most modern CPUs have multiple cores, so they can complete multiple tasks simultaneously, as if they physically were more than one CPU. A core consists of a separate set of the essential processor components (control unit, ALU, and registers). Most models of the Intel i7 processor have four cores, for example. All the CPU's cores are located on the same chip.

core A set of the essential processor components that work together (control unit, ALU, and registers). A CPU may have multiple cores.

In theory, the CPU is capable of executing a function with every tick of the system clock (called a clock cycle). However, in practice, the CPU sometimes is idle because there is a delay between the request for data to be retrieved from memory and its delivery. A delay caused by waiting for another component to deliver data is called latency.

clock cycle One tick of the system clock.

latency A period of waiting for another component to deliver data needed to proceed.

To help minimize latency, CPUs have caches. A cache is a small amount of very fast memory located near (or within) the CPU. Data that the CPU has recently used, or is predicted to need soon, is placed in the cache for temporary holding. That way, if the CPU calls for the data, it's more readily available and there is less delay.

cache A small amount of fast memory located near or within the CPU.

CPU Performance Factors

The most obvious performance factor for a CPU is its maximum speed, measured in billions of hertz, or gigahertz (GHz). Although the actual speed is dictated by the motherboard's system clock, each CPU has an advertised maximum speed, which is the highest speed at which the CPU's manufacturer assures that it will reliably function.

hertz One cycle per second, a measurement of activity speed.

gigahertz One billion hertz.

word size The number of bits that the CPU can accept as input simultaneously.

A CPU's word size also makes a difference. The **word size** is the number of bits that the CPU (or a single core of the CPU, if multi-core) can accept as input simultaneously. Most desktop and notebook PCs have 64-bit CPUs, but some tablets, netbooks, and smartphones have 32-bit CPUs; see Figure 2.2.

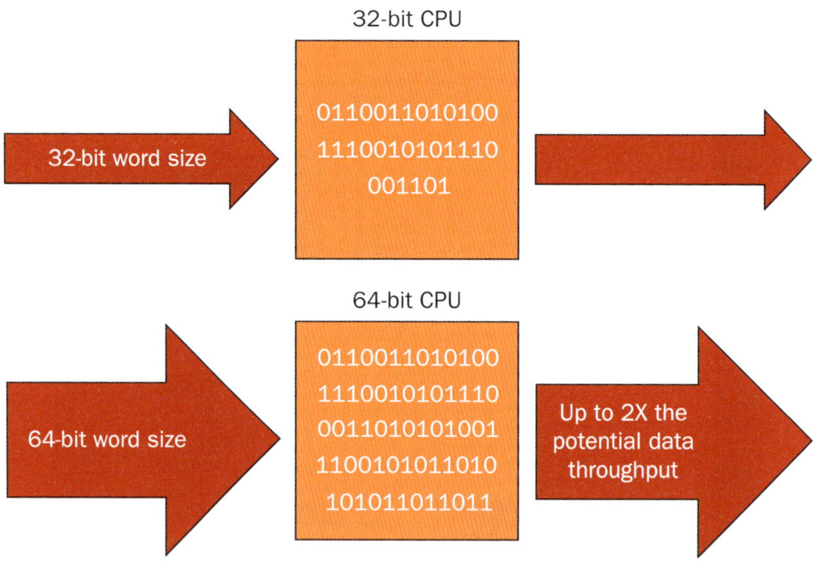

Figure 2.2 A 64-bit CPU has twice the word size of a 32-bit CPU, so the 64-bit CPU can theoretically input and output date at twice the rate. In actual use, many other factors also play a part, so the performance boost is less than 2x.

TIP Windows 7 comes in both 32-bit (x86) and 64-bit (x64) versions. When selecting a copy of Windows for a device, keep in mind that 32-bit CPUs can only run the 32-bit version of Windows. 64-bit CPUs can run either 64-bit or 32-bit versions of Windows, but run better with the 64-bit.

benchmark A consistent measurement of performance.

instructions per second A measurement of a CPU's throughput capability, taking into consideration factors such as number of cores and latency.

Because modern CPUs have many technology improvements in them, speed and word size alone do not form a reliable **benchmark** of a CPU's capability. Another way to look at performance is how many **instructions per second** the CPU can process.

The two largest manufacturers of CPUs are the companies Intel and Advanced Micro Devices (AMD). Their CPUs are roughly equivalent in performance level, but the internal architectures of the CPUs are different. A motherboard will support one or the other, but not both. Some people prefer one brand over the other, and claim that one brand or model is superior for using a certain kind of software. Such claims are a moving target, though, as each company continues to develop new and better CPUs.

Quick Review

1. What are the three main components inside a CPU?
2. What is the purpose of a cache?
3. What is a multi-core CPU?

Understanding Memory

Like the memory in the human brain, computer memory stores data. Also like human memory, there is both short-term (temporary) and long-term (permanent) memory storage. Some memory is dynamic, in that it stores data only until the computer is turned off. **Dynamic memory** (also called volatile memory) must be constantly refreshed. **Static memory** (also called non-volatile memory) retains whatever you put in it indefinitely.

dynamic memory Memory that does not retain its data unless it is constantly electrically refreshed.

static memory Memory that retains its data without electricity being constantly applied.

Another way to classify memory is whether it can be overwritten with new data or not. **Random Access Memory (RAM)** can be rewritten freely; **Read-Only Memory (ROM)** cannot (at least not in the same way that RAM can; see the following Note). All ROM is static, but RAM can be either dynamic (more common) or static.

Random Access Memory (RAM) Memory that can have its values changed freely, an unlimited number of times.

Read-Only Memory (ROM) In general, memory that cannot be rewritten. However, there are exceptions to that in newer types of ROM.

How Computers Use Memory

Computers use different types of memory in various ways. Here are some of the most common memory uses:

- **System memory:** The main memory in a computer system, such as the RAM installed on the PC's motherboard, is dynamic RAM (DRAM). System memory is installed in slots on the motherboard, perpendicular to the motherboard itself.

© iStockphoto.com/algre
System memory

- **Component memory:** Many components have a small amount of memory built in for their own use. For example, a printer might have RAM that holds the information about the page it is printing, and a display adapter might have memory to hold the data about the image it is displaying on the monitor. Component memory is typically DRAM unless the component's function requires it to be otherwise because that's the least expensive kind.

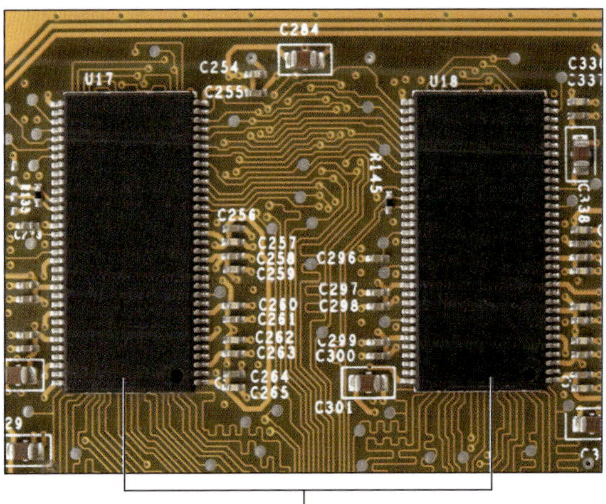

© iStockphoto.com/MauMyHaT
Component memory

Electrically Erasable Programmable ROM (EEPROM) ROM that can be erased and reprogrammed with electricity.

- ROM-BIOS: A motherboard has an EEPROM chip that contains the low-level startup instructions for the hardware. To prevent corruption that would prevent the system from starting up, this chip is not rewritable except with a special utility program.
- **Caches:** The caches in a CPU are a type of static RAM (SRAM).
- **USB flash drives, memory cards, and solid-state hard drives:** These devices use a type of EEPROM to store data. This type of EEPROM is also called flash memory; its enhanced technology allows data to be written and rewritten to it multiple times.

Understanding System Memory

system memory The main pool of dynamic RAM (DRAM) on the motherboard.

Each computer has a certain amount of system memory, also called RAM or main memory. It is dynamic RAM (DRAM), so it loses its contents if it is not constantly being electrically refreshed.

paging file The area of the hard drive set aside for use as virtual memory. Also called a **swap file**.

virtual memory Memory that is simulated by swapping data out of memory and storing it temporarily on the hard drive.

System memory forms a workspace that the operating system uses. When you open an application, that application is placed in system memory, and when you open a data file, it is placed there too. When you make changes to a data file, those changes wait in memory until you write them to a more permanent storage area by saving your work. The more system memory you have, the more applications and files you can have open at once.

NOTE

Windows also uses **virtual memory** to help prevent a computer from running out of memory. Virtual memory is a file on the hard drive used as an extension to main memory. This file is called the **paging file** or swap file. When the physical memory gets full (or nearly full), Windows moves some data to the paging file on the hard drive. When a program requests that data, Windows moves something else out of memory, swaps the old data back in again, and then responds to the request.

dual inline memory module (DIMM) A small rectangular circuit board that holds DRAM, fitting into a memory slot on a motherboard.

synchronous dynamic RAM (SDRAM) DRAM that operates at the speed of the system clock.

single data rate SDRAM (SDR SDRAM) SDRAM that performs one action per clock tick.

double data rate SDRAM (DDR SDRAM) SDRAM that performs two actions per clock tick.

Physically, system memory comes mounted on small rectangular circuit boards called dual inline memory module (DIMM). These circuit boards fit into memory slots on the motherboard. There are different types and speeds of DIMMs, so you must match the memory to the motherboard's requirements. Figure 2.3 shows two different types of DIMMs. For notebook computers, small outline DIMMs (SO-DIMMs) are used instead; they do the same thing as DIMMs but are a different size and shape.

Figure 2.3 Some DIMMs have a metal plate covering the chips for better heat dissipation.

Memory capacity is described in bytes (usually megabytes or gigabytes). SDRAM DIMMs come in different capacities, such as 2GB or 4GB. An average desktop PC might have 4GB to 8GB of system memory, which might be installed in either two or four DIMM slots.

TIP The 32-bit version of Windows can support only 4GB of RAM. If your computer has more than that, make sure you have the 64-bit version of Windows or some of your RAM will be unused. Sometimes the motherboard has a limit on the amount of RAM that can be recognized, so check this before you rush out and buy more RAM.

Quick Review

1. What is the difference between static and dynamic memory?
2. What is a DIMM?
3. In SDRAM, what does the "S" stand for, and what does it mean about the speed at which the RAM operates?

Understanding Motherboards

Both the CPU and the memory plug into the **motherboard** (see Figure 2.4). Motherboards vary in many ways, including the CPUs and memory they support, the technology used in their chipset, the expansion slots they have, and the external ports they support.

motherboard A large circuit board inside a computer that controls the operations of all other components.

Figure 2.4 A typical motherboard.

chipset The controller chip on a circuit board.

The motherboard's capabilities are determined by its **chipset**. The chipset contains the controllers that direct the traffic along the motherboard's buses, specify which memory and CPUs the motherboard can accept, and route data to expansion slots and ports as needed.

form factor The size and shape of a circuit board, such as a motherboard.

The **form factor** of the motherboard is its physical size and shape. It is significant because the motherboard must be able to physically fit into the system unit case.

Expansion Slots

expansion slot A slot in the motherboard into which an expansion card (a small circuit board) can be installed.

expansion card A small circuit board that fits into a slot on the motherboard to add functionality.

Expansion slots are plastic slots on the motherboard. Inside the slots are metal contacts that connect with metal contacts on smaller circuit boards called **expansion cards** that fit into them. You can buy many different expansion devices, adding capabilities that might not be built into the motherboard, or adding a more feature-rich version of a built-in device. For example, you might add a Wi-Fi adapter to a desktop PC with an expansion card, or a dial-up modem, or you might replace the on-board display adapter built into your motherboard with a model that has a faster graphics processor.

Different motherboards have different numbers and types of slots. Each slot type has its own separate bus, delivering its own combination of width and speed.

Peripheral Component Interface (PCI) A motherboard slot that accepts PCI expansion boards. PCI is considered a legacy interface (mostly obsolete).

PCI Express (PCIe) A new and updated version of the PCI motherboard slot. Different numbers of channels are used in different sized PCIe slots, such as 16, 4, or 1.

A typical motherboard might have three or more expansion slots: conventional **Peripheral Component Interface (PCI)** slots (an older type of slot, for backward compatibility with older devices) and several newer **PCI Express (PCIe)** slots. Figure 2.5 shows some slots in a motherboard; this one has one x1, one x4, and two x16 slots (which are all different sizes of PCIe slots), as well as one regular PCI slot.

ExpressCard A metal cartridge inserted into an externally accessible slot in a notebook PC that adds a capability to the system, such as wireless networking.

Notebook PCs are more likely than desktops to have a wide variety of built-in components, so there is less need for expansion slots. Because there's not much room for them internally, There might be an externally accessible expansion slot called an **ExpressCard** (or PC Card or CardBus) slot. ExpressCards are small circuit boards encased in a metal cartridge.

PCI Express Mini Card A small circuit board that can be installed in a notebook PC's PCI Express Mini expansion bay to add a capability to the computer, such as wireless networking.

There also might be a removable panel on a notebook PC with a **PCI Express Mini Card** socket, into which you can install a small expansion board that uses the motherboard's internal PCIe bus. One common use for this type of socket is to add a Wi-Fi adapter. Figure 2.6 shows a PCI Express Mini Card and its connector.

Photo by Snickerdo; licensed under Creative Commons.

Figure 2.5 PCI and PCIe slots in a motherboard.

Photo by Bastiaan van den Berg; licensed under Creative Commons.

Figure 2.6 A PCI Express Mini Card.

Built-in Components

Motherboards can also have built-in components for video, audio, and networking. Having these components built in means that you don't need to buy separate circuit boards for those capabilities, and you don't need expansion slots for such cards.

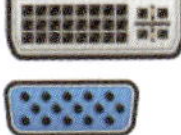

Each of those three built-in components has its own external ports built into the motherboard. The display adapter may have a **Digital Visual Interface (DVI)** connector, a **Video Graphics Adapter (VGA)** connector, or both. DVI is the newer, digital type of monitor connector used with digital monitors (which include most flat-screen LCD monitors); VGA is the older, analog type used with the boxy older CRT style of monitor and with some older or inexpensive LCD monitors.

Digital Visual Interface (DVI) A digital port for connecting a monitor to a PC.

Video Graphics Adapter An analog port for connecting a monitor to a PC.

The audio component support results in several small (3.5mm) round external connectors for plugging in speakers, headphones, and microphones. They are usually color-coded: pink for microphone, green for speakers or headphones, and blue for line input.

The Ethernet support results in an RJ-45 jack as an external connector. An RJ-45 jack looks like a telephone connector but is slightly wider and has eight metal contacts in it, rather than the two or four of a telephone connector.

Other Common External Connectors

Universal Serial Bus (USB) A general-purpose port for connecting external devices to a PC.

The motherboards typical of newer systems have only a few types of external ports. **Universal Serial Bus (USB)** is the most common multipurpose port type; many devices use USB ports, including keyboards, mice, and printers. There are different generations of USB, with different speeds.

IEEE 1394A A connector used to connect certain types of devices to a computer that require high-speed connection, such as some external hard drives and video cameras. A competitor to USB. Also called FireWire.

A motherboard can also support **IEEE 1394A** ports, also called FireWire ports. FireWire is a competitor to USB. It has not caught on quite as widely, but it is used for some external hard drives and digital video equipment.

Older systems may have a variety of other external ports, for backward compatibility with older devices. Motherboards with these older ports are still available today, but they are becoming less and less common. The most common legacy ports are:

PS/2 A connector used to connect some older keyboards and mice to a computer. PS stands for Personal System. This connector was first introduced with the IBM PS/2 computer in 1987.

parallel port A port used to connect some older printers to a computer. It is sometimes called an LPT port, which stands for Line Printer.

serial port A port used to connect some very old external devices to a computer. It is sometimes called a COM port, which stands for communications (although actually many types of ports operate serially, not just this one).

- **PS/2 port:** This is a small round port that was used for mice and keyboards before USB became popular. They are usually color-coded: purple for the keyboard and green for the mouse.
- **Parallel (LPT) port:** This is a 25-pin connector, with the holes arranged in two rows. It was used for printers before USB became the dominant interface for printers. The port on the computer is a female connector, meaning it has holes; the connector on the cable that plugs into it is a male connector, containing pins that fit in the holes. This type of connector is sometimes called a DB-25 connector.
- **Serial (COM) port:** This is a 9-pin connector (DB-9), with the pins arranged in two rows. It is a male connector on the motherboard, and the cable that plugs into it is female. This type of port used to be an all-purpose port for a variety of external devices, much like USB is today.

Drive Connectors

ATA Short for AT Attachment. The IBM PC AT was an early type of computer (1984) that was among the first to support modern hard drive technology.

Parallel ATA (PATA) A type of connector used for older disk drives and optical drives such as CD and DVD drives.

Serial ATA (SATA) A type of connector used for newer disk drives.

Most motherboards have two types of drive connectors. The older type is **Parallel ATA (PATA)**, and it is used with older hard drives and most CD and DVD drives. This type of connector has 40 pins arranged in two rows, and uses a ribbon cable to connect the device to the motherboard.

The newer type is **Serial ATA (SATA)**, a more compact connector that uses a thin round cable. SATA is used with newer hard drives. You will learn more about drive connectors in Chapter 3, "Input, Output, and Storage."

Step by Step

Exploring Your Motherboard

Use this procedure to see what components and connectors your motherboard has. Use a desktop computer for this exercise.

1. Shut down the computer, and open up the system unit. You may need a Phillips screwdriver. Ask your instructor for assistance if needed. **Do not touch anything inside the system unit.**
2. Locate the following components. Ask your instructor to confirm that you are correct:
   - CPU (may be under a heat sink)
   - System memory
   - Built-in USB ports
   - Other built-in ports (name them if you can)
   - Expansion slots (identify the type if you can)
3. Trace each cable from the motherboard to the components to see how components such as the hard drive and power supply attach to the motherboard.
4. Close the system unit's case and replace any screws you removed.

Quick Review

1. If you see a DVI port built into a motherboard, what type of capability can you assume is built into the motherboard?
2. What is PCI Express (PCIe)?

Understanding Power Supplies

The power from your wall outlet is alternating current (AC), and is either 110 volt (v) or 220v, depending on the country in which you live. Computer components require direct current (DC) and require much lower voltages. A power supply has two jobs:

- It converts AC to DC power.
- It decreases the voltage to the amount required for each component.

power supply A component that converts AC power from a wall outlet to DC power and decreases the voltage to the level needed for the computer to operate.

In a desktop PC, a power supply is a large silver metal box mounted in one corner of the system unit, with many bundles of colored wires and connectors emerging from it (see Figure 2.7). The wire colors are significant; each wire color carries a different voltage. Each connector has the appropriate wires running to it to deliver the exact voltage required for each connected device. The most common wire colors are red, yellow, and black. The connector shown in Figure 2.8, for example, uses one red wire, one yellow wire, and two black wires. The power comes in on the red and yellow wires, and the black wires are for grounding.

A desktop PC's power supply has a fan in it, and when you start up the PC, the fan starts up too. The fan pulls hot air out of the power supply, and has a side benefit of circulating air through the entire system unit too.

© iStockphoto.com/DonNichols

Figure 2.7 A desktop PC's power supply.

© iStockphoto.com/aarrows

Figure 2.8 A power connector for a Serial ATA (SATA) hard drive. The drive requires both +5 and +12 power, supplied on the red and yellow wires, respectively.

In addition to the several types of connectors that go to internal devices such as drives, the power supply also has one big connector, containing 20 or more wires arranged in two rows. Figure 2.9 shows an example. This connector plugs directly into the motherboard, and powers all its components that do not have separate power connectors.

© iStockphoto.com/ebrink

Figure 2.9 This connector runs from the power supply to the motherboard, delivering all the different voltages that devices that connect directly into the motherboard might need.

On a notebook PC, the power supply is built in. The power cord typically contains a transformer block (sometimes called a brick) that decreases and converts the voltage. Figure 2.10 shows an example. When a notebook PC is plugged into AC power, its battery

transformer block A thick block built into a power cable for a device that handles the conversion of AC power to DC and decreases the voltage to the level needed.

© iStockphoto.com/Nickondr

Figure 2.10 A power cord for a notebook PC includes a transformer block that converts the power to the type and voltage needed.

recharges. The battery automatically provides DC power at the correct voltage, so no power conversion is needed when running on battery power.

Quick Review

1. What are the two functions of a desktop power supply?
2. What is the significance of the different wire colors on a power connector?
3. Why do notebook PC power cords have a rectangular block built into them?

Summary

Understanding CPUs

A **central processing unit (CPU)** contains a **control unit**, an **arithmetic logic unit (ALU)**, and **registers**. The CPU operates at the pace dictated by the **system clock**, executing billions of operations per second. One tick of that clock is a **clock cycle**. When the CPU sits idle during a clock cycle because it is waiting for data it needs, that wait time is called **latency**. To minimize latency, CPUs have multiple **caches**.

Physically, the CPU is a **semiconductor** wafer of silicon. Most modern CPUs have multiple **cores**; each core has its own control unit, ALU, and registers. A CPU has a maximum speed, measured in **gigahertz (GHz)**. A CPU's **word size** is the number of bits it can accept as input simultaneously. Modern CPUs in personal computers are usually either 32-bit or 64-bit. Windows is available in both 32-bit and 64-bit versions. CPU performance can be described in the number of **instructions per second** it can process, but it is more reliably measured using **benchmarking** software.

Understanding Memory

Memory can be either **dynamic** (losing its data when it loses power) or **static** (retaining its data). **Random access memory (RAM)** can be freely rewritten, and can be either static or dynamic. **Read-only memory (ROM)** is always static.

System memory resides on the motherboard and is used as a work area for the operating system. Some components also have their own memory. **Virtual memory** is hard drive space that simulates extra memory by allowing the operating system to swap data into and out of the real memory into a **swap file**.

Physically, system memory comes in **dual inline memory modules (DIMMs)**.

Understanding Motherboards

The **motherboard**'s capabilities are determined by its **chipset**. A motherboard's **form factor** is its physical size.

Motherboards have **expansion slots**, each type of slot having its own **bus** on the motherboard. **Peripheral Component Interface (PCI)** is an older type of expansion slot; a newer type is **PCI Express (PCIe)**, which comes in a variety of sizes based on the number of channels, such as x1, x4, or x16. Some notebook computers have **ExpressCard** slots or **PCI Express Mini Card** slots.

Some of the ports that a motherboard may have built in include **Digital Visual Interface (DVI)** and **Video Graphics Adapter (VGA)** for video, 3.5mm analog plugs for audio, and **RJ-45** for Ethernet networking. Internally, a motherboard has connectors for disk drives, including **Parallel ATA (PATA)** and **Serial ATA (SATA)**.

A Universal Serial Bus (USB) port is a general-purpose expansion port. **IEEE 1394A**, also called FireWire, is an alternative to USB, and is used on some external hard drives and digital video cameras. Older ports that a system might have include **PS/2**, **parallel (LPT),** and **serial (COM)**.

Understanding Power Supplies

The computer's **power supply** converts AC to DC power and decreases the voltage to the amount required. The colors of the wires on the connectors on the power supply are significant, indicating different voltages. On a notebook PC, a **transformer block** built into the power cable provides the same functions as the power supply in a desktop PC.

Key Terms

benchmark
cache
Central Processing Unit (CPU)
chipset
core
Digital Visual Interface (DVI)
double data rate (DDR)
dual inline memory module (DIMM)
dynamic memory
Electrically Erasable Programmable ROM (EEPROM)
expansion card
expansion slots
ExpressCard
form factor
gigahertz (GHz)
heat sink
hertz
IEEE 1394A
instructions per second
latency
motherboard
paging file
Parallel ATA
parallel port
PCI Express (PCIe)
PCI Express Mini Card
Peripheral Component Interface (PCI)
power supply
PS/2
Random Access Memory (RAM)
Read-Only Memory (ROM)
semiconductor
Serial ATA
serial port
single data rate (SDR)
static memory
swap file
synchronous dynamic RAM (SDRAM)
system memory
transformer block
Universal Serial Bus
Video Graphics Adapter (VGA)
virtual memory
word size

Test Yourself

Fact Check

1. The ______ in the CPU does the actual processing.
   a. cache
   b. ALU
   c. control unit
   d. register
2. Some CPUs have multiple _____, each with its own control unit, ALU, and registers.
   a. caches
   b. cores
   c. clocks
   d. DIMMs
3. ________ memory loses its data when not continuously supplied with electricity.
   a. Dynamic
   b. Static
   c. Synchronous
   d. Non-volatile

4. The memory in a USB flash drive is a type of ________.

   a. DRAM

   b. EEPROM

   c. SRAM

   d. CPU

5. A(n) _____ is a circuit board containing memory chips.

   a. CPU

   b. DDR

   c. DIMM

   d. SDR

6. The motherboard's capabilities are determined by its chipset.

   a. True

   b. False

7. Which of these is a type of expansion slot on a motherboard?

   a. DVI

   b. EEPROM

   c. DDR

   d. PCIe

8. DVI and VGA are both types of _______ ports.

   a. sound

   b. network

   c. display

   d. printer

9. Which port type is a similar competitor to USB?

   a. FireWire

   b. DVI

   c. RJ-45

   d. Legacy serial (COM)

10. The two main functions of a _________ are to convert AC power to DC power and decreases the voltage of the electricity entering the computer.

Matching

Match the memory-related term to its definition.

a. DIMM

b. L1 cache

c. ROM-BIOS

d. SDRAM

e. system memory

f. virtual memory

1. ________The main memory in a computer, used as the RAM installed on the motherboard.

2. ________The EEPROM chip that contains the low-level start-up instructions for the hardware.

3. ________Static RAM inside the CPU that holds data that may be needed again shortly.

4. ________A swap file on the hard drive for data temporarily removed from memory.

5. ________A rectangular circuit board containing memory chips.

6. ________RAM that operates synchronously with the system clock.

Sum It Up

1. What are the two basic components inside a CPU?
2. What is the difference between static and dynamic memory?
3. What are four ways in which one motherboard may differ from another?
4. Why does a power supply have different colored wires?

Explore More

Benchmarking

Download the free 2014 version of SiSoftware SANDRA, a benchmarking utility, from `www.sisoftware.net`.

If you have time (at least 30 minutes), run the Overall Score test. If not, run only the Processor Arithmetic test and the Cache & Memory Latency tests. Examine the results, and compare them to the results of your classmates who are using different computers.

What is the Aggregated Score for processor arithmetic? This score is represented in GOPS (giga-operation per second).

What is the rated speed and type of the CPU? In Windows, click the Start button, and then right-click Computer and choose Properties. Note the processor information that appears on that screen. Does it match what the utility detected?

What is the memory latency score? Notice the L1, L2, and L3 cache scores are expressed in "clocks." This means that those caches, on average, take that many clock cycles to retrieve from memory.

If time permits, run other benchmarks using this utility; your instructor may assign additional tests to complete.

Completing a System Inventory

Using the features described in this chapter, create a description of your system's motherboard, as completely as you can describe it. If you can find its model number (usually stamped on the board itself), look it up online to see if its specs are available. If not, do your best to deduce its characteristics by looking at what ports are built in and by using the System Information utility in Windows.

Exploring Power Voltages

To do this exploration, you will need a desktop PC and a voltmeter (or a multimeter that measures DC volts). Your instructor may need to guide you through the process.

1. Turn on your meter and set it to DC volts. You should have a red probe and a black probe.
2. Open the system unit case, and locate the large connector that joins the power supply to the motherboard.
3. Turn on the PC.
4. Insert the black probe down into one of the sockets where a black wire connects, so that the probe touches the bare metal wire.
5. Insert the red probe down into one of the sockets where a red wire connects, so that the probe touches the bare metal wire.
6. Read the display on the meter. It should be approximately +5v.
7. Repeat Steps 4–6 with several other wire colors, and record the readings you get.
8. Turn off the meter and put it away.
9. Turn off the computer, and close the system unit case.

Think It Over

Is Faster Always Desirable?

Is it important to you, when buying a new computer, to have the fastest and best CPU available, even if it costs more? Does it make more financial sense to pay more now for a CPU that will become obsolete less quickly a few years in the future? Or is it better to buy a lesser CPU, even if you have to replace the computer sooner because it will no longer be powerful enough to run the latest programs in a few years?

Shopping with Expandability in Mind

If you were buying a computer today, what expansion slots and ports would be important for your new computer to have, and why? That is, what device would you plan to install later that might need those slots or ports?

Chapter 3

Input, Output, and Storage

Selecting and Using Input Devices

Selecting and Using Output Devices

Choosing Appropriate Storage Devices

Learning objectives

- Define input and describe the available types of keyboards and pointing devices
- Describe scanning and image-capturing device types and features
- Define output and explain the types of output devices available
- Differentiate between types of monitors and explain their features
- Differentiate between types of printers and identify the best printer for a task
- Classify storage devices according to their capacities, interface, and media
- Explain cloud and network storage and identify online and network-based storage technologies

Chapter 2, "The System Unit," explained the inner workings of a computer inside the mysterious box known as the system unit. In this chapter, you'll look at how data moves into and out of that system unit—via input and output devices.

Different kinds of computers accept input from different sources. For example, a desktop PC might have a keyboard and mouse, whereas a tablet PC or smartphone might have a touch screen and some built-in buttons. Output can include messages and data that appear on the monitor screen, a hard-copy printout, and audio cues or prompts the computer might generate, such as a warning beep or the playback of your favorite song. Storage devices hold information for later use; they vary by capacity, interface, and the medium used to store the files.

In this chapter, you will learn about the types of input, output, and storage devices available, and how to choose the right one for a particular computer system and task.

Careers in IT

Database Administrator

Businesses store large amounts of data, and that data is often much more valuable than the hardware on which it is stored. Information about customers, orders, product inventory, suppliers, and market trends must be readily and reliably available for the business to thrive. A database administrator is an expert in managing, summarizing, and safeguarding large amounts of data. Database administrators also plan and create well-organized database systems for storing new and existing data. For this career, a bachelor of science or associate of science degree in an information technology-related field would be useful.

Selecting and Using Input Devices

input device Hardware that enables the computer to accept commands or data from a human user.

Whenever you type a letter in a word processor, or issue the command to open or close the word processing program, you use an **input device**. Input devices allow the user to communicate with the operating system and applications. In this section, you will learn about several types of input devices.

Keyboards

A keyboard enables you to enter typed data—letters, numbers, and symbols. A keyboard can be a separate device that plugs into the system unit (as with a desktop PC) or a built-in keyboard (as with a notebook PC).

QWERTY The standard layout for English-language keyboards.

There are many sizes and types of keyboards, but most English-language keyboards use the same key arrangement, called **QWERTY**. The name comes from the first six letter keys on the top row, from left to right. Figure 3.1 shows a QWERTY keyboard.

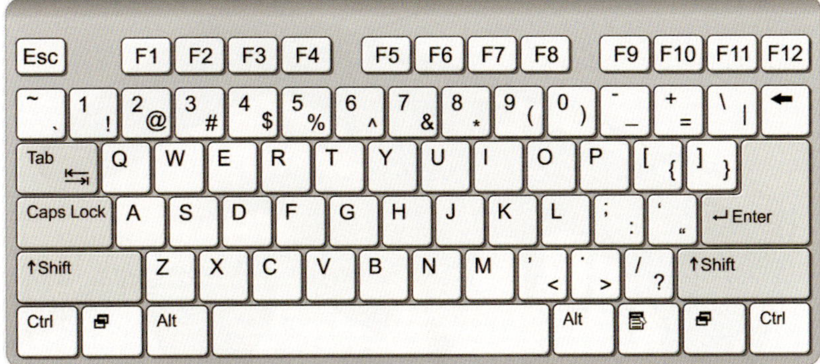

© iStockphoto.com/Youst

Figure 3.1 The QWERTY keyboard layout.

This type of keyboard has a number of specialty keys as well as the numbers, letters, and symbols. Specialty keys include:

- **Function keys** (F1 through F12) perform special actions when pressed. The action assigned to each key depends on the operating system or application you are using.
- **Toggle keys** turn a feature on or off each time they are pressed. For example, the Caps Lock key toggles between upper- and lowercase letter typing mode, and the Num Lock key toggles between the numeric keypad on the keyboard (if it has one) providing number entry or functioning as a set of directional arrows.
- **Modifier keys** change the meaning of other keys when they are pressed in combination with them. For example, the Shift key, when pressed in combination with a letter, makes that letter uppercase. Other keys, such as Ctrl and Alt, can be used with other keys to issue special command shortcuts. For example, a common keyboard shortcut in Windows 7 is Ctrl+C (press both keys simultaneously) for copying selected content.

NOTE

On a notebook computer, an Fn key may be present; it's an extra modifier key that allows you to access special functions assigned to certain keys. For example, you might see a sun symbol and an up arrow on one of the function keys. You could hold down Fn and press that function key to increase the brightness of the display. Check the manual that came with your notebook computer to find out more about the actions you can take with the Fn key.

- **Positional keys** such as the Home, End, Page Up, and Page Down keys, as well as the directional arrow keys, scroll the display or move the insertion point in applications.

A wireless keyboard does not require a cable connection to the computer, allowing for greater ease of use. An ergonomic keyboard is a keyboard that is designed to minimize the stress on the user's body (see Figure 3.2). It may have a built-in palm or wrist support, for example. A bilingual keyboard has characters in more than one language on its keys, so when you switch to a different keyboard layout in the operating system, the characters on the keyboard match what you are typing.

insertion point The flashing vertical line that indicates where typed text will appear.

wireless keyboard A keyboard that connects to the computer wirelessly rather than with a cable.

ergonomic keyboard A keyboard that is designed with features that help reduce stress on the user's hands and wrists.

© iStockphoto.com/pengpeng

Figure 3.2 An ergonomic keyboard.

virtual or onscreen keyboard A replica of a keyboard on the screen that users can tap or click to simulate typing.

Step by Step

Using a Virtual Keyboard

Devices that don't have physical keyboards, like tablets and smartphones, use a **virtual keyboard**, which is a software replica of a keyboard that pops up on the touch screen. Even if you have a regular keyboard, you can still try out a virtual keyboard in Windows if you like. Follow these steps to use the virtual keyboard in Windows 7:

1. Click the Start button and type **key** and then click On-Screen Keyboard. A window appears showing a virtual keyboard.
2. Open an application in which you can type text, such as Notepad. To open Notepad, click the Start button, type **notepad** into the Search field, and then click Notepad.
3. Experiment with the keyboard by clicking keys to type the letters.
4. When you are finished, click the Close (X) button in the upper-left corner of the On-Screen Keyboard window.
5. Close the application you opened in Step 2 without saving your changes.

Pointing Devices

A pointing device is a piece of hardware that enables you to move an onscreen pointer in a graphical user interface like Microsoft Windows. A mouse is the most common pointing device. It is a palm-sized object that you move across a flat surface to move the pointer on the display. A mouse has one or more buttons on it; you press the buttons to act upon whatever the pointer is pointing at.

mouse A pointing device that the user moves with his or her hand across a flat surface to move an onscreen pointer.

A mouse can be either mechanical or optical. A mechanical mouse has a chamber on its underside with a rubber ball in it. As you roll the mouse across a flat surface, the ball turns, activating sensors inside the chamber that translate the ball's movement to onscreen pointer activity. An optical mouse has a light-emitting diode (LED) and a sensor on its underside, as shown in Figure 3.3. The light bounces off the surface

mechanical mouse A mouse that operates by rolling a rubber ball inside a chamber containing sensors.

optical mouse A mouse that operates by bouncing light off a flat surface and measuring the reflection.

and the sensor measures it, and those measurements are reported back to the computer to tell the pointer how to move. Mechanical mice need frequent cleaning; optical mice are maintenance-free and have virtually replaced the mechanical type.

Figure 3.3 The underside of an optical mouse contains a red light and a sensor that measures its reflection from the surface the mouse is used on.

Like a keyboard, a mouse can have a wire (cord) connecting it to the computer, or it can be wireless. A **wireless mouse** communicates with a **transceiver** connected to a USB port to exchange data with the computer, or uses a technology called Bluetooth to communicate via radio waves. A wireless mouse requires a battery, whereas a wired mouse draws the small amount of power it needs from the computer via its cord.

wireless mouse A mouse that communicates wirelessly with a transceiver connected to the computer, so it does not need a cord.

transceiver A unit that provides the wireless transmission for a cordless device like keyboard or mouse, usually plugged into a USB port.

Other pointing devices are also available. For example, a **trackball** is a stationary device with a ball on top (or on the side) that you roll with your fingers. See Figure 3.4. A trackball requires less space on a desk to operate and some people find it more comfortable to use than a mouse. Many notebook computers have a built-in **touchpad**, which is a small rectangular touch-sensitive pad with buttons below it. See Figure 3.5. You can drag your finger on the pad to move the onscreen pointer, and press the buttons to click.

trackball A pointing device in which the user moves the pointer by rolling a ball with his or her fingers.

touchpad A pointing device consisting of a touch-sensitive pad on which the user drags a finger to move the pointer.

Figure 3.4 A trackball is stationary; the user moves the ball with his or her fingers.

© iStockphoto.com/vincomfoto

Figure 3.5 A touchpad is a touch-sensitive area that the user drags a finger across to move the pointer onscreen.

touch screen A touch-sensitive display monitor that functions both as an input and an output device.

A touch screen can enable you to use your finger as a pointing device. Tap or drag your finger across a touch screen to perform mouse-equivalent operations.

joystick A pointing device consisting of a vertically mounted stick that can be tilted in any direction.

A joystick, shown in Figure 3.6, is a specialized pointing device used primarily in gaming. It consists of a vertically mounted stick that can be tilted in any direction. A set of buttons on the base of the joystick enable you to perform actions, such as shooting or jumping in a game.

© iStockphoto.com/chrisboy2004

Figure 3.6 A joystick.

Drawing Tablets

drawing tablet A flat rectangular touch-sensitive surface on which a user can draw with a stylus to create onscreen artwork.

stylus A pen-shaped pointer used to drag across the surface of a touch-sensitive screen.

A drawing tablet, also called a digitizing tablet, is a specialized type of touchpad designed for drawing. The user draws on the tablet with a pen-shaped pointer called a stylus, and the drawing shows up onscreen. Professional graphic artists use drawing tablets to draw directly into a computer program to create both technical and artistic drawings. Figure 3.7 shows a drawing tablet.

© iStockphoto.com/ppart

Figure 3.7 A drawing tablet.

Sensory Input

New Technologies

Many portable devices, such as smartphones and tablets, have new types of input technology that detect direction, motion, and/or location. For example, some devices have a **global positioning system (GPS)** to detect your location, an **accelerometer** to tell how fast you are moving, a **compass** to report what direction you are facing, and a **gyroscope** to report the orientation of the device. It is the gyroscope, for example, that tells a phone or tablet when you turn it on its side so it can change the orientation of the screen.

Scanning Devices

A scanner digitizes hard-copy photos and documents and stores them electronically. Scanners work by shining a bright light on the surface of the page and measuring the amount of light that bounces back from it using a photosensitive charge-coupled device (CCD). Lighter areas bounce back more light than darker areas. For color scanning, multiple sensors are used, each one picking up a different color: red, green, and blue.

digitize To convert something from hard-copy to digital (computerized) form.

charge-coupled device (CCD) The light-sensitive sensor in a scanner that records the amount of light bounced back from the image.

NOTE

A scanner can be a stand-alone device, or it can be a component in a multi-function device (MFD) that combines the functions of a printer, copier, and scanner into one unit.

Most scanners are flatbed models, as in Figure 3.8, where you place the image on a flat piece of glass and then a sensor and light bar moves beneath it to capture the image. A flatbed scanner may optionally have a document feeder on it so multiple pages can be queued for scanning. There are also smaller portable scanners that either feed in one sheet at a time past a stationary sensor and light bar, or that you hold in your hand and manually move across the image to be scanned.

When you scan text, you can use optical character recognition (OCR) software to convert the scanned image to text that you can work with in a text editing program.

multi-function device (MFD) A device that combines the functions of a printer, a copier, and a scanner into one unit, and also a fax in some models.

flatbed scanner A scanner that has a large flat glass surface on which the page to be scanned is placed.

document feeder A mechanical feature of some scanners that enables multiple pages to be scanned consecutively without user intervention.

© iStockphoto.com/nicolas_

Figure 3.8 A flatbed scanner.

CAUTION OCR software is not perfect; it sometimes makes mistakes in conversion, so you must proofread scanned text carefully.

bar code reader A scanner that reads and interprets bar codes such as UPC symbols.

Universal Product Code (UPC) A bar code system used for identifying products for sale.

One very simple type of scanner is a **bar code reader**, shown in Figure 3.9. Bar codes are vertical stripes of varying widths and spaces that represent numeric values. The most common type of bar code is a **Universal Product Code (UPC)**, the bar code that identifies a product that consumers buy at a store.

A bar code reader examines the bars and inputs their numeric values into the computer. A bar code reader can be hand-held, like a gun-type unit that a warehouse worker might use to look up an item, or stationary, like the scanner in a grocery store checkout kiosk. Bar codes are used everywhere that numeric accuracy is important for tracking physical items. For example, they are used in many manufacturing businesses to track parts, finished products, and orders. Shipping services use them to track the packages as they move from their origin to their destination, and retail stores use them at the cash registers to scan purchased items and look up their prices.

© iStockphoto.com/UltraONEs

Figure 3.9 A bar code reader.

QR code (which stands for Quick Response) is a new type of scanner-readable code that is replacing UPCs in many places. It's a two-dimensional barcode. Whereas a standard bar code is read in only one direction (analyzing the width and spacing of the bars), a QR code is a square panel with encoded data in both directions. QR codes can store more data than bar codes, making them more useful for providing information about an item. Figure 3.10 shows an example of a QR code being scanned by a smartphone.

QR code A two-dimensional variant of a bar code, containing more information than a traditional bar code.

© iStockphoto.com/pinstock

Figure 3.10 QR codes can be scanned by smartphones (with an appropriate app installed) as well as by specialized scanners.

Put It to Work

Scanning QR Codes

Many smartphones with cameras have QR readers built into them, so your phone can serve as a QR scanner. When you scan a QR code that you see on an advertisement, for example, you might be taken to the company's website or to a coupon for the product. If you have a smartphone, see if it has a code reader app. If it doesn't, download a free one. Then locate a QR code (look in magazines, on billboards, on subways, and anywhere else that companies advertise) and scan it with your phone to see what happens.

magnetic card reader A scanner that reads and deciphers the information on the magnetic strip on a credit card or other ID card.

radio frequency identification (RFID) chip A computer chip that communicates wirelessly with a device to authenticate a user.

Another type of scanner used in many businesses is a **magnetic card reader**, shown in Figure 3.11. You use one of these every time you swipe a credit card to pay for a purchase, for example. Magnetic card readers read the encoded data on the magnetic strip on the back of your credit card or ID card and transfer that data into a computer. Some credit cards have a **radio frequency identification (RFID) chip** in them that enables you to pass them in front of a radio frequency card reader to read the card's data without it physically touching a reader. RFID chips are also used in security systems to allow employees access to secure areas of a building if they are wearing an RFID-equipped ID badge.

© iStockphoto.com/ugurhan

Figure 3.11 A magnetic card reader.

Security and Privacy

Fingerprint Readers

A fingerprint reader is a type of biometric scanner—that is, a scanner that scans something about a human body that is used to identify that person. Many computer systems use fingerprint readers as a form of user authentication. The fingerprint of the person logging in is compared to a database of pictures of the fingerprints of authorized users. Other types of biometric scanners include facial recognition, voice recognition, and retina scanners.

© iStockphoto.com/LongHa2006

optical mark recognition A scanner that detects the presence of a pencil or ink mark on certain areas of a standardized form.

magnetic-ink character recognition (MICR) The scanning system used in the banking industry to read routing and account numbers on checks and deposit slips.

Certain industries use specialized scanners to simplify data entry. For example, companies that grade standardized testing use an **optical mark recognition (OMR)** system that detects the presence of a pencil or ink mark on certain spots on a standardized form. Banking institutions save time and cut down on entry errors by using a **magnetic-ink character recognition (MICR)** system to read the routing and account numbers on checks and deposit slips, as in Figure 3.12.

© iStockphoto.com/jimd_stock

Figure 3.12 The routing numbers on checks are written with magnetic ink so they can be read by MICR machines.

Capture Devices

The scanners you have learned about so far read existing data and scan existing photographs and documents. Image capture devices, on the other hand, capture new content.

A capture device can capture either still images or motion video. Some devices do both, but most are designed primarily for one type or another. A **digital camera** is designed primarily for still photos, and looks much like a film camera; a **digital video camera** is designed primarily for motion video. See Figure 3.13. Both work using the same basic technology; the digital video camera captures many **frames** (individual still images) per second and stores them in a single file. When you play back the still images in chronological order, the image appears to be moving. Digital video cameras can also capture sound to accompany the video clips, which can be played back synchronously with the images. Many modern smartphones have built-in cameras that can take still photos and record video clips.

digital camera A camera that captures and stores still images in digital form.

digital video camera A video camera that captures and stores motion video in digital form.

frame A still image that makes up part of a digital video clip.

© iStockphoto.com/Chiyacat (left), © iStockphoto.com/arsenik (right)

Figure 3.13 A digital camera (left) and a digital video camera (right).

Some digital video cameras are stand-alone; you can take them out into the world and capture video, and then connect the video camera to a computer to transfer, edit, and save the video clips. Other cameras are **webcams**, as in Figure 3.14, which are simple video cameras that lack their own storage and capture controls. They remain permanently

webcam A digital video camera that must remain connected to a computer as it operates.

attached to the computer, and store their video clips or still images directly on the computer's storage drives. They rely on video capture software on the computer to start and stop the capture process. Webcams are often used for online video chatting through services such as Skype.

© iStockphoto.com/temniy

Figure 3.14 A webcam.

Audio Input Devices

audio adapter Also called a sound card. A component of a computer system that accepts and processes audio input and delivers audio output.

Most personal computers support audio input, either through a built-in **audio adapter** on the motherboard or through an add-on sound card. A computer's audio ports may support speakers, headphones, microphones, and both analog and digital external audio device input. An example of an external audio input device is a home stereo system; an external digital audio device might be a digital piano keyboard.

If you have a microphone and voice input software, you can speak into the microphone to issue commands to the computer and to input text into a word processing program. Some people with disabilities use voice input to control the computer as a substitute for a keyboard or mouse, and some people who have a lot of text to enter but don't type very quickly may find voice input more efficient than trying to type all the text. People who use audio input frequently find that it is worthwhile to buy a high-quality microphone headset, as in Figure 3.15, because it provides more accurate voice pickup.

voice recognition software Software that recognizes spoken words that match words in its database to digitize spoken language.

speech recognition software Software that can learn an individual's pronunciation and vocal inflection and translate it into digitized text.

There are two kinds of voice input software: voice recognition and speech recognition. **Voice recognition software** recognizes spoken words that match words in its database. It does not pay attention to the tone or inflection of the speaker's voice. People who speak with a heavy accent may have difficulty with such software. Voice recognition is included with Microsoft Windows and Microsoft Office. **Speech recognition software** is teachable software that learns an individual's pronunciation and vocal inflection. Each user trains the software by reading long passages of text into the microphone; the software records what each word sounds like when that person pronounces it, and can also learn new words.

Figure 3.15 A headset microphone works well for voice input software use.

Quick Review

1. Name three kinds of pointing devices.
2. Besides numbers, letters, and symbols, what other kinds of keys are found on a keyboard and what do they do?
3. What hardware is required for audio input?
4. What is the difference between a digital video camera and a webcam?

Selecting and Using Output Devices

Output devices make the computer's processed information available to a human user. Without output devices, there would be little reason to have a computer, because it wouldn't produce anything you could use. The most common types of output devices are display screens, printers, and speakers.

Display Screens

A **display screen** is a video screen that the computer uses to provide information to a human user. A display screen can be built into a device, as it is with smartphones, tablets, and notebook PCs, or it can be a separate unit (a monitor), as it is with the majority of desktop PCs.

display screen A video screen that a computer uses to provide output to a human user.

Display screens create their images by filling in tiny dots called **pixels** with different colors. The pixels are so small and so close together that the human eye sees them as continuous color gradients rather than individual blocks. Monitors differ in the technology they use to illuminate those pixels.

pixel An individual colored dot in a raster graphic or on a display screen.

Built-in display screens are thin and flat, and most of them use **liquid crystal display (LCD)** technology. Most modern stand-alone monitors are also LCD, like the one shown in Figure 3.16. This technology has two polarized filters, with a liquid crystal substance between them. One filter is at an angle, so light doesn't pass through it automatically. When electricity hits a crystal, it twists, refracting the light so that it passes

liquid crystal display (LCD) A flat-screen display technology that passes electricity through liquid crystals to create a display image.

through the second filter and lights up the display in a certain spot. Color displays have separate filters for red, green, and blue. Some new mobile devices use **organic light-emitting diode (OLED)** technology, which uses organic matter that lights up in response to an electrical current.

organic light-emitting diode (OLED) A flat-screen technology that uses organic matter that lights up in response to electrical current to create a display image.

© iStockphoto.com/dem10

Figure 3.16 An LCD monitor has a thin, flat screen.

Flat-screen displays vary in the number of transistors used to create the display image. In an **active matrix**, each individual pixel in the display is actively maintained by a separate transistor. Almost all LED screens today are an improved variant of an active matrix called **thin-film transistor (TFT)**. In a **passive matrix** (which is cheaper to manufacture), each pixel maintains its state on its own until it decays or is refreshed. An OLED screen may be active matrix or passive matrix, depending on the model.

active matrix An LCD type in which each pixel is actively maintained by a separate transistor.

thin-film transistor An improved type of active matrix common in modern monitors and display screens.

passive matrix An LCD type in which each pixel maintains its state on its own until it decays or is refreshed.

NOTE A **high-definition TV (HDTV)** can also be used as a computer monitor by connecting the computer to one of its **high-definition multimedia interface (HDMI)** input ports.

Cathode ray tube (CRT) is an older monitor technology that uses a large vacuum tube and electron guns to create a display image on a phosphor-covered glass. See Figure 3.17. The electrons strike phosphors on the monitor glass and briefly light up. The display is refreshed many times per second to maintain the image. The phosphors are arranged in **triads**: red, green, and blue, as shown in Figure 3.18. Depending on what color a particular pixel should be, different phosphors illuminate within that triad. CRT monitors are heavy and bulky compared to LCDs, and have mostly been replaced by LCD monitors. You may still see one in use with an older computer, however.

high-definition TV (HDTV) A television that displays at least 1920 × 1080 resolution (also known as 1080p).

high-definition multimedia interface (HDMI) A type of connector used to connect an HDTV to another device, such as a computer or a home theater system.

cathode ray tube (CRT) An older type of monitor technology that uses a vacuum tube and electron guns to create a display image.

triad A cluster of three phosphors: one red, one green, and one blue.

© iStockphoto.com/KonstantinPetkov

Figure 3.17 A CRT monitor is housed in a large plastic boxlike case.

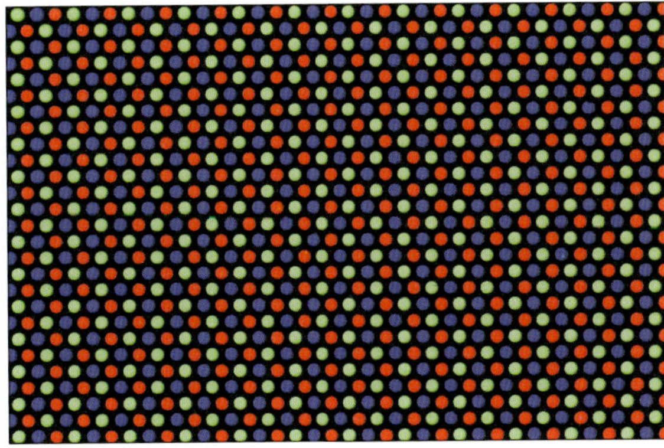

© iStockphoto.com/Pillon

Figure 3.18 An extreme close-up of part of a CRT monitor's screen, showing how triads of red, green, and blue appear.

You also may encounter a few specialized monitor types. For example, some e-book readers have a special type of screen called electronic paper (**e-paper**). This type of screen retains its image but is unpowered except when the display changes, so it uses much less power than a device with an LCD screen. A **digital** or smart whiteboard is a large writing board in a conference room or other meeting area that is connected to a computer, so that whatever is written on the board is also saved on the computer. Digital tools and buttons also appear on the screen for interacting with the data collected, as shown in Figure 3.19.

e-paper A monitor technology used in book readers in which the screen retains its image but is unpowered except when the display changes.

digital whiteboard A whiteboard that is connected to a computer, so that whatever is written on the board is saved on the computer.

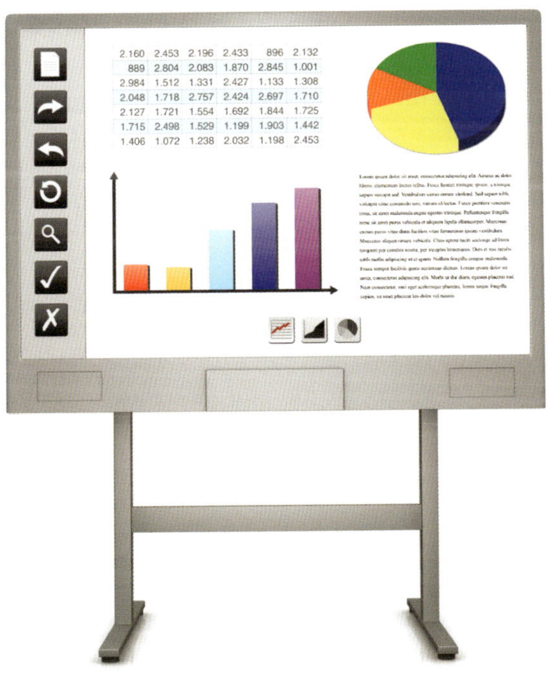

© iStockphoto.com/lucadp

Figure 3.19 A digital whiteboard.

resolution The number of pixels that comprise a display, horizontally and vertically.

maximum resolution The highest display mode (the greatest number of pixels) a display can support.

A display screen has a maximum **resolution**, which is the highest display mode it can support. Display modes are expressed as *horizontal number of pixels* × *vertical number of pixels*, such as 1600 × 900. On an LCD monitor, **maximum resolution** is sometimes called native resolution. See Figure 3.20.

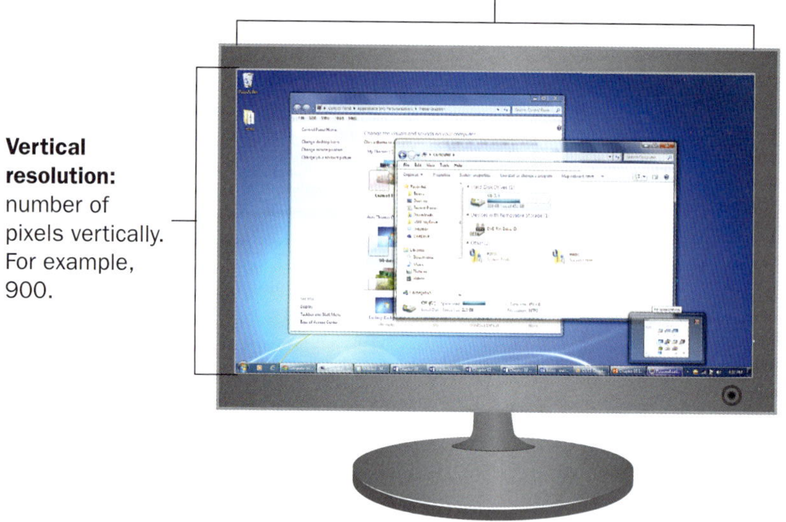

Figure 3.20 A screen's resolution is described as horizontal x vertical pixels.

TIP One quirk of LCD monitors is that if you use any resolution that is lower than the native one, the display may not appear as sharp and crisp. Therefore, you should run an LCD in its native resolution whenever possible. If the icons and text are too small to read, adjust the text and icon size in the operating system's settings.

aspect ratio The ratio of width to height on a display screen, such as 4:3 (standard) or 16:9 (wide).

When selecting a display mode in the operating system, you should choose one that matches the aspect ratio of the display screen. The **aspect ratio** is the ratio of width to height—in other words, the relative dimensions of the screen. Some monitors have a traditional 4:3 aspect ratio, but many LCD screens use a wide-screen 16:9 aspect ratio instead.

refresh rate The number of times each pixel in a display is refreshed per second.

All display screens have a maximum **refresh rate**, the number of times each pixel is refreshed per second. The operating system's display mode determines the actual refresh rate that is used. On a CRT, using a high refresh rate (greater than 80 Hz) makes the monitor flicker less, resulting in less eyestrain for the user. On an LCD monitor, the refresh rate is somewhere around 60 Hz but is not as important because an LCD monitor is not prone to flickering.

display adapter The computer component that communicates instructions from the operating system to the display.

A display screen relies on the computer's **display adapter** to tell it what to do. The display adapter, in turn, takes its orders from the operating system to specify the display mode (resolution, refresh rate, and color depth). The display adapter requires its own memory, which it uses to hold the color information for each pixel as it operates, and which it uses to render 3D objects and control special video effects in certain applications. If the display adapter is built into the motherboard, the display adapter may reserve some of the motherboard's memory for its own use. If the display adapter is a separate circuit board, it has its own memory mounted directly on the circuit board.

Resolutions and LCD Monitors

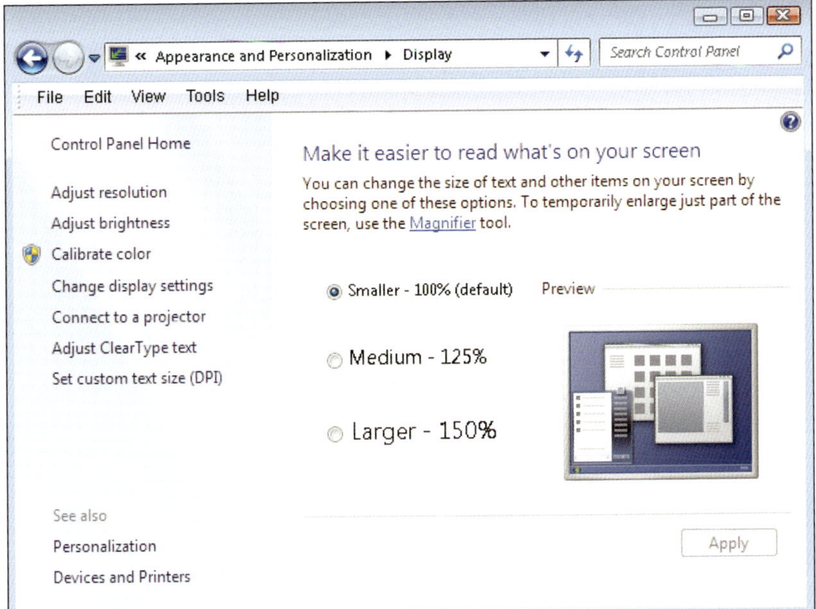

Most LCD displays look fuzzy at any resolution other than their highest one. However, the highest resolution display mode may make the text and icons so small that they are difficult to see and work with. As a workaround, you can change the text and icon size in Windows. After switching to the highest resolution for your display, right-click on the desktop and choose Screen Resolution. Click the Make Text and Other Items Larger or Smaller hyperlink. Then choose one of the available sizes: Smaller, Medium, or Larger. You may have to restart your computer after making this change before the new setting will take effect.

Troubleshooting

Step by Step

Exploring Display Modes in Windows 7

Follow these steps to see the current display settings in Windows 7:

1. Right-click on the desktop and choose Screen Resolution.
2. Make a note of the Resolution setting. Open the Resolution drop-down list and see what other settings are available. Are you currently using the highest setting?
3. Click the Advanced Settings hyperlink.
4. In the dialog box that appears, on the Adapter tab, click the List All Modes button.
5. In the List All Modes dialog box, scroll through the list to see what modes your display adapter supports. Notice that a display mode consists of three factors: resolution (for example, 1600 × 900), color depth (for example, True Color [32-bit]), and refresh rate (for example, 60 Hz).

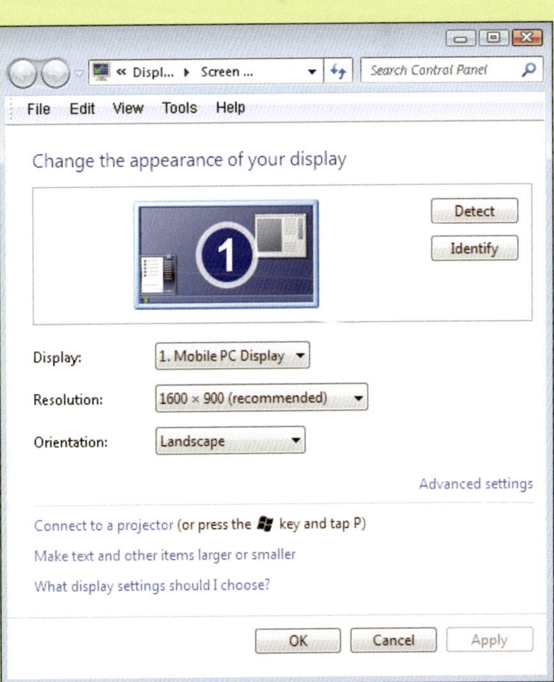

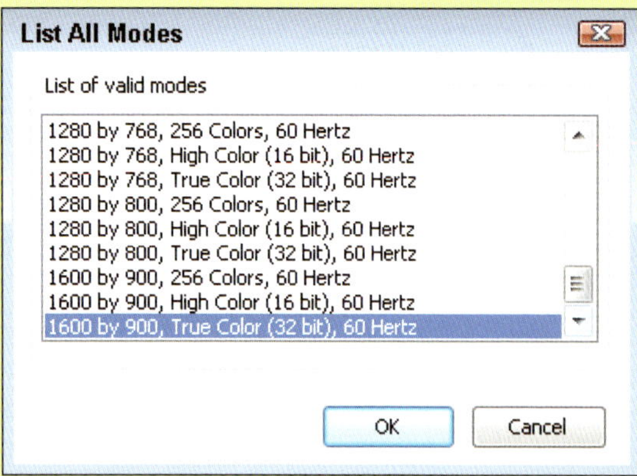

6. Click Cancel to close the dialog box without making a change.
7. Click the Monitor tab, and note the current Screen refresh rate setting and the Colors setting.
8. Click Cancel to close the dialog box.
9. Click Cancel to close the Control Panel window.

Printers

hard copy Physically printed pages of a document or a printed photo; the opposite of soft (electronic) copy.

Printers generate **hard copy**—that is, physical printed pages you can hold in your hands. Over the years, there have been many different printer technologies, each with its own characteristics and benefits. In this section, you'll learn about several printer types and find out what differentiates one printer from another.

Printer Features

When selecting a printer, there are a number of factors to consider:

consumables Printing supplies that must be replaced with use, such as paper and ink.

dots per inch (dpi) A measurement of printed image quality, the number of individually colored dots in one row (or column) of one inch of the printed file. A printout can have a different horizontal and vertical dpi, although this is not common.

- Initial cost: How much does the printer cost?
- Per-page cost: How much does it cost to print a page, taking into account the price of the **consumables**? How much does the ink, toner, or ribbon cost, and how many pages will it print before you have to replace it? Are there other parts in the printer that wear out and have to be replaced after a certain number of pages?
- Resolution: How many individual **dots per inch (dpi)** does the printed image consist of? A higher resolution results in a sharper image, as shown in Figure 3.21. A low-resolution printer might output at 300 dpi, while a high-resolution printer might output at 1200 dpi.
- Speed: How many pages per minute can the printer output? A typical printer might output at somewhere between 10 and 20 pages per minute for black-and-white and slightly less than that for color.
- Color: Does the printer print in color, or just in black-and-white? If it prints in color, can it print photos well? Some printers are designed specifically for photos and have special inks for them and/or use special glossy paper for photos.

Figure 3.21 A high-resolution printout uses more pixels per inch, resulting in smoother lines and finer details.

- Paper handling: Does it have multiple paper trays, so you can have two sizes of paper loaded at once? How much paper can it hold at once? How well does it print on heavy cardstock or envelopes without bending or creasing them? Does the printer have any special paper-handling features, such as the capability to print on both sides of the paper (**duplexing**) without the user manually flipping the paper over? What is the largest size paper it can accept?
- Interface: Most printers use the USB interface to connect directly to a computer. Can the printer also connect to a network? Does it require a cable to connect it to the network, or can it connect wirelessly?
- Multi-function: Is it just a printer, or can it perform other tasks too, like scanning, copying, and/or faxing? A multi-function device (MFD) can save you money and space if you would otherwise have to buy separate machines for those functions.

duplexing To print on both sides of the paper.

Inkjet Printers

An **inkjet printer** sprays liquid ink onto a page through a set of very small nozzles (ink jets). The depending on the model, an ink jet printer uses either heat or electricity to make the ink squirt out of the nozzles. Figure 3.22 shows an inkjet printer.

inkjet printer A printer that squirts ink onto paper with small nozzles (jets) to form the page image.

Most inkjet printers are color models, having four separate ink cartridges: black, cyan, magenta, and yellow. Some models designed for photo printing have even more cartridges for greater photo realism, and may also have a memory card slot so you can print photos directly from the card rather than having to go through a computer.

© iStockphoto.com/gmnicholas

Figure 3.22 An inkjet printer.

Inkjet printers are popular in homes and small businesses because the cost of the printer is very low, so it's economical to get started. However, the ink cartridges are expensive and don't last for very many pages, so high-volume printing on an inkjet printer can be very expensive. The special glossy paper needed for best-quality photo printing can also be expensive.

CAUTION If an inkjet printer sits idle for weeks at a time, the ink in the nozzles dries out, and you may see quality problems with your printouts. Running the printer's self-cleaning cycle may restore the print quality, but doing so wastes some ink, driving up the cost per page even higher. Unfortunately there is not much you can do to prevent this; it's just something to be aware of when selecting a printer technology.

Laser Printers

laser printer A printer that forms the page image by transferring toner to the paper via a rotating drum with electrical charges.

Laser printers are popular in business because they are fast, they handle high-volume printing well, and the cost per page is low. They also produce good quality, high-resolution output, and both color and black-and-white models are available. The main drawback is the initial cost, which can be higher than for other printer types. Figure 3.23 shows a laser printer.

drum The rotating cylinder inside a laser printer, on which the page image is formed with electrical charges.

toner The powdered mixture of plastic and iron used to form the image on a laser printer.

fuser The heating element in a laser printer that melts the toner, fusing it to the paper.

A laser printer prints by creating an image of the page on a rotating drum using varying levels of electrical charges. The drum is negatively charged, and then a laser neutralizes the charge in some spots. When the drum rotates past a reservoir of toner (a powdered mixture of colored plastic particles and iron), the toner is attracted to the neutralized areas, and clings to the drum. Then the paper rotates past positively charged paper, and the toner is pulled off the drum and onto the paper. A fuser element heats the paper, melting the plastic particles in the toner so that the particles stick to the paper permanently.

Figure 3.23 A laser printer.

Specialty Printers

In addition to the printer types discussed so far, a variety of special-purpose printers exist. You may see some of these printers in businesses, schools, and government offices.

Thermal printers transfer images to paper using heat. For example, some cash registers use a special thermal-coated paper for receipts; the cash register contains a simple direct thermal printer that heats certain areas of the paper so that it turns black and forms the text for your receipt. A thermal wax transfer printer melts a wax-based ink onto paper in tiny dots, using dithering to create different colors. It's a high-cost, medium-quality printout that was popular before color laser printers became economically feasible for ordinary users, but is seldom seen today. A thermal dye transfer printer, sometimes called a dye sublimation printer, heats ribbons containing dye and then diffuses the dye into specially coated paper. The print quality is outstanding, but the paper and the dye are both expensive. Some small-format snapshot printers use this technology.

thermal printer A printer that transfers images to paper using heat.

direct thermal printer A printer that heats certain areas of specially coated paper so that it turns black and forms the image.

thermal wax transfer printer A printer that melts a wax-based ink onto paper in tiny dots.

dithering Placing different colored dots side by side in an image so that from a distance they appear to be a third color.

thermal dye transfer printer A printer that heats ribbons containing dye and then diffuses the dye onto specially coated paper.

A plotter is a large-format printer that excels at creating high-precision drawings like blueprints, maps, and engineering drawings. Figure 3.24 shows a plotter. Plotters that use a variety of printing technologies, including variants of inkjet and laser, are available. On the other end of the size spectrum, some small-format specialty printers work with their own software to accomplish specific tasks, such as printing labels, postage, or work orders.

plotter A large-format printer that creates high-precision documents such as maps and engineering drawings.

© iStockphoto.com/loonger

Figure 3.24 A plotter.

Audio Output Devices

The audio adapter in a computer handles both input and output. You learned earlier in this chapter how audio input comes in from microphones and digital musical instruments. The most common audio output devices are speakers and headphones.

Speaker systems designed for computers are somewhat different from speaker systems designed for home stereo and home theater systems. Typically, a single 3.5mm plug connects to an output port on the computer; you don't plug in the speakers separately to the computer. On a two-speaker system, one speaker connects to the computer and the other speaker connects to the first speaker. A system with more speakers than that usually has a central gathering point, such as a subwoofer into which all the speakers connect.

Step by Step

Adjusting Sound Output Volume in Windows

Window 7 provides a Volume control in the notification area that you can easily use to adjust the overall sound coming from your computer's speakers or headphone, and also mute or unmute the sound. You can also adjust the volume levels for individual components. Follow these steps to explore your computer's sound controls:

1. In the notification area, click the speaker icon. A slider appears.
2. Click the speaker graphic at the bottom of the slider. A red X appears on the button, indicating the sound is muted.
3. Click the Mixer hyperlink at the bottom of the slider. A dialog box opens showing individual sliders for each adjustable sound-producing item on your system. You may have different ones than shown here.

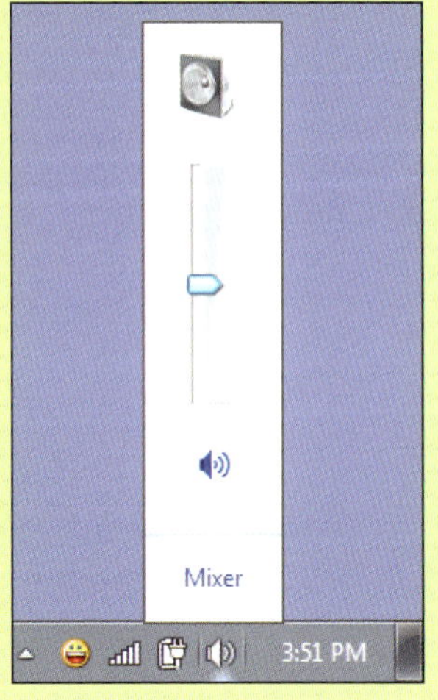

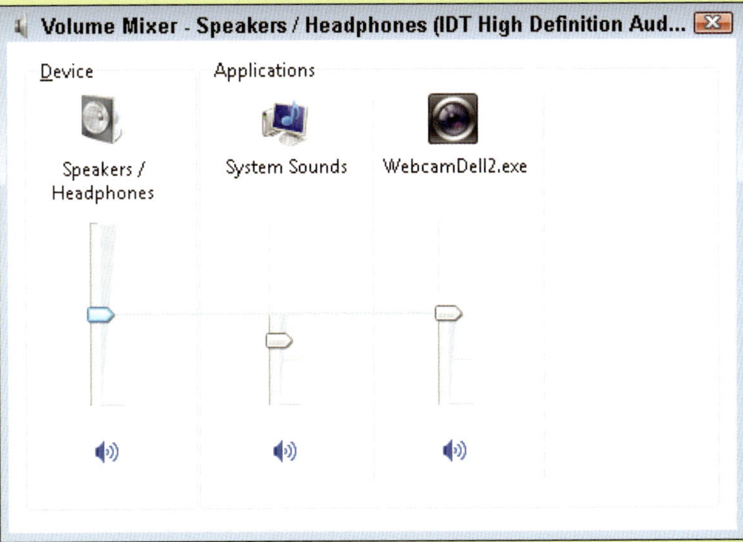

4. Adjust any of the sliders as needed and then close the dialog box.

NOTE

Audio can also be output to a portable digital media player such as an iPod or iPhone, but that type of output is not the same as sending the audio to a speaker system. When you output music to a digital player, you are transferring files to the player, so the process is much more like copying files to an external drive than it is setting up sound output. The next section of this chapter discusses file storage and transfer.

Quick Review

1. What is LCD technology?
2. Define monitor resolution, and explain how it is measured.
3. Name three types of printers, and give an example of an appropriate use for each.

Choosing Appropriate Storage Devices

As you learned in Chapter 2, when a computer processes data, RAM (Random Access Memory) holds that data temporarily. RAM is known as **primary storage** because it's where the data must be in order to interact with the CPU. Data waits for the CPU's attention in memory, and then it waits again in memory when the CPU has finished processing it.

primary storage System RAM in a computer, where processed data is first stored after it exits the CPU.

For data to be safely and permanently stored, however, it must be placed in **secondary storage**. Secondary storage devices are nonvolatile, so they don't lose their contents when the computer's power is turned off. Secondary storage can include hard disk drives, solid state drives, CDs, DVDs, and network and cloud-based storage.

secondary storage Storage that retains data after the computer is turned off, such as a hard disk drive, DVD, or USB flash drive.

Storage devices are evaluated in these ways:

- Capacity: How much can it hold?
- Cost: How much does the storage cost per megabyte or gigabyte?

- Access speed: How quickly can the data be written and retrieved?
- Interface: How does it connect to the computer, and how fast is that connection?
- Media type: Is it magnetic, optical, or solid state?
- Portability: Is the storage inside the system unit, or connected to it externally?
- Removability: Is the disc removable from the drive that reads and writes it, or are they one inseparable unit?

In the following sections, you will learn about storage in general, and about several types of storage devices and their characteristics.

Data Storage Basics

file A group of related bits stored together under a single name.

folder A logical organizing unit for grouping related files together.

subfolder A folder within another folder.

volume A physical storage device, or a portion of one, that is assigned an identifying letter. Sometimes used interchangeably with *drive,* but a physical drive may actually contain multiple volumes.

disk One or more platters on which data is stored. Spelled *disc* when referring to the optical type (DVDs, CDs).

drive The mechanical components that read and write the data on a disk.

A file is a named collection of bits that work together to represent a single object, such as an executable program, a spreadsheet, a picture, or a system file. Folders are logical organizing units for files. For example, a Windows-based computer has a Windows folder containing the system files needed to run Windows, a Users folder containing the data files and settings for each user account, and a Program Files folder containing the files needed for each installed application. A folder within a folder is called a subfolder; each of the aforementioned folders contains multiple subfolders. Files and folders are stored on volumes. Each volume has a letter followed by a colon, such as C: or D:. Figure 3.25 summarizes this structure.

Some people use the terms disk (or disc), drive, and volume interchangeably, but they have different meanings. The term disk refers to a platter or set of platters on which data is stored. Examples include a hard disk drive (HDD) and a DVD. When referring to a CD, DVD, or Blu-ray, it is customary to spell the term *disc*. The term drive refers to the mechanical components that read and write the data on a disk. In some cases, such as with an HDD, the drive and its platters are physically inseparable, so the terms disk and drive have come to be synonymous; *hard disk* and *hard drive* refer to the same thing. When the disc is removable from the drive, however, as with a CD or DVD, the terms are separate. See Figure 3.26.

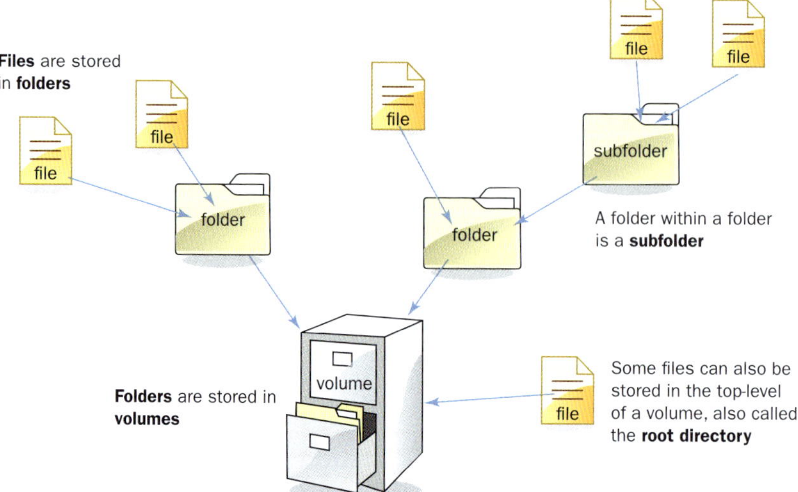

Figure 3.25 Files are stored in folders, which are stored on volumes.

Figure 3.26 In hard disk drives, the disk and drive are one unit; in optical drives, the disc and drive are separate.

Solid-state storage devices such as USB flash drives are technically neither discs nor drives, because they have no platters and no moving parts. However, they are commonly referred to as drives anyway, as in the term *solid-state drive (SSD)*.

Most commonly, each physical storage device acts as a single volume. For example, your DVD drive might have a volume letter of E: assigned to it. However, some high-capacity storage devices such as hard disk drives can be partitioned into multiple volumes, each of which appears in the operating system to be a separate storage device with its own letter.

Hard Disk Drives

A **hard disk drive (HDD)** is the most popular type of secondary storage for personal computers. Although newer technologies are emerging, HDDs remain the standard because of their high capacity and low cost.

hard disk drive (HDD) A mechanical drive with an integrated set of disk platters that store data in patterns of magnetic polarity.

An HDD consists of a stack of metal platters (usually four to six) that are coated with iron dust. These platters spin on a common spindle inside a sealed metal casing. A set of **read/write heads** inside the HDD casing reads and writes data on the platters; there are heads on each side of each platter. The arms move in and out to reach different spots on the platters, and the disks move past the heads as they spin. The most common platter sizes are 3.5" in diameter on HDDs for desktop systems and 2.5" on HDDs for notebooks. Figure 3.27 shows the inside of a hard disk drive case.

read/write head A component in a disk drive that reads and writes to the disk(s).

© iStockphoto.com/rhambley

Figure 3.27 The inside of a hard disk drive.

track One of the concentric rings in a disk's organizational system.

cylinder All the tracks at a single position of the read/write heads' actuator arm.

A precise system exists for describing the physical locations on an HDD. The platters are divided into concentric circles, like the rings on a tree trunk cross-section, called tracks. Each platter's first track is track 0, the next one track 1, and so on. The track number tells the drive where to position the actuator arm that controls the position of the read/write heads. All the heads move together, so if one head is reading track 1 on one side of one platter, all the other heads are also reading track 1 on their side of their platter too. For this reason, tracks are not referred to individually, but as cylinders. A cylinder is the group of all the tracks at a single arm position. Figure 3.28 illustrates the relationship between these parts.

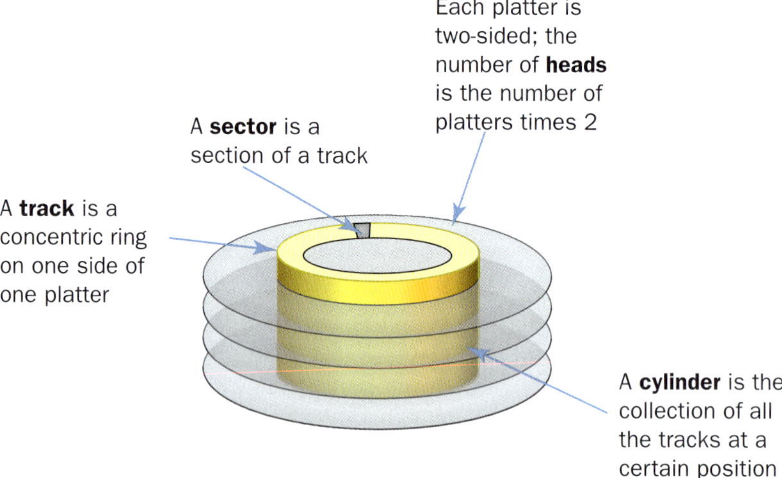

Figure 3.28 A hard disk drive is organized into tracks, cylinders, heads, and sectors.

sector The smallest addressable unit of storage on a disk drive, at 512 bytes

cluster A grouping of sectors. The number of sectors in a cluster depends on the file system and the disk size.

Each track is divided into segments called sectors. A sector holds exactly 512 bytes. Because there are so many sectors, and because almost every file is much larger than 512 bytes, sectors are grouped together into clusters, and the drive's controller addresses clusters rather than individual sectors. The number of sectors per cluster is determined by the drive's size and formatting, but most modern HDDs have 32 sectors per cluster.

An HDD can be internal or external, but most are internal, installed inside the system unit. An internal HDD connects to the motherboard using either a parallel ATA (PATA) or serial ATA (SATA) cable. An external HDD connects to a port on the outside of the system unit, and depending on the model may use a USB port, a FireWire (IEEE 1394a) port, or an external SATA (eSATA) port. You can buy enclosures that will convert an internal HDD to an external one.

See "Drive Connectors" in Chapter 2 for more information about PATA and SATA. See the section "Other Common External Connectors" in Chapter 2 to learn more about USB and FireWire.

Optical Drives

An optical drive uses a light beam and sensor to read the data. The surface of a blank optical disc is shiny and reflects light strongly. When data is written to an optical disc, certain areas are burned with a laser so they are less reflective. The shiny areas are called *land*, and the less-shiny areas are called *pits*. Recall from the preceding section that on an HDD, transitions between positive and negative magnetic polarity indicate a 1 bit, and lack of transition indicates a 0 bit. On an optical disc, transitions between areas of greater and lesser reflectivity indicate a 1, and a consistent level of reflectivity indicates a 0. See Figure 3.29.

optical drive A drive that reads discs that are stored in patterns of greater and lesser reflectivity, such as a DVD or CD.

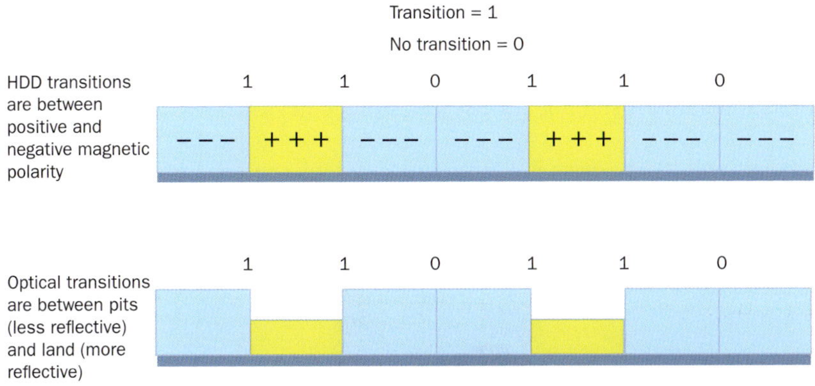

Figure 3.29 Magnetic and optical storage both look for transitions in the state of the disc surface.

There are several types of optical drives and discs. The oldest and most basic type is a compact disc (CD), which holds up to 900MB of data. CDs are used for small amounts of data and also for audio recordings. A digital versatile disc (DVD) can store up to 4.7GB per disc (single-sided, single layer). DVDs can also be double-sided, with recordings on both sides rather than recording on one and a label on the other. DVDs can also be dual-layer, where the top layer is semitransparent and read using a laser and sensor at a different angle than the lower layer. A double-sided, dual-layer DVD can hold up to 17GB of data. DVDs are used to distribute large applications, large amounts of data, and standard-definition movies. Blu-ray discs (BD) can store up to 128GB in up to four layers. They are used to distribute even larger amounts of data, or high-definition movies.

compact disc (CD) An optical disc used for storing music and data, holding up to 900 MB.

digital versatile disc (DVD) An optical disc used for storing standard-definition movies and data, holding up to 4.17 GB per side per layer.

Blu-ray disc (BD) An optical disc used for storing high-definition movies and data, holding up to 25 GB per layer.

All three types of discs can be read-only (ROM), recordable once (R), or rewriteable (RW). To record or rewrite a disc, you must have a drive with that capability that supports the type of disc you are using.

DVDs come in two competing recordable and rewriteable standards, abbreviated as plus and minus signs, like this: DVD+R and DVD-R. Some older home stereo systems do not support reading from +R and +RW discs, but otherwise the differences are unnoticeable to most consumers.

CAUTION Optical discs are sturdy, but scratches, dirt, and fingerprints can prevent them from being read accurately. Store discs in a protective sleeve or case when you are not using them, and hold discs only by their edges. Don't let anything touch the shiny side of the disc, especially anything sharp or abrasive. If you need to write on a disc, write only on the label side, and use only a suitable soft marking pen.

Solid-State Drives

A solid-state drive (SSD) uses a type of EEPROM to store data in tiny transistors. As you learned in Chapter 2, electrically erasable programmable read-only memory (EEPROM) is a type of memory that stores its contents permanently; it is nonvolatile. Because it is electrically erasable, the computer can erase what's written there and rewrite it. The type of EEPROM used in solid-state drives can be erased and rewritten in small blocks, making it suitable for use as a storage device.

solid-state hard drive (SSHD) A high-capacity solid-state storage device that substitutes for an HDD as the main storage drive in a computer.

When a solid-state drive is a large-capacity replacement for an HDD, it's sometimes called a **solid-state hard drive (SSHD)** to distinguish it from lower-capacity portable solid-state storage, such as USB flash drives. Figure 3.30 shows a solid-state hard drive.

© iStockphoto.com/scanrail

Figure 3.30 A solid-state hard drive looks much like an HDD from the outside.

Solid-state drives are silent because they don't have any moving parts, and the access time is very fast because there are no read/write heads that have to move anywhere to get to the data. SSDs are more expensive than HDDs, though; you get much less capacity for the money. For this reason, SSHDs are found mostly in high-end desktop and notebook computers. Solid-state storage is common in tablets and smartphones, where high-capacity storage is not needed and being lightweight is a primary concern.

To balance between performance and cost, some systems have both a small SSD and a larger HDD. The SSD contains the start-up files and the operating system, and the HDD holds everything else. Hybrid drives are also available that combine the two technologies in a single physical unit.

Network Volumes

As you've seen so far in this chapter, most computer storage is directly attached to the individual computer. This is known as local storage, or direct-attached storage (DAS). However, computers can also use a network to access storage that's not physically nearby.

direct-attached storage (DAS) Storage that is directly connected to the computer that accesses it.

Network storage can enable multiple users to access the same up-to-the-minute information simultaneously. For example, in a retail business with multiple checkout areas, all the checkout computers access a common database containing the item prices so that when the price of an item changes, all cashiers immediately have that information available. On a smaller scale, a family could store its movie and music collection on one computer, which then can share the collection with all the other computers in the household via the family's wireless network. Storage that is available via a network is called network-attached storage (NAS).

network-attached storage (NAS) Storage that is accessed via a network.

Generically speaking, network-attached storage can be a volume on a file server in a business network or a shared folder on an individual's personal computer. However, the term is most often applied to a NAS appliance, which is a specialized computing device built specifically for network file sharing. The appliance connects directly into the network, and can be remotely configured from any computer, so it doesn't need its own input or output devices. NAS appliances are available for consumers as well as businesses; for example, you could connect an inexpensive NAS appliance to your home network to provide everyone in your family with always-on access to shared files.

NAS appliance A specialized device that provides storage space to network users.

Some large companies employ storage-area networks (SANs) to make central access to large amounts of data simple. A SAN logically combines the contents of multiple remote storage devices so that each individual computer connected to the SAN sees that storage pool as a single local drive.

storage-area network (SAN) A distributed storage system that appears to each individual computer as a local volume on that computer.

When it is essential that data be kept safe and readily available, some companies store that data on a redundant array of inexpensive disks (RAID). There are several types of RAID systems, and each type offers improvements over a single disk drive in performance, in data safety, or in both. Usually, when you store data on a disk you write to one disk at a time. RAID systems have the capability to spread the data across multiple drives so each physical disk contains part of the data; this is called striping. For example, RAID0 stripes data across multiple physical disks to improve the speed at which data is accessed, and RAID1 mirrors the contents of a physical disk on another identical disk so that the data is always available even if the original disk fails. RAID5 combines the striping from RAID0 with a data storage method that enables the RAID unit to reconstruct lost data on any of the physical disks in the event of a disk failure.

redundant array of inexpensive disks (RAID) A multi-disk storage system that optimizes performance, data safety, or both, depending on the type.

striping Spreading the data across multiple drives to improve performance or protect the data.

Cloud-Based Storage

A cloud is a secure computing environment consisting of a set of remote servers that users access via the Internet. A cloud can include applications, communication with other users, and storage space (cloud storage).

cloud A secure computing environment accessed via the Internet.

cloud storage Storage that is accessed from a cloud environment.

One of the most popular individual cloud storage systems is Microsoft OneDrive. If you have a Microsoft account (which is free), you automatically get several gigabytes of OneDrive storage online. It is a secure storage environment, and you can optionally choose to share certain folders or files with specific other people or with the public. Google also offers free cloud-based storage to users, as do many other online companies.

Businesses of all sizes also employ cloud storage. For example, a business with many locations might create a cloud-based information system for all employees to access, regardless of where they are. This information system might include customer and product information, order information, access to human resources data such as vacation schedules, and company-wide announcements and memos. A large company might maintain its own online server for implementing its cloud environment, or might contract with a third-party company to host its cloud.

Quick Review

1. Explain the difference between primary and secondary storage.
2. How does an HDD store data?
3. Differentiate between CDs, DVDs, and BDs in terms of capacity.
4. What is a solid-state hard drive (SSHD)?

Summary

Selecting and Using Input Devices

Input devices allow the user to communicate with the computer. The most common input devices are a **keyboard** and **mouse**, both of which can be either wired or wireless. A keyboard can have an **ergonomic** design to prevent hand and wrist strain. Devices that lack a real keyboard use a **virtual keyboard** (software-based) to enable user input.

A pointing device controls the onscreen pointer in the user interface. A mouse can be **mechanical** or **optical**. Other pointing devices include **trackball** and **touchpad**. Some computers have a **touch screen** on which your finger can serve as a pointing device. A **drawing tablet** enables you to input drawings using a **stylus**.

A scanner **digitizes** a hard-copy photo using a **charge-coupled device (CCD)**. A scanner can be part of a **multi-function device (MFD)** that also includes a printer and copier. A **bar code reader** is a specialized type of scanner used for reading **Universal Product Code (UPC)** symbols. **Magnetic bar code readers** and **radio frequency identification (RFID) chips** are other types of scanning devices, as are **optical mark recognition (OMR)** systems and **magnetic-ink character recognition (MICR)** systems.

A capture device captures new content, rather than scanning existing content. Examples include **digital cameras** and **digital video cameras**. A **webcam** is a digital video camera that must remain connected to a computer in order to function.

Audio input can be used to control a computer with commands and to input music and sounds. Audio input requires an **audio adapter** (sound card). When using a microphone for audio input, **voice recognition software** interprets speech by matching words in a database; **speech recognition software** is teachable software that learns an individual's pronunciation.

Selecting and Using Output Devices

A **display screen** is a video screen the computer uses for outputting information to the user. A stand-alone display screen is called a **monitor**. **Liquid crystal display (LCD)** is a popular type of flat-screen monitor technology. A newer alternative is **organic light-emitting diode (OLED)**. An LCD screen can be either **active matrix** (a version of which is **thin-film transistor**) or **passive matrix**. In active matrix, each **pixel** has its own transistor. A **high-definition TV (HDTV)** can also be used as a computer monitor via a **high-definition multimedia interface (HDMI)**.

Cathode ray tube (CRT) is an older monitor technology that uses a vacuum tube and electron guns to light up colored phosphors on a glass screen. Phosphors are arranged in triads of red, green, and blue.

Some specialized display types include **e-paper** (for book readers), **digital whiteboards**, and **digital projectors**. Projector brightness is measured in lumens.

A display screen has a **maximum resolution**, expressed as a number of pixels horizontally and vertically. The ratio of horizontal to vertical is its **aspect ratio**. The **refresh rate** is the number of times per second the display is refreshed. The number of bits needed to describe the color of a pixel is the **color depth**. A **display adapter** tells the display screen what to do.

The key factors in selecting a printer include initial cost, cost per page for **consumables**, print resolution (expressed in **dots per inch**), speed, color, interface, and paper handling.

An **ink jet printer** squirts liquid ink onto paper. The printer is inexpensive to buy, and produces good quality color graphics, but the cost per page is high because of the cost of the ink cartridges. A **laser printer** transfers **toner** to a **drum** and then to paper, and then **fuses** the toner to the paper. It is economical per page and produces good quality output, but is expensive to buy initially. Specialty printers include **direct thermal**, **thermal wax transfer**, **thermal dye transfer**, and **plotters**.

Audio output comes through speakers and headphones. Speakers designed for computer use are **powered**, and have shielding to prevent **electromagnetic interference (EMI)**.

Choosing Appropriate Storage Devices

Primary storage is RAM; **secondary storage** is permanent storage, such as a disk. A **disk** is a platter (or multiple platters) that stores data; a **drive** is the mechanical component that reads and writes the data. In some storage types, the disk and drive are inseparable.

A **hard disk drive (HDD)** is the most popular type of secondary storage for personal computers. It is magnetic and mechanical, and usually internal to the system unit. Read/write heads store the data in **sectors** on **tracks**. A group of sectors is a **cluster**. A group of tracks at a specific read/write head position is a **cylinder**. HDDs can use either PATA or SATA connectors internally, or USB, FireWire, or eSATA externally.

An **optical drive** uses a light beam and sensor to read data on **compact discs (CD)**, **digital versatile discs (DVD)**, and/or **Blu-ray discs (BD)**.

A **solid-state drive (SSD)** uses EEPROM to store data in tiny transistors. **Solid-state hard drives (SSHD)** are a substitute for traditional HDDs as the main secondary storage in a computer.

Local drives are **direct-attached storage (DAS)**. Network-accessible storage is **network-attached storage (NAS)**. **NAS appliances** are simple computers designed to be used as network storage. A **storage-area network (SAN)** makes remote storage appear as a local volume on each individual computer.

A **redundant array of inexpensive disks (RAID)** is a system that uses multiple physical HDDs to increase performance and reliability by spreading the data out across all the disks and implementing schemes for reconstructing the data in the event of one disk's failure.

Cloud storage is storage that the user accesses online via a **cloud**, which is a secure computing environment online.

Key Terms

active matrix
aspect ratio
audio adapter
bar code reader
Blu-ray disc (BD)
cathode ray tube (CRT)
charge-coupled device
cloud
cloud storage
cluster
compact disc (CD)
consumables
cost per page
cylinder
digital camera
digital versatile disc (DVD)
digital video camera
digital whiteboard
digitize
direct thermal printer
direct-attached storage (DAS)
disk
display adapter
display screen
dithering
document feeder

dots per inch (dpi)
drawing tablet
drive
drum
duplexing
e-paper
ergonomic keyboard
file
flatbed scanner
folder
frame
fuser
hard copy
hard disk drive (HDD)
high-definition multimedia interface (HDMI)
high-definition TV (HDTV)
inkjet printer
input device
joystick
laser printer
liquid crystal display (LCD)
magnetic card reader
magnetic-ink character recognition (MICR)
maximum resolution
mechanical mouse
mouse
multi-function device
NAS appliance
network-attached storage (NAS)
optical drive
optical mark recognition (OMR)
optical mouse
organic light-emitting diode (OLED)
passive matrix
pixel
plotter
primary storage
QR code
QWERTY
radio frequency identification (RFID) chip
read/write head
redundant array of inexpensive disks (RAID)
refresh rate
resolution
secondary storage
sector
solid-state hard drive (SSHD)
speech recognition software
storage-area network (SAN)
striping
stylus
subfolder
thermal dye transfer printer
thermal printer
thermal wax transfer printer
thin-film transistor (TFT)
toner
touch screen
touchpad
track
trackball
transceiver
triad
Universal Product Code (UPC)
virtual or onscreen keyboard
voice recognition software
volume
webcam
wireless keyboard
wireless mouse

Test Yourself

Fact Check

1. The Ctrl key on a keyboard is an example of what type of key?
   a. positional
   b. modifier
   c. function
   d. toggle
2. A(n) _______device communicates with the computer via a transceiver.
   a. ergonomic
   b. mechanical
   c. optical
   d. wireless

3. The scanning technology used by banks to read the routing numbers on checks is

   a. magnetic-ink character recognition (MICR)

   b. optical mark recognition (OMR)

   c. Universal Product Code (UPC)

   d. magnetic card reader (MCR)

4. The ____ ratio for a monitor is the ratio of width to height, such as 4:3 or 16:9.

   a. resolution

   b. aspect

   c. refresh

   d. depth

5. The main drawback to an inkjet printer is:

   a. high cost per page

   b. high initial cost

   c. does not print in color

   d. does not print graphics

6. Which of these is primary storage?

   a. HDD

   b. SSHD

   c. RAM

   d. DVD

7. On an HDD, data is stored in

   a. sectors

   b. transistors

   c. pits

   d. optical tracks

8. Which type of optical disc holds the most data?

   a. CD-R

   b. DVD-RW

   c. BD

   d. DVD

9. What kind of storage is remote but appears to each individual computer as a local volume?

   a. DAS

   b. SAN

   c. NAS

   d. RAID

10. If a file is stored in a cloud, where is it located?

    a. Local local area network

    b. Internet

    c. Local local HDD

    d. USB flash drive

Matching

Match the term to its description.

a. CRT

b. HDD

c. LCD

d. OLED

e. NAS

f. SSD

1. ________A type of flat-screen monitor that twists liquid crystals using electricity to form the display image
2. ________A type of flat-screen monitor that applies electricity to organic matter to form the display image
3. ________A type of monitor that uses electron guns to illuminate phosphors to form the display image
4. ________A type of storage that uses rigid metal platters to store data magnetically
5. ________A type of storage that uses solid-state memory to store data
6. ________A type of storage that is accessed via a network

Sum It Up

1. List three input devices and three output devices.
2. How do wireless input devices communicate with the computer?
3. Explain briefly how LCD and CRT technologies form screen images.
4. List three types of printers and give an example of an appropriate use for each one.
5. Explain how HDD and SSHD differ internally.
6. Differentiate between DAS, NAS, SAN, and cloud storage.

Explore More

Input and Output Devices in Your World

For the next 24 hours, notice what computer input and output devices you see in use at school, at work, in your community, and at home. For example, at your local grocery store, you might see a digital cash register with a bar code scanner and a thermal receipt printer, and you might see a magnetic card reader for credit card processing. See how many devices from this chapter you can identify, and submit a list to your instructor of what you saw and where you saw it.

Speech Recognition in Windows 7

In Windows 7, turn on speech recognition. To do so, open the Control Panel and type **speech** in the search box. Next, click Windows Speech Recognition and work through the wizard to configure the feature. Then start Speech Recognition by saying **Start Listening**.

Next, open Microsoft Word, start a new blank document, and speak the following text into your microphone:

I am learning to use a microphone as an input device in Windows 7. I am dictating this text aloud, and Microsoft Word is typing it for me. Speech recognition is part of Windows 7's Ease of Access features.

When you are finished speaking, correct any errors. Then either save or discard the Word document, as your instructor directs you to do.

Think It Over

How Much Does Printing Really Cost?

Suppose your employer needs to print about 3,000 invoices a month. He asks you to recommend a printer type and to prepare a cost estimate for the purchase of a printer. Weigh the options available, and do some Internet research to find suitable models and their prices. Research the cost of the consumables for the printers as well.

Prepare a report that summarizes the initial cost to buy the printer as well as the cost of consumables. Check the printer's documentation online to find out if there are any other parts that periodically need to be replaced (for example, the drum in a laser printer may need replacing at some point) and the number of pages the printer can produce before that replacement is necessary. Present the consumable cost per page, as well as an estimate of the monthly and yearly consumable cost.

Optional: Find a printer that has a lower cost per page than the printer you initially chose, and prepare the same report as before with the new cost data.

Solid-State Drives

Solid-state hard drives (SSHD) are more expensive than HDDs, as you learned in this chapter. Nevertheless, some businesses are adopting them as the main storage devices for new personal computers that the companies buy. What might be the reasoning behind this? Brainstorm a list of the benefits you get with an SSHD compared to an HDD.

Optional: Use the Internet to research what other consumers who have purchased solid-state hard drives have said.

Backing Up Your Files

Suppose you want to back up your entire MP3 and home video collection, which currently occupies 100 GB on your computer's main HDD. Would it be better to buy an external HDD to do the backup, or to back the files up onto optical discs? Consider not only cost, but also convenience, reliability, and ease of retrieving the files later. If you chose optical discs, which type would you use, and how many of them would you need? If you chose an external HDD, what size would you buy—one that the files barely fit on, or one with room for more files you might acquire later?

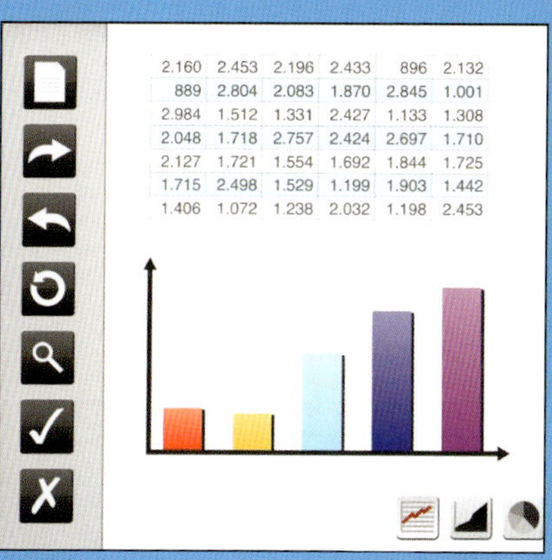

Part II

Software

2.160	2.453	2.196	2.433	896	2.132
889	2.804	2.083	1.870	2.845	1.001
2.984	1.512	1.331	2.427	1.133	1.308
2.048	1.718	2.757	2.424	2.697	1.710
2.127	1.721	1.554	1.692	1.844	1.725
1.715	2.498	1.529	1.199	1.903	1.442
1.406	1.072	1.238	2.032	1.198	2.453

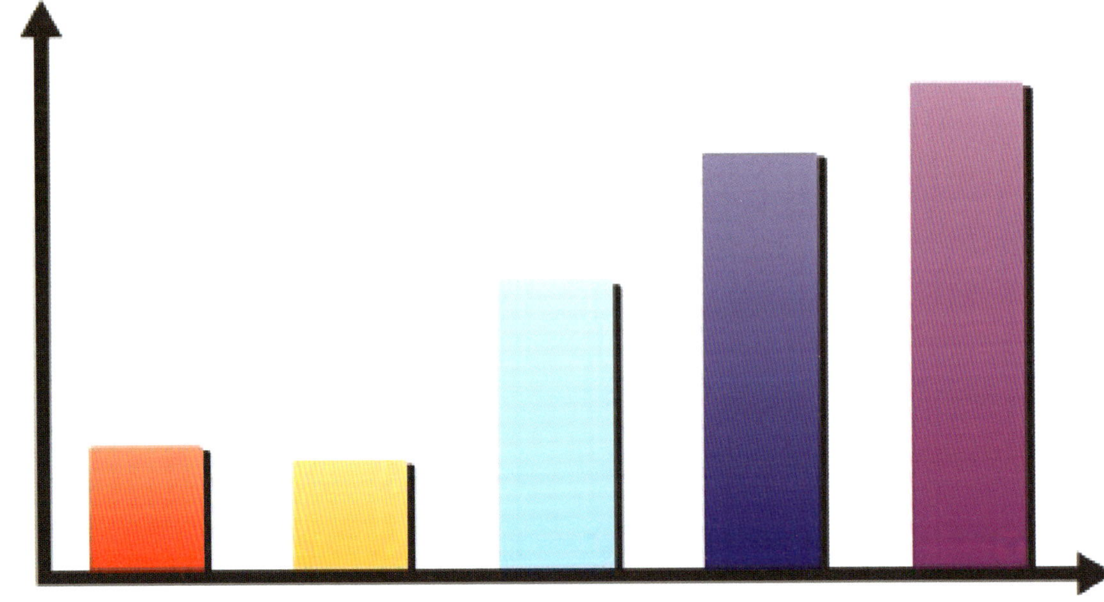

Chapter 4

Operating System Basics

Learning objectives

- Understand the types of operating systems available
- Differentiate among the major desktop operating systems
- Explain computer file storage concepts

When you think about using a computer, you probably think about performing some useful task with it, or playing a game. Behind the scenes, though, is the software that keeps the computer running and responding to commands: the operating system (OS).

The operating system you use can make a big difference in how the computer behaves, how it responds to commands, what applications it can run, and what add-on hardware you can attach. By understanding the available operating systems and their benefits, you can make the right choice in selecting an operating system—or you can choose to purchase a device with the right operating system already built in.

In this chapter, you will learn about system software in general and how operating systems work. You'll survey several popular operating systems, and learn how they communicate with hardware, with the Internet, and with the user. You will also find out how computers store and manage files.

Careers in IT

Programmer

A programmer writes the instructions that become computer programs. Whether it's an operating system, a utility, or a game, a programmer takes a general concept like "open a dialog box with user controls for adjusting the graphics quality" and makes it a reality by writing the exact instructions needed, line by line. The programmer then compiles those instructions into a usable program, or combines them with the instructions written by another programmer or group of programmers to make a larger program. More experienced programmers may also participate in developing the requirements for a program. A programmer should have at least an associate degree in Computer Technology, Computer Science, or Information Technology, and should be familiar with at least two or three different programming languages.

© iStockphoto.com/nullplus

Understanding System Software

system software Software that starts the computer and keeps it running, performing basic system tasks such as running applications, managing files, and correcting errors.

System software includes BIOS, the operating system, and utility programs that perform system maintenance and protection tasks such as error correction and backup. Let's look at each category in more detail.

The System BIOS

As you learned in Chapter 2, "The System Unit," the Basic Input/Output System (BIOS) is the built-in software on the motherboard that starts the computer. It performs a power-on self-test (POST) at startup, which ensures that all the critical hardware devices are functioning properly, including the CPU, the RAM, and the motherboard. If the hardware passes the tests, the BIOS looks for an operating system on one of the available drives, and then passes off control to the operating system to complete the boot process. The BIOS has a list of default settings it uses for managing memory and devices, but those settings can be overridden by user settings that you specify.

The Operating System

The BIOS starts the computer at a basic level, but the operating system does the bulk of work to keep it running and to help the user accomplish tasks. Remember from Chapter 1, "Computer Basics," that the operating system performs these important functions (see Figure 4.1):

- It provides the user interface that humans use to communicate commands and receive feedback.
- It communicates with the hardware, instructing it to take action to accomplish tasks. For example, it communicates with the keyboard and mouse to accept input, and it communicates with the display screen to show output.
- It runs applications and enables humans to interact with them.
- It controls and manages the file storage system.

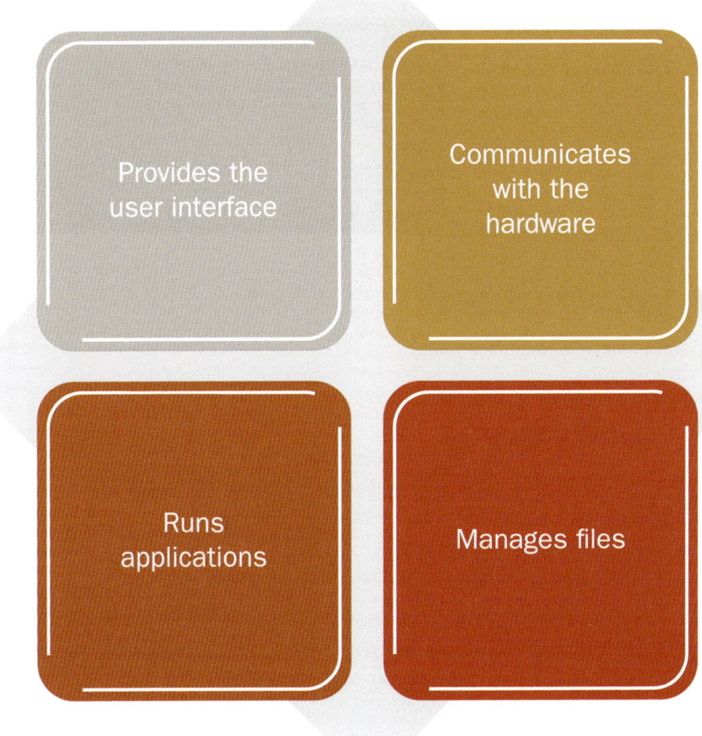

Figure 4.1 The functions performed by an operating system.

There are many kinds of operating systems, suited for a wide range of devices, from supercomputers to smartphones. Each operating system is optimized for the hardware it runs on and the tasks the user is likely to want to perform. For example, the operating system on a tablet computer is designed to be compact (because there is limited storage space in the tablet), easy to operate (because most users are not computer professionals), and fast to respond to simple commands, whereas the operating system in a server is designed to give computer professionals many options for managing and configuring the server and supporting users and databases.

An operating system can have either a **graphical user interface (GUI)** or a **command-line interface**. GUI interfaces are the norm in operating systems designed for most personal computing devices, such as desktops, notebooks, tablets, and smartphones. Users interact with the graphics they see onscreen by using a keyboard or mouse, or using a finger or stylus on a touch screen. In a command-line interface, users employ a keyboard to type commands at a prompt; the interface is text-only. Command-line operating systems were common in the early days of computing, but nowadays they are confined mostly to server operating systems. Figure 4.2 compares a GUI to a command-line interface.

graphical user interface (GUI) A user interface based on a graphical environment, in which users interact with it using a pointing device or touch screen as the primary input device.

command-line interface A user interface based on typing text at a command prompt.

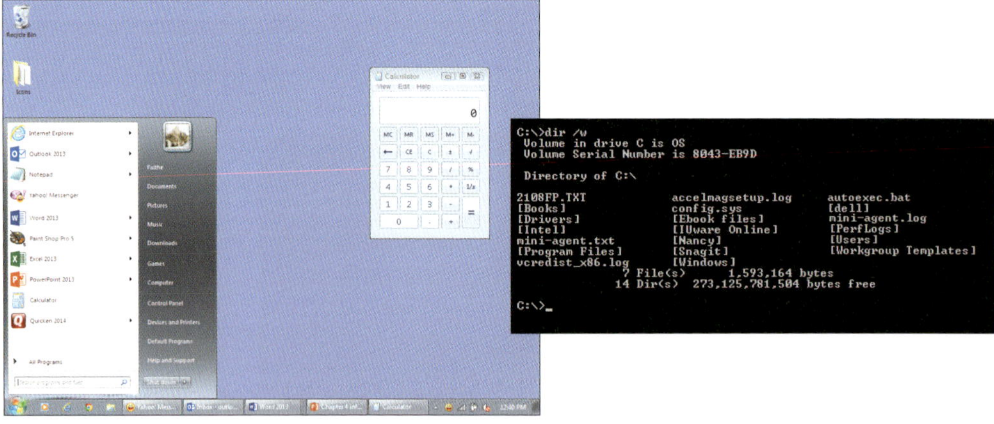

Figure 4.2 A GUI (left) and a command-line interface (right).

Utility Software

utility software Software that performs some useful service to the operating system, such as optimizing or correcting the file storage system, backing up files, or ensuring security or privacy.

Utility software performs a task (or set of tasks) that optimizes, repairs, or safeguards the computer or its data. The difference between utility software and the operating system is sometimes not clear-cut, because most operating systems come with many utility programs built-in. For example, Microsoft Windows comes with utilities for checking a disk for errors and optimizing the way files are stored on an HDD (hard disk drive). Third-party utility software is also available, and may do a more thorough job at the task, combine multiple functions in a single interface, or have more advanced options for configuring how the tasks will run. Figure 4.3 shows the Norton Security Suite, which provides security, identity protection, a backup utility, and a PC tune-up utility.

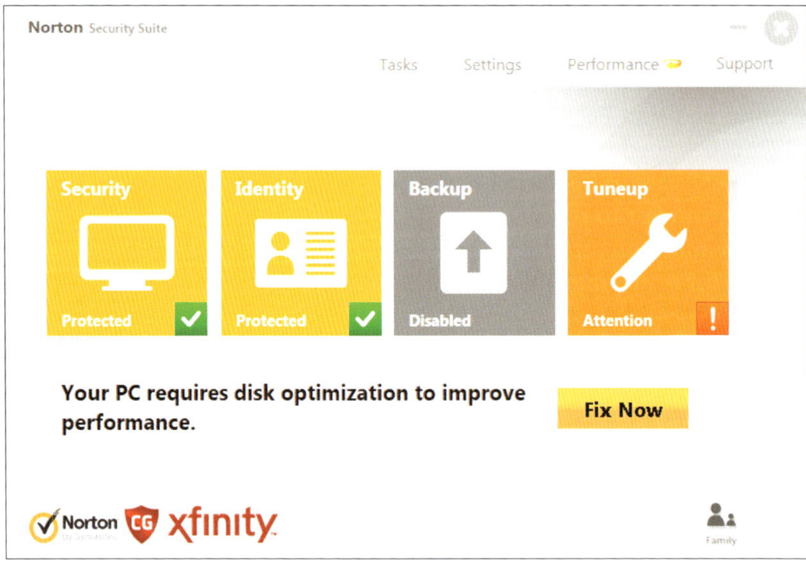

Figure 4.3 A third-party application such as Norton Security Suite provides several different utilities.

There are many types of utilities that protect the computer from attack by malware (harmful or maliciously created software). Antivirus programs find and remove viruses, for example; anti-spyware software finds and removes spyware and adware; firewall software blocks hackers from invading your system; and anti-spam software detects and segregates junk email. Some all-in-one protection suites such as Norton Security Suite protect against many types of threats at once. You will learn more about the different types of malware and their detection and removal in Chapter 11, "Network and Internet Privacy and Security."

Other utilities detect problems with the computer's operation. For example, a disk checking program can find and fix errors in the file system on a volume, and a registry cleanup program can find and fix inconsistent or unneeded entries in the registry, which is the system configuration database that Microsoft Windows uses. An uninstaller utility removes installed software along with any associated files and registry entries.

Backup software makes backup copies of your important files on a separate drive, for safekeeping. You can automate and schedule the backup process so it occurs without your intervention at whatever interval you specify.

malware Malicious software that consists of programs designed to disrupt the normal operation of computer systems.

virus A type of malware that attaches itself to an executable file and spreads to other files when the program is run.

spyware A type of malware that spies on the user's activities and reports them back to the spyware's developer.

adware A type of malware that pops up unwanted ads on the screen.

firewall software Software that blocks hackers from accessing a computer by closing unnecessary services and ports.

anti-spam software Software that rejects junk email messages.

disk checking program Software that finds and fixes errors in the disk storage system.

registry cleanup program Software that analyzes the Windows registry and deletes unneeded entries.

registry The main system configuration database for Microsoft Windows.

uninstaller utility Software that removes installed software along with its associated files and registry entries.

Quick Review

1. Name two types of system software other than the operating system.
2. Name five types of utility programs.

Comparing the Major Operating Systems

When you think about operating systems, you probably think first of Microsoft Windows, which is the operating system used on more than 90 percent of all desktop and notebook PCs. You will learn a lot about Microsoft Windows in upcoming chapters. However, there are many other operating systems, designed for a variety of computers and computer-related devices.

Desktop and Notebook Operating Systems

There are two main hardware platforms for desktop and notebook computers: Apple and Intel (IBM-compatible). The Apple Macintosh platform supports only the Apple operating system: Mac OS X (pronounced *Mac O-S-X,* although the X technically is the Roman numeral 10). This operating system has an attractive GUI and is easy to understand and use. Apple assigns the versions of Mac OS X code names as well as version numbers. The most recent version at this writing is called Mavericks (version 10.9). Figure 4.4 shows the Mavericks version of Mac OS X.

platform A type of computer hardware that is compatible with certain operating systems.

Mac OS X The graphical operating system designed for Apple's desktop and notebook computers. Newer versions now run on the Intel platform.

Mavericks The code name for Mac OS X 10.9.

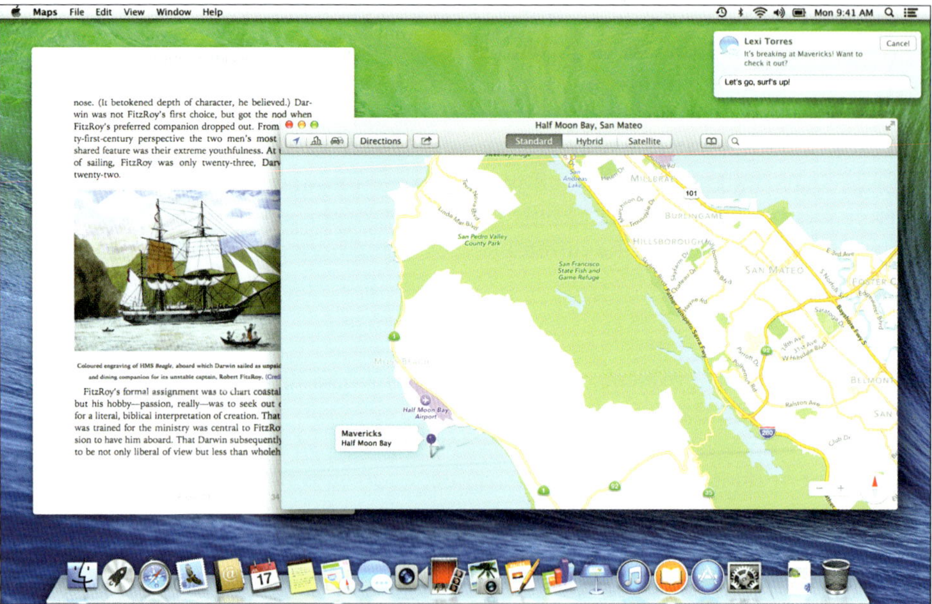

Figure 4.4 Mac OS X 10.9 (Mavericks).

The Macintosh platform has been popular with graphics professionals for decades, and much of the best page layout and graphics editing software was originally developed for the Mac. However, in recent years, similar software has become available for both Windows and Mac, so there is no reason to choose a Mac based on software compatibility anymore. Although Mac hardware is not cross-compatible with Windows software, Mac software is cross-compatible with the Intel platform. The latest version of Mac OS X will run on both Macintosh and Intel computers.

Microsoft Windows The graphical Microsoft operating system designed for Intel-platform desktop and notebook computers.

Most Intel-based systems use **Microsoft Windows**. Like Mac OS X, Windows also has an attractive GUI and is easy to learn and use. Windows has the advantage of being the most popular OS, and therefore the one that more applications are written to run on.

The most recent version at this writing is Windows 8.1, but Windows 7 is still widely used worldwide, and is the version featured in this book. Chapter 5 ("Introduction to Windows 7") introduces you to Windows 7; you will learn there how to run programs and manage files. Figure 4.5 shows the Windows 7 user interface.

Linux An open-source, cross-platform operating system that runs on desktops, notebooks, tablets, and smartphones.

Linux (pronounced *LIN-ucks*) is an operating system that looks and feels very similar to UNIX. It can run on a variety of platforms, including Intel-based desktops and notebooks, servers, and handheld devices. (Android, a popular OS for smartphones and tablets, is a variant of Linux.)

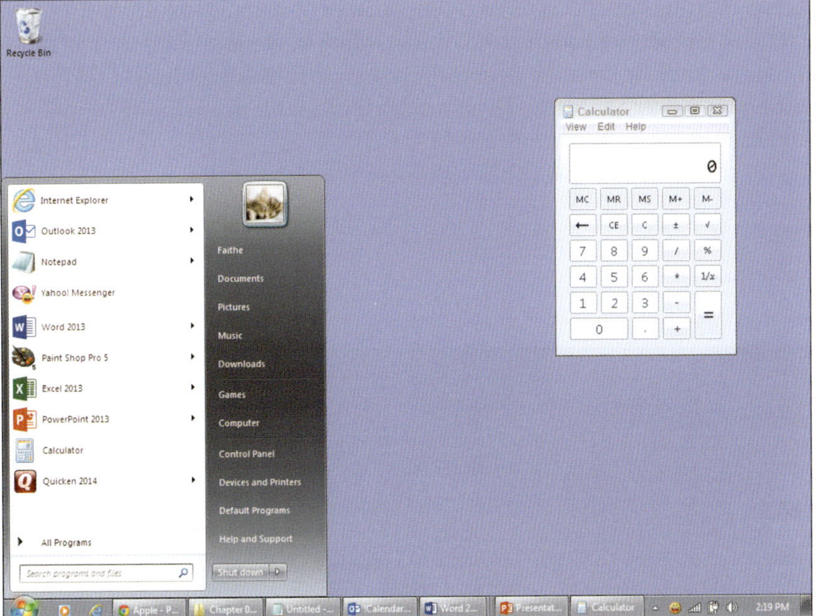

Figure 4.5 Windows 7.

Linux was developed by Linus Torvalds. The name *Linux* is a combination of the words Linus and UNIX. Linux is open-source, which means that Mr. Torvalds retains ownership of his original code, but it is free to the public to use in any way they see fit. Users are free to modify the code, improve it, and redistribute it. Developers are not allowed to charge money for the Linux kernel itself (the main part of the operating system), but they can charge money for **distributions** (**distros** for short), which are packaged collections of add-ons and utility programs for Linux. Some of the most popular distros include SUSE Linux, Ubuntu Linux, and Red Hat Linux.

distribution or **distro** A packaged collection of an open-source kernel such as Linux along with helpful add-ons and utilities.

multi-boot The ability to have more than one OS installed and to choose at startup which one to run.

virtualization Running a different operating system in a windowed environment within another operating system.

virtual machine An operating system running within another operating system.

Put It to Work

Running More than One OS

If you want to run multiple operating systems on a single PC, one way is to set it up to **multi-boot**. Each time you start the computer, a menu appears asking which operating system you want to start up. Each operating system must be on a separate volume in order to multi-boot. Windows supports multi-booting; install the non-Windows OS first, and then when you install Windows, its Setup program will ask whether you want to set up multi-booting. The drawback to multi-booting is that each time you want to switch operating systems, you have to restart the computer.

Another way to experience multiple operating systems on the same PC is to use a virtualization program. **Virtualization** enables you to create an entire **virtual machine** inside an application, and install a different operating system on it. The main operating system of the PC is the host OS, and the one inside the virtual machine is the guest OS. You can easily switch back and forth between the host and guest operating systems. VMWare (`www.vmware.com/products`) is the most popular virtualization software; versions are available for individual PCs as well as for large-scale commercial use, such as running several server OS versions on the same server.

shell The user interface for an operating system. Some operating systems, like Windows, do not separate the shell from the kernel; others, like Linux, give you a choice of shells.

Linux is, at its core, a command-line operating system, as is UNIX. However, nearly all the distros contain multiple **shells**—utilities that allow a user to interact with the operating system. Most distros have a GUI sitting on top of the shell. These are highly graphical, and as attractive and easy to use as Windows and Mac OS X. Figure 4.6 shows the Ubuntu Linux shell, for example. Although most Windows and Mac OS X applications will not run in Linux, plenty of free, open-source equivalents for most software types are designed specifically for Linux, or have Linux versions.

Figure 4.6 The Ubuntu Linux GUI.

thin client A computer with minimal hardware, designed for a specific task. For example, a thin web client is designed for using the Internet.

Some portable computers, such as netbooks, don't require a powerful operating system like Windows for the simple tasks they are designed to perform, like checking email and surfing the web. On such computers, performance is better, and more storage space remains when a **thin client** operating system is used. A thin client is an operating system that is "thinner" (that is, smaller and more agile) than a regular desktop operating system. It doesn't have a lot of utilities or features, but it has the right ones for the system on which it is installed.

Chrome OS A thin client operating system created by Google for small notebook computers (netbooks).

One popular thin client operating system is **Chrome OS**. Chrome is the name of both an operating system and a web browser, both produced by Google. Chrome OS is a variant of Linux, and was developed through an open-source project called Chromium OS. This simple operating system comes preinstalled on some thin clients. It contains a simple file manager, the Google Chrome web browser, and a media player. It doesn't run most applications designed for other operating systems. Figure 4.7 shows a Chrome OS screen.

Figure 4.7 Google Chrome OS.

New Thin Client Operating Systems

New Technologies

Chrome OS is far from the only operating system for thin web clients. Several other open-source operating systems have recently been released, such as Haiku (`www.haiku-os.org`), openThinClient (`openthinclient.org`), and ThinStation (`www.thinstation.org`). These operating systems require less powerful computers than Windows or Mac OS X because they are leaner and have fewer features. Using a thin client operating system on an older computer can make it perform better when doing activities like browsing the web or managing email. The downside of using a non-standard operating system is that few applications are available for it, so you may be limited to the applications that come with it (usually a text editor, a web browser, an email program, and a music player, at the minimum).

Operating Systems for Tablets and Smartphones

Tablets and smartphones have special operating system needs. They use solid-state storage, which is expensive, so the amount of storage space is limited. Therefore, a large operating system is impractical; the operating system must be simple, easy to use, and above all, compact in size. The operating system comes preinstalled on a static memory chip on tablets and smartphones, so these platforms are often referred to as **system-on-chip (SoC)**. A separate memory chip (or set of chips) is used to hold the data you create and the extra applications you install.

system-on-chip (SoC) An operating system that comes preinstalled on a chip on a portable device such as a smartphone.

For most of their capabilities, tablet and phone operating systems rely on third-party applications (**apps**) purchased or downloaded for free from an online store. Because users can freely select their own apps, there is no need to provide lots of preinstalled apps with the operating system, and each person's device can be customized for his or her preferred activities.

app An application, such as for a personal computer, tablet, or smartphone.

Portable Apple devices (iPhone and iPad) use an operating system called **iOS**. Its main advantage is its popularity—because it is so popular, thousands of apps are available for it via the Apple Store. Figure 4.8 shows an iPad screen with iOS as the operating system.

iOS The Apple-created operating system for Apple tablets and phones.

Figure 4.8 The iPad runs the iOS operating system.

Android An open-source operating system used on a variety of portable devices, including tablets and smartphones.

The main competitor to iOS is **Android**, an open-source OS created by Google. Android is popular on low-end tablets because it is free, and because many apps are available for it and most of them are free. Many smartphones also use a version of Android.

Windows RT The Windows version designed for SoC tablet computers.

Windows Phone The Windows version designed for smartphones.

Microsoft has two different versions of Windows for portable devices. For tablets, there is **Windows RT**, which is much like the desktop version of Windows but designed for SoC devices. Most desktop applications won't run on a Windows RT system. For smartphones, there is **Windows Phone**, an operating system designed specifically for phone use. Figure 4.9 shows a Windows Phone display.

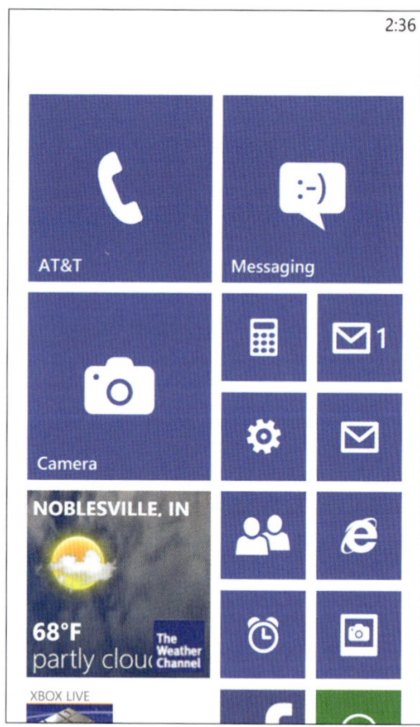

Figure 4.9 The Windows Phone operating system.

Quick Review

1. Name the Windows version designed for each of these platforms: desktop computer, tablet, smartphone, and server.
2. Name three operating systems for smartphones.

Understanding Digital Storage

Most operating systems save and store files using the same basic principles, although the individual file formats may differ between platforms and operating systems. The following sections describe the logical organization of computer file systems.

Drives, Volumes, and File Systems

A drive is a physical storage unit, such as an HDD, a SSD, or a DVD drive. As you learned in Chapter 3, "Input, Output, and Storage," some drives are separate from their discs, as a DVD drive is. Other drives have the discs built-in, like in an HDD. And some drives are not technically "drives" at all, in that they have no moving parts, but are called drives for consistency; solid-state drives are an example of that. The term *hard drive* generically refers to both HDD and SSHD storage in popular usage.

Each drive has one or more volumes, which are logical divisions of storage areas. Volumes are represented by letters, such as C:. A small-capacity, removable storage device like a DVD or a USB flash drive has a single volume letter. A large-capacity storage device like an HDD or SSHD may be divided into multiple volumes.

To prepare a hard drive for use, it must first be partitioned. **Partitioning** creates the logical divisions of the available space. A physical drive can logically be a single volume (one big partition with one volume letter assigned), or it can be split up into many pieces, each with its own volume letter. Each volume must then be formatted. **Formatting** organizes the available space by creating a **file system** on it. The file system determines how the files will be stored and retrieved logically.

partition To create logical divisions of the available space on a storage medium such as an HDD; or, a logical division of space on a storage medium.

format To create the file system on a volume.

file system A set of rules for storing and managing the files on a volume, such as NTFS or FAT32.

Depending on the operating system and the utility you are using to partition and format the drive, different file systems may be available. Table 4.1 lists several popular file systems. Modern versions of Windows prefer the **New Technology File System (NTFS)** for the **system volume** (that is, the volume on which Windows itself is installed), but can also support **FAT32**, a file system used in earlier Windows versions. Mac OS X uses a file system called **Hierarchical File System Plus (HFS+)**. Linux supports several different file systems, and the default file system installed depends on the distro. CDs and DVDs commonly use the **ISO 9660** (also called CD File System, or CDFS) or the **Universal Disc Format (UDF)** file system.

New Technology File System (NTFS) The proprietary Microsoft file system used in modern versions of Windows.

system volume The volume on which the operating system files are stored.

FAT32 A file system used in Windows 95, Windows 98, and Windows Millennium Edition. FAT stands for File Allocation Table.

Hierarchical File System Plus (HFS+) The file system used with Mac OS X.

ISO 9660 A file system used on optical media such as CDs; also called CD File System, or CDFS.

Universal Disc Format (UDF) An extension of the ISO 9660 file system, a file system used on optical media such as CDs and DVDs.

Different file systems offer different features and benefits. NTFS, for example, provides features like file encryption, file compression, support for long filenames (up to 255 characters), and support for large-capacity volumes (up to16 TB). You will learn about file encryption and compression later in this chapter.

Table 4.1 Popular File Systems

File System	*Type of Disc*	*Operating System*	*Notes*
NTFS	HDD, SSHD	Windows 2000 and higher	
FAT32	HDD, SSHD	Windows 95 and higher	Obsolete because it can't support volumes over 4GB in size
FAT16	HDD, SSHD	MS-DOS, all Windows versions	Obsolete, replaced by FAT32
FAT12	Floppy disks	MS-DOS, all Windows versions	Obsolete because floppy disks are obsolete
HFS+	HDD, SSHD	Mac OS X	
ISO 9660	Optical	Various	
UDF	Optical	Various	

Windows uses a Disk Management utility to provide information about the system's disks and drives and to allow users to perform disk-based maintenance operations.

How Files Are Organized in Folders

root directory The top-level folder on a storage volume.

The top level of storage for a volume is its **root directory**. The root directory is like the lobby of a building. All other locations within the volume are accessed by going through it. The term *root directory* is a carryover from an earlier time when folders were called directories. Another name for the root directory is *top-level folder*.

path The complete descriptor of a file's location, including the volume and folders.

A file's **path** is the complete descriptor of its location. A file named Budget.txt located in the root directory of the E: drive, for example, would have a path like this:

```
E:\Budget.txt
```

The colon (:) in the preceding example path indicates that the letter preceding it is a volume letter. The \ follows a folder (directory) name. The example has no name before the \ because the root directory has no name.

Now suppose that file were in a folder called Personal. Its path would look like this:

```
E:\Personal\Budget.txt
```

As you learned in Chapter 3, a folder within a folder is called a subfolder. Suppose that the Personal folder had a subfolder called Financial, and our example file was in that folder. The path would look like this:

```
E:\Personal\Financial\Budget.txt
```

folder tree A graphical representation of a volume's storage hierarchy, with subordinate branches for folders and subfolders.

A volume's folder hierarchy can be complicated. There can be hundreds of folders in the root directory, and each of them can contain many levels of subfolders. A file management utility, such as Windows Explorer in Windows 7, provides a visual picture of the structure that you can browse. For example, in Figure 4.10, the example file appears in the Financial folder. The **folder tree** in the navigation pane at the left shows the complete path taken to get to that file.

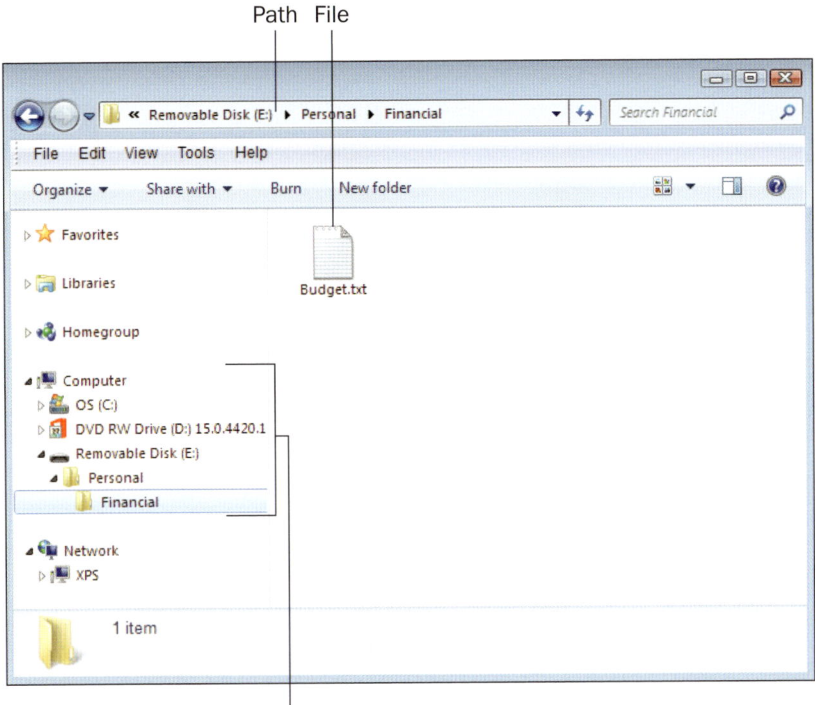

Figure 4.10 The Budget.txt file's complete path is illustrated in the navigation pane.

In Windows 7, you can jump directly to any location by clicking its name in the navigation pane. You can expand and collapse folders there by double-clicking their names. You can also navigate by using the path that appears in the Address bar at the top of the Windows Explorer window. In Figure 4.10, the path appears like this:

Removable Disk (E:) ⇨ Personal ⇨ Financial

That's simply an alternative way of writing the path. If you click in the Address bar, you see the traditional version of the path instead, like this:

E:\Personal\Financial

Step by Step

Examining the Folder Structure in Windows 7

Follow these steps to use the Windows Explorer tool to browse the contents of the volumes folders on your computer:

1. Click Start and then click Computer. Windows Explorer opens, showing all the volumes that it recognizes on your computer. Some volumes may not appear, so this may not be an exact one-to-one match with the volumes you saw in Disk Management earlier in the chapter. In this example, you see an HDD, a DVD, and a USB flash drive.

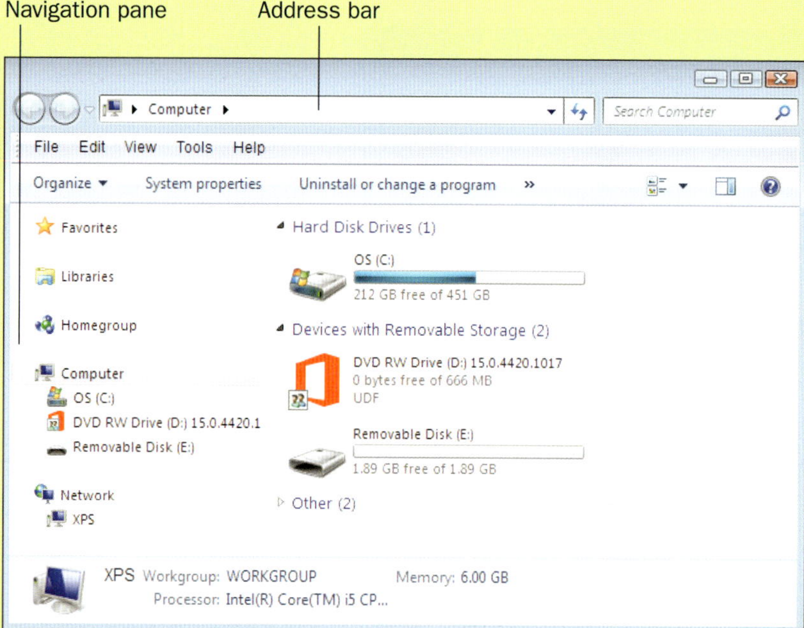

2. Double-click the C: drive in the main window. Its content appears. The folders appear first, followed by any files that are stored in the root directory.
3. Double-click the Windows folder. Its content appears, which includes many subfolders and many files.
4. In the Address bar at the top, click Computer to return to that screen.
5. In the navigation pane at the left, under the Computer heading, double-click the C: drive.
6. Scroll down in the navigation pane and locate the Users folder and double-click it.
7. In the navigation pane, double-click the Public folder. Then double-click the Public Documents folder.
8. In the Address bar, click the arrow to the left of Computer and then click Libraries.
9. Click the Close (X) button in the upper-right corner of the window to close it.

File Extensions and File Types

file extension A code at the end of a filename that indicates the file's type.

Each application has a specific format in which it saves the files you create in it. To help identify the file format, some operating systems (including Microsoft Windows) use file extensions. A **file extension** is a code following the name of the file that indicates its type. Extensions are separated from the filename by a period, like this: Myfile.docx. In this example, docx is the extension, and it indicates the Microsoft Word format.

Almost all files have file extensions in Windows, not just data files. For example, the executable files that run applications also have extensions, as do the Windows system files and their helper files. Table 4.2 lists some of the most common file extensions and their applications.

TIP You might not see a file's extension in Windows Explorer. By default, Windows 7 hides extensions for known file types. If you want to display them, from Windows Explorer, open the Tools menu and click Folder Options. Click the View tab, and then clear the Hide Extensions for Known File Types check box, and click OK.

Table 4.2 Common File Extensions

Extension	*File Type*	*Associated Application*
txt	Text	Notepad, WordPad, Microsoft Word
gif, png, jpg, tif	Photo or graphic	Paint, Photoshop, or almost any other photo editing program
doc, docx, docm	Word processing document	Microsoft Word, some other word processing programs also support
rtf	Word processing document	WordPad, Microsoft Word, or almost any word processing program
xls, xlsx, slxm	Spreadsheet	Microsoft Excel
ppt, pptx, pptm	Presentation	Microsoft PowerPoint
mdb, accdb	Database	Microsoft Access
pdf	Portable document format (platform-independent formatted document)	Adobe Reader, Adobe Acrobat, limited support in Microsoft Word
xps	XML document format (Microsoft-specific platform-independent formatted document)	XPS Viewer, Windows 7, Windows 8, limited support in Microsoft Word
exe, com, bat	Executable program files	n/a
dll, ini, dat	Helper files for programs and for Windows itself	n/a
zip	Compressed archive file	Windows Explorer, or a third-party program such as WinZip

Table 4.2 shows some common default application assignments, but the actual application assigned to a particular extension depends on the settings in your operating system. You can configure the OS to associate a file type with any of the applications you have installed on your computer. When an extension is assigned to an application, and you double-click a data file with that extension, the data file automatically opens in the associated application (provided, of course, that the application is capable of handling that file type).

Backups

Because storage media sometimes fail, it's important to back up important files frequently. Businesses spend thousands of dollars on robust, automated systems that back up their servers nightly, as well as key files on individual computers in some cases. Home and small-business users can use smaller backup systems designed for individual PCs.

backup software Software that enables and automates the process of backing up files to external media.

Backup software can save your backup files to external media, such as a writeable DVD or an external hard drive, or to a network or Internet location. To save space on the backup media, backup software creates its own compressed archive files in its own proprietary format. To restore from the backup, you must use the same backup software that was employed to create the backup. A backup can span multiple discs or volumes, and can include multiple archive files. The collection of archive files created for a single backup instance is called a **backup set**.

backup set A set of backup files created during a single backup operation.

Each time backup software runs, only a small portion of the files will have changed since the last backup was created. In order to reduce the amount of time the backup takes, not all storage is fully backed up every time. Instead, the backup software reads each file's **archive attribute** (sometimes called an archive flag). When a file is backed up, its archive attribute is turned off. When the file changes, its archive attribute turns

archive attribute A file attribute that indicates whether or not a file has changed since its last backup.

on again. The operating system manages the archive attribute for each file automatically. The backup software can be configured to skip any files where the archive attribute is off, which omits any unchanged files from the backup set.

full backup A backup operation that backs up all files and sets their archive attribute to Off.

differential backup A backup operation that backs up all files that have the archive attribute set to On but does not change that attribute.

You can do a full backup or a partial one. A **full backup** backs up every file in the specified list, and clears each one's archive attribute (that is, sets it to Off). There are two types of partial backups. A **differential backup** backs up only files that have changed since the last full backup. Backing up the files does not change their archive attributes, so that the next time you do a backup, they are still marked to be backed up again. If you need to restore the files, you would need the last full backup set and then the most recent differential backup set. This method saves on media because you only have to keep two backup sets, and you can reuse the same media each time you perform a differential backup. However, the differential backup set gets larger every time you run it because more files will have changed, and over time the differential backup set can get fairly large. Therefore, a full backup should be done periodically (for example, every week or two) to keep the size of the differential backup set small.

incremental backup A backup operation that backs up all files that have the archive attribute set to On and then sets the attribute to Off.

An **incremental backup**, on the other hand, turns off the archive attribute for each file as it backs it up. Therefore, each time you run an incremental backup, it backs up only the files that have changed since the last incremental backup. If you need to restore the files, you would need the last full backup set and every incremental backup set that has been done since then. The backup runs quickly each time because only the most recently changed files are backed up. However, the user has to maintain many backup sets to have a complete and current backup. Running a full backup creates another full set, and all the previous incremental backups can be discarded or overwritten.

Windows 7 comes with a backup utility called Backup and Restore. You can use it to back up your important files, and to schedule full, differential, or incremental backups to occur at regular intervals. You can also invest in third-party backup programs that have more features.

TIP Users who have just a few important files to back up may prefer to manually copy them to an external drive periodically rather than using backup software, especially if the files do not frequently change. Another way to ensure your important files are always available is to store them in a cloud storage system such as Microsoft's OneDrive (formerly known as SkyDrive) or Apple's iCloud. Companies that offer cloud storage use RAID systems, as described in Chapter 3, to make sure data is constantly available, even if one or more drives fail.

Quick Review

1. Define the terms volume, root directory, and folder, and explain how they work together.
2. Explain how a single physical drive can have multiple volumes with different file systems on them.
3. Describe the difference between full, incremental, and differential backups.

Summary

Understanding System Software

System software includes the BIOS, the operating system, and utility programs that perform system maintenance and protection.

A computer's **platform** is its type of hardware. Only certain operating systems can run on certain platforms. The **Intel platform**, also called IBM-compatible, is the most popular platform; this platform's most popular operating system is Windows.

There are many types of **utility software** for performing various system maintenance tasks. **Antivirus**, **firewall**, and **anti-spyware** programs protect from outside attacks and malicious software (**malware**). **Anti-spam** programs cut down on the amount of junk email you receive. A **disk checking program** can find and fix file system errors, and a **registry cleanup program** can find and fix inconsistent or unneeded entries in the **registry**. **Backup software** can automate the process of backing up important files.

Comparing the Major Operating Systems

Mac OS X is the operating system on most Apple desktop and notebook computers. Its latest version is OS X 10.9, code named **Mavericks**. Its main competitor is **Microsoft Windows**, which is the most popular operating system in the world, used on more than 90% of all desktop and notebook PCs.

Linux is an open-source operating system based on UNIX. The basic version is free, but you can purchase a packaged collection of add-ons and utility programs with it called a distribution (**distro**). A distro typically includes a GUI, as an alternative to Linux's native command-line interface.

You can run multiple operating systems on a single computer by setting it up to **multi-boot**, or to use a **virtual machine** to run the secondary operating system within the first one.

A **thin client** operating system such as Chrome OS is designed for small portable notebook computers that are used primarily for going online.

Tablets and smartphones have an operating system that is preinstalled on a chip (**system-on-chip**, or **SoC**). Users can download **apps**, which are add-on applications that extend the device's capabilities. The popular SoC operating systems are **iOS**, **Android**, **Windows RT**, and **Windows Phone**.

Understanding Digital Storage

A **drive** is a physical storage unit. It can be **partitioned** into one or more logical **volumes**. **Formatting** a volume places a **file system** on it, which it will use to store its files. **NTFS** is the most popular file system for modern versions of Windows; **FAT32** is an older file system used in earlier versions of Windows. **HFS+** is the Mac OS X file system, and **ISO 9660** (CD File System, or CDFS) and **Universal Disc Format (UDF)** are used for optical discs.

The top level of a storage volume is its **root directory**. A file's **path** is the complete descriptor of its location, including the volume and any folders you pass through to get to it. A **folder tree** is a graphic representation of a volume's folder structure. A **file extension** is a code following the filename that indicates its type.

Backup software helps keep your data safe by backing it up to external media. The collection of files created for a single backup instance is a **backup set**. A backup can be **full**, **differential**, or **incremental**.

Key Terms

adware
Android
anti-spam software
app
archive attribute
backup set
backup software
Chrome OS
command-line interface
differential backup
disk checking program
distribution (distro)
FAT32
file extension
file system
firewall software
folder tree
format
full backup
graphical user interface (GUI)
Hierarchical File System Plus (HFS+)
incremental backup
iOS
ISO 9660
Linux
Mac OS X
malware
Mavericks
Microsoft Windows
multi-boot
New Technology File System (NTFS)
partition
path
platform
registry
registry cleanup program
root directory
shell
spyware
system-on-chip (SoC)
system software
system volume
thin client
uninstaller utility
Universal Disc Format (UDF)
utility software
virtual machine
virtualization
virus
Windows Phone
Windows RT

Test Yourself

Fact Check

1. Which of these is NOT a type of system software?
   a. word processing software
   b. backup software
   c. BIOS
   d. operating system
2. Which of these is a thin client OS?
   a. Windows Server
   b. Chrome OS
   c. Mac OS X
   d. UNIX
3. What file system is the default for Windows 7 system volumes?
   a. NTFS
   b. FAT32
   c. HFS+
   d. UDF

4. C:\Books\Current\Chapter01.docx is an example of a:
    a. volume
    b. folder tree
    c. registry entry
    d. path
5. What application would open the file Birthdays.rtf?
    a. Paint
    b. Microsoft Access
    c. Adobe Reader
    d. WordPad
6. What would you expect the extension of a compressed archive file to be?
    a. pdf
    b. xps
    c. zip
    d. docx
7. Which type of backup does NOT reset each file's archive attribute to Off after backing it up?
    a. full
    b. differential
    c. incremental
    d. none of the above
8. A virtual machine allows you to:
    a. Run one operating system inside of another
    b. Run more applications than you have memory to run normally
    c. Speed up the CPU
    d. Run a 64-bit operating system on a 32-bit platform
9. What does changing to a different shell do?
    a. Changes the applications that can be run
    b. Changes the way the OS communicates with hardware
    c. Changes the kernel
    d. Changes the user interface
10. Which type of backup backs up every file in the specified list and clears each one's archive attribute?
    a. full
    b. differential
    c. incremental
    d. none of the above

Matching

Match the term to its description.

a. GUI

b. Linux

c. shell

d. SoC

e. UDF

f. root directory

1. ________ A user interface that uses pictures and a pointing device to issue commands
2. ________ An open-source operating system used on a variety of platforms
3. ________ An operating system's user interface
4. ________ The file system used on DVDs
5. ________ An operating system that comes preinstalled on a chip on a portable device
6. ________ The top-level folder on a volume

Sum It Up

1. List three types of system software.
2. List five types of utility programs.
3. List three operating systems that would run on an IBM-compatible desktop PC.
4. Name three operating systems used on smartphones.
5. Explain the purpose of partitioning a drive.
6. Give an example of a complete path to a file, and explain the parts of the path.

Explore More

Linux Distros

Suppose you want to put Linux on an older desktop PC and give it to a relative who wants to use the Internet. But that person doesn't know much about computers, so you must find a Linux distro that is very easy to use, even for a beginner. Do a web search on the terms *Linux distro beginner*. Based on the information you find, choose two Linux distros you think would meet your needs, and explain why you chose the ones you did.

Examining File Associations

Windows 7 has default extension associations for various file types. For example, when you double-click on a file with a txt extension, Windows 7 opens it in Notepad because Notepad is the default application for the txt extension.

When you have more than one application that is capable of opening a certain type of file, you may want to change the Windows default setting for that extension. For example, if you have both Microsoft Word and WordPad, you might prefer one over the other for opening files with an rtf extension.

You can work with file associations in either of two ways. You can browse a list of applications and see what extensions are associated with each one, or you can browse a list of extensions and see what applications are associated with each one. Open the Control Panel in Windows 7, click Programs, and click Default Programs. Then examine the settings and options available there. To browse by program, choose Set Your Default Programs. To browse by extension, choose Associate a File Type or Protocol with a Program.

Think It Over

Backup Scheduling

Suppose you were designing your own backup schedule for your computer. Which folders or files would you back up? Regarding the files you did not choose to back up, why did you exclude them? How often would you perform a full backup? How often would you perform a differential or incremental backup—and which would it be? Think about your answers, and give a reason for each one.

Chapter 5

Introduction to Windows 7

Learning objectives

- Understand the Windows 7 interface
- Be able to start up and shut down Windows
- Know how to run programs
- Perform common file management tasks

In Chapter 4, "Operating System Basics," you learned about operating systems in general—what they do, how they work, how they differ from one another. In this chapter, you will turn your full attention toward one operating system in particular: Windows 7.

Windows 7 is a popular operating system, installed on millions of personal computers worldwide. This chapter starts with a tour of the Windows 7 desktop, so you can familiarize yourself with its paths. You'll learn how to start up and shut down a Windows computer, and how to use special power-saving and security modes. You'll see how to run programs in Windows 7. Finally, you'll learn how to manage files using Windows Explorer, and perform common operations like copying, moving, renaming, and deleting files.

Careers in IT

Health IT Specialist

In many countries, governments have recently enacted laws that require health-care providers to computerize certain parts of their practices. For example, patient health records, medical billing, supply and drug inventories, and medical equipment maintenance records will soon need to be in electronic form if they are not already. This requirement opens up many job opportunities for health IT specialists. A health IT specialist plans and sets up health-care recordkeeping systems that meet all government requirements and keeps such systems up to date and in good repair. This job requires at least an associate's degree in a computer-related field, with a bachelor's or master's degree preferred for supervisory positions.

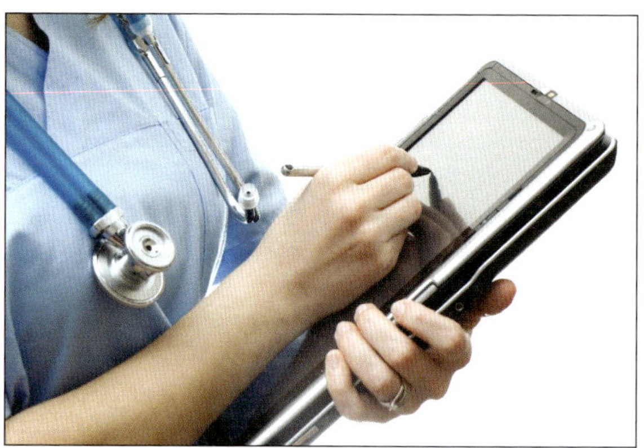

© iStockphoto.com/mkurtbas

A Tour of Windows 7

desktop The Windows 7 interface, on which windows open containing applications. Can also refer specifically to the background image.

The Windows 7 interface, called the **desktop**, is your starting point for most of the activities you perform in Windows 7. From the desktop, you can run programs, manage files, access the Internet, check the status of devices, and more.

Your Windows desktop is like a physical workspace in some ways. You can have multiple files and projects open at the same time, spread out on the desktop so you can see each one of them. The desktop can be changed to suit your personal style. The desktop background can be a solid color, as in Figure 5.1, or it can be a picture of your choice.

taskbar The bar along the bottom of the Windows desktop, from which you can start programs and manage running programs.

Start button The button that opens the Start menu.

icon A small picture representing a file, folder, application, or other object.

pinned Attached to a fixed feature onscreen, such as to the taskbar or the Start menu.

notification area The area to the left of the clock on the taskbar, containing icons for programs running in the background. Also called the **system tray**.

The **taskbar** is the thin bar across the bottom of the screen. It is used to start programs and manage the programs that are already running. At the far-left end is the **Start button**. The small graphics you see on the desktop are called **icons**. An icon can sit on the desktop, as the Recycle Bin icon does in Figure 5.1, or it can be **pinned** to the taskbar for easy access. For example, in Figure 5.1, four pinned icons appear to the right of the Start button. The center of the taskbar is blank in Figure 5.1, but if any programs were running or windows open, buttons for those programs or windows would appear there. Some other icons are at the right end of the taskbar, but these aren't pinned there. That area is called the **notification area** (or **system tray**), and the icons there represent information from programs or system components that are running in the background, such as the Volume Control and the Battery Meter. At the far-right end of the taskbar is a clock.

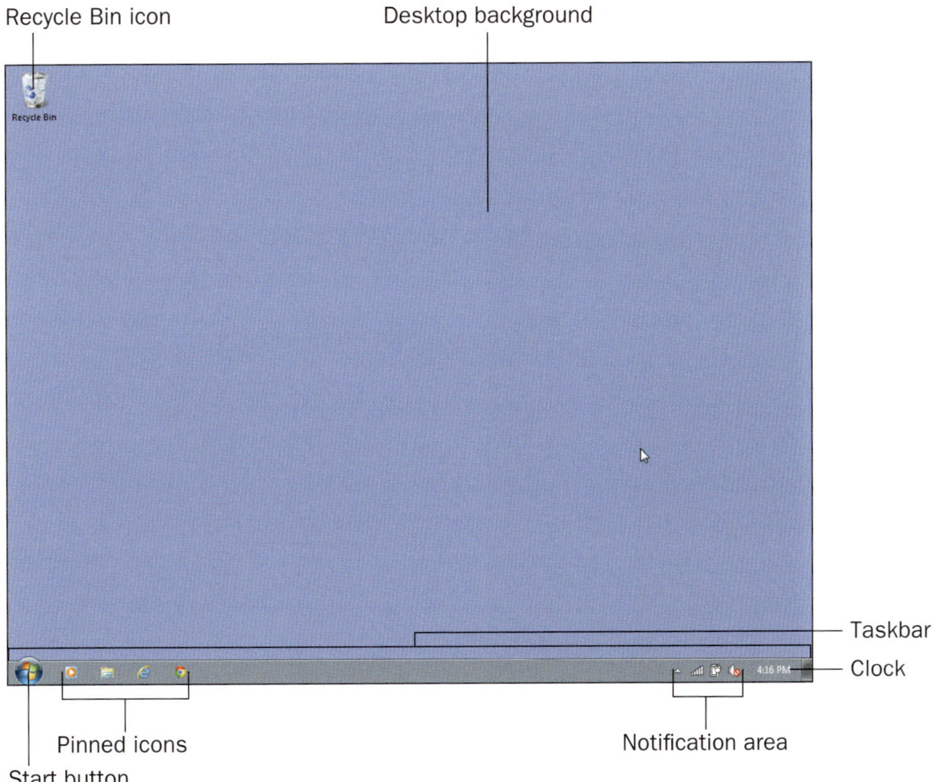

Figure 5.1 The Windows 7 desktop.

When you click the Start button, the **Start menu** opens, as shown in Figure 5.2. It has two columns. In the left column, the top section contains pinned shortcuts to applications. By default, there might not be any pinned shortcuts here; Figure 5.2 shows pinned shortcuts for Internet Explorer and Outlook. The bottom section of the left column contains shortcuts to recently or frequently used applications. This list changes depending on your usage. Below that is the **All Programs** command. It opens a hierarchical menu of all the installed programs on your system; you'll learn more about it in the section "Running Applications" later in this chapter. At the bottom of the left column is a **Search box**; you can type in this box to narrow down what appears on the Start menu to find what you are looking for.

Start menu The menu that opens when you click the Start button, containing shortcuts to applications, storage locations, and settings.

All Programs The command at the bottom of the Start menu that opens up a hierarchical menu system of all the installed applications on the computer.

Search box The box at the bottom of the Start menu that enables you to type the name of a program or feature you are looking for to narrow down the Start menu's listing.

In the right column are links to commonly accessed locations and settings, described in Table 5.1.

Table 5.1 Locations and Settings on the Start Menu

Link	*Opens*
User's name	The user's personal folders: C:\Users\username
Documents	The user's Documents library
Pictures	The user's Pictures library
Music	The user's Music library
Games	The Games folder, which is a virtual folder that shows shortcuts to all installed games in one place
Computer	The Computer view of Windows Explorer, showing the local volumes
Control Panel	The Control Panel (top level)
Devices and Printers	The Devices and Printers section of the Control Panel
Help and Support	The Windows 7 Help and Support window

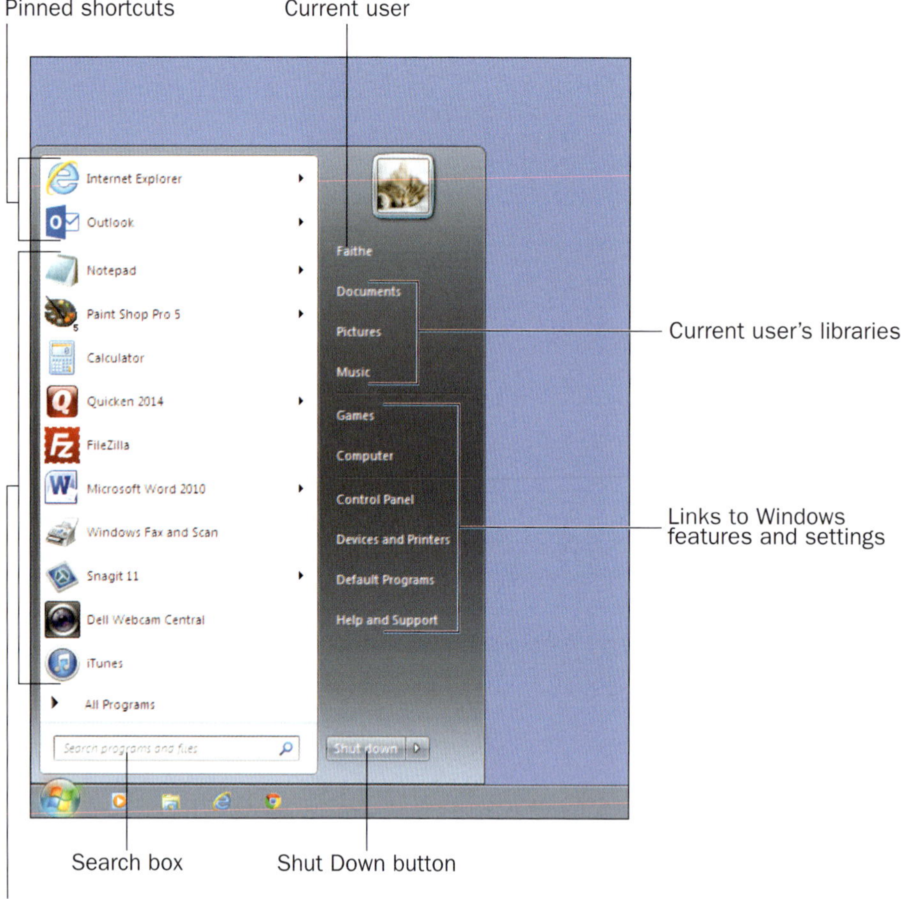

Figure 5.2 The Start menu.

Quick Review

1. How do you open the Start menu?
2. What is the notification area?
3. Name two places where pinned shortcuts appear.

Starting Up and Shutting Down

When you turn on the computer's power, Windows 7 loads automatically. Depending on the way your copy of Windows is configured, the desktop might appear automatically, or you might see a login screen.

NOTE Windows 7 boots directly to the desktop without prompting for a user account or password if ALL the following conditions are true: 1) There is only one user account set up on this PC (excluding the built-in Guest and Administrator accounts); 2) that user account has no password; and 3) the Guest account is disabled.

At the login screen, if your username appears with a password box under it, type the password and press Enter to log in. If several different usernames appear, click your account to select it. The options available at the login screen may vary depending on the edition of Windows 7 you have, and depending on whether the PC you are using is connected to a domain-based network.

Shutting Down or Restarting the PC

When you shut down the PC, Windows shuts down and the computer stops using power. The next time you start the computer, Windows must reload itself into memory, which takes a minute or two. You should shut down a computer completely before moving it, storing it, or servicing it. You should also shut down the computer when prompted to do so by Windows itself. (A complete shutdown and restart is sometimes required to complete the installation of certain updates.) When you shut down the computer and then turn it back on again later, that's called a **cold boot** because the computer's circuitry has been off (and is therefore cold).

cold boot To start up a computer from a power-off state.

When you restart the PC, Windows shuts down, but the computer's power remains on, and Windows immediately restarts. Restarting is also called a **warm boot** because the computer stays on (warm) as it reboots. You should restart when Windows prompts you to do so (for example, after updates have been installed), and also as a troubleshooting technique if you begin to experience problems with Windows. To restart Windows, choose Restart from the Shut Down button's menu, as shown in Figure 5.3.

warm boot To restart a computer that is already powered on.

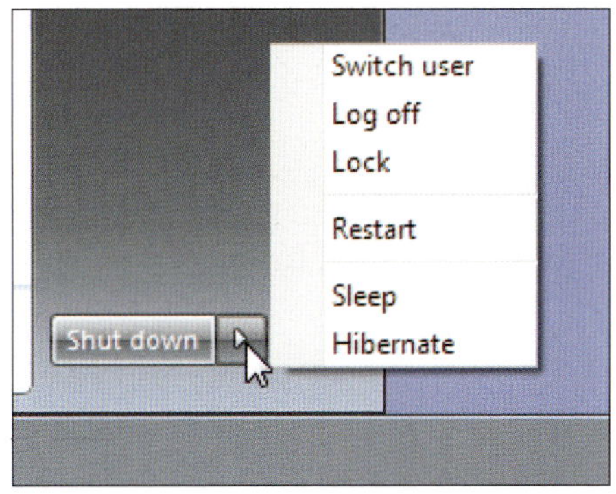

Figure 5.3 The Shut Down button has a menu of additional options; Click the arrow to open the menu.

Restarting Helps!

Troubleshooting

If you talk to any computer professional about a problem you are having with your computer, the first thing he or she will probably ask you is: *Have you tried restarting?* That's because restarting Windows can cure a variety of one-time or occasional problems that may occur. For example, suppose your mouse pointer starts jumping around wildly as you move the mouse. That's a problem with the display adapter, and it can almost always be cured by restarting the PC. Another common problem that restarting usually fixes is a keyboard that suddenly starts sending the wrong characters to the PC as you type.

Besides shutting down, there are several other ways to make the computer use less (or no) power. You will learn about them in the section "Placing the PC in a Low-Power Mode," later in this chapter.

Step by Step

Shutting Down a Windows 7 Computer

Follow these steps to shut down the computer completely and turn its power off:

1. Click Start, and then click the Shut Down button.
2. If any programs have unsaved files, a prompt appears for them. Respond to the prompt as needed.

Restarting a Windows 7 Computer

Follow these steps to restart the computer:

1. Click Start, and then click the arrow to the right of the Shut Down button. A menu appears, as shown in Figure 5.3.
2. Click Restart.
3. If any programs have unsaved files, a prompt appears for them. Respond to the prompt as needed.

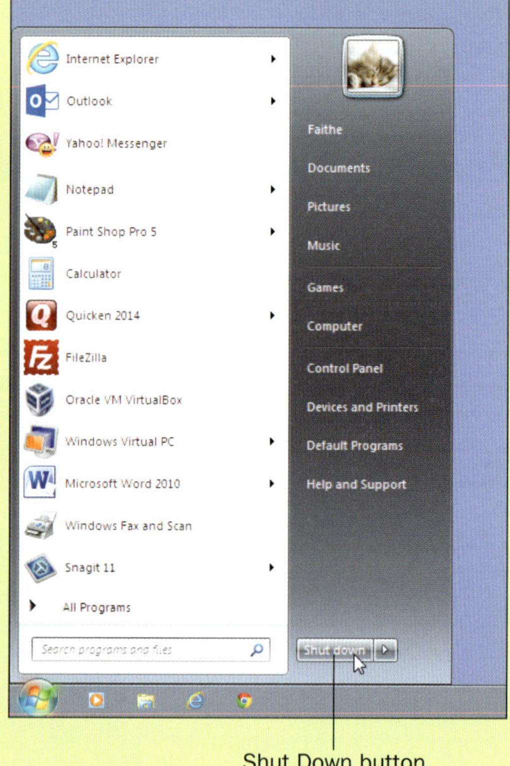

Placing the PC in a Low-Power Mode

Windows supports two special modes that you can place the computer in as an alternative to shutting down completely. In each of these modes, when the computer resumes operation, the desktop is just as you left it, including any open programs, windows, and files. This saves you time because you don't have to wait as long for Windows to start up as you normally would, and when it does start up, you don't have to reopen the applications and windows you want to continue working with.

Sleep mode A power-saving mode that keeps RAM powered but turns off everything else to save power.

Hibernate mode A power-saving mode that saves the contents of RAM to the hard drive and then shuts down all power. When the computer wakes up, it reads the saved data back into RAM so the computer does not have to restart completely.

Sleep mode is a low-power state. It keeps the RAM powered, but shuts down all other components. RAM doesn't use much memory, so the computer consumes very little power. On a desktop computer, that means it uses less electricity. On a battery-powered computer, that means the battery lasts much longer. Waking up from Sleep mode is very quick—only a few seconds. Hibernate mode is a no-power-needed state. It copies the contents of RAM to a reserved area on the hard drive, and then shuts the power down completely. When the computer starts back up again, instead of booting normally, it reads the stored data back into memory, so you can pick up where you left off. Hibernate mode takes more time to wake up from than Sleep mode does (about 30 seconds, on the average), but that's less time than it would take to start the computer from being completely shut down.

To place the computer in one of these modes, select it from the Shut Down button's menu on the Start menu, as shown in Figure 5.3. Closing the lid on a notebook computer usually puts the system into Sleep mode automatically; you may see the power light flashing intermittently as an indication the computer is sleeping.

To wake up from Sleep mode, press any key on the keyboard. To wake up from Hibernate mode, press the computer's Power button.

CAUTION

Not all computer hardware supports Hibernate mode. If you experience problems with the computer entering Hibernate mode, search online for troubleshooting help for your specific computer; there may be a BIOS (Basic Input Output System) update or driver update that can resolve the problem.

Troubleshooting

Stuck?

If your computer appears completely dead when you try to wake it up from Sleep or Hibernate mode, try holding down the computer's Power button for 10 seconds. Doing so will shut the PC down completely, resetting any special power mode it was previously in. You may see an error message when you restart the computer about Windows not shutting down correctly and offering to start Windows in a special mode. Don't use a special mode; choose Start Windows Normally.

Logging Off and Switching Users

Windows 7 supports multiple user accounts. When one user is finished, he or she can log off, which shuts down any running programs, closes any open data files, unloads all personal settings for that user, and returns to the login screen, with all the available users listed. From that point another user can log in. Logging off closes the user's personal activities down, but it does not completely restart Windows. Therefore, it takes less time than a full restart.

log off To close a user account's session, closing all open programs and data files and unloading all of that user's personal settings.

If another user wants to use the computer for a short time, the first user may not want to take the time to shut down all applications and data files that he or she is working on. The Switch User command suspends the current user's session but does not end it, and returns to the login screen. Another user can then log in. The users can switch back and forth freely between the open accounts, and other users can even log in, too.

Switch User A Windows feature that enables another user to log in without the original user logging off first.

To use the Log Off or Switch User command, choose it from the Shut Down button's menu, as shown in Figure 5.3.

TIP

Why not just let another person sit down and use the computer for a few minutes, without switching? That's fine to do, as long as the first user doesn't mind the lack of privacy. Each logged-in user has his or her own separate personal files and settings, and anyone who uses the computer while you are logged in can see your files. Switching users also enables each user to have his or her own preferred settings, such as display resolution and color scheme.

Locking the PC

If you are going to be away from your computer for a while, you might not want other people to be able to see what you were working on or snoop on your computer while you are gone. To prevent such intrusion, you can use the Lock command. Locking preserves the current state of the computer but redisplays the login screen. You must retype your password when you return to the computer to continue your session. Locking is similar to switching users except the login screen that appears shows the prompt only for the user who locked the PC, and not the full list of users that you see when you use Switch User.

lock To prevent unauthorized users from using a computer by displaying a password prompt.

To lock the PC, choose the Lock command from the Shut Down button's menu, as shown in Figure 5.3. Alternatively, the PC can be locked by pressing the Windows key on the bottom left of the keyboard and the L key simultaneously.

Quick Review

1. What is the difference between Log Off and Restart?
2. What is the difference between Sleep and Hibernate?
3. What is the difference between Lock and Switch User?

Running Applications

As you learned in Chapter 1, "Computer Basics," programs that perform some useful task (other than keeping the computer itself running) are known as applications. Running applications is the main reason Windows exists. Windows comes with a variety of small applications that it calls Accessories; these include a calculator, a text editor, a simple word processor, and a drawing program. You can also buy and install other applications on your own, and some computers come with some third-party applications already installed, such as a DVD movie player or a productivity suite such as Microsoft Office.

Starting an Application

As you saw earlier in the chapter, the Start menu has a few shortcuts on it. The top section contains pinned shortcuts, and below that are shortcuts to recently or frequently used applications. If the application you want to run isn't in either of those places, you must click All Programs to open the full menu system. This menu system contains both application shortcuts and folders. If you click a folder, you see the shortcuts within it. The Start menu is hierarchically organized, just like the file system you learned about in Chapter 4. There are subfolders within folders, and files can exist at any level of the organizational structure. Figure 5.4 shows the Accessories folder expanded to show its subfolders, and the System Tools subfolder expanded below that, for example. Yours will look different because you have different applications installed than the PC illustrated here.

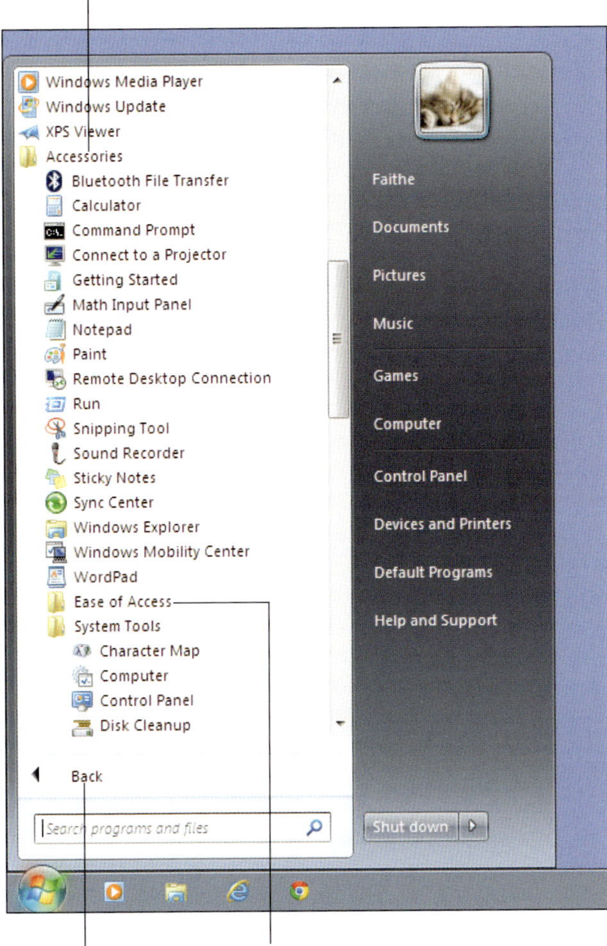

Figure 5.4 The All Programs menu with the Accessories folder expanded.

Because the Start menu can get complicated with so many folders and shortcuts, you may find it easier to search for the application you want to run rather than browsing for it. To search for an app, after opening the Start menu, start typing the application's name. The menu shows only the items that match what you typed. It is a full-featured search, and it finds all files on your hard drive, not just the applications on the Start menu. However, the Start menu applications appear at the top of the list, for easy access. In Figure 5.5, I typed **quick**, for example.

You can also start applications from shortcuts on the desktop or that are pinned to the taskbar or to the top of the Start menu. Just click the item you want on the Start menu or taskbar, or double-click the desired icon on the desktop.

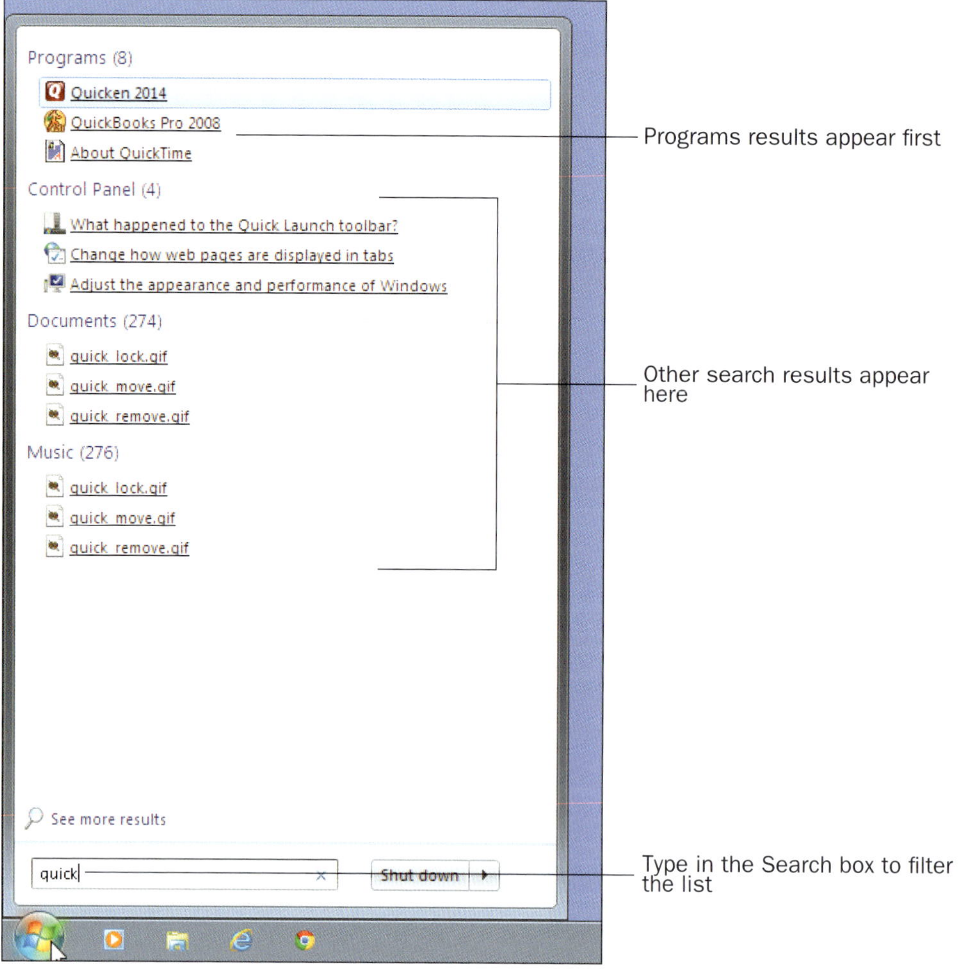

Figure 5.5 When you type a word (or part of a word), the Start menu shows the results of that search.

Put It to Work

Pinning Shortcuts

An easy way to re-find an application on the Start menu is to pin it, either to the Start menu or to the taskbar. If you pin it to the Start menu, it appears in the upper-left quadrant of the Start menu. If you pin it to the taskbar, it appears to the right of the Start button. After locating the desired item on the Start menu, but before clicking it to select it, right-click it. On the menu that appears, choose Pin to Start Menu or Pin to Taskbar.

To place a shortcut on the desktop, minimize all open windows. Open the Start menu, locate the icon you want, and then hold down the Ctrl key as you drag the application off the Start menu; a copy will be created on the desktop. Make sure you hold down Ctrl as you drag; otherwise, the shortcut will be removed from the Start menu.

Step by Step

Starting an Application

Follow these steps to start an application:

1. Click Start.
2. If you see a shortcut for the application you want, click it. Otherwise, do one of the following:

- Click All Programs and then click the application you want. Click a folder to open it if needed.
- Start typing the application name and then click the name when it appears at the top of the Start menu.

Manipulating a Window

As the name implies, Microsoft Windows is based on windows—movable rectangular blocks in which different types of content appear. When you run an application, it appears in its own window, and when you browse a file listing, that listing appears in its own window too. Figure 5.6 illustrates some basic parts of a window.

window A movable rectangular block in which content appears.

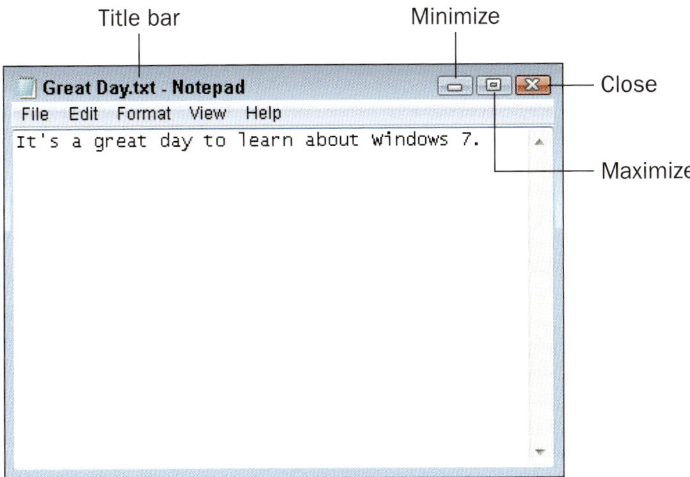

Figure 5.6 Each window has these features in common.

The title bar is the bar across the top of the window. If the window holds an application, it shows the application's name. If the application has a file open, it also shows the file's name. You can move a window around onscreen by dragging its title bar.

title bar The bar across the top of a window that shows the window's name; you can move the window by dragging it.

The buttons at the far-right end of the title bar control the window's size.

- Minimize: Hides the window by shrinking it down to a button on the taskbar. Use this button to get a window out of the way temporarily without closing it.
- Maximize: Enlarges the window to fill the entire screen. When a window is already maximized, this button changes to a Restore button, which returns the window to the size it was before you maximized it.
- Close: Closes the window, exiting the application that was open in it (if applicable).

minimize To shrink the window to a button on the taskbar.

maximize To enlarge the window to fill the entire screen.

restore To change a window from its maximized or minimized state to the size it was before it was maximized or minimized.

Each window has a border around its edges. You can position the mouse pointer over any part of the border and then drag to change the size of the window. If you drag a corner of the border, you can resize in both dimensions at once.

Step by Step

Move a Window

Follow these steps to move a window:

1. Position the mouse pointer over the window's title bar.
2. Hold down the left mouse button and drag the window to a new location.

Resize a Window

Follow these steps to resize a window:

1. Position the mouse pointer over the window's border. The pointer will turn into a double-headed arrow.
2. Hold down the left mouse button, and drag the border to change the window's size.

Navigating in an Application

Most Windows-based applications have one of two interfaces: a menu interface or a Ribbon interface. A menu interface is typical of older applications and applications not developed by Microsoft; the Ribbon interface is common in newer Microsoft applications.

menu bar A horizontal bar near the top of a window containing the names of menus that can be opened by clicking on the names.

keyboard shortcut A key combination that, when pressed, issues a command, as an alternative to selecting the command in another way.

A menu-based interface has a **menu bar** across the top of the screen, immediately below the title bar. You can click a menu name to open the menu, as shown in Figure 5.7. Notice in Figure 5.7 that some commands have **keyboard shortcuts** listed next to them. You can press those keys instead of using the menu system if you prefer.

TIP If a program does not appear to have a menu bar, try pressing the Alt key. A menu bar may appear.

dialog box A window that appears in response to selecting a command, prompting for more information about how the user wants the command to be executed.

Notice also that some commands have ellipses after them (. . .). These commands open **dialog boxes**, which are windows that prompt you for additional information. For example, if you click the Print command, the Print dialog box opens, prompting you to enter print settings, as shown in Figure 5.8.

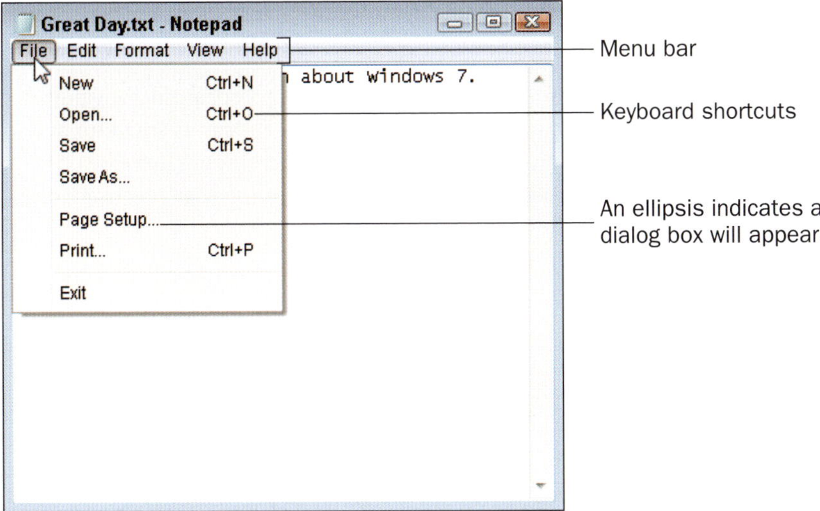

Figure 5.7 Menu-based application windows have these features.

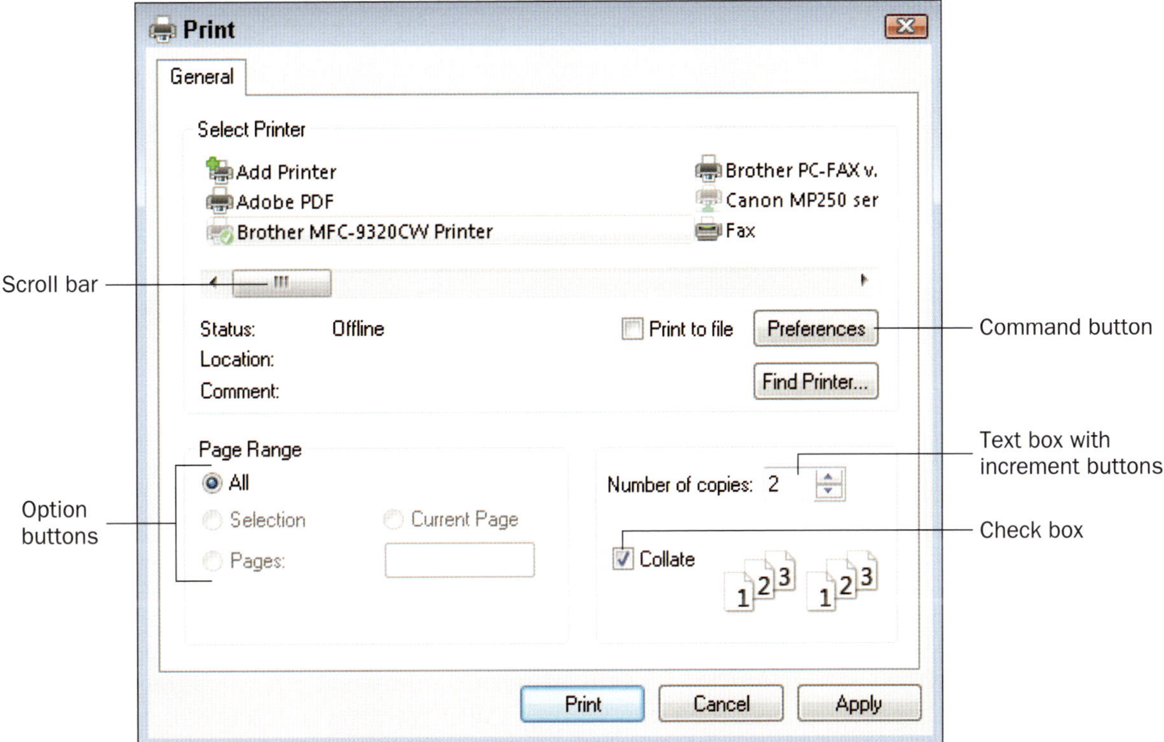

Figure 5.8 Some menu commands open dialog boxes.

Dialog boxes have various ways of asking you for information. For example, the dialog box in Figure 5.8 has the following features:

- **Scrollable list:** The list of printers at the top of the dialog box has a scroll bar beneath it. You can drag the scroll box from side to side to scroll the listing, or click the arrow at one end of the scroll bar to scroll in that direction.
- **Check box:** A check box toggles a feature on or off. Click it to change its state.

- **Text box:** A text box enables you to enter text or a number directly into it.
- **Increment buttons:** Text boxes that only accept numeric values sometimes have increment buttons, which appear as small up and down arrows. You can click an arrow to increment (increase) or decrement (decrease) the number shown in the text box as an alternative to manually typing a number.
- **Option buttons:** Option buttons present a group of mutually exclusive values. When one option button in a group is selected, the previous selection is cleared.
- **Command buttons:** Command buttons are large rectangular buttons with text labels on them. Clicking a command button performs an action, such as the Print, Cancel, or Apply buttons in Figure 5.8, or opens another dialog box, as with the Preferences and Find Printer buttons.

toolbar A group of graphical buttons representing commands.

Some menu-based applications contain one or more **toolbars**, which are groups of graphical buttons that serve as shortcuts for issuing certain commands. In most cases, you can point at a button on a toolbar to see a pop-up ScreenTip that tells the button's name or purpose, as in Figure 5.9.

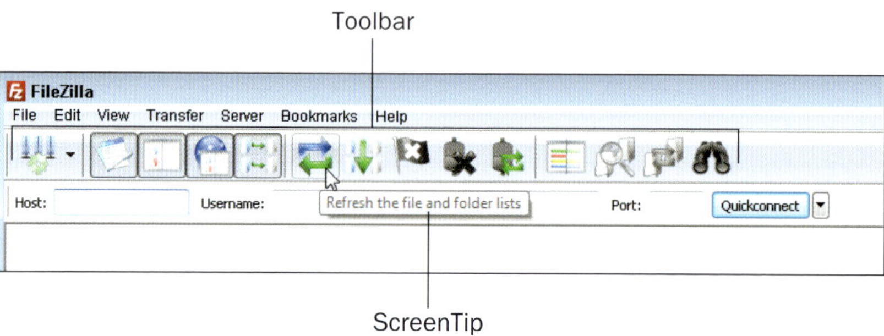

Figure 5.9 Some menu-based applications contain toolbars.

Ribbon The main toolbar in Office applications and some other Windows applications, consisting of multiple tabbed pages of commands.

Ribbon-based applications do not have a menu bar or toolbar. Instead, they have a tabbed **Ribbon**, which is somewhat like a large multi-page toolbar. Each tab represents a different page of tools. Click a tab to access the buttons and other tools on that tab. Figure 5.10 shows an app called WordPad. It has two ordinary tabs, Home and View, containing commands you can select. It also contains a File tab, which is the blue tab to the left of the other two. The File tab opens a File menu, which contains commands for saving, opening, closing, and printing files. Microsoft Office programs use this same type of interface, so you will become very familiar with it in upcoming chapters.

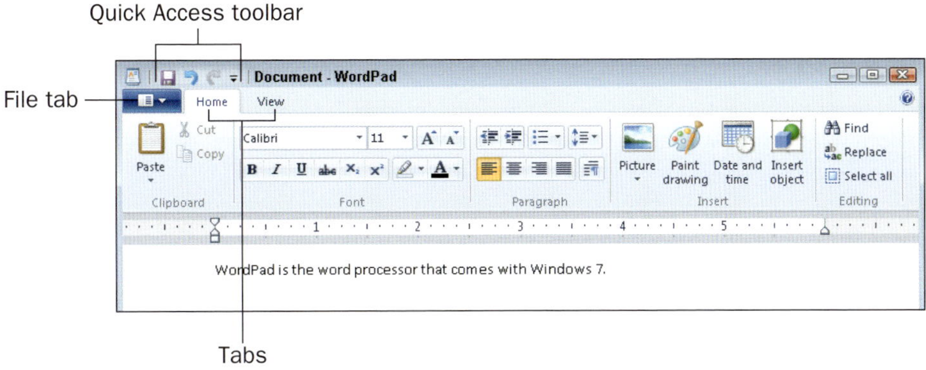

Figure 5.10 A Ribbon-based interface.

In most Ribbon-based applications, there is also a small toolbar above the tabs called the Quick Access toolbar. You can add a copy of any button to this toolbar to keep it handy. To add a button to it, right-click the button on the Ribbon and choose Add to Quick Access Toolbar.

TIP

In most applications, both menu-based and Ribbon-based, you can right-click to open a **shortcut menu** (also called a context menu) and select commands from there. The shortcut menu's content changes depending on what you right-click and what you are doing. For example, if you right-click some text that you've selected, the shortcut menu contains commands to cut and copy it, as shown in Figure 5.11.

shortcut menu A context-sensitive menu that appears when you right-click an object onscreen.

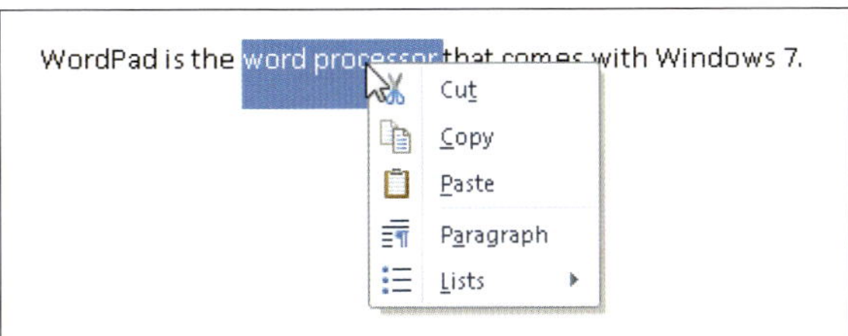

Figure 5.11 Right-clicking in an application opens a context-sensitive shortcut menu.

Exiting an Application

To close an application, close its window by clicking the Close (X) button in the upper-right corner, or open its File menu and choose Exit, or press Alt+F4 when the application window is active.

Quick Review

1. How can you search the Start menu for the application you want to run?
2. In a menu-based interface, what does an ellipsis (. . .) indicate about a command?
3. In a Ribbon-based interface, what happens when you click the File tab (the leftmost tab)?

Put It to Work

Using Internet Explorer

This book devotes an entire chapter (Chapter 10, "Web Basics") to using Internet Explorer (IE), but you will probably need to use the web before you get to that chapter to complete some of your assignments, so here is a very quick overview.

Windows 7 has a shortcut to Internet Explorer pinned to the taskbar, so you can start IE from there if you like, or you can click the Start button and click Internet Explorer at the top of the Start menu.

The page that appears initially depends on what page has been set as the default (referred to as the Home page). If you are accessing IE from your school or workplace, a page may have been assigned for you specific to that organization.

To go directly to a specific address (called a Uniform Resource Locator, or URL), type it in the **address bar**. You can also use the address bar to perform searches. Instead of entering a specific address in the address bar, type some keywords there, or even a whole sentence. Your default search engine will return a list of pages that meet your search criteria.

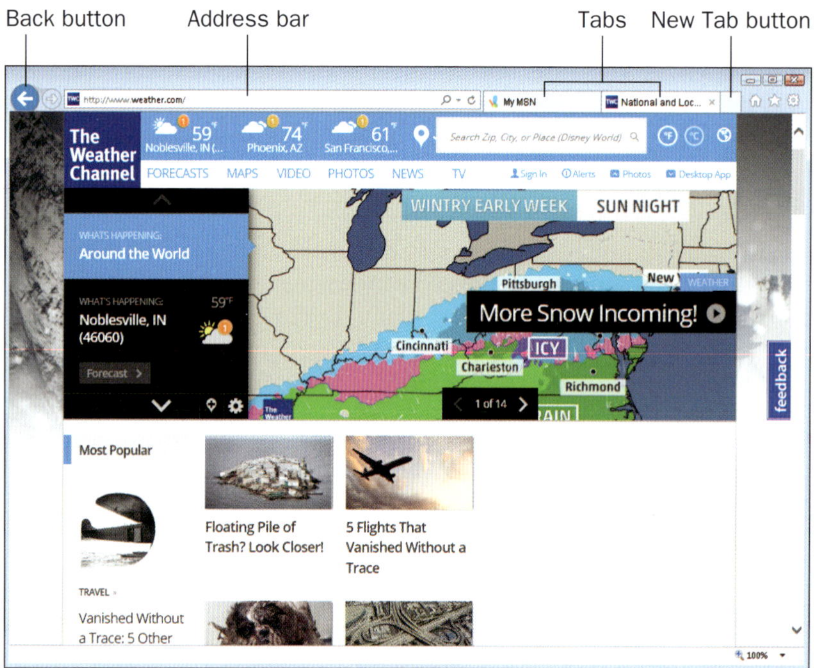

Use the Back button to return to a previous page. To go back several steps at once, hold the mouse button down on the Back button to open a menu of previously viewed pages.

To open a link in a new tab, right-click the link and choose Open in New Tab. You can then switch back and forth freely between the open pages by clicking their tabs. You can also start a new tab without specifying a page to show on it by clicking the New Tab button to the right of the rightmost displayed tab.

address bar The field above the menu bar in Windows Explorer that shows the current path.

Managing Files

As you learned in Chapter 4, a computer's file system consists of physical drives that contain volumes that have letters (with colons) assigned to them, like C: and D:. Each volume can contain folders, and each folder can contain files. Files can also exist at the top level of a volume's organization (its root directory).

In Windows 7, Windows Explorer is the tool for managing files. "Managing" is a pretty broad term, encompassing all the various operations you might perform on a file, including moving, copying, renaming, deleting, and viewing its properties. The rest of this chapter is devoted to teaching you those skills.

Understanding the Windows Explorer Interface

In many ways, Windows Explorer resembles any other window. It has a title bar, a menu bar, and window controls, all of which you learned about earlier in this chapter. It also has some extra features, though, that not every window has, shown in Figure 5.12.

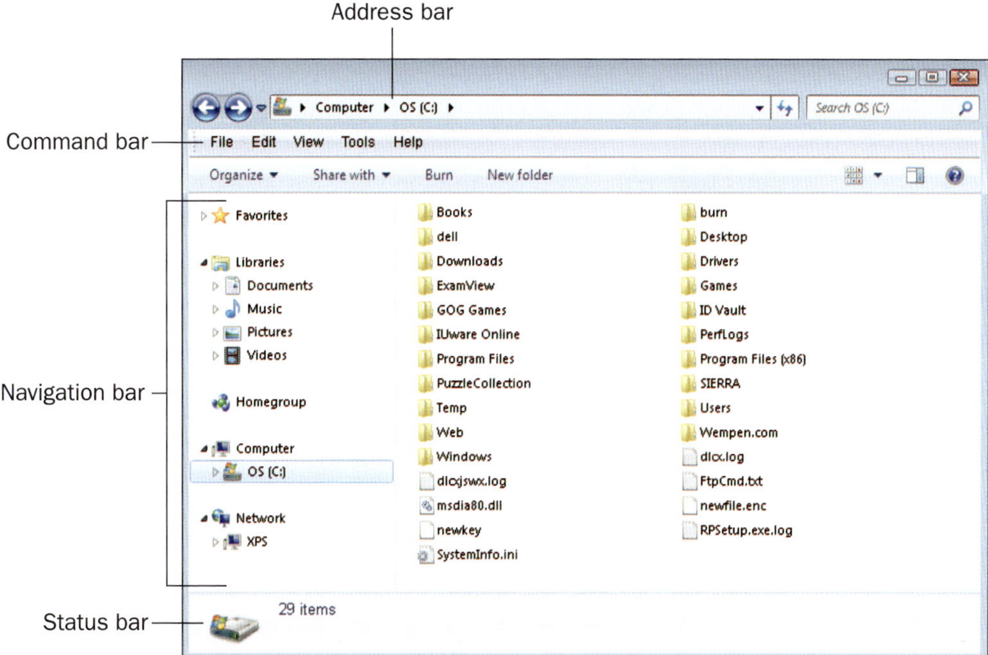

Figure 5.12 Windows Explorer has some tools and features that most application windows don't have.

- **Navigation bar:** The pane on the left side of the Windows Explorer window contains links for displaying various locations, both on your local computer and on any networks you may be connected to.
- **Command bar:** This extra bar below the menu bar contains an Organize button that opens a menu, and also other commands too, which change depending on what location you are viewing. On the far-right end of the command bar are the Change Your View button (which opens a menu of available views), a Preview Pane button (which toggles a preview pane on and off), and a Get Help button (which opens the Help system).

- **Address bar:** The address bar, which appears above the menu bar, shows the current path. You learned about paths in Chapter 4, in the section "How Files Are Organized in Folders."
- **Status bar:** This bar appears at the bottom of the window and reports information about the currently displayed or selected location or objects.
- **Search box:** To find a particular file or folder in Windows Explorer, you can type a part of its name in the Search box and press Enter. The Search feature looks in files, folders, and objects in your Outlook data file (if you have one) and looks both at the filenames and their contents.

Navigating to Different Locations

When you open Windows Explorer, the location shown depends on how you opened it. For example, the Start menu has several links on it that all open different locations (Computer, Documents, Pictures, and Music). In addition, the Windows Explorer shortcut on the taskbar opens Windows Explorer to the Libraries window. (You will learn about libraries later in this chapter.) You can easily navigate to any location in Windows Explorer, so it doesn't matter from which location you start.

One way to navigate to a different location is to click one of the links in the navigation pane (the left pane). The navigation pane contains these expandable sections, as shown in Figure 5.13:

- **Favorites:** Contains shortcuts for a few common locations, such as the desktop and Recent Places. You can also add your own location shortcuts here, for easy access to the locations you use the most.
- **Libraries:** Contains shortcuts for the Documents, Music, Pictures, and Videos libraries for the logged-in user account. (They are separate for each user account.)

homegroup A small group of mutually trusted computers on a peer-to-peer network such as in a home or small office.

- **Homegroup:** If your computer is part of a **homegroup**, a link to it appears. A homegroup is a type of networking used in home and small-business workgroup environments. You learn more about networking in Chapter 8, "Networking and Internet Basics."
- **Computer:** Contains a list of all the local volumes in an expandable folder tree.
- **Network:** Contains shortcuts for browsing a network if you are connected to one.

To expand a section, double-click its name, or point to it (so that a white triangle appears to its left) and then click the triangle to expand it. When a section is expanded in the folder tree, the triangle next to it appears black; click the black triangle to collapse the section again.

You can also navigate by double-clicking a folder in the main pane. For example, you could start out by clicking Computer in the navigation pane to display a list of volumes, and then double-click the C: volume, and then double-clicking a folder in the listing that appears, and keep double-clicking folders until you arrive at the file you are seeking.

If you want to go back one step in your navigation, click the Back button in the upper-left corner. The Forward button next to it takes you one step forward again after you have used Back.

If you want to go up one or more levels in the hierarchy, you can expand the folder tree in the navigation pane and click the folder location to jump to, or you can click the folder name in the address bar. You can also click any of the triangles between the folder names in the address bar to open a menu of locations at that same level and then click any location from the menu to jump to it.

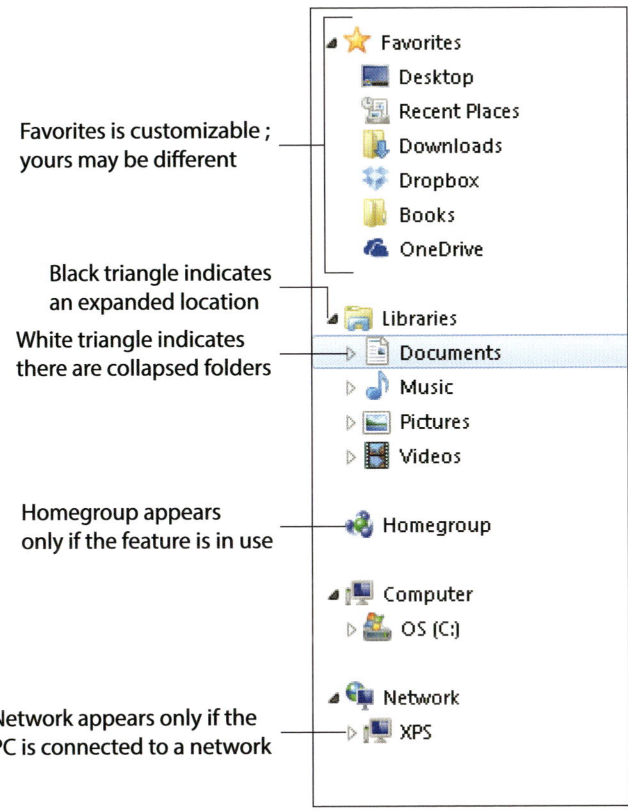

Figure 5.13 Locations in the navigation pane.

Changing the View of a Location

You can view the current location in the main pane in a number of different ways. Click the Change Your View button to toggle through the available views, or click the down arrow to the right of that button to open a menu of views and then click the one you want, or drag the slider up or down to a different view. See Figure 5.14.

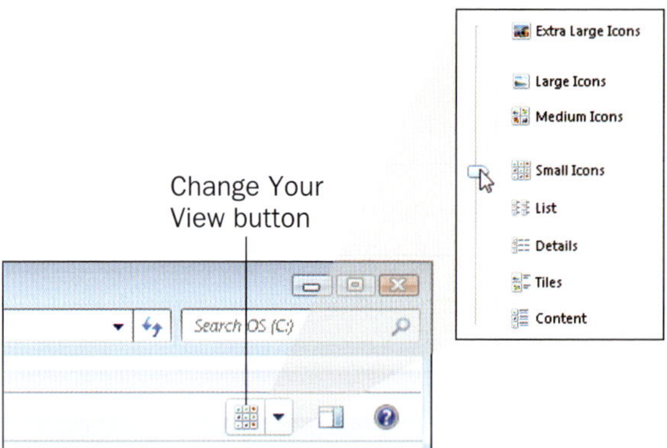

Figure 5.14 Open the Change Your View button's menu to select a view.

TIP The menu has a slider because you aren't limited to just the presets on the menu; you can position the slider halfway between two settings for additional choices. For example, if you position the slider between Large and Extra-Large, you get icons that are halfway between those two options in size.

Understanding Libraries

library A virtual folder that combines the contents of one or more specified folders into a single view.

virtual folder A view that resembles a folder but has no direct equivalent in the computer's file system.

A library is not a folder, although it looks like one. It is a virtual folder created by combining the contents of several different folders in one pane. The Libraries feature enables you to work with the contents of many different locations at once, without worrying about where a particular file is actually stored.

Windows 7 comes with four libraries already set up for you: Documents, Music, Pictures, and Videos. Your libraries are unique to your user account; if someone else logs into the same PC, he will see his own libraries instead of yours. This provides for some privacy when multiple people share a computer. You can also create other libraries if you like.

NOTE Although the default library names reflect the types of files that Windows suggests you store in them, libraries are not limited to certain file types. You can store any files in any libraries.

Each library monitors the contents of one or more locations. For example, the Documents library monitors two folders by default: the logged-in user's personal Documents folder (C:\Users*username*\My Documents) and a Public Documents folder (C:\Users\Public\Public Documents). You can set it to monitor other locations as well.

When you save a file to your Documents library, where is that file actually saved, if the library represents multiple locations? That depends on which folder is set up to be the **save location**. In the Documents library, for example, the default save location is C:\Users*username*\My Documents.

save location The location where files are saved when a user saves them to a library.

Step by Step

Setting a Library to Monitor Additional Folders

Follow these steps to add another folder to a library's Locations list:

1. In Windows Explorer, in the navigation pane, right-click the desired library and choose Properties. The Properties dialog box opens for that library.
2. Click Include a Folder.
3. Navigate to the desired folder, select it, and then click the Include button.
4. Click OK.

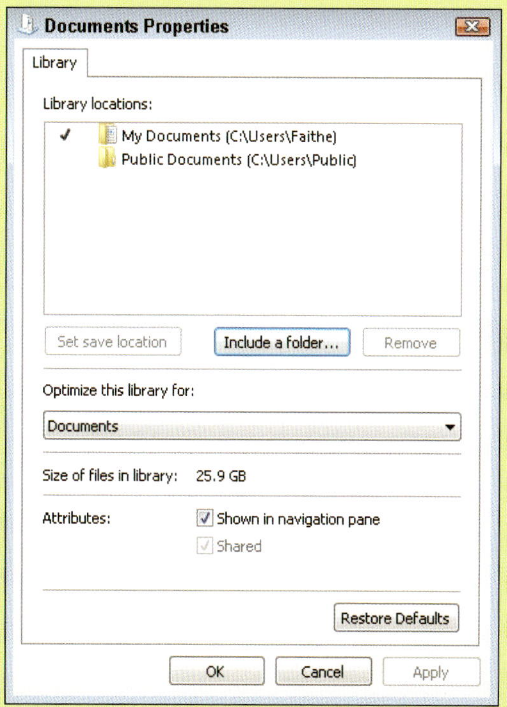

Changing the Save Location for a Library

Follow these steps to change which folder a library stores files in when you save to that library:

1. In Windows Explorer, in the navigation pane, right-click the desired library and choose Properties. The Properties dialog box opens for that library.
2. In the Library Locations list, click the folder you want to use as the save location.
3. Click Set Save Location.
4. Click OK.

Creating a New Library

Follow these steps to create a new library:

1. In Windows Explorer, in the navigation pane, right-click Libraries, and on the menu that appears, point to New and then click Library.
2. In Windows Explorer, in the navigation pane, right-click Libraries, and on the menu that appears, point to New and then click Library. A new library appears in the list, named New Library.
3. Right-click New Library and choose Properties. The Properties dialog box for the new library opens.

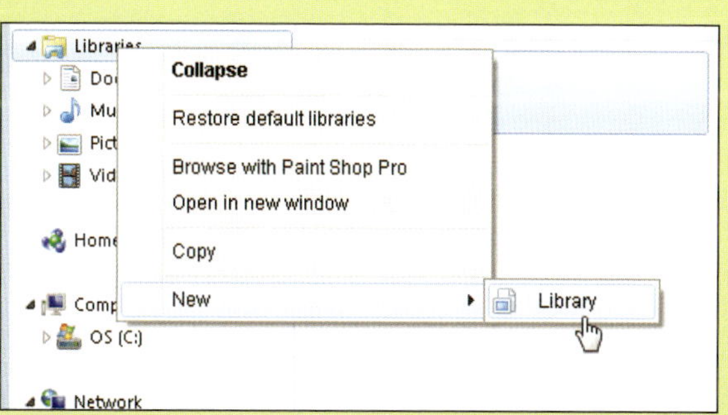

4. Add folders to the new library using the steps from "Setting a Library to Monitor Additional Folders."
5. Choose the save location using the steps from the preceding instructions for "Changing the Save Location for a Library."
6. Open the Optimize This Library For: drop-down list and choose the file type that is most appropriate for this library, or leave it set to General Items if the library will contain a variety of content.
7. (Optional) If you do not want this library to appear in the navigation pane under Libraries, clear the Shown in Navigation Pane check box.
8. Click OK.
9. You may want to change the name from New Library to one of your choosing. Right-click New Library and choose Rename, and type the new name into the text box.

Selecting Files and Folders

Before you can issue a command that affects a file or folder (for example, to move or copy it), you must first select that file or folder. If you are selecting only one file or folder, it's easy—just click it. It becomes highlighted. (The highlighting color varies depending on the color scheme you are using in Windows.) If, however, you want to act upon multiple files or folders at once, you must select them all before issuing the command.

contiguous Physically adjacent to one another.

non-contiguous Not adjacent.

When two or more files or folders are contiguous (adjacent) in the file listing, you can select them by clicking the first one and then holding down the Shift key while you click the last one. All the files between the two are also selected. When the files you want are non-contiguous (not adjacent), hold down the Ctrl key and then click individually on each one. See Figure 5.15. When you are finished making your selections, release the Ctrl key. To cancel a selection, click anywhere away from the selection.

TIP To select all the files and folders in the current location, press Ctrl+A.

Contiguous versus Non-contiguous Selection

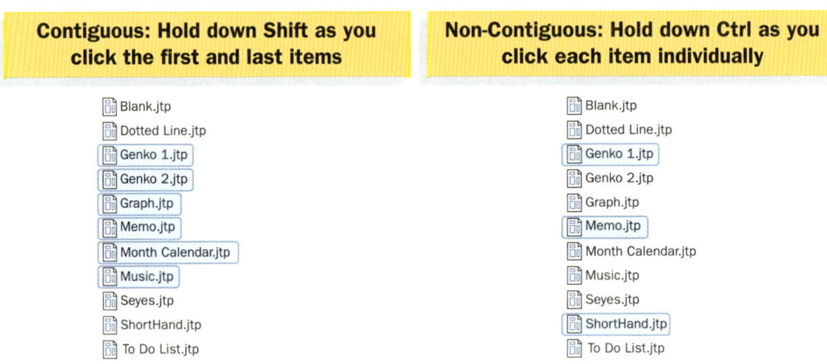

Figure 5.15 Contiguous versus non-contiguous file selection.

Creating New Folders

As you work in Windows, you may want to create new folders to organize your data. For example, you might create a separate folder for each project you work on. You could create them in your My Documents folder, so that they show up in your Documents library, or in another other location on any volume to which you have access.

command bar The bar below the menu bar in Windows Explorer that contains an Organize button that opens a menu, and also other commands, which change depending on what location you are viewing.

To create a new folder, click the New Folder button on the command bar in Windows Explorer. A new folder appears with a generic name, with the name highlighted so you can easily change it. See Figure 5.16. Type the new name and press Enter.

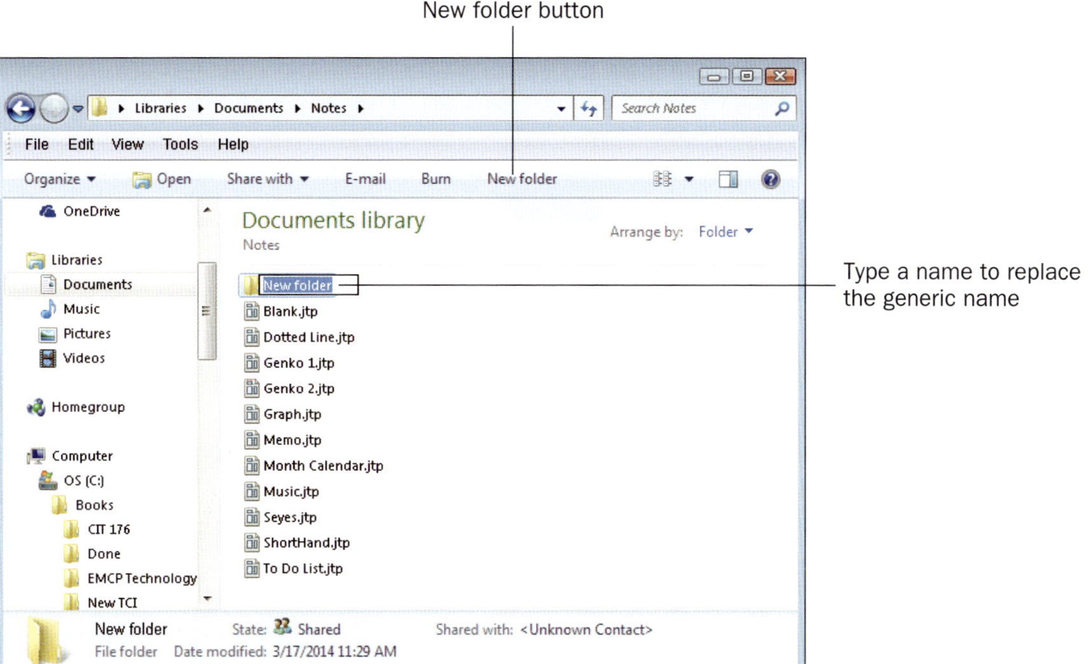

Figure 5.16 Creating a new folder.

An alternative way of creating a folder is to right-click a blank area of the file listing, point to New, and click Folder. Yet another way is to open the File menu, point to New, and click Folder.

TIP

Renaming and Deleting Files and Folders

There are many different ways to rename a file or folder. You can do any of the following:

- Select the file or folder and press F2 to make the name editable. Type the new name and press Enter.
- Click the file or folder to select it and then click it again to move the insertion point into the name. Edit the name and press Enter.
- Right-click the file or folder and click Rename. Edit the name and press Enter.
- Select the file or folder and then open the File menu and choose Rename. Edit the name and press Enter.

To delete a file or folder, select it and then do any of the following:

- Press the Delete key on the keyboard.
- Right-click the file and folder and click Delete.
- Open the File menu and click Delete.

CAUTION You can rename any file or folder. That does not mean, however, that you *should*. Many folders and files are part of installed applications or Windows itself, and if you rename them, they may no longer function as intended. To be safe, rename only files and folders that you have created.

Deleting a file sends it to the Recycle Bin, which is a temporary holding area for deleted content. You can retrieve a deleted file or folder from the Recycle Bin.

Step by Step

Restoring a Deleted Item from the Recycle Bin

Follow these steps to retrieve a file or folder that you have deleted:

1. Double-click the Recycle Bin icon on the desktop to open the Recycle Bin window.
2. Select the deleted item to restore.
3. Click the Restore This Item button on the command bar.

Click Restore this item

Select the file to restore

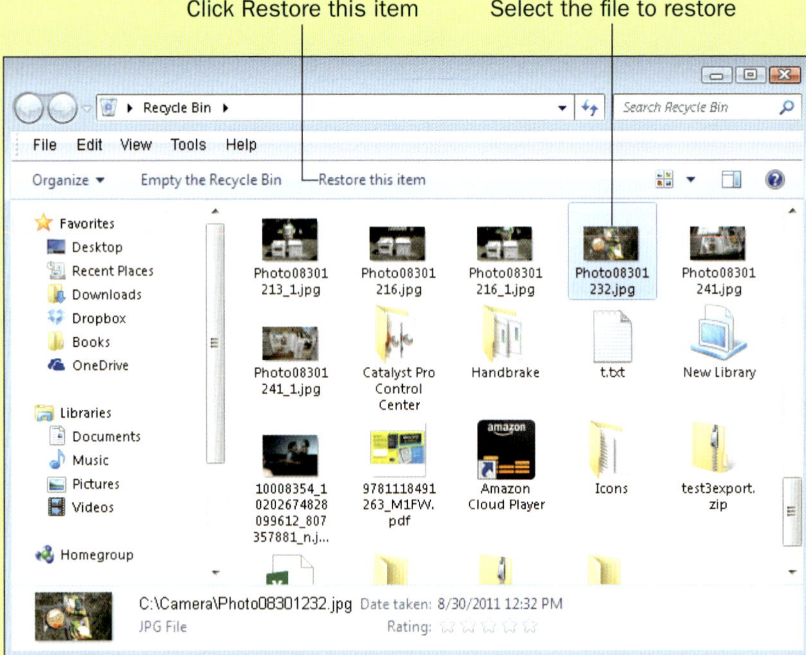

Moving and Copying Files and Folders

You can move and copy files and folders from and to any location. This enables you to transfer your data files from your hard drive to a removable drive such as a USB flash drive, for example.

CAUTION The same warning applies to moving files as to deleting them: If you move a file that an application or Windows relies on, Windows or an application may not function as expected anymore.

There are many ways to move and copy items. You can use the Windows Clipboard, or drag and drop files from one location to another, or you can use the Move to Folder or Copy to Folder command in Windows Explorer.

The Windows Clipboard is a temporary storage area in memory. When you use the Cut operation on an object (or group of objects), it is removed from its current location and placed on the Clipboard. Or, when you use the Copy operation on an object, the object remains in the current location but a copy of it is placed on the Clipboard. Then when you use the Paste operation, it is copied from the Clipboard to a new location. The object remains on the Clipboard until something else is placed there with either another Cut or another Copy operation. In this chapter, you use the Clipboard to copy and move files, but it can also be used to move or copy snippets of data from applications into other applications. For example, you can use it to copy certain cells from an Excel spreadsheet into a Microsoft Word document or into an email message you are composing.

Clipboard A reserved area in memory for temporarily holding content that has been cut or copied from an application or from Windows Explorer.

Table 5.2 lists the various ways of activating the Cut, Copy, and Paste commands in Windows 7.

Table 5.2 Using the Clipboard in Windows 7

Operation	*Keyboard Method*	*Right-Click Method*	*Menu Method*	*Command Bar Method*
Cut	Ctrl+X	Right-click and choose Cut.	Open the Edit menu and click Cut.	Click Organize and click Cut.
Copy	Ctrl+C	Right-click and choose Copy.	Open the Edit menu and click Copy.	Click Organize and click Copy.
Paste	Ctrl+V	Right-click and choose Paste.	Open the Edit menu and click Paste.	Click Organize and click Paste.

Drag-and-drop is a technique for moving items from place to place. You can open the source and the destination locations in separate File Explorer windows onscreen, and then drag items between them. When you drag between two locations on the same volume, the drag operation moves by default; if you want it to copy, hold down the Ctrl key as you drag. When you drag between two locations on different volumes, the drag operation copies by default; if you want it to move, hold down Shift as you drag.

TIP

If you are not sure whether the two locations are on the same volume, you can be sure you get the operation you want (move or copy) by always holding down Shift as you drag for a move and always holding down Ctrl as you drag for a copy. Alternatively, you can right-drag instead of dragging with the left mouse button. When you do so, a menu appears when you release the mouse button, enabling you to select a move or copy operation.

The Move to Folder and Copy to Folder commands (both on the Edit menu) are unique to Windows Explorer, and provide an alternative to the other two methods just described. They enable you to move or copy using a dialog box interface.

If you want to move items to a removable drive such as a USB flash drive, there is yet another method available. Right-click the selected item(s) and select Send To from the context menu that is displayed, and then click the removable drive from the menu that appears.

Step by Step

Moving or Copying (Clipboard Method)

Follow these steps to move or copy selected files or folders using the Windows Clipboard:

1. In Windows Explorer, select the file(s) and/or folder(s) to be moved or copied.
2. Press Ctrl+C to copy, or press Ctrl+X if you want to move. Or use one of the other methods from Table 5.2.
3. Navigate to the location where you want to paste the cut or copied item(s).
4. Press Ctrl+V to paste. Or use one of the other methods from Table 5.2.

Moving or Copying (Drag-and-Drop Method)

Follow these steps to move or copy selected files or folders using drag-and-drop:

1. In Windows Explorer, select the file(s) and/or folder(s) to be moved or copied.
2. Open another Windows Explorer window (for example, click Start and click Computer) and navigate to the destination location.
3. Arrange the two windows so that both are visible at once.
4. Hold down Ctrl to copy, or hold down Shift to move. (See the note earlier in this section about the need to use those keys.)
5. Drag the selected item(s) from the original location to the destination.

Moving or Copying (Dialog Box Method)

Follow these steps to move or copy selected files or folders using the Move to Folder or Copy to Folder command:

1. In Windows Explorer, select the file(s) and/or folder(s) to be moved or copied.
2. Open the Edit menu and click Move to Folder or Copy to Folder. The Move Items or Copy Items dialog box opens.
3. Navigate to the desired destination location. Use the same navigation techniques you use in the folder tree in the navigation pane.
4. Click the Move (or Copy) button.

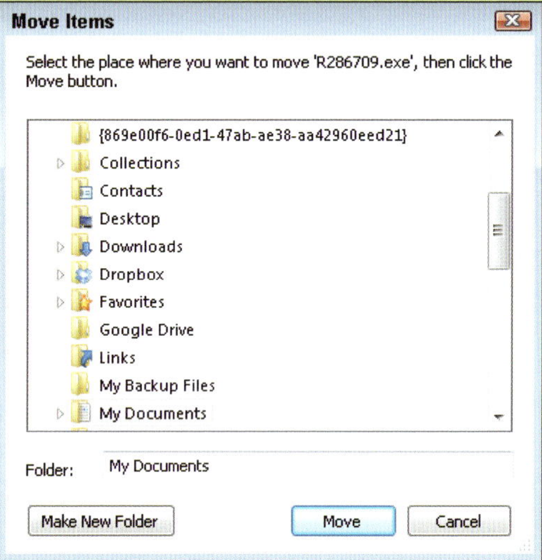

Working with Shortcuts

shortcut A pointer to a file or folder.

A **shortcut** is a link, or pointer, to the original file to which it refers. It allows a file or folder to appear to be in two or more locations at once, while maintaining a single original copy of it. For example, all the program names on the Start menu are shortcuts to the executable files that run those programs, as are the shortcut icons on the left end of the taskbar. You can also place shortcuts directly on the desktop.

Some shortcuts appear with a small arrow in the lower-left corner of the icon, indicating that the icon represents a shortcut rather than the original file, and some of them have the word “shortcut” in their name, as shown in Figure 5.17. However, not all shortcuts follow these conventions, so it is not a sure way to differentiate a shortcut from a regular file. A better method is to right-click the icon and choose Properties. If the dialog box that appears contains a Shortcut tab, the icon is a shortcut icon.

Figure 5.17 An original file (left) and a shortcut that refers to it (right).

To create a shortcut, right-drag the original file to another location. When you release the mouse button, a menu appears. On that menu, click Create Shortcuts Here. This works to create a shortcut almost anywhere. For example, you can drag an item from the Start menu or from a Windows Explorer screen to the desktop or to the taskbar.

You can work with shortcuts just like any other files. You can rename them, for example, in the same way you learned to rename files earlier in this chapter. You can move them and copy them freely. To delete a shortcut, delete it as you would any other file. Deleting a shortcut does not delete the file to which it refers.

Quick Review

1. How do you select multiple non-contiguous files?
2. Name two different ways of copying files from your hard drive to a USB flash drive.
3. What is a shortcut?

Summary

A Tour of Windows 7

The **desktop** is the heart of the Windows 7 interface. The key features of the desktop include the taskbar and icons. On the taskbar is the **Start button, pinned** icons, buttons for running application windows, the **notification area**, and the clock, from left to right.

When you click the Start button, the **Start menu** appears, with links to commonly or recently used programs and locations appear. Click **All Programs** to see the full list of programs you can run, or type the first few letters of what you seek into the **Search box**.

Starting Up and Shutting Down

Windows starts up automatically when you turn on the computer. You are prompted to log in with your user ID and to type a password if your account has one assigned to it. A **cold boot** is one where the computer has been off; a **warm boot** is a restart with the computer already on.

Sleep mode is a power-saving mode that keeps RAM powered but turns off everything else. **Hibernate mode** saves the contents of RAM to the hard drive and then shuts down all power.

When a user is finished with the computer, he or she can **log off**, which shuts down any running programs, closes open data files, and unloads that user's personal settings. To allow someone else to log in without the first user logging out, use **Switch User**. To return to a login screen without closing out of programs and applications, use the **Lock** command.

Running Applications

To start an application, choose it from the Start menu. If you don't see it on the top level menu, click All Programs to find it, or type its name in the Search box.

A **window** is a movable rectangular block in which content appears, such as an application or file listing. Each window has a title bar at the top of it. In the right corner of the title bar are window control buttons: **Minimize**, **Maximize** (or Restore), and **Close**. To resize a window, drag one of its borders. To move a window, drag its title bar.

To navigate within an application, use its **menu bar**. Some commands have **keyboard shortcuts** for speeding up your work. Some commands open **dialog boxes** for providing more information. Programs with a menu bar sometimes have a toolbar, which is a row of clickable icons. A Ribbon is a multi-page, more sophisticated version of a toolbar.

To exit an application, click the window's Close button, or open the File menu and choose Exit, or press Alt+F4.

Managing Files

The parts of a Windows Explorer window include the **navigation bar**, **command bar**, **address bar**, **status bar**, and **Search box**.

You can navigate to different locations using the shortcuts in the navigation pane in the **Favorites** list, or select one of the libraries from the **Libraries** list. If you are connected to a network, you can browse network locations from the **Homegroup** or **Network** lists. Use the **Computer** list to browse local volumes. To change the view of a location, click the Change Your View button, or click the down arrow to the right of that button to open a menu of views and then click the one you want.

Libraries are **virtual folders** that combine the contents of several locations into one window. The default libraries are Documents, Pictures, Music, and Videos for each user. You can create your own libraries too, and set up libraries to monitor additional folders. Each library has a **Save Location**, which is the folder that files are placed in when saved to the library.

To select **contiguous** files and folders, hold down Shift as you click the first and last ones. To select **non-contiguous** files and folders, hold down Ctrl as you click each one individually. To create a new folder, click the New Folder button on the command bar.

To rename a file or folder, select it, press F2, type the new name, and press Enter. To delete a file or folder, select it and press the Delete key. Deleted files go to the Recycle Bin; you can retrieve them from there.

You can move and copy files using the Clipboard, drag-and-drop, or use the Move to Folder or Copy to Folder command.

A **shortcut** is a pointer to a file or folder. To create a shortcut, right-drag an object to a new location and on the shortcut menu that appears when you release the mouse button, choose Create Shortcuts Here.

Key Terms

address bar
All Programs
Clipboard
cold boot
command bar
contiguous
desktop
dialog box
Hibernate mode
homegroup
icon
keyboard shortcut
library
lock
log off
maximize
menu bar
minimize
non-contiguous
notification area
pinned
restore
Ribbon
save location
Search box
shortcut
shortcut menu
Sleep mode
Start button
Start menu
Switch User
taskbar
title bar
toolbar
virtual folder
warm boot
window

Test Yourself

Fact Check

1. What is the area immediately to the left of the clock in the taskbar?

   a. Start box

   b. notification area

   c. pin area

   d. application area

2. If a program does not appear on the top level of the Start menu, click _______ to see a list of other programs.

   a. Accessories

   b. System Tools

   c. All Programs

   d. More Programs

3. Which link would you choose from the Start menu to see a list of local volumes?

   a. Control Panel

   b. System Tray

   c. Computer

   d. All Programs

4. What mode turns off all components except RAM?

   a. Log off

   b. Hibernate

   c. Lock

   d. Sleep

5. What do you drag to move a window?

   a. border

   b. title bar

   c. Ribbon

   d. menu bar

6. To exit an application, open its File menu and choose

   a. Close

   b. Exit

   c. Quit

   d. End

7. A _________ is a virtual folder that combines the contents of several locations.

   a. library

   b. panel

   c. sync pane

   d. compressed folder

8. To select multiple non-contiguous files, hold down the ______ key.

   a. Shift

   b. Alt

   c. Ctrl

   d. Home

9. The _________is a temporary storage area that holds content that you copy to it with the Cut or Copy command.

   a. Desktop
   b. Control Panel
   c. Clipboard
   d. Recycle Bin

10. To create a shortcut on the desktop, _______ the file to the desktop.

   a. Ctrl+drag
   b. Shift+drag
   c. right-drag
   d. Alt+drag

Matching

Match the feature to its function.

a. hibernate
b. lock
c. log off
d. restart
e. shut down
f. sleep
g. switch users

1. ________Shuts off all power except to memory.
2. ________Copies the content of memory to the hard drive and then powers off all components.
3. ________Exits Windows and turns the computer's power off.
4. ________Closes all open applications and files and unloads user-based settings.
5. ________Exits Windows and then restarts Windows.
6. ________Returns to a login screen without closing open applications, for security. The same user logs in to resume.
7. ________Returns to a login screen without closing open applications, so a different user may temporarily log in also.

Sum It Up

1. Describe the major features of the Start menu and desktop.
2. Explain the alternatives available to completely shutting down your computer at the end of your work session.
3. Explain how to start and exit an application.
4. Describe how to move, resize, minimize, maximize, and close a window.
5. Describe the controls used in dialog boxes.
6. Explain how to move, copy, rename, and delete files and folders.
7. Demonstrate how to navigate between storage locations using Windows Explorer.
8. Explain the difference between a folder and a library.

Explore More

Sorting File Listings

Windows Explorer enables you to sort the file listing by name, date, or other characteristics. To do this, right-click a blank area of the file list, point to Sort By, and click the characteristic by which you want to sort. If you display the file list in Details view, you can also click one of the column headings to sort by that heading (for example, Type or Size). Try this out for yourself. Display the contents of the root directory of the C: volume in Details view, and sort the listing by Type. Sorting a file listing can make the files you want to work with contiguous, so you can use the Shift key method of selecting them that you learned about earlier in this chapter.

Looking at File Properties

Each file has properties that you can view by right-clicking it and choosing Properties from the menu. In a file's Properties box, you will find a General tab that has file attributes on it and a Security tab that enables you to configure its security settings. Depending on the file type, there may also be other tabs, such as Details and Previous Versions (for some types of data files). If it's an application, there may be a Compatibility tab, on which you can configure the program to run with settings compatible for an earlier version of Windows. If it's a shortcut, a Shortcut tab offers settings for changing the shortcut's properties. Working on your own, open C:\Program Files in Windows Explorer and examine the properties of at least one folder and at least three files, and compare the tabs and settings that are available to view and adjust.

Compatibility Mode

Some older applications do not run well under Windows 7, but there's a work-around. You can set an application to run in Compatibility mode with settings that simulate an earlier Windows version of your choice. To set this up, follow these steps:

1. Right-click the executable file for the program, or a shortcut that you use to run the program (such as its shortcut on the Start menu) and choose Properties.
2. On the Compatibility tab, tick the check box next to the Run This Program in Compatibility Mode.

3. Open the drop-down list of versions and choose an earlier Windows version. If you know which version the program was designed for, choose that. Otherwise, choose Windows XP (Service Pack 3). If that one doesn't work, you can come back later and try the next-latest version, and so on, until you find the one that works.
4. Click OK. Then try running the program again to see if the new settings help.

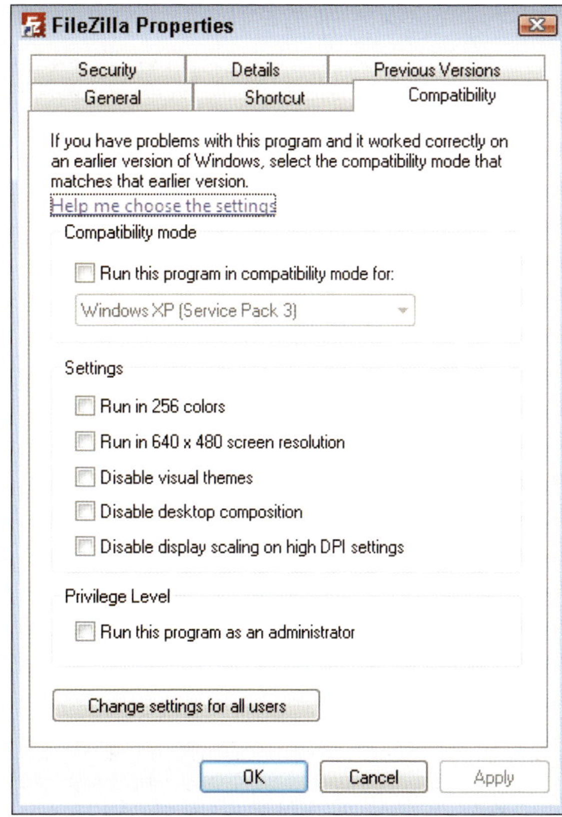

Think It Over

Desktop Shortcuts

Some people like to have shortcuts for all the applications they use on the desktop, so they can access them easily without having to use the Start menu. Their desktops become covered with dozens of icons over time. Other people prefer to keep the desktop clean, showing only the Recycle Bin, and they pin shortcuts only to the taskbar and Start screen. What is your preference, and why? Are there any drawbacks to pinning lots of icons to the desktop? To the taskbar? To the Start screen?

Security versus Convenience

How important is your privacy on your computer? Is it worth it to you in terms of privacy to have a separate user account from everyone else who uses your computer? Do you feel more comfortable stepping away from the computer while you are logged in if you use the Lock feature to password-protect it from others? Or would you rather have the computer be completely open to everyone in your family, with no private information?

New Applications

Suppose you bought a new application and it doesn't use either a Ribbon or a menu system, at least not like the ones you have encountered before. How would you figure out how to use the program? What are some of the resources that might be available to you?

Chapter 6

Understanding Application Software

Learning objectives

- Identify the various types of application software
- Understand the basics of business productivity applications
- Explore graphics and photo-editing programs
- Understand system requirements and the uninstall process

As you learned in Chapter 1, "Computer Basics," *software* is a broad term for any program that runs on a computer. This can include the operating system and all its helper files, utilities that keep the computer healthy and running well, and applications. Another name for software is a program.

Application software is software that enables you to perform a useful task on your computer. Some programs are classified as productivity software because they allow you to get things done. Other application software is designed to entertain you or help you learn something.

Business Productivity Software

Businesspeople typically use a collection of applications known as an office suite to perform the most common tasks involved in their jobs, such as writing reports and correspondence, calculating numbers, giving presentations, and maintaining databases of information.

application software Software that helps a human perform a useful task for work or play.

word processor A program used to create or view text-based documents.

Understanding Word Processing and Desktop Publishing

The most popular type of productivity software is the word processor. This type of program is used to create text-based documents. A word processor contains many features designed to help improve text, such as spell-checking, grammar correction, and formatting tools. In fact, Microsoft Word is the world's most widely used word processor and one of the most advanced examples of this type of program.

In addition to creating and editing your own work, you can also open word-processing documents that other people have created. Word can open and save documents in a variety of formats, enabling you to exchange documents with people who use other word-processing applications. You will learn how to save and open files in Word and other Office applications in Chapter 7, "Understanding Microsoft Office 2010."

A word-processing program provides a wide variety of text formatting options. For example, you can make the text larger, change its color, or use different fonts. You can structure the page to emphasize important elements by using a larger type size. You can specify how the text is arranged, so that all the words start at the far left or far right of the page in a neat vertical arrangement. Figure 6.1 shows a document in Microsoft Word that includes several types of formatting, including shading, different fonts, and multiple columns.

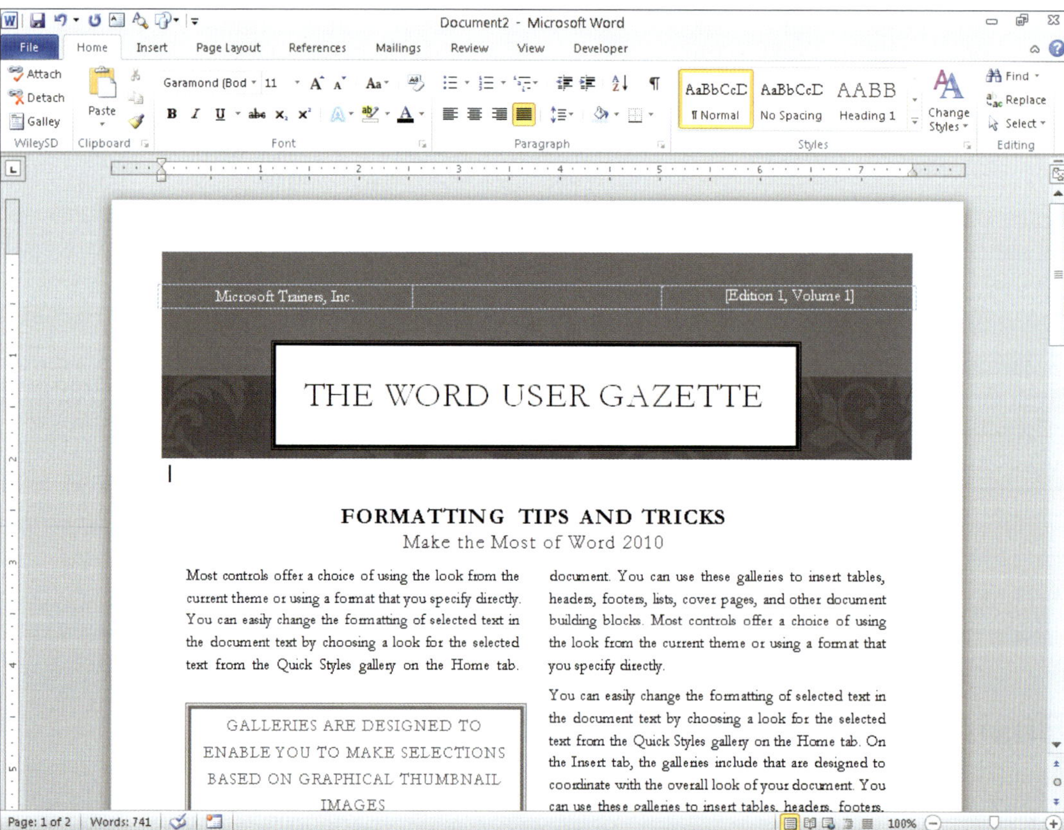

Figure 6.1 Word-processing software provides strong formatting tools that are ideal for producing newsletters and reports.

For even more control over page layout, you can use a **desktop publishing** program, sometimes called page layout software. Some popular desktop publishing programs include Microsoft Publisher for casual home users and QuarkXPress and Adobe InDesign for professionals.

desktop publishing software Software that helps create page layouts with text and graphics.

Desktop publishing software enables users to precisely position the text and other elements on a page or across a double-page spread (facing pages) to create an attractive design. The text can be creatively wrapped around embedded images, and graphics can be made transparent, or "ghosted," behind text so the words aren't obscured.

The main difference operationally between word processing and desktop publishing is that a word-processing program typically enables you to type directly on the page onscreen, and it flows the text automatically based on the margins, indents, and number of columns you specify. Desktop publishing, on the other hand, uses movable and resizable frames for everything, including text. This gives you more control over the precise positioning of each element, as shown in Figure 6.2.

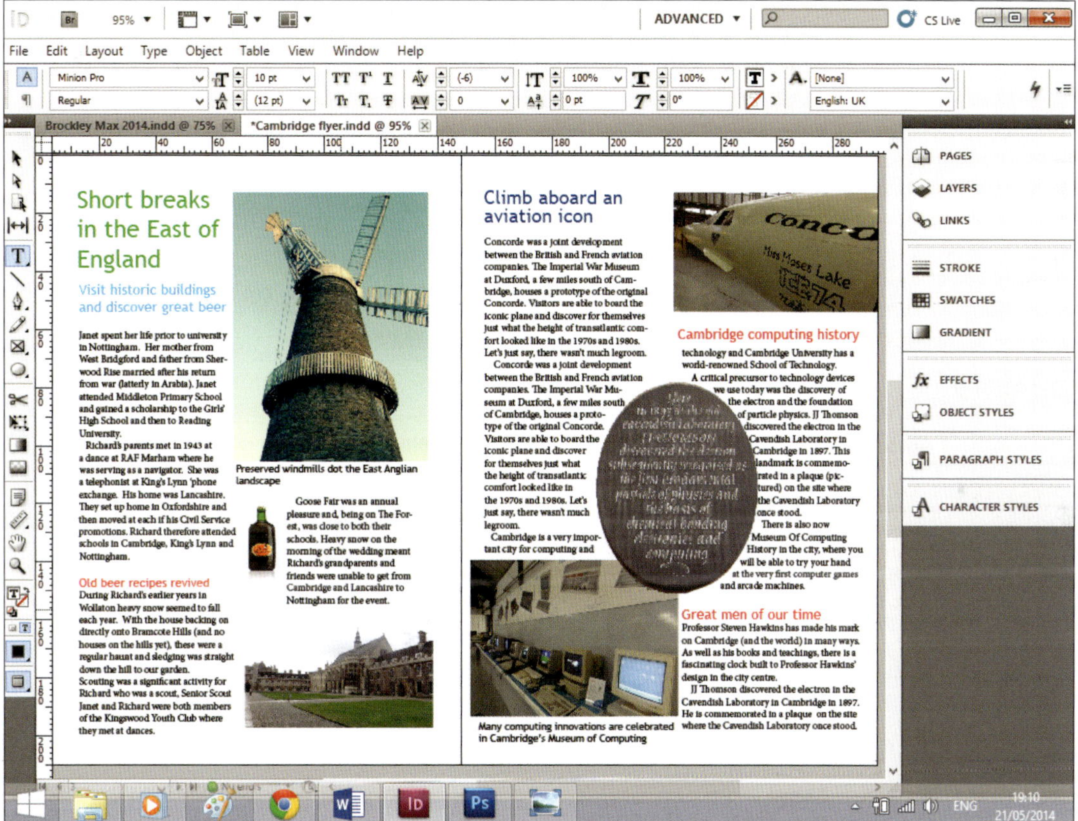

Figure 6.2 Page layout software offers more sophisticated formatting and design tools than word processing software.

Careers in IT

Administrative Assistant

An administrative assistant provides office and document support to a manager or executive. He or she is expected to know how to use a word processor to create and format documents. The templates supplied with word-processing software make the formatting and spell-checking processes much easier, but an administrative assistant should be familiar with how they work and be capable of producing neatly formatted reports with charts and graphs. An administrative assistant's duties may also include creating printed materials in other applications, such as Excel and PowerPoint, and combining content from multiple applications into reports and presentations.

All administrative support roles require a solid understanding of office productivity programs and strong organizational skills. A diploma in administration, information technology, or business management is also expected. A business administration or IT degree plus vocational courses will help progress your career into office management.

Understanding Spreadsheets

spreadsheet A program that presents rows and columns of figures and other items against which time and other variables can be plotted.

A **spreadsheet** program is used to analyze and present numeric data. For example, you might use a spreadsheet to create a budget, summarize sales data, or compare mortgages. Figure 6.3 shows a sales summary report with a chart created in Microsoft Excel, the most popular spreadsheet program available today.

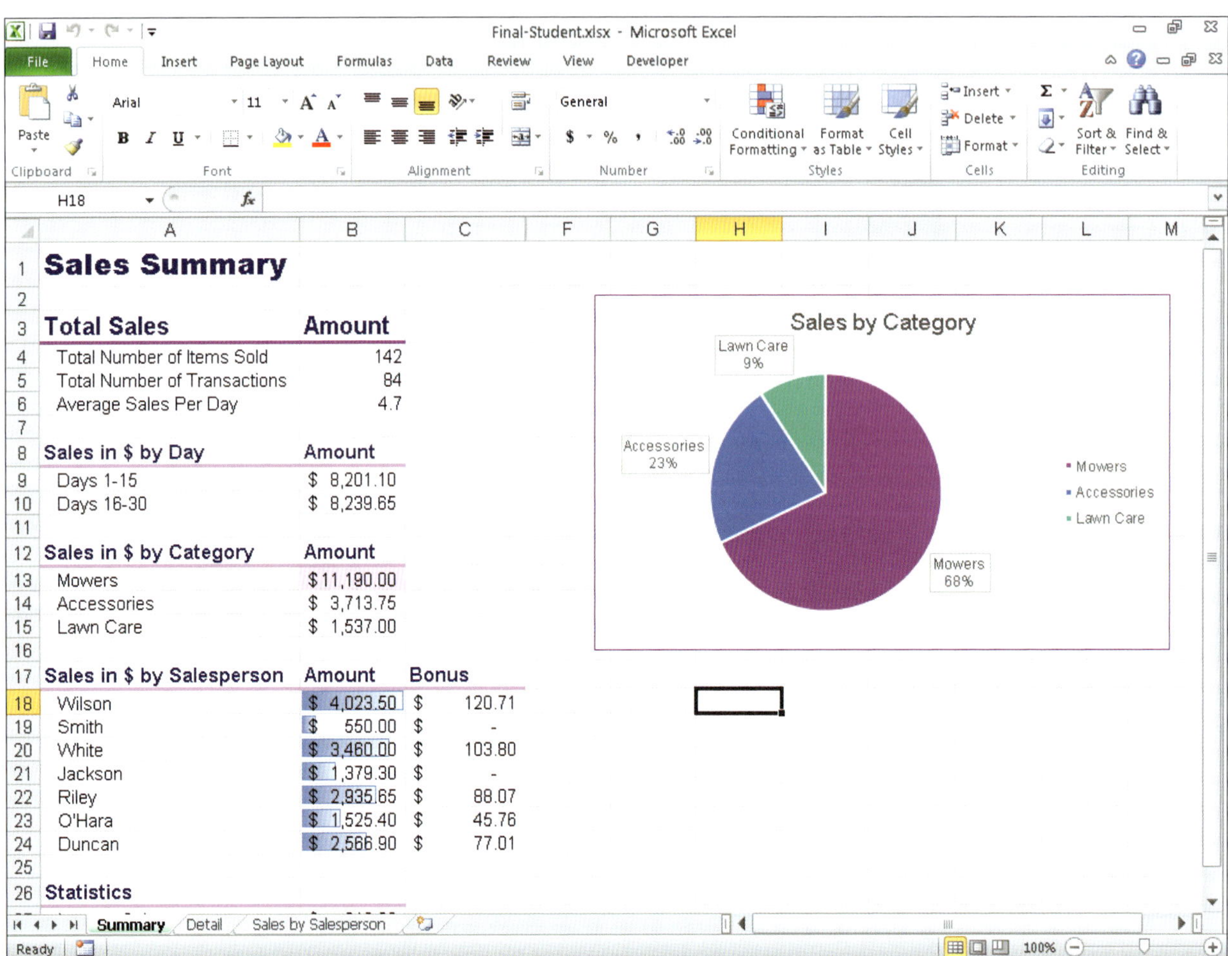

Figure 6.3 Use spreadsheets to record everyday expenses and make simple calculations.

Spreadsheet data is entered into **cells** in rows and columns. You can enter text, numbers, or a combination of the two. If you enter numbers, you can apply number formatting that makes the numbers appear as currency, percentages, or any of several other number types.

cell The intersection of a row and a column in a worksheet.

Spreadsheet software does more than just record lists of text and data, however. It also supports **formulas** that calculate and manipulate the numeric data. For example, in Figure 6.4, each of the expense figures in column B is summed in the formula in cell B9: =SUM(B3:B7).

formula A mathematical calculation to be performed in an Excel cell. It may refer to other cells for its values.

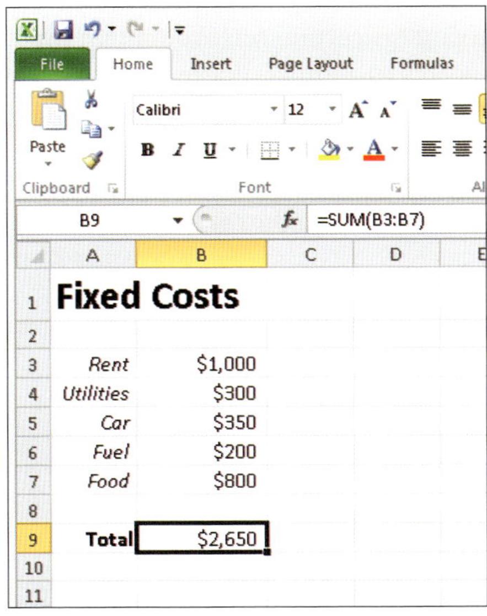

Figure 6.4 A formula is used in cell B9 to sum the values in cells B3 through B7.

Spreadsheets can produce a range of charts and graphs based on the data they contain, like the one shown in Figure 6.3. These charts can then be exported and used in a report such as a word processing document or a presentation.

Careers in IT

Data Analyst

Accountants, tax advisors, business owners, and managers all depend on spreadsheets for their work. However, as with word-processing skills, it's likely you'll need to use spreadsheets in almost any type of job. The ability to "crunch numbers" comes in useful for analysis, planning, and forecasting, too.

Spreadsheets are incredibly useful when working with a large amount of data. A data analyst must have the ability to categorize and process large volumes of information and draw meaningful conclusions from them. Databases and spreadsheets are both used to process and draw out information.

Data analysts may have a degree in statistics, mathematics, or business, but they also need an in-depth knowledge of spreadsheets in order to work with such large amounts of information and variables.

Understanding Databases

A **database** is a structured collection of data, such as the inventory of a store or a collection of personnel files. A database contains one or more **tables**, each of which contains records. For example, you might have a table called Employees that contains a record for each employee.

database A collection of data stored in a structured format, with the same facts stored about each instance. A database stores data in a way that enables you to search and locate it quickly.

table A collection of records, arranged in a row-and-column format.

record A row in a table, storing information about a specific person, place, or thing.

field A column in a table, storing one particular kind of information, such as Phone or Name.

database management system (DBMS) An application that helps users create and manage databases.

A **record** is information about one instance of the data being stored, such as one employee, one inventory item, or one sales transaction. Each record contains one or more individual pieces of information, called a **field**. For example, in an Employees table, one of the fields might be Badge Number, and another might be Hire Date. The software used to create and control a database is a **database management system (DBMS)**. For small, simple databases, many people use Microsoft Access. For large-scale databases, a company might use an enterprise-level database system like Oracle.

data mining Extracting information from a database to zero in on certain facts or summarize a large amount of data.

A database program makes calculations and extrapolates information using combinations of data and varying instruction sets. You might use it to see how one item or person compares to another. For example, your school uses a database to keep track of how well you're doing in comparison to your classmates across different subjects. Extracting information from a database is known as **data mining**. Web searches make use of data mining to provide search results based on the search query the user enters.

relational database A spreadsheetlike database that shows how items in a database are connected or have attributes in common.

The most common type of database is called a **relational database**. In a relational database, there are multiple tables that have relationships to one another. For example, in a sales database, there might be a Customers table, an Orders table, and an Order Details table. Because an individual customer can have multiple orders, and an individual order can contain multiple items, the details about the customer are stored separately from the details about the order, and the order line items are stored separately from both. Figure 6.5 shows these tables and their relationships in Microsoft Access. Using related tables allows a salesperson to pull up the customer's shipping and payment information whenever he or she starts a new order, rather than having to reenter it each time. Microsoft Access creates relational databases.

node (database) The point of intersection in a diagram or in a database; where several items share a node, the node itself becomes important.

hierarchical database A way of organizing data from a single starting point or premise in a treelike parent and child relationship format. All records are shown in terms of how they relate to the originating point at the top of the tree.

A hierarchical type of database has a tree structure in which elements consist of **nodes**. The database starts from a single point, known as the parent node. The database branches out and has multiple levels. Items on a branch are known as child nodes. There may be one or several child nodes. A **hierarchical database** works by narrowing down a search starting with the entire set of records and successively excluding any that the search doesn't apply to. Family historians would use a hierarchical view to see all the descendants of a single ancestor.

Put It to Work

How an Online Store Uses Databases

When you buy something online, the online store uses an application program to manage the purchase process that will connect to the database to check stock levels. When you arrive at the site and log in, the application will look for you in the customer database and check that your password and email address match the details for your account. When you add an item to your shopping cart, a database query is run to check the stock levels and, if applicable, the application places the requested item in your cart and instructs the database stock level to decrease by one. When you click Checkout to go the payment page, the site will ask you to confirm or revise your payment details and then issue a request to your bank for the funds. Assuming the request is accepted, the online shopping application will confirm your purchase and send you an electronic receipt before issuing an instruction to the warehouse to send out your goods.

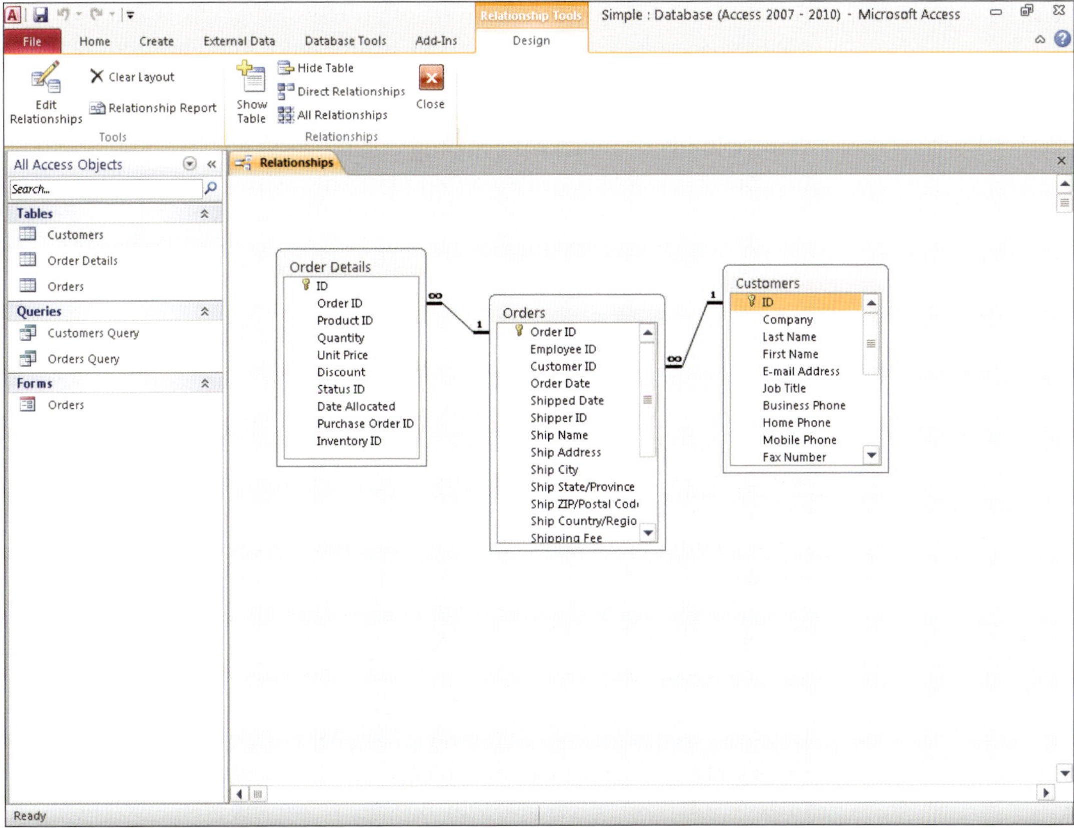

Figure 6.5 A relational database contains multiple tables with relationships between them.

Personal Information Management Software

It can be a challenge to keep track of where you need to be, what you need to do, and whom you need to contact. Personal information management (PIM) software helps people stay organized by providing a calendar, an address book, and a to-do list. Some PIM software also functions as an email program, and allows you to send, receive, store, and organize email messages.

Microsoft Outlook is a very popular email application that includes a full set of PIM capabilities. You can also get some of the individual PIM functions in other applications. For example, you can buy separate calendar, task list, and email applications, or use free versions online, such as Google Calendar and Gmail.

Software Suites

Some software manufacturers, such as Microsoft, offer multiple related products that are designed to work well together. They are sometimes sold together as a **suite**, which is a collection of related applications. The Microsoft Office suite is a very popular suite of business applications; you will learn more about it in Chapter 7. It includes Word, Excel, PowerPoint, and Outlook, plus some extra applications in some versions, such as Access and Publisher. All the applications in the Office suite have similar user interfaces, and can exchange content freely. You can buy each application separately, but it is much less expensive to buy the suite.

suite A group of applications by the same manufacturer purchased as a group.

Adobe also makes a well-known set of professional graphics and publishing tools, Creative Suite. In Creative Suite, the Photoshop, Dreamweaver, Illustrator, InDesign, and Director programs provide photo-editing, web design, vector graphics, desktop publishing, and video-editing capabilities. Each program in Creative Suite supports the proprietary file formats of the other programs, so a Photoshop file can be imported into Illustrator, where further elements can be added before the file is again opened for final edits to be completed in Photoshop.

Accounting and Personal Finance Software

accounting software Software that enables a small business to manage and track its financial health and transactions.

Whether you are doing the accounting for a small business or just keeping track of your own personal bank account, there is software available that can help you. **Accounting software** simplifies the entire process of managing a business's finances, including creating invoices and purchase orders, processing payments, and running reports. QuickBooks is one of the most popular accounting applications for small businesses; larger businesses may use their own proprietary accounting software. An online version is also available on a pay-as-you-go monthly fee plan. Other accounting programs include FreshBooks and Outright, both of which are web based.

personal finance software Software that enables individuals to track and manage their bank accounts and investments.

If you are looking to track your own personal finances, you might want to consider a program such as Quicken, the most popular **personal finance software**. It can not only manage your bank accounts, but also your investments and loans. Microsoft also has a free online tool called Mint that can perform many of the same functions, and your bank may have its own web-based interface that you can use for free.

tax software Software that enables individuals and small businesses to calculate the taxes they owe and file the needed forms with the government.

If you live in a country where you have to file a yearly income tax statement, you may want to get help from **tax software**. TurboTax and H&R Block are two popular tax applications, each of which comes in various versions for different levels of tax filing complexity. This software can help you print the forms you need to mail, or in some cases to file the required forms electronically for you online.

Quick Review

1. What kind of software is useful for creating budgets and charts?
2. Explain how the following items are related: database field, database record, and database table.
3. What is a suite?

Graphics Software

graphics software Software that enables you to create and manipulate visual images.

Graphics software includes any application that enables you to create and manipulate visual images. This broad category includes drawing programs, photo manipulation programs, presentation creation programs, and video capture and editing software. The products available include both professional-quality software used in entertainment and advertising, and consumer-quality software that the average computer hobbyist might experiment with.

Desktop publishing software, which you learned about earlier in this chapter, can straddle the line between text and graphics software because it enables you to combine text and graphics to produce page layouts.

NOTE

Vector Image Drawing Programs

There are two main categories of graphic images: vector and raster. Although they may look similar, they are structured quite differently, and require entirely different types of software to create them.

A **vector-based illustration** is created with math formulas, like in geometry class. A rectangle, an oval, a straight line—they all have a math formula that plots them on a two-dimensional grid. A three-dimensional vector graphic, such as a 3D representation of a cube or sphere, plots the image in a three-dimensional grid space. (The software does all the math, so you don't have to worry about that part—you just draw by dragging your mouse to create the lines and shapes you want.) Professional-quality programs such as Adobe Illustrator create very sophisticated vector graphics for commercial uses, such as technical drawings and architectural plans. At a much simpler level, Microsoft Office products like PowerPoint, Word, and Excel all come with basic vector drawing tools you can use in their data files. Vector graphics also figure prominently into many video games.

vector-based illustration A drawing that is constructed of mathematically created lines.

Vector images have many advantages. They do not take up much disk space to store because the information needed to display them is very simple and compact. They can also be resized to any size without any loss of quality, because the math formulas behind them are simply recalculated and the shape redrawn. The main disadvantage of a vector graphic is that even the best quality drawings don't look completely real. Most people would never mistake a character from a game like "Second Life" or "The Sims" for a video of a real person, for example.

Step by Step

Creating Vector Graphics

Follow these steps using Microsoft PowerPoint to explore the vector graphic tools in Microsoft Office 2010:

1. Open PowerPoint 2010. A new presentation opens.
2. On the Home tab, click the Layout button, and click Blank.
3. On the Insert tab, click the Shapes button, and then click one of the shapes in the Basic Shapes section of the menu.

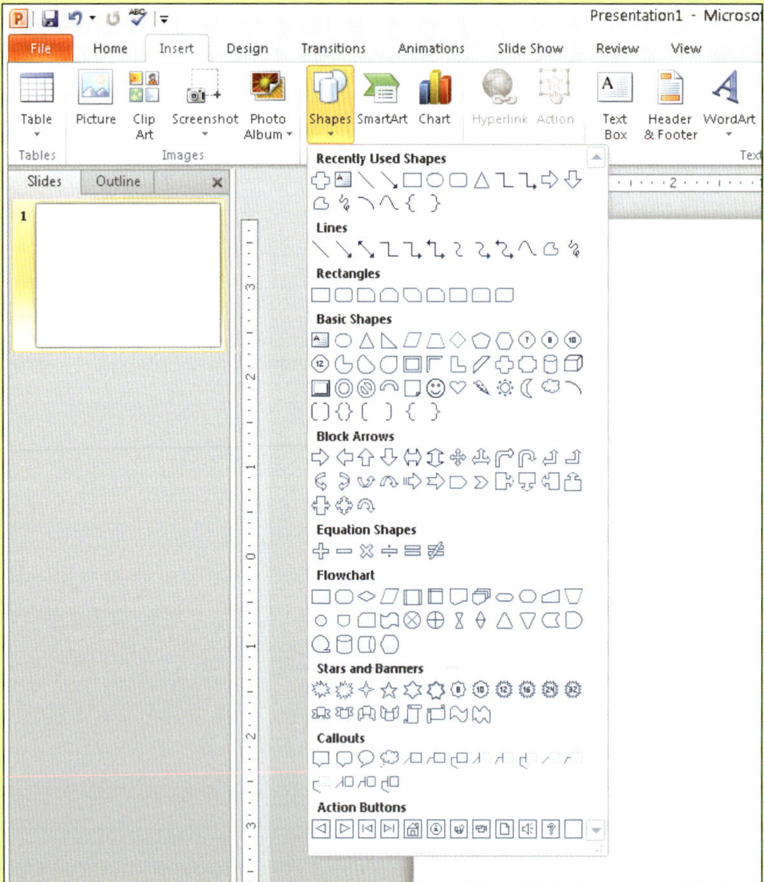

4. Drag to draw the shape on the blank slide.
5. Drag one of the corners of the image's frame to resize the image.

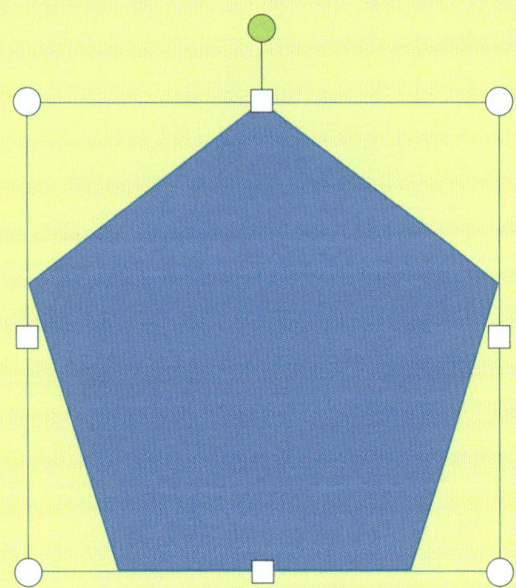

6. Drag the center of the image to move the image.
7. Draw at least three other shapes and at least one straight line (from the Lines section of the Shapes menu).
8. Select one of the shapes, and then on the Drawing Tools Format tab, click Shape Fill. On the palette of colors that appears, click a different color.

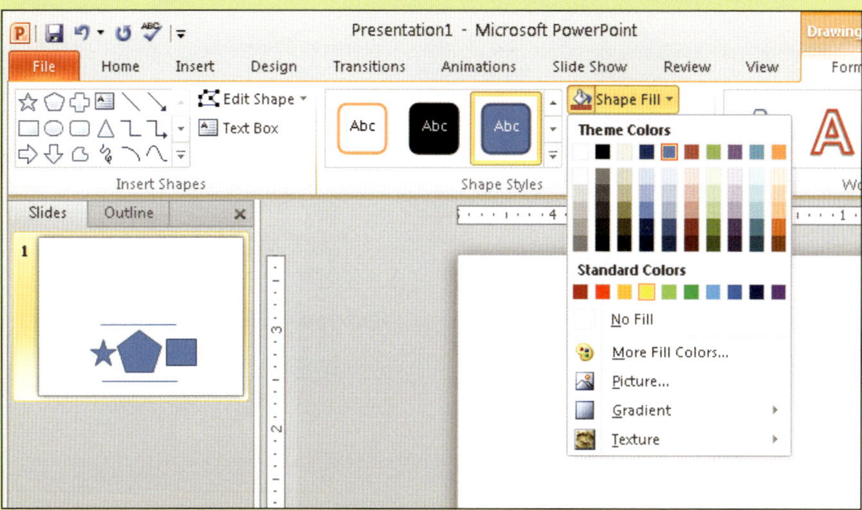

9. Close PowerPoint without saving your changes.

Raster (Photo) Editing Programs

A raster graphic, also called a bitmap image, is one that's composed of a grid of colored pixels. When you use a scanner or digital camera to capture an image or take a photo, the result is a raster graphic. Raster graphics can also be created from scratch using a program such as Paint (the free raster image-editing program that comes with Windows) or, on the higher end, Adobe Photoshop (or the consumer-level version, Photoshop Elements, shown in Figure 6.6).

raster graphic A graphic that consists of a grid of colored pixels that collectively form an image.

pixel An individual colored dot in a raster graphic or on a display screen.

A raster graphic has a native size, known as its resolution. Resolution is measured in number of pixels horizontally by number of pixels vertically, like this: 1024 × 768. This is the same way monitor screen resolution is measured, as you may remember from Chapter 3, "Input, Output, and Storage." The higher the resolution, the better the picture will look when printed at a large size.

resolution The number of pixels that comprise an image horizontally and vertically.

A raster image also has a color depth, which means the number of bits required to describe each pixel's color. A standard color depth is 24-bit, which uses 8 bits for red, 8 bits for green, and 8 bits for blue. There are 2^{24} (that is, 2 to the 24th power, or about 16 million) unique colors possible in 24-bit color. The human eye can only detect about 10 million different colors, so this is more than enough for full photorealism.

color depth The number of bits needed to describe the color of each pixel in a certain display mode, such as 16-bit or 32-bit.

One disadvantage of raster graphics is that they take up a lot of disk space. Each pixel requires 24 bits to describe it, at a minimum, so a 1024 × 768 image would take up at least 2,359,296 bytes (about 2.3 MB) in an uncompressed file—maybe more, depending on the file format. Because raster images can be so large, some file formats employ compression.

compression The process of reducing the size of a data file by encoding information using fewer bits than the original file.

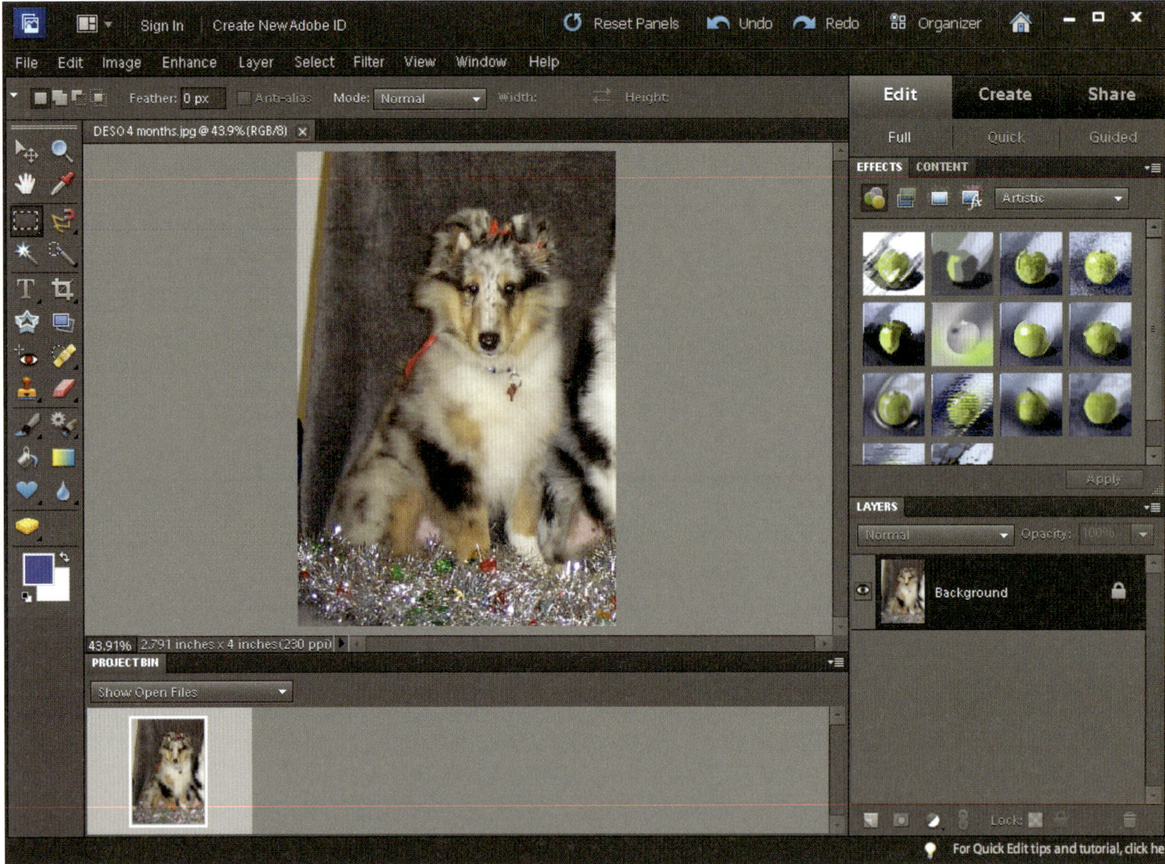

Figure 6.6 Photoshop Elements, a simpler version of the popular Adobe Photoshop, can be used to create and edit raster graphics.

Depending on the file format, compression can either be lossless (no loss of image quality) or lossy (some loss of image quality).

The other major problem with raster graphics is that they tend to lose their quality when resized—especially when enlarged beyond their original dimensions. This happens because when you enlarge a raster image, the pixels don't change size, so the software must simulate a particular pixel's color, taking up more space than it originally did. The trouble is, it's not nearly as simple as just adding another pixel of the same color next to the original, because resizing is often done in odd multiples, like 15%. Therefore, the image-editing software must do its best to simulate the enlargement by doubling some pixels but not others, and the result is a jagged or fuzzy image. In Figure 6.7, for example, see how this image, originally with crisp lines, becomes **pixilated** (that is, you can see the jagged edges of individual pixels) when it's enlarged.

pixilated The effect of seeing the jagged edges of individual pixels that occurs when a raster image is enlarged.

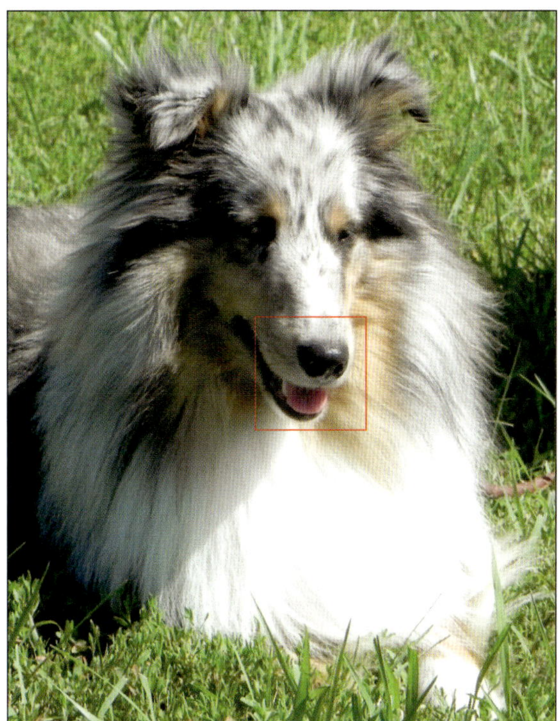

Figure 6.7 When you resize a raster image, jagged or fuzzy edges may appear.

Step by Step

Creating Raster Graphics

Follow these steps using Paint to experiment with raster graphic creation and editing:

1. Open the Paint program in Windows. (Click Start, type Paint, and then click Paint on the results list that appears.)
2. Click the Color 1 button and then click the color of your choice. This will be the outline color.
3. Click the Color 2 button and then click the color of your choice. This will be the fill color.

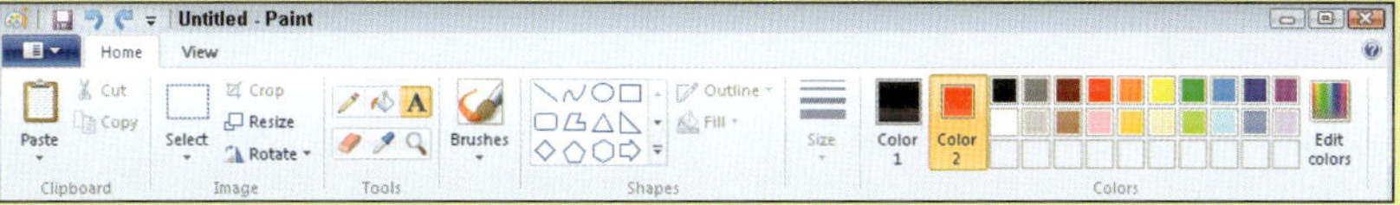

4. In the Shapes group, click the shape of your choice and then drag on the blank work area to create the shape.
5. Click the Fill button and then click Watercolor. The shape receives a fill of the color you chose in Step 3, in the Watercolor style.
6. In the Tools group, click the Zoom tool (the magnifying glass) and then click repeatedly on the image's border until the border looks jagged.

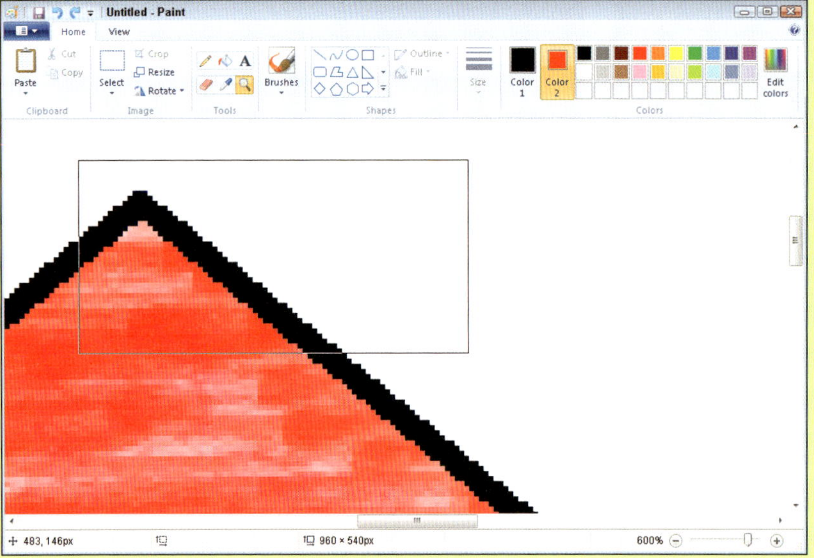

7. Right-click until the zoom returns to 100%. (The Zoom percentage appears in the lower-right corner of the window.)
8. Click the down arrow under the Brushes button, and click a brush of your choice.
9. In the Tools group, click the Text tool (looks like an A). Then click in the center of the shape.
10. On the Text tab, in the Font group, change the font size to 48 and then type a question mark.

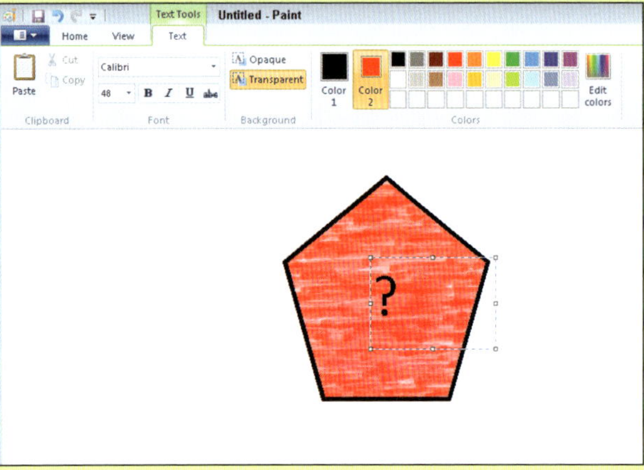

11. Click the Color 2 button and choose white as the color.
12. On the Home tab, in the Tools group, click the Eraser tool. Then drag the mouse pointer across part of the shape to erase it.
13. Close Paint without saving your changes.

Presentation Graphics Software

At various points in your working life, you're likely to be asked to give a presentation or make a speech. It's a daunting prospect. However, you can deflect some of the attention by giving your audience something else to look at. They will also find it easier to digest what you have to say if you provide a visual representation of key facts and figures you're discussing. Presentation graphics software is the ideal tool for this purpose. It enables you to create screen-sized slides containing a mixture of words and images that you can move through on demand as you deliver your presentation. You can incorporate audio and video clips, corporate branding such as company logos and color schemes, and other special elements and features. (See Figure 6.8.)

presentation graphics software A program that combines charts, graphics, and bulleted lists of information as a series of slides that summarize a report or verbal presentation. Microsoft PowerPoint is the most widely used program.

slide A screen of information that is displayed in a static fashion while a presenter elaborates on its contents. Often, the slide will be part of an electronic presentation file and the presenter can move through successive files on demand.

Figure 6.8 A PowerPoint presentation is used to summarize the speaker's information.

Most presentations are created and delivered using the Microsoft PowerPoint part of the Microsoft Office productivity suite. On an Apple computer, the equivalent program is Keynote; there is also a version of Microsoft Office available for Apple devices such as Macs and iPads.

Presentation graphics generally distill what the speaker says into bulleted summaries, and bar and pie charts. Such presentations may accompany a detailed report or be used as part of a marketing pitch—for example, showing why a company is better to do business with than its rivals. The most effective presentations have only a handful of slides and feature minimal details, allowing the audience to focus on what the presenter says. To make your point effectively, avoid creating long and boring presentations crammed with far too much information.

Computer-Aided Design Software

computer-aided design (CAD) The process of using computer software to produce technical drawings that include the product's precise scale, simulate its textures, and show it in full three-dimensional detail.

Computer-aided design (CAD) software is used when designing any sort of item that has a physical form (rather than being flat like a photo). It uses the same basic idea as the two-dimensional vector graphics that you learned about earlier in this chapter, but it models them to have height, width, and depth. This is also known as *3D modeling*.

wireframe A 3D vector drawing that consists only of drawn lines, without any surface textures applied.

Three-dimensional drawings are built around a **wireframe**. This is a sort of skeleton on which details of the computerized object or character are overlaid. The wireframe is created by extruding the flat shape to give it volume and depth.

The object is also given mass and assigned textures and properties such as skin, hair, bones, or fabric. Each of these elements has a predefined (but separately editable) set of attributes. For instance, the attributes of a brick wall would include strength, inflexibility, and resistance to wind and people bumping into it. The wireframe can be rotated so the designer can check that all the design elements and perspective are correct.

render To apply a surface texture and fill to a wireframe image to give it a solid appearance.

Once all the attributes have been added to an object created using a CAD program, the object is **rendered** to give it the appearance of a solid form by applying surface texture and color. For example, in Figure 6.9, which shows a rendered image in AutoCAD, notice how the image surface of the handheld vacuum includes two different surface textures: One looks like solid plastic, and the other looks semi-transparent.

Rendering can require huge amounts of computer power. Especially detailed designs can take many hours to render. If you want to design in 3D, you will need a powerful desktop computer with a multi-core CPU, lots of memory, and a high-quality graphics card.

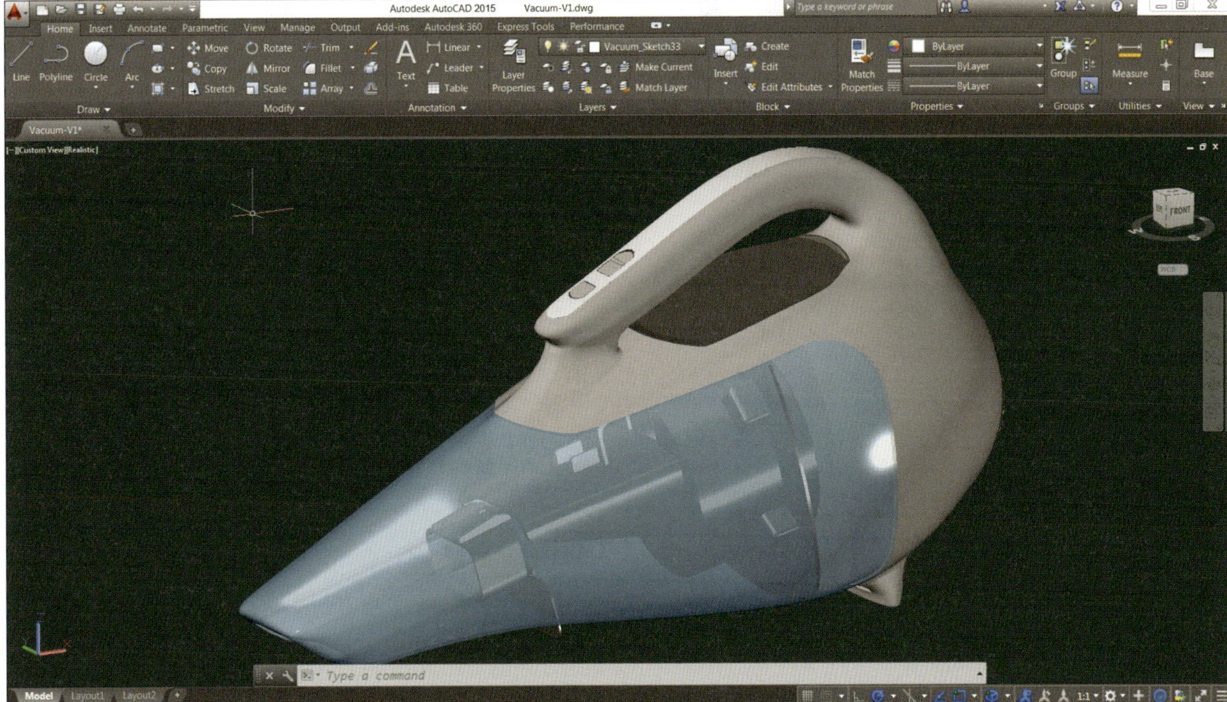

Image courtesy of Autodesk

Figure 6.9 Wireframe images are created in 3D vector modeling programs and then covered with surface textures to make them appear more realistic.

Computer-Aided Designer

Many creative industries depend on computers for their work. The computer games and film industries make extensive use of 3D design. Almost every new product that's created is prototyped using CAD software, too. A CAD designer needs strong technical drawing and creative graphics skills.

Developments in CAD software and a new type of printer have made it possible to prototype objects much more cheaply. A 3D printer uses plastic rather than ink to lay down layer upon layer in order to build up three-dimensional objects. Consequently, there is a greater demand for people who can produce the designs for the objects that will be printed in 3D. 3D printers such as the Makerbot Replicator 2X (pictured) are being used in classrooms and by hobbyists to create 3D models.

Photo courtesy of Makerbot.com

Careers in IT

Quick Review

1. What are the advantages of vector graphics?
2. What are the advantages of raster graphics?
3. Explain the relationship between a wireframe and rendering in a CAD program.

Other Types of Software

Besides the big categories of software we've looked at so far in this chapter, there are many smaller categories, such as lifestyle and hobby programs, and educational software. The following sections only scratch the surface of what's available; you will want to explore the many types of applications available on your own.

Music and Video Players

If you have a Windows computer, you'll find that Windows Media Player can play music you've downloaded and any music CDs you insert. It will also play some video clips and movies. As an alternative to Windows Media Player, you might use iTunes, which is a free download from Apple's website. iTunes, shown in Figure 6.10, can play music, videos, podcasts, audio books, and more. You can also use online services, such as Pandora, to listen to music.

Figure 6.10 iTunes is one example of an application that can play music and video clips.

Your computer may come with a DVD movie player application, or you might choose to buy one, such as RealPlayer Plus, WinX, or CyberLink PowerDVD. This software provides an interface you can use to watch movies on DVD and Blu-ray discs (provided, of course, you have an appropriate disc drive).

Can't Play DVDs?

If Windows Media Player won't play DVDs, it may be because you are missing a codec. A **codec** is a translation file; codec is short for *coder/decoder*. Different file formats require different codecs, and not all versions of Windows 7 come with the one you need to play DVD movies. (If you have Windows 7 Home Premium, Ultimate, or Enterprise, you should have it already.) You can choose to buy and install the needed codec (see `http://windows.microsoft.com/en-us/windows/windows-media-player-plug-ins`), but before you do that, see whether there is some other application installed on your PC that will play DVD movies. Most PCs that come with a DVD drive also come with such software.

codec A translation file used to play back a certain audio or video format. An abbreviation of coder/decoder.

Audio and Video Editing Software

If you want to create your own videos and music, you'll need a camera and instruments to do so. You can easily capture video and record audio on a smartphone and then transfer them to your computer for editing.

Many applications are available for editing audio tracks. For example, the freeware program Audacity (`audacity.sourceforge.net`) lets you import multiple audio tracks, trim out the parts you don't require, and then splice everything together. Mac users can record and mix digital piano, guitar, and drum tracks in the excellent GarageBand application. You can also buy more full-featured products, such as Adobe Audition.

Windows Live Essentials (`windows.microsoft.com/en-gb/windows-live/essentials`) contains a free Windows Movie Maker program that you can use to trim and combine video clips and photos and to add a sound track or commentary (see Figure 6.11). On a Mac, iMovie offers slick tools to quickly create your own mini movie. Neither of these programs will tax your computer's processor, but if you want to create professional-looking movies you'll need to use a dedicated video-editing program such as Sony Vegas Pro or Adobe Director. As with the animation and 3D graphics programs described earlier, you need a powerful computer; a quad-core or eight-core processor and powerful graphics card are essential.

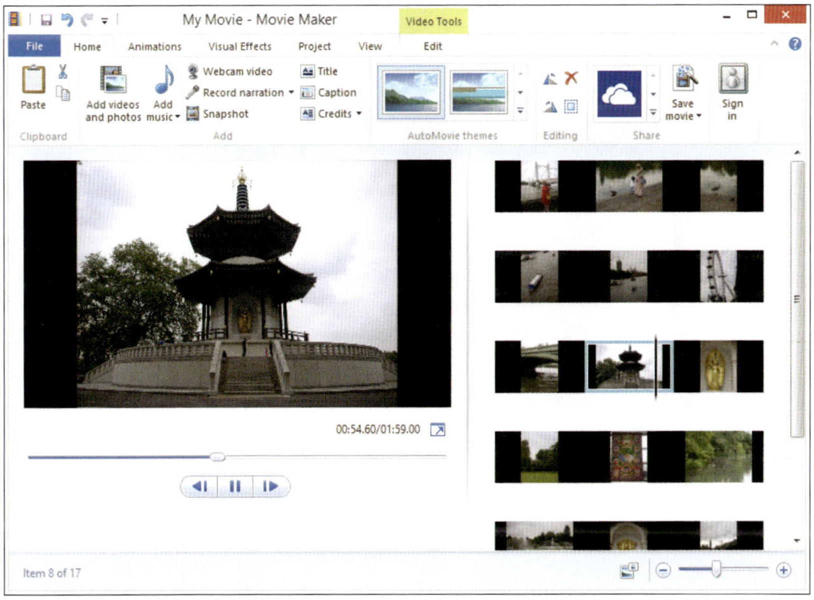

Figure 6.11 You can use a free video editor such as Windows Movie Maker to make video clips from your photos.

Personal Enrichment and Education Software

legal software Software that guides the user in creating legally binding contracts and forms.

Just about anything that you want to accomplish, you can find software to help you do it. For example, you can buy legal software that will help you draw up basic legal documents that are valid in your location, such as a will, a power of attorney statement, a lease, and a loan agreement.

reference software Software that provides access to established facts and information on a variety of topics.

You can also improve your life by using reference software, such as dictionary and encyclopedia programs. These are mostly found online these days because it is easier to keep them current that way; you might choose to use free resources or to pay for a subscription to an online encyclopedia with premium content.

NOTE With so many free online reference sources today, why would someone want a reference tool such as an online encyclopedia with premium content? One important reason is that a commercial source of reference materials offers more accuracy and higher quality because they can afford to pay full-time fact-checkers and professional writers. Online sources that are collaboratively maintained, such as Wikipedia, do not provide any assurance of accuracy, and the writing quality varies a great deal among entries.

educational software Software that teaches or trains an individual in a particular type of knowledge or skill.

Educational software can teach new skills and expand your knowledge on a variety of subjects. When you think of educational software, you might at first think of software designed for children, but there are many adult education programs too, such as Rosetta Stone for learning new languages (see Figure 6.12). Many colleges and universities offer online courses that have their own proprietary learning interfaces, including video lectures, interactive tutorials, and text and graphical lessons.

Figure 6.12 Learn a new language using Rosetta Stone software.

A Free Education

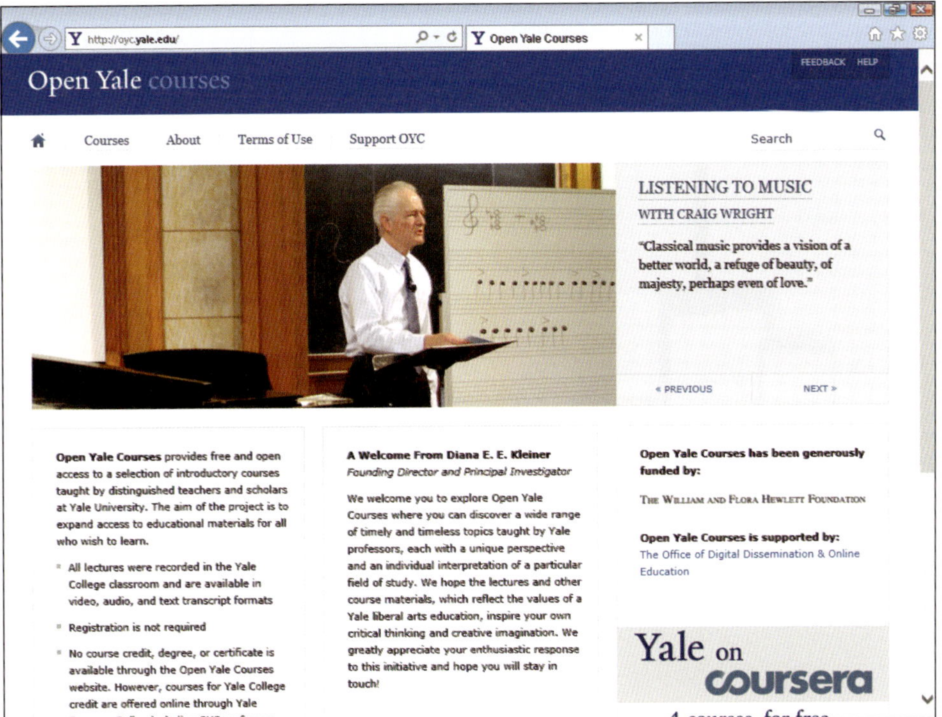

Do you know someone who would like to be better educated but doesn't have the money to spend on higher education? Direct her to Open Yale, a service of Yale University, at `http://oyc.yale.edu`. To quote from its website: "Open Yale offers free and open access to a selection of introductory courses taught by distinguished teachers and scholars at Yale University. The aim of the project is to expand access to educational materials for all who wish to learn. All lectures were recorded in the Yale College classroom and are available in video, audio, and text transcript formats. Registration is not required." This program does not issue any credit, degree, or certificate.

Communication Software

Communication software provides various ways of communicating with other people, usually via the Internet.

An **email application** helps you send and receive email messages. You might choose a stand-alone application like Eudora, a combination email and PIM application like Outlook, or an online web-based service like Outlook.com or Gmail.

email application Software that assists in sending and receiving email.

Most operating systems come with a web browser application, but you can also download and install others, most of them for free. Popular browsers include Internet Explorer (which comes with Windows), Google Chrome (which comes with the Chrome OS), Safari (which comes with Mac OS X and iOS), Opera, and Firefox. Figure 6.13 shows the Google Chrome browser.

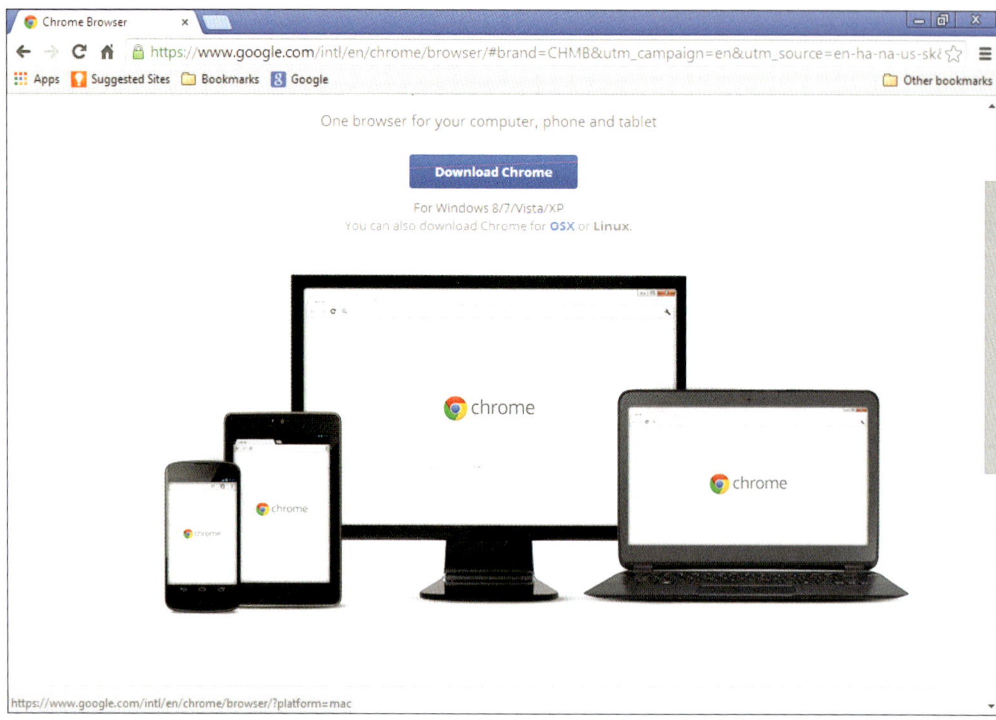

Figure 6.13 Versions of the Chrome browser are available for a variety of operating systems.

instant messaging Sending and receiving short text messages in real-time over the Internet.

video chat Having an online conversation that includes both audio and video.

Free instant messaging applications such as Yahoo! IM and AOL Instant Messenger enable you to have text conversations with your friends and family from your computer desktop. Some of these programs also have some video chat capabilities. Services such as Skype are designed specifically for video chat; they enable you to have person-to-person video chats with other people, provided you both have webcams and microphones on your computers.

videoconferencing A means of conducting a video conversation remotely using an Internet connection and the webcam or camera on your laptop, phone, or tablet.

Businesses use videoconferencing programs to hold meetings involving multiple people at multiple locations. These programs are the full-featured business version of video chat; they not only allow you to see and hear other participants, but also allow you to share computer screens, collaborate on documents in real-time, draw on a virtual whiteboard, and more. A company that does a lot of remote conferencing may have its own server with its own conferencing software.

groupware Software that helps people collaborate on business projects and work together in a team environment when they are not physically together.

Groupware helps people who are working on projects together to keep in touch. Users can post shared files that can be collaboratively edited, exchange messages, hold online meetings, and more in this environment. Microsoft SharePoint is one example of groupware software.

Web Authoring Software

web authoring software Software that helps create website designs and content.

what you see is what you get (WYSIWYG) A feature in an application that allows users to see their work exactly as it will be when it is distributed to others, such as in print or online.

Want to create your own website? There are many ways to do it. You can code your own files in a plain text editor like Notepad and then check your work in a browser, but most people (including most professionals) use web authoring software that provides a what-you-see-is-what-you-get (WYSIWYG, pronounced *wizzy-wig*) interface. Using this software, you don't have to constantly switch back and forth between your code and a browser window to see what you're doing. One popular application that professionals use is Adobe Dreamweaver; there are many free and low-cost alternatives for the casual user, including tools found on websites that will host your web page for free or very cheaply.

Quick Review

1. What is a codec?
2. What is groupware?
3. What is WYSIWYG?

Managing Your Applications

In the following sections, you'll learn some important information that will help you choose the right software and manage your software collection.

Application System Requirements

Before you purchase an application, you should check its system requirements. The **system requirements** represent the minimum hardware configuration required in order to successfully install and run the application. You can find the system requirements printed on the software box if you buy it at a retail store; if you buy it online, you can find them on the application's website. System requirements usually include a minimum CPU speed, a minimum amount of RAM, and certain standards for sound and video support. They may also specify Internet access, a particular type of input device (such as a joystick), and a certain amount of free hard drive space. Figure 6.14 shows the system requirements for the World of Warcraft video game under Windows, for example. It is common for the system requirements for games to be more restrictive than for business applications because of the intense graphic processing needed for games that have complex motion graphics. As you can see in Figure 6.13, this application has two sets of specs: one for the minimum requirements, and one that is recommended for best performance.

system requirements The minimum hardware required to install and run an application.

Windows

	MINIMUM REQUIREMENTS	RECOMMENDED SPECIFICATIONS
Operating System	Windows® XP / Windows Vista® / Windows® 7 / Windows® 8 / Windows® 8.1 with the latest service pack	Windows® 7 / Windows® 8 / Windows® 8.1 64-bit with latest service pack
Processor	Intel® Pentium® D or AMD Athlon™ 64 X2	Intel® Core 2 Duo 2.2 GHz, AMD Athlon™ 64 X2 2.6GHz or better
Video	NVIDIA® GeForce® 6800 or ATI™ Radeon™ X1600 Pro (256 MB)	NVIDIA GeForce 8800 GT, ATI™ Radeon HD 4830 (512 MB) or better
Memory	2 GB RAM (1 GB Windows® XP)	4 GB RAM
Storage	25 GB available hard drive space	
Internet	Broadband internet connection	
Media	None for the recommended digital installation	
Input	Keyboard and mouse required. Other input devices are not supported.	Multi-button mouse with scroll wheel
Resolution	1024 x 768 minimum display resolution	

Figure 6.14 The system requirements for World of Warcraft.

Installing and Removing Applications

Installing an application is easy. To install an application that came on CD or DVD, simply insert the disc into your computer. The Setup utility should run automatically. If it does not, browse the content of the drive and double-click the Setup.exe file. To install an application that you downloaded, double-click the downloaded file after it has finished downloading.

To remove an application in Windows 7, you use the Control Panel, as described in the following steps.

Step by Step

Uninstalling a Windows Application

Follow these steps to uninstall an application in Windows 7:

1. Click Start, and click Control Panel.
2. Under the Programs heading, click Uninstall or Change a Program.
3. Click the program to uninstall on the list of programs that appears.
4. In the bar at the top of the list, click Uninstall.

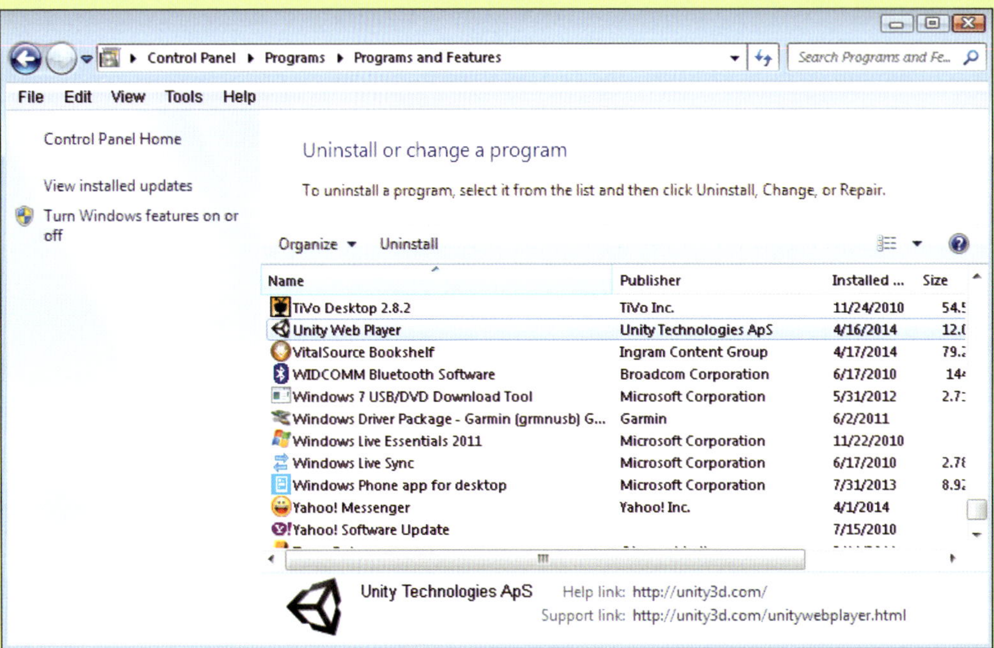

5. Follow the prompts that appear to uninstall the application. They will vary depending on the application.
6. If prompted to restart the computer after the uninstall has completed, click Yes to do so.

Updating Applications

Application developers frequently release free updates to their products. These updates may add new features, fix problems, or both. Some updates even patch security holes that make your computer vulnerable to online attack. It is almost always a good idea to install any available updates right away.

Some applications are set up to automatically notify you when an update is available. The notification may pop up in a dialog box, or as a balloon near the notification area. Click in the message that appears and follow the prompts. Some Microsoft products, such as Microsoft Office, update themselves automatically as needed through Windows Update.

Other applications must be checked manually for updates. For example, some applications have a Check for Updates command on the Help menu, as in Figure 6.15. Select the command to allow the program to check its home website for updates. Then follow the prompts that appear if an update is available. You might have to go to the website manually to look for updates.

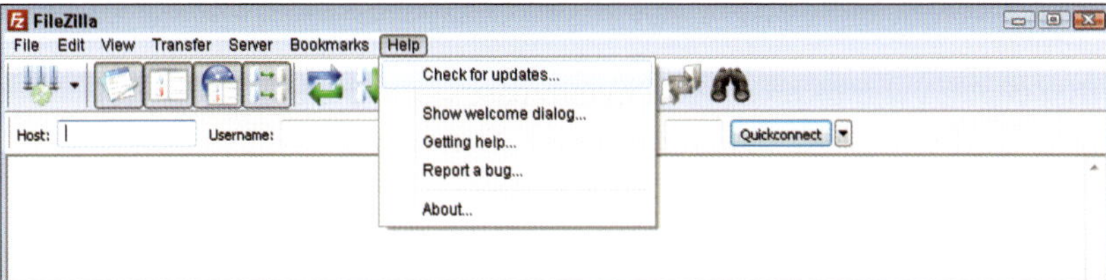

Figure 6.15 Some programs require you to manually check for updates.

Quick Review

1. How do you install an application in Windows?
2. How can you tell whether your computer meets an application's requirements before you buy the application?

Summary

Business Productivity Software

A **word processor** is used to create text-based documents. **Desktop publishing** software provides more control over page layout than a word processor. A **spreadsheet** is a grid used to analyze and present numeric data in **cells**. Spreadsheets use **formulas** to perform calculations.

A database is a structured collection of data. The data resides in **tables**, each of which contains **records** and **fields**. An application that creates databases is a **database management system**. **Data mining** is the process of extracting useful information from a database. The most common type of database is a **relational database**, which has multiple tables with relationships between them; another type is a **hierarchical database**, which uses a tree structure made up of **nodes**.

A suite is a group of related applications, such as the applications in Microsoft Office. There are other suites too, such as Adobe Creative Suite.

Accounting software helps small businesses maintain their financial records. **Personal finance software** helps individuals and families do the same. **Tax software** helps individuals and businesses file their tax forms.

Graphics Software

Graphics software is software that enables you to create and manipulate visual images. **Vector graphics** are lines and shapes drawn mathematically, like in geometry. Vector graphics are small and easily resizable but not realistic.

Raster graphics, or bitmaps, are composed of a grid of colored **pixels**. They are large and don't resize well but can be photorealistic. A raster graphic's size is its **resolution** (number of pixels horizontally and vertically). It has a **color depth**, which is the number of bits required to describe each pixel's color. Some file formats support **image transparency**, **image animation**, and/or **compression**. When a raster image is resized, it may become **pixelated**.

Presentation graphics software enables you to create **slides** to use as visual aids in presentations.

Computer-aided design (CAD) software is used to design 3D objects using vector-based drawings. An object drawing starts out as a **wireframe** and then is **rendered** by having surface textures and colors applied to it.

Other Types of Software

Music applications such as iTunes can plan and manage not only music but also videos, podcasts, and audio books. DVD player software can play movies from DVD discs on your computer. For Windows Media Player to play DVDs, you must have a supported version of Windows or purchase a **codec**. To edit your own audio and video files, a variety of free and low-cost programs are available, as well as higher-end professional tools.

Legal software helps people draw up basic legal documents that are valid in their location. **Reference software** provides a collection of information, such as a dictionary or an encyclopedia. **Educational software** can teach new skills and expand your knowledge through lessons and tutorials.

Communication software includes **email applications**, **instant messaging**, and **video chat.** Professional-quality video chat for groups is called **videoconferencing**. **Groupware** is software that helps people work together as a team from remote locations.

Web authoring software helps people create web pages and sites. Some are simple text editors, but most are **what-you-see-is-what-you-get (WYSIWYG)**, for easier viewing of the edits.

Managing Your Applications

The **system requirements** of an application explain the minimum hardware configuration required to run the application successfully. It may include specs for CPU, memory, graphics, and hard drive space.

To install an application, insert its CD/DVD or run its Setup file. To remove an application, use the Uninstall a Program feature in the Control Panel in Windows.

Some applications update themselves automatically; with others, you must locate and run a Check for Updates command in the software interface or visit the manufacturer's website to see if updates are available.

Key Terms

accounting software
application software
cell
codec
color depth
compression
computer-aided design (CAD)
data mining
database
database management system
desktop publishing software
educational software
email application
formula
graphics software
groupware
hierarchical database
instant messaging
legal software
node
personal finance software
pixel
pixilated
presentation graphics software
raster graphic
record
reference software
relational database
render
resolution
slide
spreadsheet
suite
system requirements
table
tax software
vector-based illustration
video chat
videoconferencing
web authoring software
what-you-see-is-what-you-get (WYSIWYG)
wireframe
word processor

Test Yourself

Fact Check

1. Which software creates page layouts by arranging text and graphics in movable frames?
   a. desktop publishing
   b. word processing
   c. spreadsheet
   d. DBMS
2. What does a spreadsheet use to do math calculations?
   a. macros
   b. formulas
   c. charts
   d. records
3. Which of these is *not* associated with a database?
   a. table
   b. record
   c. field
   d. formula
4. What kind of graphic can be resized without losing image quality?
   a. raster
   b. tabular
   c. vector
   d. pixilated
5. What are the individual dots that make up a raster image called?
   a. formulas
   b. pixels
   c. vectors
   d. hexagons
6. In CAD, a 3D object is first created as a _______ and then rendered to give it a surface.
   a. wireframe
   b. pixel
   c. vector
   d. record
7. __________ is software that enables team members to collaborate online.
   a. Freeware
   b. Groupware
   c. Shareware
   d. Teamware

8. ________ refers to applications by the same manufacturer purchased as a group.

   a. Legal software
   b. Desktop publishing software
   c. A suite
   d. System requirements

9. You can remove applications from Windows from the

   a. Device Manager
   b. Control Panel
   c. Dock
   d. Taskbar

10. Cells and formulas are most closely associated with which type of application?

   a. CAD
   b. Spreadsheet
   c. Word processor
   d. Photo editing

Matching

Match the software type with an appropriate use for it.

a. 2D vector drawing software
b. CAD software
c. database
d. desktop publishing software
e. raster editing software
f. spreadsheet
g. word processor

1. ________Technical drawing of a building floor plan.
2. ________Retouching a photo.
3. ________Creating a 3D model of a new product being developed.
4. ________Creating a layout for a magazine.
5. ________Analyzing sales figures for the last three months.
6. ________Storing information about a company's inventory.
7. ________Writing a research paper for a class.

Sum It Up

1. For each of the following, name two types of work you could accomplish: word processor, spreadsheet, desktop publishing software, database.
2. What are the advantages of a software suite?
3. How is data stored in a relational database?
4. If a raster graphic had a resolution of 800 × 600, how would you determine the number of pixels in it?
5. Explain the process of rendering in a CAD application.
6. Explain the difference between instant messaging and videoconferencing.

Explore More

Making Older Software Work in Windows 7

Applications originally written to run under earlier versions of Windows may not always perform well under Windows 7. One work-around is to set up Compatibility Mode for an application. Compatibility Mode can simulate any of several earlier Windows versions when interacting with that application. Using the Help and Support in Windows 7, look up information about Compatibility Mode to learn how it works and how to enable it.

With your instructor's permission, download a shareware or freeware game from `www.download.com`, where the system requirements do not include Windows 7, and install it on your computer. As you are locating a game to download, look at the system requirements for the game to find out the highest Windows version it supports. Then configure Compatibility Mode to emulate that version. Try the game to make sure it works with these settings. When you are finished, uninstall the game.

Other Software Types

There are many other software types besides the ones presented in this chapter. Using the Internet to help provide ideas, make a list of at least seven types of software that weren't covered in this chapter, and write a brief description of each type, including who might use it and what they might use it for. If you can't think of seven types, look at a website that sells software, such as Amazon.com, for ideas.

Think It Over

Paying for Application Software

Some types of software application cost hundreds of dollars, while other programs can be used for free. What are the advantages and disadvantages of paying for software? How do you think makers of free software make any money? What pricing model would you use if you were writing a program, and how would you make money from it? How would you provide customer support and make sure improvements to the program were made?

Chapter 7

Understanding Microsoft Office 2010

Understanding the Office 2010 Interface

Using Basic Features of Office Applications

Saving, Opening, and Creating Files

Printing and Sharing Files

Learning objectives

- Identify the basic parts of an Office application's interface
- Use common features that all Office applications share
- Save, open, and create data files
- Print your work

Microsoft Office is the most popular suite of business applications in the world. Its core products—Word, Excel, and PowerPoint—are considered the standard tools in millions of offices. In many companies, newly hired business professionals and support staff are expected to come into their positions already knowing how to use these tools.

Because Microsoft Office is a suite, the applications share many common features. You will learn about the common features in this chapter, including using the interface, managing the application window, saving and opening files, creating new files, and distributing your work to others.

Careers in IT

Microsoft Office Specialist

© iStockphoto.com/cmcderm1

After you have mastered the Microsoft Office products, you may want to pursue Microsoft Office Specialist certification. Candidates take a series of tests that show their mastery of the applications, and after passing the exams, earn a certificate. Potential employers will see this certification as proof that you can use Office applications productively to tackle whatever tasks are given to you.

There are three levels of certification. You can earn a Microsoft Office Specialist certification in each application. For Expert level certification, you must pass the Expert level exams for Word and Excel. For Master level, you must pass the Expert level exams for Word and Excel plus the basic level exam for PowerPoint and one other basic level exam of your choice (Outlook, Access, or SharePoint). See `http://www.microsoft.com/learning/en-us/mos-certification.aspx` to learn about the certification program.

Understanding the Office 2010 Interface

Each Office 2010 application has the same basic controls, so once you have mastered one application, learning another application is easy.

Ribbon The main toolbar in Office applications and some other Windows applications, consisting of multiple tabbed pages of commands.

tab A tabbed page of a Ribbon, or the name of a particular tabbed page.

group A named section of a Ribbon tab.

dialog box launcher An icon in the lower-right corner of a group on the Ribbon; when clicked, it opens a dialog box or task pane.

The heart of each Office application's controls is a thick toolbar across the top called the **Ribbon**. The Ribbon has multiple **tabs**; click a tab to display a different set of controls. The Home tab is displayed by default when you open the application. Each tab of the Ribbon is organized into groups. A **group** is a named section; the group names appear at the bottom of each group. Some groups have a **dialog box launcher** in the lower-right corner. Clicking this button opens a dialog box or task pane with more extensive options than are shown on the Ribbon itself.

Some tabs are common to all applications, such as Home, Insert, and View; others are unique to a particular application, such as the Mailings tab in Word and the Formulas tab in Excel. Figure 7.1 shows the Ribbons in Word 2010 and Excel 2010.

Backstage view The area of an Office application where you select commands that affect the entire active document or the application itself. Access it by clicking the File tab on the Ribbon.

To the left of the regular tabs is a File tab, which opens **Backstage view**. Within Backstage view, you can select a command for saving, opening, or closing a file, or click a category and then select commands on the right. The commands change depending on which category you choose. For example, in Figure 7.2, the Save & Send category has been selected.

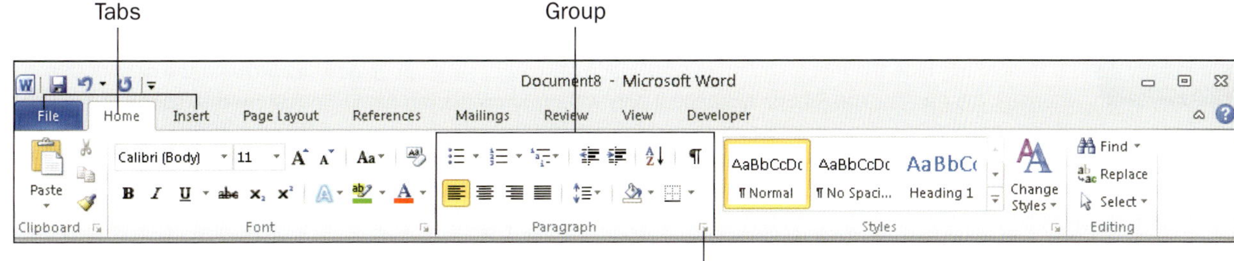

Dialog box launcher

Excel's first two groups are the same as in Word

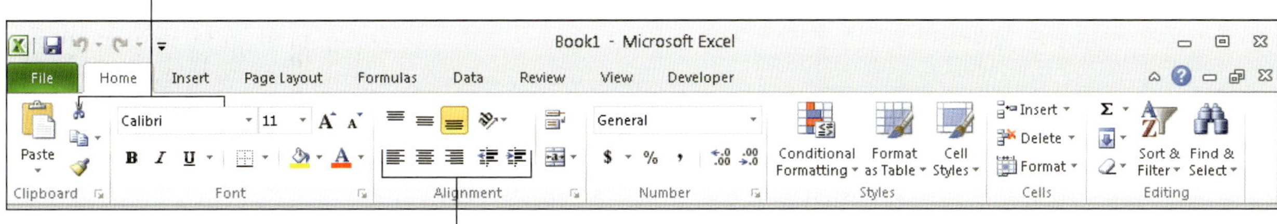

Some of the buttons in Excel's Alignment group are the same as those in Word's Paragraph group

Figure 7.1 The Ribbon in Word 2010 (top) and Excel 2010 (bottom).

Commands for saving, opening, and closing

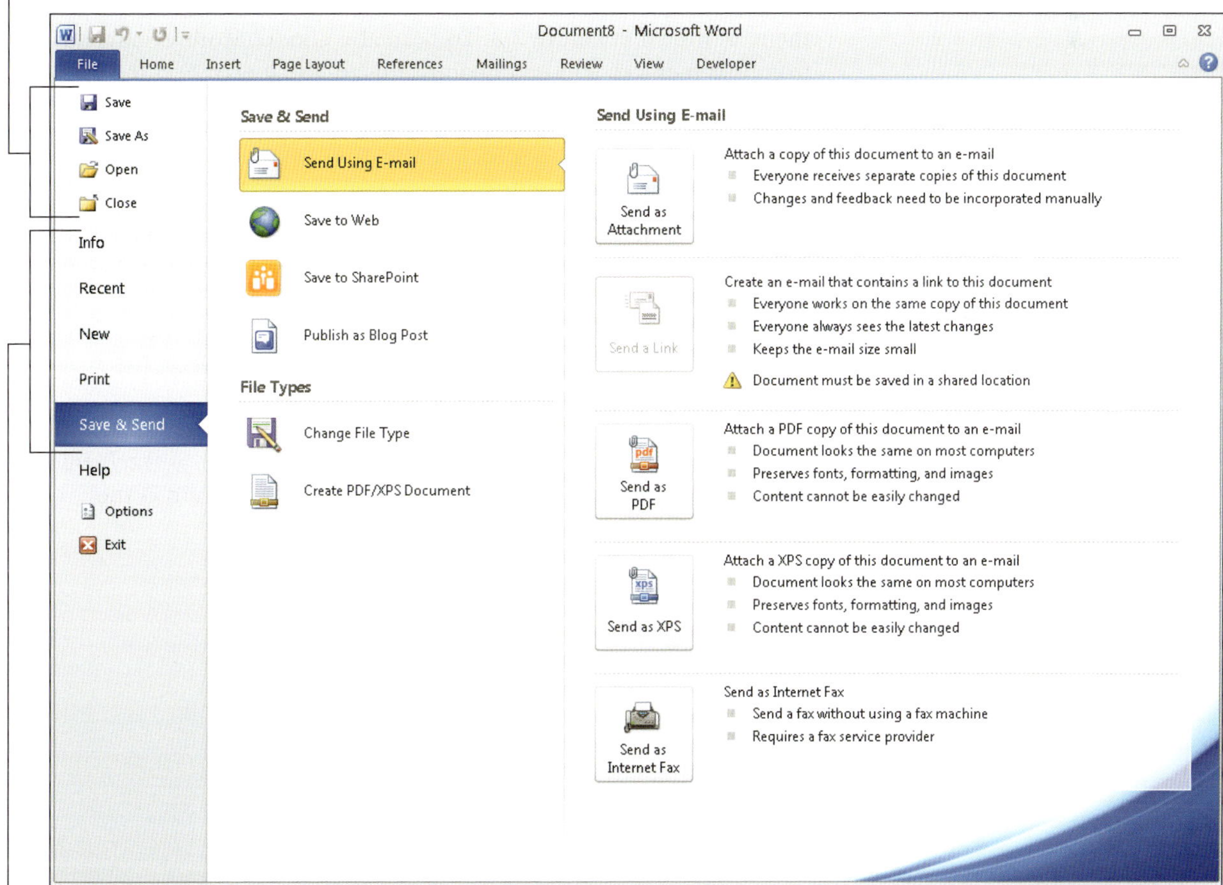

Categories

Figure 7.2 Backstage view provides access to commands and options that affect the entire file.

TIP To temporarily hide the Ribbon for more workspace onscreen, click the up-pointing arrow to the right of the Ribbon's tab names. The Ribbon will appear only when you click a tab name. To restore the Ribbon to being always on, click the down-pointing arrow (which replaced the up-pointing arrow you clicked earlier).

Click here to hide the Ribbon

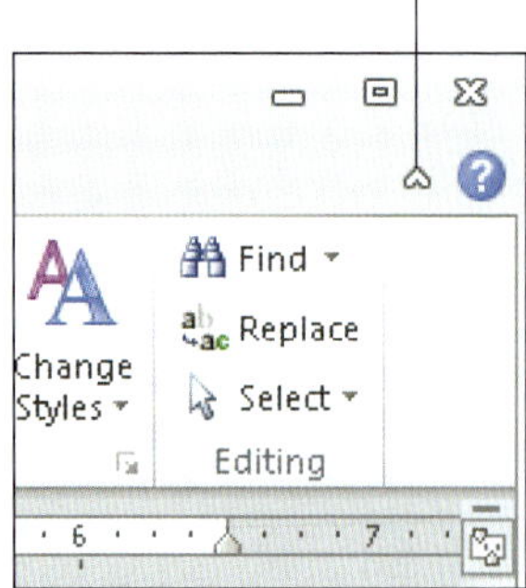

Quick Access Toolbar (QAT) The small, customizable toolbar above the Ribbon tabs in an Office application's interface.

Above the Ribbon, on the left end of the title bar, is the **Quick Access Toolbar (QAT)**. You can customize this toolbar by adding and removing commands from it. This toolbar remains constant no matter which tab is displayed, so you can keep your favorite commands close at hand on the QAT without having to remember which tab contains them. The down-pointing arrow at the right end of the QAT opens a menu of common commands that you can toggle on and off on the QAT by selecting them, as shown in Figure 7.3. You can also choose More Commands from that menu to add other commands to it that aren't on the list.

Quick Access Toolbar

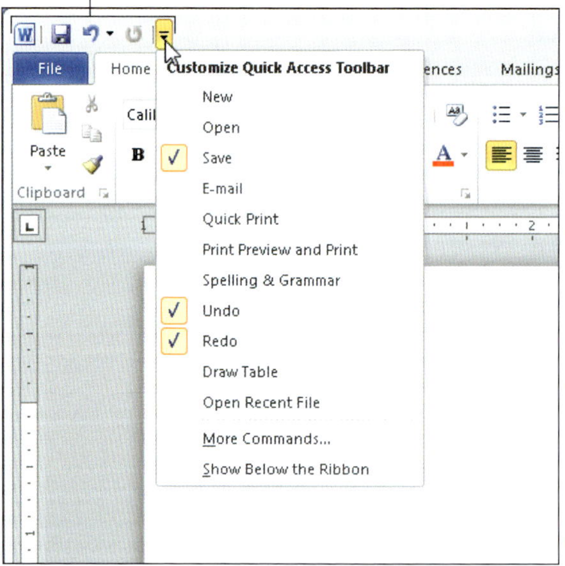

Figure 7.3 Customize the QAT by selecting commands from its menu.

Ribbon Doesn't Look Right?

Troubleshooting

If the Ribbon in an application doesn't appear to have the same commands on it as your classmates' computers, yours may have been customized. To reset the Ribbon, right-click any button on the Ribbon and choose Customize the Ribbon. In the lower-right corner of the dialog box that appears, click Reset and then click Reset All Customizations. Then click OK. Your Ribbon will be back to its original state.

When you right-click, a **shortcut menu** appears (also called a *context menu*). Its commands depend on what you right-clicked. If you right-click a selected block of text, for example, commands appear that will help you format it, move or copy it, and check its spelling, as shown in Figure 7.4. If you right-click on a graphic, commands appear for formatting and positioning the graphic. The shortcut menu that appears when you right-click a button on the Ribbon offers an option to add that command to the Quick Access Toolbar.

shortcut menu The context-sensitive menu that appears when you right-click an object.

Figure 7.4 The shortcut menu is different depending on what you right-clicked. The menu shown here is displayed when you right-click a block of text.

When you hover the mouse pointer over a button or command on the Ribbon, a **ScreenTip** appears, telling you its name and purpose. In some cases, ScreenTips also contain **keyboard shortcut** prompts. For example, when you point at the Justify button on the Home tab, you find out that Ctrl+J is the keyboard shortcut setting that alignment, as shown in Figure 7.5. To use a keyboard shortcut, hold down the first key while you tap (press and release) the second key.

ScreenTip The information that appears about a command or button when you hover the mouse pointer over it.

keyboard shortcut Two or more keys that, when pressed in combination, issue a command.

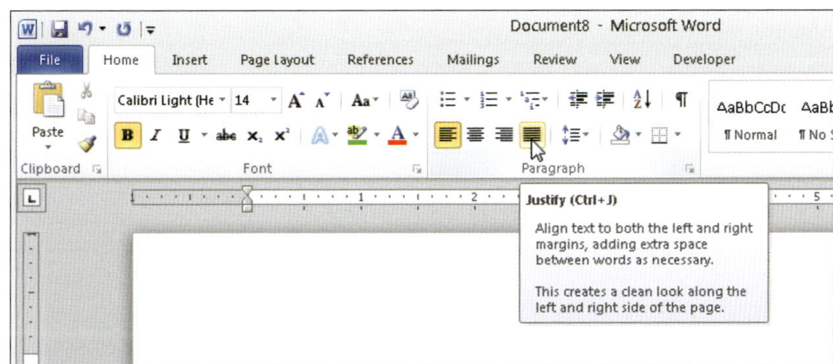

Figure 7.5 A ScreenTip provides information about a Ribbon command or button.

TIP

For a list of all the available keyboard shortcuts in an application, open the application's Help window (F1) and search for *keyboard shortcuts*. The **status bar**, at the bottom of the application window, provides several pieces of status-related information. In a Word document, for example, it tells you how many pages are in the document and what page number you are working with at the moment. It also tells you how many words are in the document. See Figure 7.6. The exact details the status bar provides depend on the application.

Figure 7.6 The Status bar in Word 2010.

status bar The bar at the bottom of an application's window that reports status information.

Zoom controls Controls at the right end of the status bar that adjust the magnification at which the data is displayed.

At the right end of the status bar are the **Zoom controls**. The Zoom controls enable you to zoom in and out to view your work at different magnifications. You can drag the slider, or you can click the - (minus) or + (plus) button on its ends to increment the zoom out (-) or in (+). The current zoom level is reported to the left of the Zoom slider; click the current Zoom level to open a Zoom dialog box in which you can set the zoom level more precisely. You can see the Zoom and View controls in Figure 7.6. The View tab also has Zoom controls that perform the same functions (plus a few others).

As with any window, you can adjust an Office application window's size. To resize a window, drag its border, and to move a window, drag its title bar. You can maximize it by clicking its Maximize button (in the upper-right corner of the window), and then restore it to pre-maximized size by clicking the Restore button, which replaces the Maximize button when the window is maximized. You can minimize the window down to a button on the taskbar with the Minimize button, and you can close the window (which closes the application and any open files) by clicking the Close button. Figure 7.7 points out the window controls in an Office application's window.

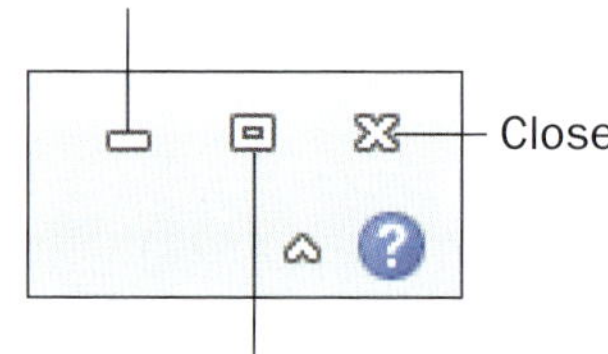

Figure 7.7 Office application windows have the same window controls as other windows in your operating system.

Quick Review

1. What are the buttons above the tab names on the Ribbon?
2. What is Backstage view and what kinds of commands are found there?
3. How do you display a context-sensitive shortcut menu for an object?

Using Basic Features of Office Applications

Office applications have many commands and features in common. For example, the procedures for getting help, changing views, cutting and pasting, formatting text, and undoing mistakes are nearly identical. In the following sections, you will learn about some features that work the same way in each of the main Office applications.

Getting Help

To get help in any Office application, do any of the following:

- **Press the F1 key.** If you do this while a dialog box is open, the help provided is context-sensitive.
- **Click the Help button.** It's the question mark in a blue circle above the right end of the Ribbon. You can see it in Figure 7.7, below the Close button.
- **Click the File tab and click Help.**

In the Help window that appears, you can search for a particular topic by typing a keyword in the Search box, or you can browse the Help system by clicking on one of the hyperlinks on the home page of the Help system. Figure 7.8 identifies the buttons on the Help window's toolbar.

Figure 7.8 Use the Help window to look up information about using the active application.

Changing Views

Each application has its own unique set of views that you can switch among while working with your data. Different views are useful in different situations. For example, in PowerPoint, you use Normal view for general slide editing and Slide Sorter view to reorder and organize the slides. In Word, you use Print Layout view for most editing, but you can switch to Outline view to organize sections of a document or Web Layout to see how a document will appear when saved as a web page.

To switch views, select the desired view from the View tab on the Ribbon. See Figure 7.9. You can also switch to certain views using the Views buttons on the status bar (just to the left of the Zoom controls).

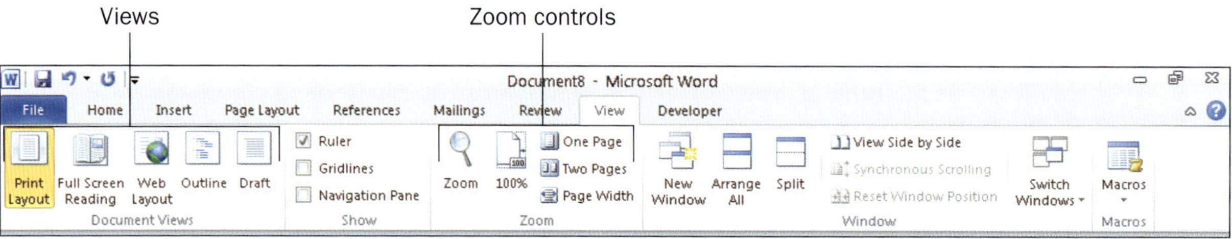

Figure 7.9 Choose an appropriate view for the task at hand from the View tab.

Moving Around

scroll To page through the document so that a different part of it becomes visible.

scroll bar The horizontal or vertical bar to the bottom or right of the document, containing scroll arrows and a scroll box, which you can use to scroll.

As you create content in an application, you might have more content than you can see onscreen at once, so you might need to scroll to view different parts of it. You can scroll using the scroll bars with your mouse. Figure 7.10 shows a scroll bar.

In Excel, the vertical and horizontal scroll bars are always available. In Word and PowerPoint, the vertical scroll bar is always available, but the horizontal one only appears if the displayed document is wider than the screen width.

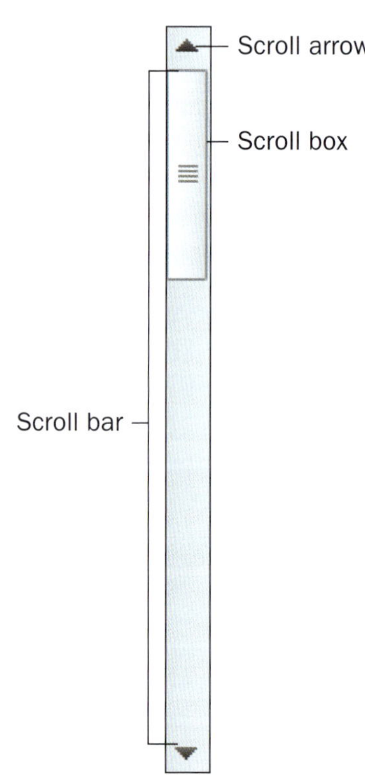

Figure 7.10 A scroll bar in Microsoft Word.

TIP

Here are some ways to use a scroll bar:

- Click the arrow at the end of a scroll bar to scroll the display slowly in the direction of an arrow (a small amount each time you click).
- Drag the box in the scroll bar to scroll quickly.
- Click in the empty space on the bar to one side or the other of the scroll box to move one screenful at a time in that direction.

The size of the **scroll box** indicates how much content you can't see at the moment. For example, in Figure 7.10, the scroll box occupies about one-third of the scroll bar; that means that about one-third of the document's content is currently visible. In a very large spreadsheet or document, the scroll box might be very small.

scroll box The box in the scroll bar that you can drag to scroll the display. You can also click above or below the scroll bar to scroll one screenful at a time.

You can also move around using keyboard shortcuts. As you gain experience with the applications, you might find using keyboard shortcuts more convenient than using the scroll bar. For example, pressing Ctrl+Home takes you to the beginning of the file in most Office applications.

Scrolling the display does not move the insertion point. To move the **insertion point**, click where you want it to go, or use the directional arrow keys on your keyboard to move it. In Excel, there is no insertion point, but a thick outline around the active cell shows the cell in which content will be entered.

insertion point The flashing vertical line that indicates where typed text will appear.

Selecting Content

Most of the commands you issue apply to whatever text or object is selected. For example, to italicize text, you first select the text to affect. Then when you click the Italics button, only the selected text is affected.

When you select in Excel, you usually want to select entire cells rather than individual characters of text. When a cell is selected, any formatting or other commands that you issue apply to everything in that cell. You can select a contiguous range (all in one rectangular block area) or a non-contiguous range (multiple cells that are not adjacent to one another). To select an object (such as graphic), click it.

Step by Step

Selecting Text in Word or PowerPoint

Do any of the following to select text:

- Drag the mouse pointer across it (holding down the left mouse button).
- Click where you want to start and then hold down Shift as you press the arrow keys to extend the selection.
- Click where you want to start and then hold down Shift and click where you want to end the selection.

Selecting Cells in Excel

To select a contiguous range of cells:

- Drag the mouse pointer across the cells (holding down the left mouse button).
- Click the first cell to select it and then hold down Shift as you press the arrow keys to extend the selection.
- Click the first cell to select it and then hold down Shift and click the last cell.

To select a non-contiguous range of cells:

- Click the first cell to select it and then hold down Ctrl and click each individual cell to select.

Using the Office Clipboard

In the section "Moving and Copying Files and Folders" in Chapter 5, "Introduction to Windows 7," you learned about the Windows Clipboard. This temporary holding area enables you to cut or copy an item from one location and then paste it into another location, effectively moving or copying it. The Clipboard can also be used to cut, copy, and paste snippets of data from different applications and data files into a single file. For example, you can copy a paragraph from a Word document and paste it into an Excel worksheet or PowerPoint slide, or into a different location in Word (either in the same document or a different document).

Table 7.1 provides a quick summary of the ways to cut, copy, and paste in Office applications.

Table 7.1 Methods of Cutting, Copying, and Pasting in Office Applications

Action	Keyboard shortcut method	Ribbon method	Right-click method
Cut	Ctrl+X	Home⇨Cut	Right-click and choose Cut from the shortcut menu.
Copy	Ctrl+C	Home⇨Copy	Right-click and choose Copy from the shortcut menu.
Paste	Ctrl+V	Home⇨Paste	Right-click and choose Paste from the shortcut menu.

Office Clipboard The enhanced version of the Windows Clipboard that appears in Office applications. It can hold up to 24 items at once.

Microsoft Office has an enhanced version of the Clipboard called the **Office Clipboard**. It uses the Windows Clipboard as its basis, but adds the capability to store up to 24 objects at a time. (On the Windows Clipboard, when you cut or copy another object, the previously saved object is removed from the Clipboard.)

To display the Office Clipboard's task pane, click the dialog box launcher in the Clipboard group on the Home tab. Each time you cut or copy something to the Clipboard from an Office application, it is placed on the list in the task pane. If you want to paste the most recently cut or copied item, you can use the standard methods of pasting from Table 7.1. However, if you want to paste one of the earlier items, display the Clipboard task pane and then click the item you want to paste. Figure 7.11 shows the Clipboard task pane with several items on it. The Office Clipboard is shared among all Office applications, so you can, for example, copy several cell ranges or charts from Excel and have access to them in PowerPoint or Word on the Office Clipboard.

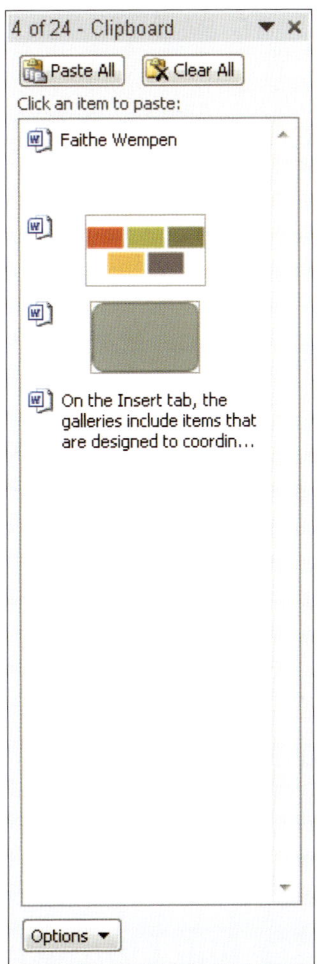

Figure 7.11 The Office Clipboard task pane enables you to store up to 24 items to be pasted.

Clearing the Office Clipboard

Privacy and Security

If you don't exit from all Office applications before stepping away from your computer, anyone who sits down at your computer can see the items on the Office Clipboard. If you have any concerns about privacy, click the Clear All button at the top of the Clipboard task pane to remove all items from it after you are finished using the Clipboard.

Using Undo and Redo

If you make a mistake in an Office application, you can easily undo your last action with the Undo command. You can either click it on the Quick Access Toolbar (see Figure 7.12) or press Ctrl+Z, its keyboard shortcut. You can do this multiple times in a row to go back multiple steps.

There's an easy way to undo multiple actions at a time. The Undo button has a down arrow to its right; click it for a drop-down list of recent actions, and then drag across the ones you want to undo.

After you have used Undo, a Redo button becomes available to its right on the QAT. Redo undoes the Undo operation. You can use Redo as many times in a row as you used Undo. For example, if you just clicked Undo three times to undo the last three actions, you can then click Redo three times to redo those actions. The shortcut for Redo is Ctrl+Y.

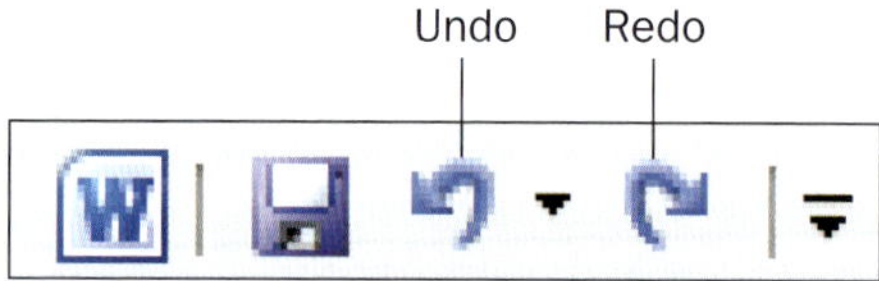

Figure 7.12 Undo and Redo buttons on the Quick Access Toolbar. The Undo button's menu enables you to go back multiple steps.

When Redo is not available, its button on the QAT turns into a Repeat button, which enables you to repeat the last action you took. If you aren't sure which button is active in that spot (Redo or Repeat), hover the mouse over the button and see what name appears in the ScreenTip.

Text Entry and Formatting

To enter text, click in an area that accepts text, moving the insertion point there, and begin typing. In Excel, you type in cells; in PowerPoint, you type in object placeholder frames. In Word, you can type text directly on the document page. To edit, use the Backspace key to delete the character to the left of the insertion point, or use Delete to delete the character to its right. You can also select blocks of text, or cells containing content, and press the Delete key to clear the text. See "Selecting Content" earlier in this chapter. In Excel, rather than an insertion point, there's a **cell cursor**, a thick outline that indicates the active cell.

cell cursor The thick line around the active cell in Excel, indicating that this is where typed text will appear.

Put It to Work

Click and Type

In Word, when you start a new document, the insertion point is in the upper-left corner of the page. What if you want to type something in the center of the page, or at the bottom? One method is to press Enter until you get to the desired vertical position. An easier way is to use Click and Type. Move the mouse pointer to the spot where you would like to place the insertion point, so that the mouse pointer turns into an I-beam with an image of one of the alignment buttons next to it (from the Home tab's Paragraph group). Depending on where on the page horizontally you move, the alignment symbol changes to show how the text will be set to align if you click and type in that spot. Click, and the insertion point jumps to the spot you clicked, and Word automatically creates the needed paragraph breaks to get the insertion point to that spot. This only works in Word, not in Excel or PowerPoint.

All the Office applications have similar controls for text formatting. After you select some text, you can use the commands in the Font group on the Home tab to change the font, size, and color of text, as well as apply attributes like bold, italics, and underlining. Figure 7.13 shows the Font group in Word and points out the buttons that are common to all the applications. To find out what the other buttons are in this group, point at each one to view the ScreenTip.

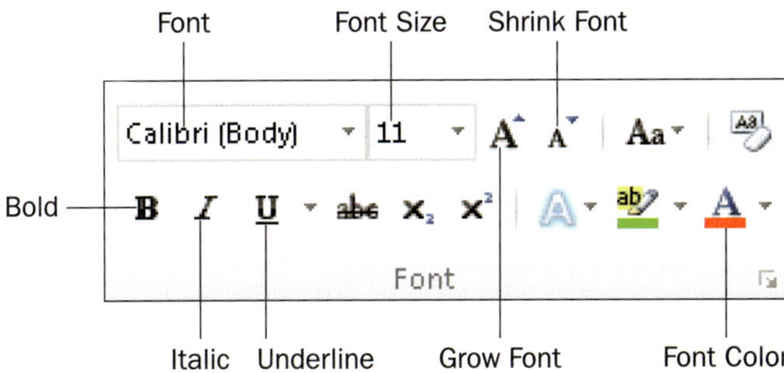

Figure 7.13 Use the Font group's commands to format text.

Understanding Themes and Color Palettes

Each application enables users to apply themes, which are groups of formatting presets. A **theme** contains definitions of three key formatting aspects: fonts, colors, and effects (applied to graphic objects). In some applications, a theme may contain additional elements; for example, in PowerPoint, a theme may contain a background image that is applied to each slide. You can override a theme's settings in one or more of those areas by applying a color theme, font theme, or effect theme (which are like themes but more limited, affecting only that one aspect of the formatting).

theme A named set of formatting presets, governing font, color, and object effect choices.

Each document, workbook, or presentation has a set of 12 color placeholders: 10 colors for standard use, and 2 colors that define the colors for followed and unfollowed hyperlinks. The choice of theme (or color theme) dictates what those colors will be.

Commands for selecting colors (such as the Font Color button on the Home tab) open a **color palette** from which you can select a color, like the one shown in Figure 7.14.

color palette A grid of color choices that opens when you click a button for a feature that is color-related.

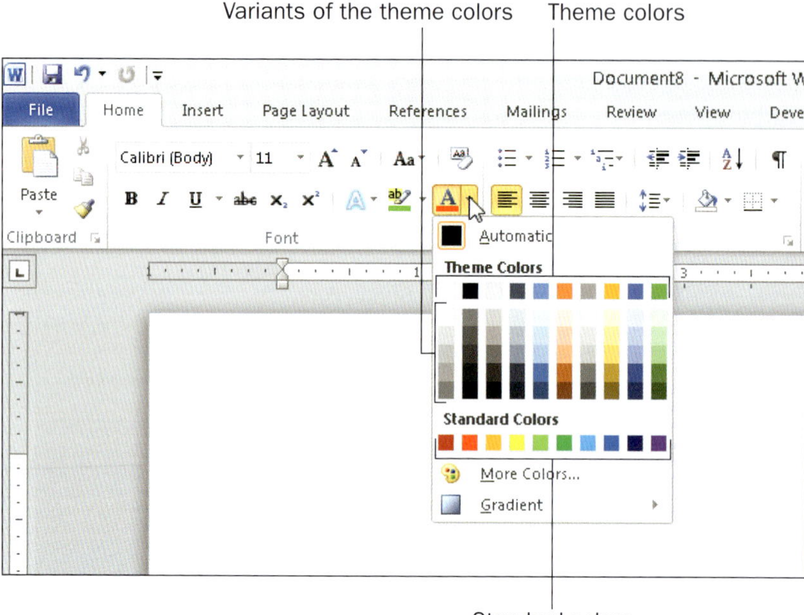

Figure 7.14 Select a color from a palette of choices.

On this palette, you see the following choices:

theme colors The colors assigned to the color placeholders in a theme.

- **Theme Colors:** The top row in this section contains **theme colors**, color swatches for the colors assigned to each placeholder position in the theme. Beneath the top row are variants of the theme colors, either lighter or darker than the original color by a specified amount. When you apply colors from this area, you are not choosing actual colors—you are choosing placeholder positions. If you change to a different theme or color theme, those colors will change.

standard colors Fixed colors that are not affected by the theme in use.

- **Standard Colors:** **Standard colors** are fixed, and are not affected by the theme or color theme.
- **More Colors:** If you want a fixed color but none of the color swatches in the Standard Colors section are right, choose More Colors to open a Colors dialog box from which you can select a color more specifically. On the General tab of this dialog box is a larger assortment of swatches. On the Custom tab, you can specify a color by number using one of the standard color models.

There may be other choices at the bottom of the palette, depending on the object you are applying color to. For example, there may be a Gradient option for applying a blend of colors.

Moving and Resizing Objects

Each application includes the capability to insert content in movable and resizable frames that either float over the top of the regular content (as is the case in Excel) or interact with the text on the underlying page in a way you specify (as in Word). In PowerPoint, all content is in frames.

The content within one of these frames is known as an object. An object can be a graphic, a chart, a drawing, or any of several other items. A text box can also be an object.

object An item that is separate from the rest of the document, with its own movable and resizable frame.

selection handles The markers on the border of an object that allow the object to be resized.

To resize an object, drag one of its selection handles. A selection handle is a small marker in a corner of the object's frame or at the midpoint along one side of the frame. Depending on the application and the type of object, the selection handles may be either white or colored (black, pale blue, or bluish-green), and may be either round or square. Figure 7.15 shows the selection handles around a text box, for example.

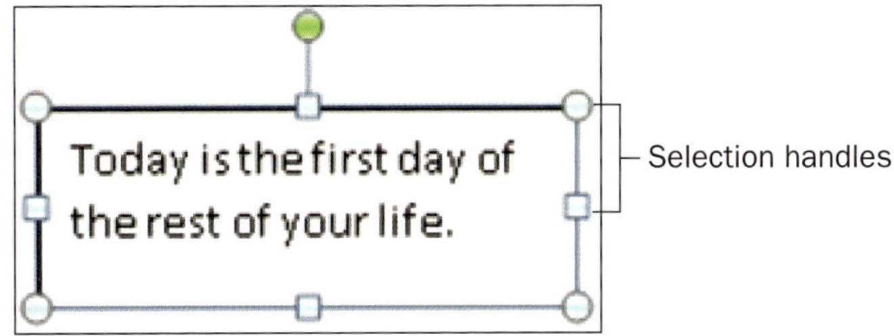

Figure 7.15 Drag a selection handle to resize an object.

CAUTION

As you resize an object, its aspect ratio (proportion of height to width) may change. If the object is a graphic, the graphic may become distorted. To avoid changing the aspect ratio when resizing an object, hold down the Shift key as you drag a corner selection handle. Some object types maintain their aspect ratio automatically when you drag a corner selection handle, even if you do not hold down the Shift key.

To move an object, drag it with the mouse. You can position the mouse pointer over any part of the object and then drag. (Exception: If the object is a text box, you must drag it by any part of its border that is *not* near a selection handle.)

Quick Review

1. How do you resize an object?
2. What key do you press to get help?
3. How do you change to a different view?
4. What is the difference between the Windows Clipboard and the Office Clipboard?

Saving, Opening, and Creating Files

Each application has similar procedures for working with data files. You can create, save, and open files in much the same way. In the following sections, you will learn the basic techniques for these operations.

Saving Files

As you work in an application, the content you create is stored in the computer's memory. This memory is only temporary storage. When you exit the application or shut down the computer, whatever is stored in memory is flushed away forever—unless you save it.

The steps for saving and opening data files are almost exactly the same in each application, so mastering it in one program gives you a head start in other programs.

TIP Ctrl+S is the keyboard shortcut for the Save command; Ctrl+N is the shortcut for the New command (to start a new file); and Ctrl+O is the shortcut for the Open command (to open an existing file).

Navigating the file system is the same in the Save and Open dialog boxes as it is in Windows Explorer, which you learned to use in Chapter 5. You can move between volumes and folders, select favorite locations from the Favorites list, and so on. Figure 7.16 points out the navigation controls in the Save As dialog box in Word, for example.

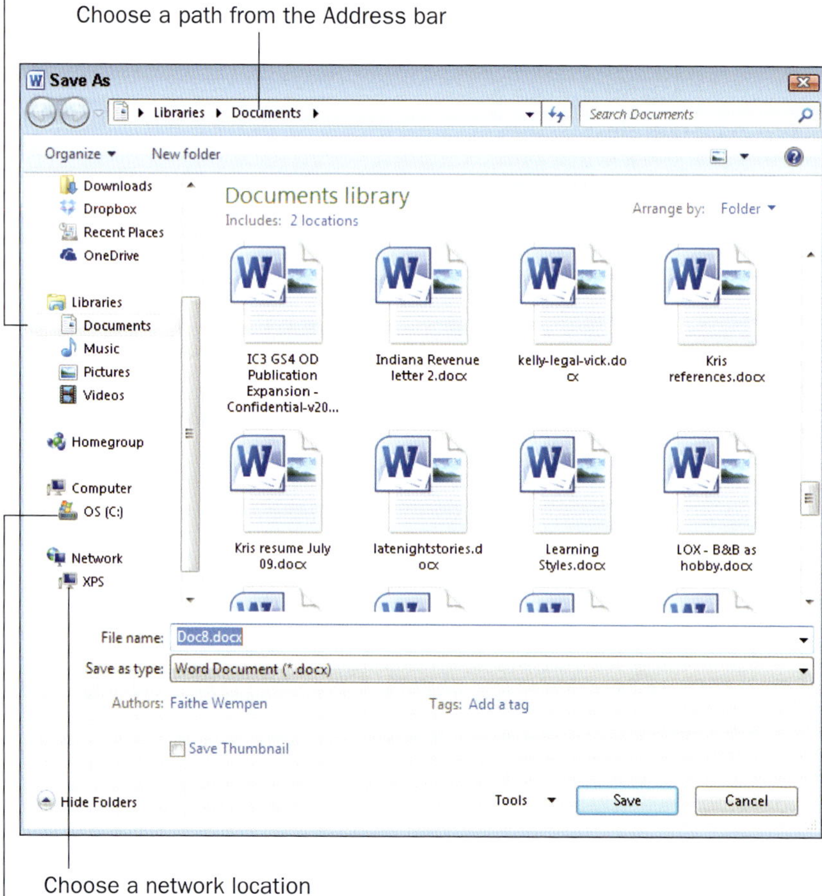

Figure 7.16 Use the Save As dialog box controls to navigate to different locations.

Saving to the OneDrive Cloud

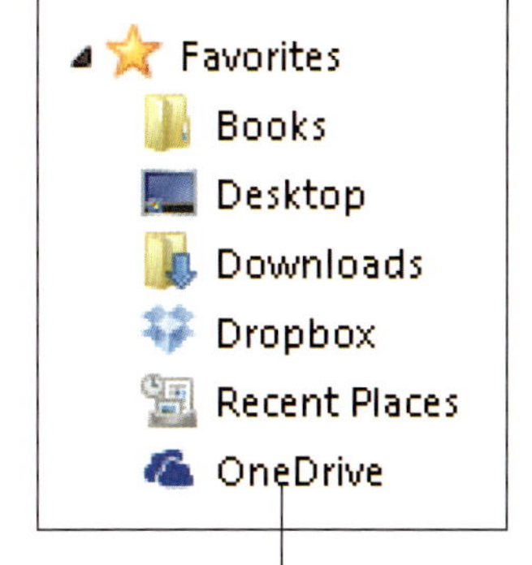

If there is no OneDrive (or SkyDrive) shortcut here, the utility is not installed.

If you use Microsoft OneDrive (formerly called SkyDrive) for cloud storage, you can easily save to it directly from any Office application by using the OneDrive shortcut in the Favorites list in the Save As or Open dialog box. (If you don't see a OneDrive shortcut there, go to `https://onedrive.live.com/about/en-us/download` and download the utility for Windows 7 that integrates OneDrive with Windows Explorer.)

Put It to Work

Step by Step

Saving a File for the First Time

Use these steps the first time you save a new file:

1. Click the File tab and click Save, or click the Save icon on the QAT.
2. In the Save As dialog box, navigate to the desired location, as shown in Figure 7.16.
3. Type the desired filename in the File name box.
4. (Optional) Change the file type if desired.
5. Click Save.

Re-Saving a File Subsequent Times (Same Settings)

Do the following to save a file again using the same settings:

1. Click the File tab.
2. Click Save, or click the Save icon on the QAT. The file is immediately saved with the same settings as before.

Re-Saving a File Subsequent Times (Different Settings)

Follow these steps to save another copy of an existing file in a different location, or with a different name, or with a different file type:

1. Click the File tab and click Save As.
2. In the Save As dialog box, navigate to the desired location.
3. Type the desired file name in the File name box.
4. (Optional) Change the file type if desired.
5. Click Save.

Understanding Data Formats

Each application has its own data formats, summarized in Table 7.2. When you save a file, you can open the File type drop-down list and select a file format.

TIP When you don't have a reason to do otherwise, use the native file format for an application (the one where the extension ends in "x"). The resulting files are smaller and you ensure that you have access to the full set of application features that way. Some program features aren't supported in backward-compatible file formats, and you won't be able to use them (or save them) in a backward-compatible file.

Each application's native format is the default format in which new content is saved. Each application also has a macro-enabled option, for files that contain macros. (Most don't.) Making the general format non-macro-enabled cuts down on the risk of spreading macro viruses. Each application can also save and open files from earlier versions for backward compatibility. (Use the format that has 97-2003 in its name.)

Table 7.2 Office Application File Formats

Application	*Native format*	*Macro-enabled format*	*Backward-compatible format (97-2003 format)*
Word	.docx	.docm	.doc
Excel	.xlsx	.xlsm	.xls
PowerPoint	.pptx	.pptm	.ppt

Password-Protecting Files

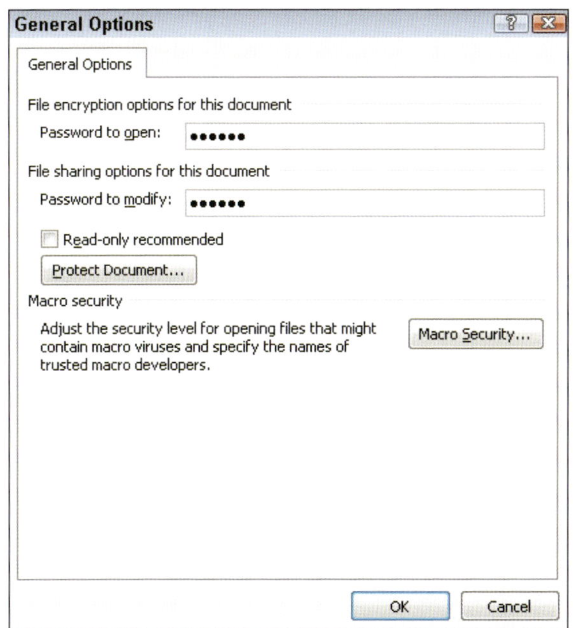

You can password-protect an Office application's data file as you save it. To do so, from the Save As dialog box, click the Tools button, and then choose General Options from the menu. In the dialog box that appears, you can assign a password to the file. There are two password prompts: Password to Open and Password to Modify. The former allows read-only access; the user cannot save changes back to the same file. The latter enables changes to be saved. You can assign two different passwords to allow some people one type of access and others the other type.

Opening and Closing Files

To open an existing file, click the File tab and click Open and then make your selection in the Open dialog box, after navigating to the location where the file is stored. After you have created a file and saved it, you can reopen the file to review or edit it.

> **NOTE**
>
> You can open files when you are not already in an application. In Windows Explorer you can double-click a data file to open it in its native application.

If you want to open a recently used file, there's a quicker method. After clicking the File tab, click Recent, and then click the shortcut for one of the recently used files that appear on the list, as shown in Figure 7.17.

When you are finished with a file, you can close it by clicking the File tab and then clicking Close. Closing a file frees up some of your computer's memory for other uses. When you exit the application, all open files are automatically closed, and you are prompted to save any unsaved changes to them.

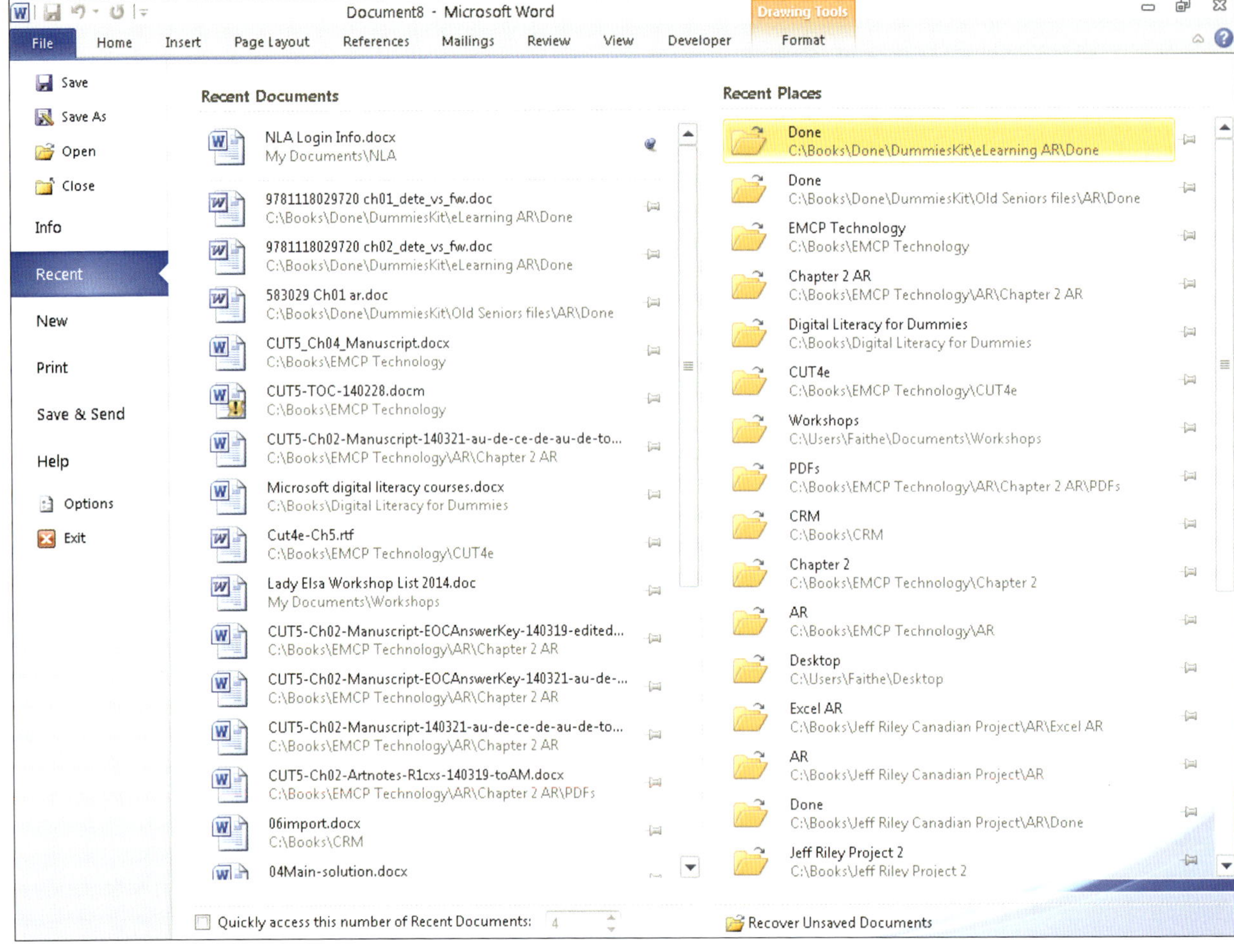

Figure 7.17 Select a file from the Recent list as an alternative to choosing it from the Open dialog box.

Quick Review

1. Name two different ways of accessing the Save command.
2. How can you quickly reopen a recently used file?
3. How do you close an open document without exiting the application?

Printing and Sharing Files

Each application has a similar Print function that you can use to generate hard copies of your work. You can also share your work electronically with others by sending it to people via email.

Printing a File

To print a file, first set it up the way you want it in the application, including hiding or collapsing any content you don't want to show, setting font sizes and spacing, and so on. Then click the File tab and click Print, and make your selections of the options that appear.

The options are slightly different in each application; Figure 7.18 points out some of the common features. You can choose which printer to use, the number of copies to print, whether those copies should be collated, what page orientation to use, and more.

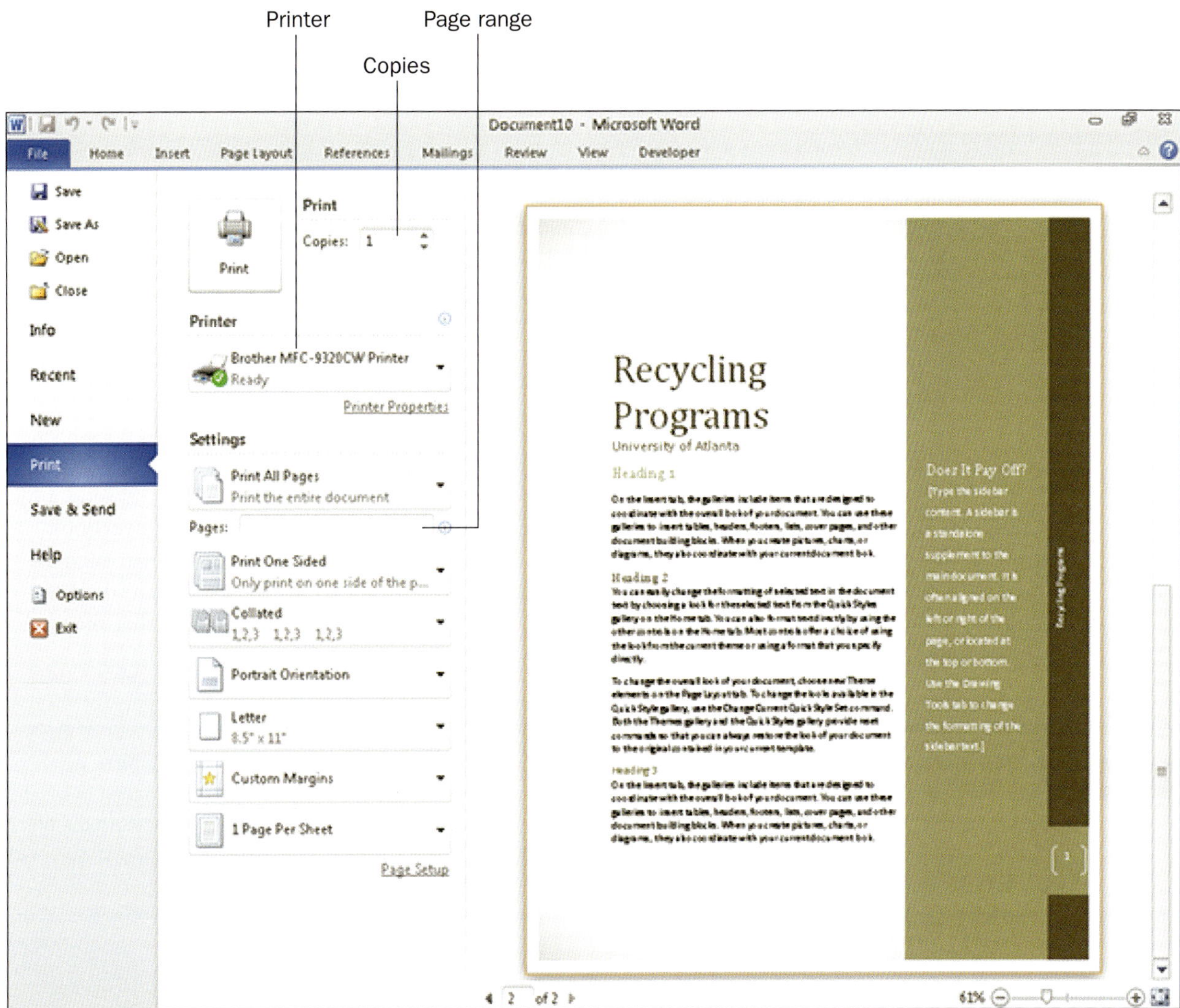

Figure 7.18 Print from the Print category in Backstage view.

In the Pages text box, you can specify certain page numbers to print. To print individual pages, separate the numbers by commas, like this: 1, 3, 7. To print a range, use a hyphen, like this: 3-6. Other print options may be available, depending on the application; click the Print All Pages button to open a menu.

The largest portion of the Print screen consists of a Preview pane, on which you can see the document exactly as it will be printed. Use the arrow buttons below the preview to move between pages. If you don't like the preview, click any other tab to return to normal viewing and fix the document as needed before you print.

Step by Step

Printing a File

Follow these steps to print a file:

1. Click the File tab and click Print. Options appear for the print job.
2. Adjust any settings as desired, including choosing a different printer, number of copies, and page range.
3. Click Print.

Sending a File as an Email Attachment

In your email software, you can attach files to your outgoing messages, but you can also attach and send files directly from within Office applications, without opening your email software separately. You can send a file in its native format (for example, docx for Word, pptx for PowerPoint, and so on), or you can choose to send it in some other format, such as PDF. When the recipient gets your attached file, he or she can double-click it to open it in whatever application is associated with that file type on his or her PC.

NOTE

PDF (Portable Document Format) is a page layout format that is platform-independent; people often use it to send files to people who may not have the appropriate software to open the file in the application in which it was originally created. Sending a file as a PDF also makes it harder for others to make changes to the file, so it is useful for sending contracts and other official documents for review. XPS is the Microsoft equivalent of PDF. Office 2010 applications can save and send in either PDF or XPS.

Step by Step

Sending a File via Email

Follow these steps to send a file as an email attachment:

1. With the file open in its Office application, click the File tab and click Save & Send.
2. In the center pane, click Send Using Email.
3. In the right pane, click the appropriate button to indicate the way you want the file sent. To send it in its native format, choose Send as Attachment.

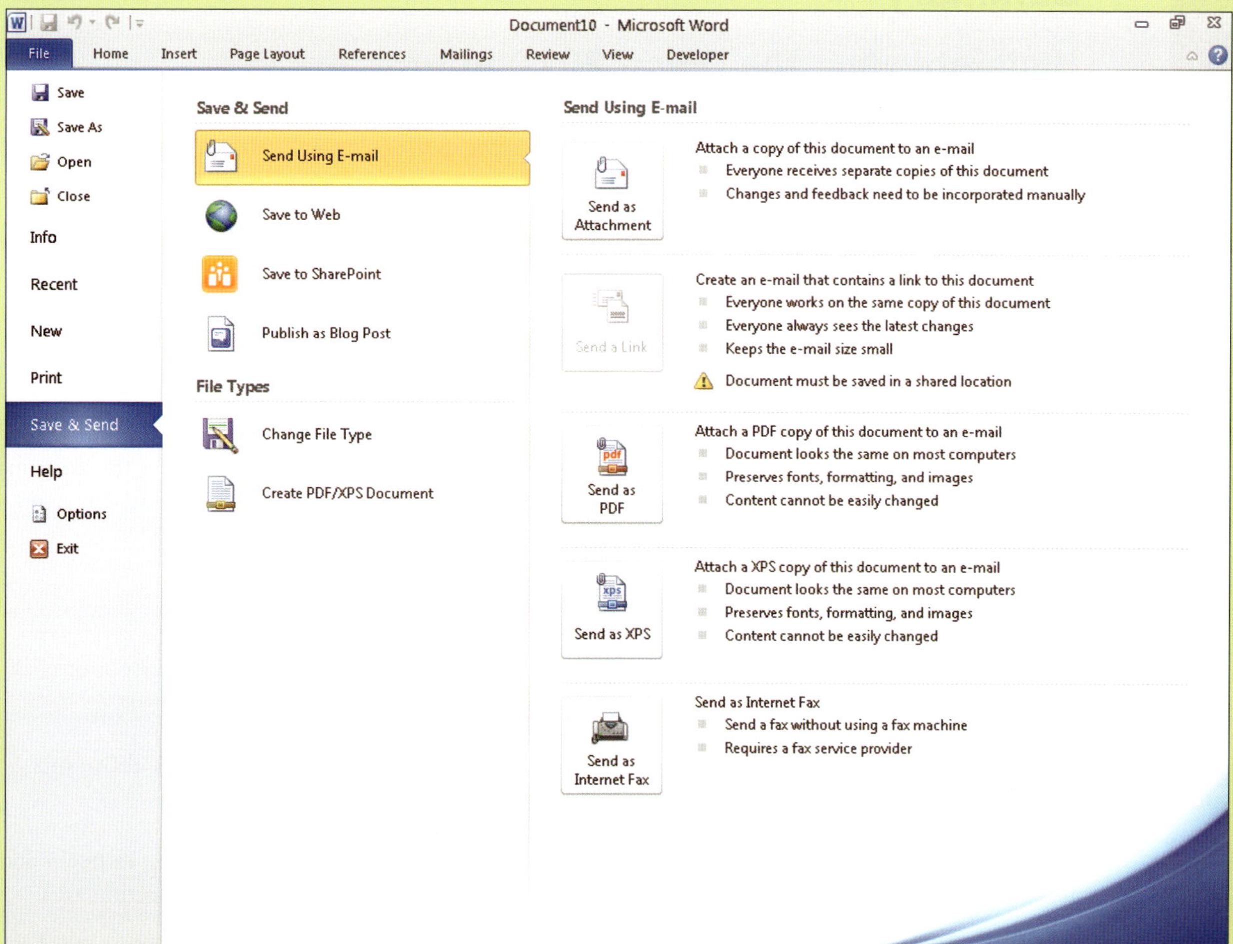

4. Follow the prompts to complete the send operation. The exact steps from this point depend on what format you chose in Step 3.

Quick Review

1. How do you preview a print job before it is actually printed?
2. How can you send a file to someone else as an email attachment?

Summary

Understanding the Office 2010 Interface

The **Ribbon** is the large, multi-tabbed toolbar at the top of each Office application window. It contains **tabs** (pages) of commands. Commands are organized in **groups** on each tab. A **dialog box launcher**, found in some groups, opens a dialog box related to that group.

When you click the File tab, **Backstage view** opens, which contains multiple categories in a navigation bar along the left side. Click a category to see a page of options relating to file management. The **Quick Access Toolbar (QAT)** is the small, customizable toolbar that appears above the Ribbon. When you right-click, a context-sensitive **shortcut menu** appears, from which you can select commands relating to what you right-clicked.

When you hover the mouse over a button, a **ScreenTip** appears explaining its name and purpose. Some ScreenTips contain **keyboard shortcut** prompts too. The **status bar** appears at the bottom of the application's window. **Zoom controls** adjust the magnification at which you see your work. Zoom controls appear on the right end of the status bar and also on the View tab.

Basic Features of Office Applications

To open the Help system in an application, press F1, or choose Help from the File menu, or click the Help icon in the upper-right corner of the application window.

To **scroll** in the document, use the **scroll bars**. You can drag the **scroll box**, or click above or below the scroll box, or click one of the scroll arrows.

To select content, drag across it with the mouse, or click where you want the selection to begin and hold down Shift as you click at the other end, or use the arrow keys to extend the selection area.

The **Office Clipboard** is like the Windows Clipboard except it has more features, and is available only in Office applications. It can hold up to 24 items.

Undo reverses the last action. Use the Undo button on the QAT or press Ctrl+Z. Redo reverses the reversal; press Ctrl+Y or use the Redo button on the QAT.

The **insertion point** is where text you type will appear. You can move it by clicking where you want it. In Excel, a **cell cursor**, a thick line around a cell, indicates that it is active, and text you type will be placed in it.

Office files can have **themes** applied, which are sets of formatting presets. They consist of font, color, and graphic effect choices. You can also apply each of those separately (color theme, font theme, effect theme). When you choose colors, you select from a color palette that contains **theme colors**, variants of theme colors, and **standard colors**.

A framed object within an Office document is called an **object**. Objects can include charts, graphics, and text boxes. Drag a **selection handle** on an object to resize it, or drag the object itself to move it. Drag the border to move a text box.

Saving, Opening, and Creating Files

To save a file, use the Save command on the File menu. The first time you save a file, you are prompted for a name, location, and type in the Save As dialog box. When you save subsequent times, you are not prompted. If you want to be prompted, use the Save As command instead.

To open a file, use the Open command on the File menu. Navigate to the location of the file in the same way you do in Windows Explorer. To close a file, use the Close command.

Printing and Sharing Files

To print your work, open the File menu and click Print. Then use the controls that appear to specify the options for the print job.

You can email a file to others in native format, or in PDF or XPS format. These are both page layout formats that people can read even if they do not have the original applications.

Key Terms

Backstage view
cell cursor
color palette
dialog box launcher
group
insertion point
keyboard shortcut
object
Office Clipboard
Quick Access Toolbar (QAT)
Ribbon
ScreenTip
scroll
scroll bar
scroll box
selection handle
shortcut menu
standard colors
status bar
tab
theme
theme colors
Zoom controls

Test Yourself

Fact Check

1. What is found in the lower-right corner of some groups on the Ribbon?
    - a. status bar
    - b. dialog box launcher
    - c. list box
    - d. Close button
2. How do you enter Backstage view?
    - a. Click the Home tab.
    - b. Press Ctrl+B.
    - c. Press Ctrl+X.
    - d. Click the File tab.
3. How do you display a shortcut menu?
    - a. Double-click
    - b. Triple-click
    - c. Right-click
    - d. Press Ctrl+S

4. How do you display a ScreenTip?

   a. Hover the mouse over the item.

   b. Double-click the item.

   c. Right-click the item.

   d. Triple-click the item.

5. How do you display the Office Clipboard?

   a. Ctrl+K.

   b. Click the Paste button.

   c. Click the dialog box launcher in the Clipboard group.

   d. Any of the above.

6. Which of these is NOT stored in a theme?

   a. effect choices

   b. color choices

   c. font choices

   d. page size and orientation choices

7. In a color palette, what are the colors that appear below the row of theme colors?

   a. variations on the theme colors

   b. standard colors

   c. fixed colors

   d. recently used colors

8. To resize an object, drag its

   a. border, but not on a selection handle

   b. selection handle

   c. rotation handle

   d. title bar

9. Which of these is the default file format for saving your work in Excel?

   a. .xlsm

   b. .xls

   c. .xlsx

   d. .xlss

10. When sending a file as an attachment, you can send it in its native format, in XPS format, or as a(n)

    a. .png

    b. .mov

    c. .pdf

    d. .mp3

Matching

Match the feature to its function.

a. dialog box launcher

b. object

c. QAT

d. ScreenTip

e. selection handle

f. shortcut menu

g. theme

1. ________Toolbar that appears above the Ribbon
2. ________What you see when you right-click an item
3. ________The small icon in the lower-right corner of a group
4. ________Content that has its own resizable frame
5. ________What appears when you hover the mouse over a button on the Ribbon
6. ________A named set of formatting settings
7. ________What you drag to resize an object

Sum It Up

1. Explain how to save and open files in Office applications.
2. Describe the main features that the user interfaces of all Office applications have in common.
3. Describe how colors are arranged on a palette and how they relate to the active theme.
4. Name three things you can customize in an application via its Options dialog box.
5. Explain how to change the default save location.
6. Describe how to move the insertion point.
7. Contrast the Windows Clipboard to the Office Clipboard.

Explore More

Customizing the Status Bar

The status bar's content varies, not only between applications, but also with customization. Right-click the status bar in any application for a menu of items you can show or hide on it (see Figure 7.19).

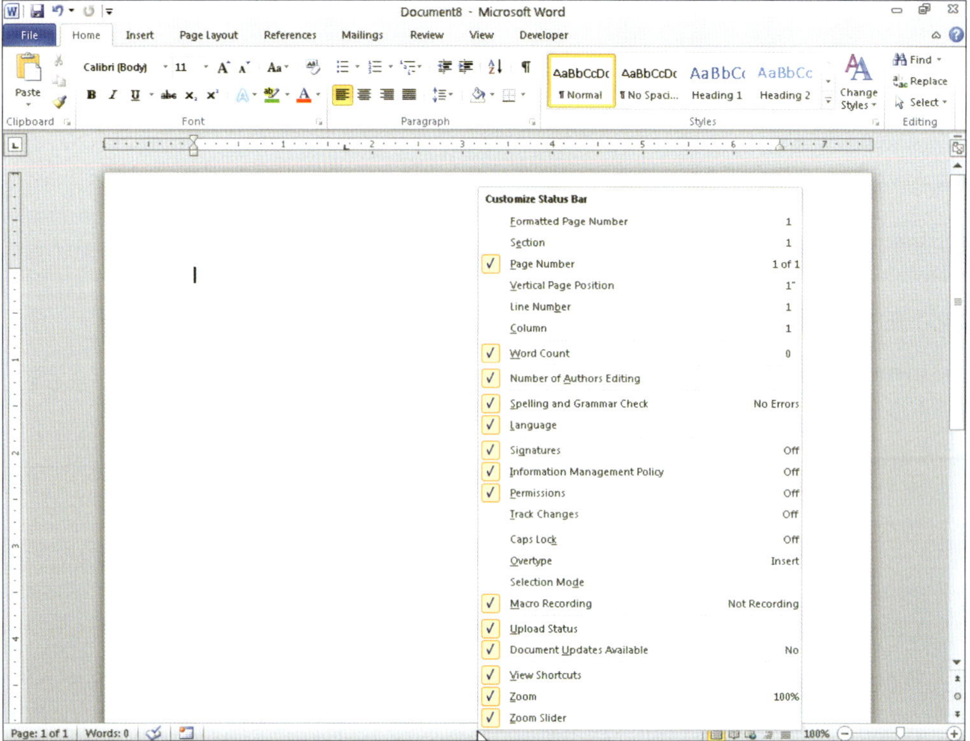

Figure 7.19 Right-click the status bar to choose what information should appear there.

More Keyboard Shortcuts

Each application has an extensive set of keyboard shortcuts available. Open the application's Help system and search for *Keyboard Shortcuts* to see an article that lists the complete set. There are separate sets of shortcuts for various situations. For example, there are shortcuts for moving the insertion point, shortcuts for scrolling, shortcuts for selecting, shortcuts for commands, and so on.

Can't get enough of working with the keyboard? Each Ribbon tab and command has a keyboard equivalent too. To see them, press the Alt key, as shown in Figure 7.20. Key tips appear next to each tab and command name. Then press that key to choose that command. (You have to press Alt each time to use these shortcuts.) This is how people who can't use a mouse navigate in Office applications, by the way.

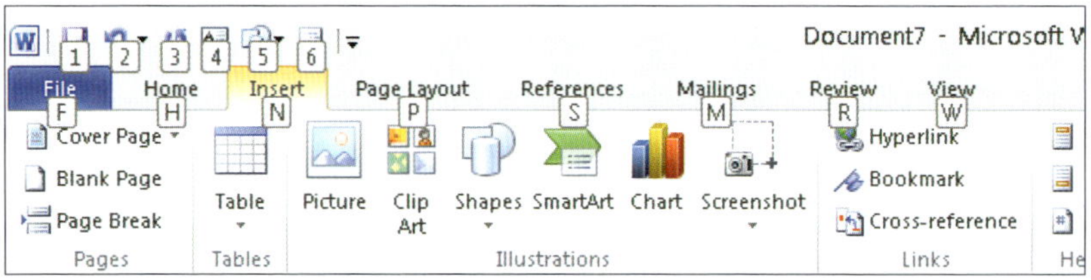

Figure 7.20 Press Alt to see keys you can use to select Ribbon tabs and commands.

More Application Options

For some of the more obscure settings in an application's options, check out the Advanced category in the Options dialog box. You might be surprised at some of the changes you can make. For example, in Word, you can set default behaviors for cutting, copying, and pasting data, and in PowerPoint you can disable right-clicking during a slide show as a security measure to keep people from stopping a slide show at an interactive kiosk.

Think It Over

Ribbon Customization

Some people may find an application easier to use when the Ribbon is customized, but if multiple people share a computer, customizations can be a problem. If you were in charge of your school's or workplace's computers, would you allow people to customize the Ribbon, or not? Explain your answer.

Theme Colors versus Standard Colors

When choosing colors for a project, would you rather use theme colors or standard colors? What are the trade-offs?

Sharing Files

You can share files in ways other than attaching them to email. What are some other ways you can share files, and how do they compare? What are the pros and cons of each method you identify?

Part III

Connectivity and Communication

Chapter 8

Networking and Internet Basics

Learning objectives

- Identify communications networks in daily life
- Distinguish among types of networks
- Identify common types of network hardware
- Understand the Internet and choose a connection method

When computing first began, each computer was separate, and data was moved between computers only with difficulty. Today, however, computers connect to both local and global networks that make information sharing easy, whether you're sharing data with your brother's computer in the next room or with a file server halfway around the world.

This chapter explains the basics of modern networking, both large and small networks, both wired and wireless, and both private and public. You will learn how networks are structured, how network resources are identified, and how network security helps keep your data safe. You'll also learn how to troubleshoot some common network-related problems.

Our Connected World: Communication Systems

Networking is everywhere, and many of our everyday activities are enabled or assisted by computer networking, even the activities that might not on the surface seem to have anything to do with it. For example, when you withdraw funds at your local bank branch, the bank verifies your account balance on the bank's main server at the home office. When you buy an item at your local discount chain store, and you pay for your purchase with a credit card, the cash register's software checks a credit card verification server to make sure your card is valid before charging your purchase. It then sends the information to the store's internal inventory management system via the local network. The local server then sends an updated inventory report to the company's web server, so that someone ordering from the store's website will know that the item is no longer in stock. When you call your mother on your cell phone on the way home to tell her about your purchase, your call goes through the wireless network for your cell phone provider.

Let's start out this chapter by looking at some of the large-scale networks that make up our connected world.

Public Telephone and Data Networks

circuit-switched network A network that creates a point-to-point connection between locations that remains open for the duration of the communication.

public switched telephone network (PSTN) The worldwide network of circuit-switched telephone lines.

packet-switched network A network that transfers data by breaking it up into separately transferred packets.

The first worldwide network ever created was the telephone network, predating computers by many decades. This network is an example of a **circuit-switched network**. It works by creating a point-to-point circuit between the two locations. The telephone network creates a pathway between the two points, and that pathway remains open for the duration of the phone call. Networks can be public or private. The public telephone system—the whole of the world's circuit-switched telephone networks—is known as the **public-switched telephone network (PSTN)**.

In contrast, computer networks are **packet-switched networks**. A communication channel does not remain open between two points for an entire conversation; instead, the data is broken up at the sending end into small packets, each with an electronic envelope around it that states the source and the destination, and sent individually to the receiver. Depending on the network traffic, each packet may take a different route to the destination, but when they arrive they are unpacked and reassembled into the original message.

The Internet

Internet A global packet-switched network created cooperatively by multiple companies, governments, and standards organizations.

protocol A rule or custom that governs how something is done. In a computer context, it refers to a standard for transferring data.

Internet service provider (ISP) A company that maintains a direct connection to the Internet and leases access to it to individuals and companies.

protocol stack A related group of protocols—for example, TCP/IP.

TCP/IP The protocol suite (set of rules) that defines how data will move on the Internet and on most other modern networks.

The **Internet** is the world's largest network. It is not owned or maintained by any one company; instead, it is a cooperative effort among many companies and governments, with multiple standards organizations managing the rules for its operation. The Internet is a packet-switched network with a worldwide addressing system. The Internet uses various **protocols** (rules) that all participating computers have standardized on, so that services like the web, email, and instant messaging work the same everywhere. Most companies and individuals don't connect directly to the Internet; instead, they connect to an **Internet service provider (ISP)**, which in turn connects to the Internet. For example, if you have cable Internet at home, your ISP is your cable provider.

The Internet is based on a **protocol stack** (a set of protocols) called **Transmission Control Protocol/Internet Protocol (TCP/IP)**. TCP/IP provides a common set of standards by which data can be sent and received. It is used not only on the Internet, but in most private networks today as well. One of the key features of TCP/IP is IP addressing, which is a means of uniquely identifying each connected computer on the network by a numeric value.

Private Digital Networks

Many companies maintain high-speed connections between their locations. They can do so by leasing a line, running their own cables, or using the existing pathways of the Internet. Using the Internet is the most cost-effective method, but not the most reliable method, because the connection can be affected by Internet traffic problems and connections that other companies control and maintain.

Using the Internet is also not very secure; it's an open system and data being sent and received can easily be snooped. To tighten the security when using the Internet as a conduit, many companies use a software technology called **virtual private networking (VPN)**. VPN technology creates a secure, tamper-resistant data tunnel between two points on the Internet, so that sensitive information can be exchanged securely, as in Figure 8.1. A VPN allows an employee who is working outside of the company's main building to connect to any of the internal network resources, just as if he or she were in the building.

virtual private networking (VPN) A method of creating a secure, private communication tunnel using a public communications channel such as the Internet.

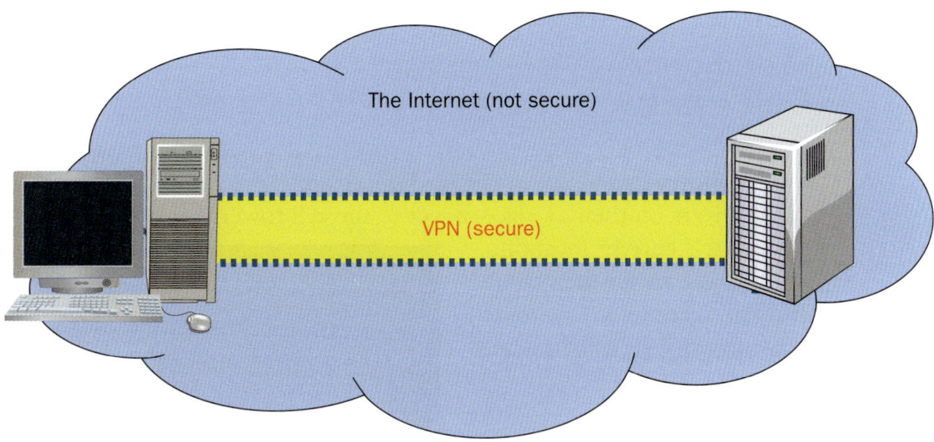

Figure 8.1 A VPN creates a secure connection between two points using the Internet's infrastructure to physically carry the data.

Satellite Data Networks

A **satellite** is a transmitter/receiver unit that orbits the Earth, more than 22,000 miles up. Satellites are in geosynchronous orbit (that is, their orbit is synchronized with the Earth's orbit), so they do not appear to change in position compared to any location on Earth. A satellite contains transponders, which are two-way radios that communicate with stations on the ground. Satellites are used to quickly send information between two points on Earth that are physically separated by a great distance. For example, when the Olympics are held in one country, satellites are used to broadcast the video of each competition nearly instantly to every other country. Satellites are also used for services like satellite radio (Sirius/XM, for example) and satellite TV broadcasts such as DirecTV and Dish Network (see Figure 8.2). Some Internet services also use satellites to provide Internet access to areas where other high-speed connection technologies are not available.

satellite A data transmitter/receiver in geosynchronous orbit with the Earth.

© iStockphoto.com/Petrovich9

Figure 8.2 Satellites can be used for broadband communications.

Cell Phone Networks

Cellular telephone companies have their own data networks, using a combination of satellites, cables, and on-ground towers with transmitters and receivers on them. Calls connect to the cell tower that is closest to the phone's current location, and that cell tower then taps into the larger telecommunications network via satellites and cables.

Some cell phone networks can also be used to access the Internet (see Figure 8.3). You can access the Internet on a smartphone (a cell phone that includes computer functionality), and you can tether (connect) a smartphone to a computer and use the phone as a modem to allow the computer Internet access.

smartphone A cellular phone that includes computer applications and Internet access capability.

tether To connect a smartphone to a computer so that the computer can use the smartphone's Internet access.

© iStockphoto.com/amete

Figure 8.3 Cell phone networks can carry both voice and data.

© iStockphoto.com/a_Taiga

Tethering a Computer to a Smartphone for Internet Access

Put It to Work

If your phone has Internet access, you can probably share its Internet access with a notebook or tablet computer. The exact steps depend on you phone's operating system. On an iPhone, the feature is called Personal Hotspot. On a Windows Phone, it's called Internet sharing. On Android, it's called Tethering & Portable Hotspot. Check out your phone now and see whether that feature is available. It's not cost-effective as a long-term Internet access solution, but it works great when you don't have other access available, such as in a car or boat.

Quick Review

1. How does a circuit-switched network differ from a packet-switched network?
2. What is an ISP?
3. What is the benefit of creating a VPN as opposed to sending data directly over the Internet?

Ways of Classifying Networks

As you learned in the previous section, the world is full of networks of various types. Most of the rest of this chapter, however, focuses specifically on networks that help personal and business computers connect with one another.

There are several ways to classify computer networks. You can look at them according to their geographical scope, the way the network is physically laid out, the way data travels through the network, and whether the network is wired (that is, connected with cables) or wireless. In the following sections, you will look at networks in several of these ways.

Geographical Range

One way to classify networks is according to the geographical range that they cover, from a few feet within a single person's office to a huge area that covers multiple countries or even multiple continents. Figure 8.4 provides a graphical explanation of some of these ranges.

Figure 8.4 The geographical range of linked devices determines the type of network that connects them.

Personal Area Networks

personal area network (PAN) A network formed when devices are connected to an individual computer.

A personal area network (PAN) consists of devices that directly connect to a single computer. For example, if you are showing a presentation in a conference room during a business meeting, you might connect your notebook PC to the projector in the room. You might also form a PAN by connecting your smartphone to your computer.

Local Area Networks

local area network (LAN) A network that connects devices housed in the same physical location.

A local area network (LAN) is a network in which all the devices are located within the same physical location, such as a single building or a group of adjacent buildings. A key characteristic of a LAN is that it is contained within a relatively small area. For example, your home network is a LAN, and so is the network at your school.

Metropolitan Area Networks

metropolitan area network (MAN) A network that connects devices within the area of a city or town.

A metropolitan area network (MAN) is a network that spans an entire town or city—or, as the name implies, a metropolitan area that might span a major city and its suburbs. A city might invest in a network infrastructure, for example, and then businesses and individuals within that area might sign up to use the network.

Wide Area Networks

wide area network (WAN) A network that spans at least two geographical locations; a business with two or more offices may have a LAN at each site but use a WAN to connect them all to the same network.

A wide area network (WAN) is a geographically dispersed network, usually consisting of at least two LANs connected together by an external link. A business or college with multiple separate campuses might link all the individual LANs together to form a WAN, for example. A WAN is not necessarily managed by a single organization and may include architecture and communications hardware from several different service providers. In this sense, the Internet is a form of global WAN.

Peer-to-Peer and Client/Server Networks

peer-to-peer (P2P) network A network that consists only of clients (no servers).

Another way to classify networks is to look at whether or not a server is involved in their management. As you learned in Chapter 1, "Computer Basics," a *server* is a computer that is dedicated to providing network and sharing services to the other computers on the network. Very small networks (10 computers or fewer) can get by without a server by operating as a peer-to-peer (P2P) network, also called a *workgroup*. In a P2P network, each computer shares in the administrative burden of maintaining the network, as shown in Figure 8.5. Each computer is responsible for authenticating other users who want to share its resources (files and printers) and for making those resources available. A P2P network slows down each computer slightly because of the overhead involved in the network. It is not usually noticeable with just a few computers, but the more computers there are, the greater the slowdown.

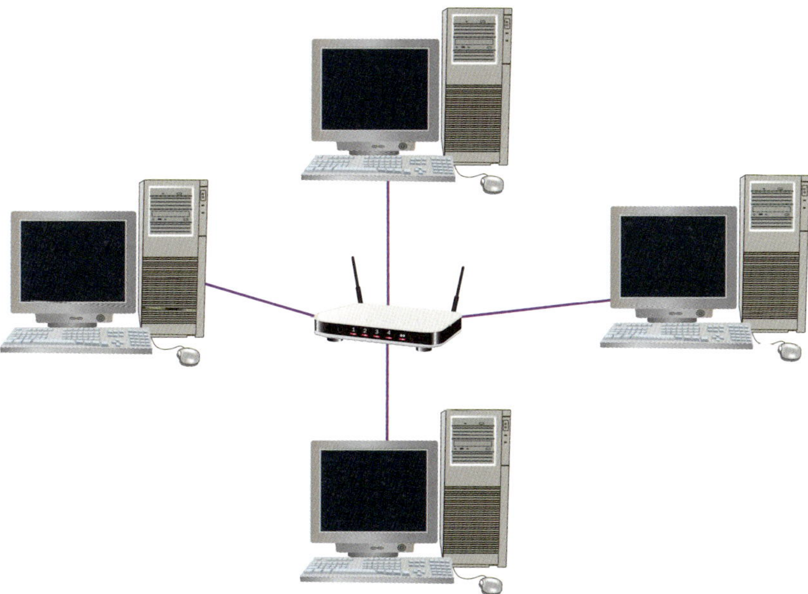

Figure 8.5 Every computer shares administrative responsibilities on peer-to-peer networks, which have no servers.

For larger networks, a client/server model is more effective. A **client/server network**, such as the one shown in Figure 8.6, is a network that consists of one or more servers plus one or more **clients**—that is, computers with which individuals run applications. Client/server networks can be any size and can have multiple servers. Each server may perform a different type of network task, such as a file server or a print server. Each server may also serve a subset of the total pool of clients.

client/server network A network that contains one or more servers.

client A computer used by an individual to run applications.

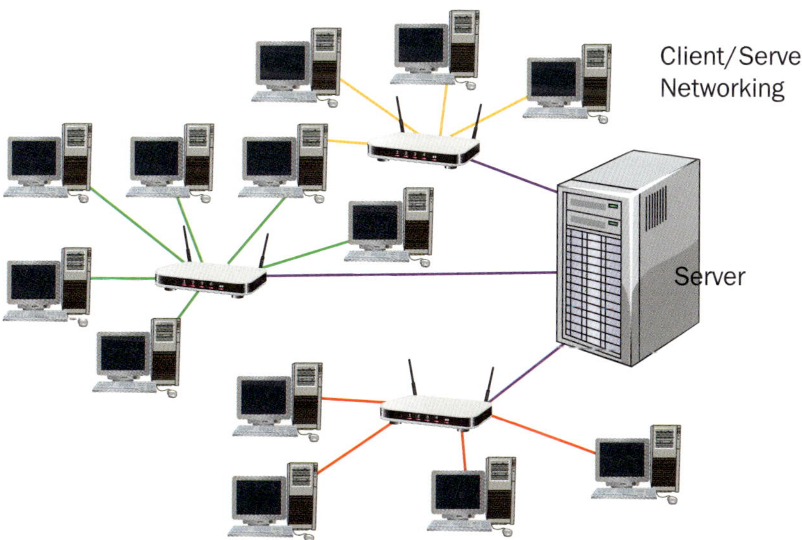

Figure 8.6 Client/server networks have one or more servers through which multiple computers can perform various tasks.

Intranets and Extranets

intranet A special network that only staff within the company network can access. For security reasons, an intranet can only be accessed onsite and not remotely.

Some organizations have a part of the network that can only be accessed from within the organization. This sub-network is known as an intranet. The network administrator may enable intranet users to share message board items, link to external web pages, and comment on photos or news items that are posted. The intranet cannot be accessed by anyone outside the organization and can't be accessed when staff are not physically located in the office unless they are given specific permission for remote access.

extranet A special network set up by a business for its customers, staff, and business partners to access from outside the office network; may be used to share marketing assets and other non-sensitive items.

In contrast, a company may maintain an extranet, a separate network that is specifically intended for people outside the organization. An extranet may be used by the company's business partners, contract employees, or customers to get real-time information, such as about products it supplies that might soon need restocking.

Ethernet

Ethernet The current dominant standard for local area networking devices.

Over the years since networking began, there have been several popular networking technologies—that is, different sets of standards for networking hardware and software. All of those technologies have become obsolete except Ethernet. Most network hardware that you buy in stores today can be assumed to be Ethernet-compatible unless it specifies otherwise.

Ethernet can technically be either wired or wireless, but it is becoming increasingly common to refer to only the wired type as Ethernet; wireless Ethernet is popularly called **Wi-Fi**. (See the following section for more information about Wi-Fi.)

Wireless Networking Technologies

A network can connect devices using either wired or wireless connections. A wired connection runs a cable between the points, whereas wireless connects the two points via radio frequency (RF) or infrared.

Wireless communications have two main uses. The first use is at the endpoints of network connectivity, where a device such as a smartphone or laptop computer connects wirelessly to a router or other device that provides network and/or Internet access. The second use is as a source of transferring data between locations when using cables is not practical, such as with satellite and microwave systems.

NOTE A single network can contain a mixture of wired and wireless connections, as long as they are the same network technology. For example, if you have a router in your home through which all the computers share an Internet connection, some of the computers can connect to it with wired Ethernet and others can connect to it via Wi-Fi. Because they all share a common network technology (Ethernet), they work together seamlessly. However, networks using different technologies cannot communicate with one another. For example, you can't use a Bluetooth device to connect to an Ethernet network.

Wi-Fi

Wi-Fi is short for wireless fidelity. It's the common name for the wireless networking technology that's used for almost all home and business networks today, often referred to by its standard number: IEEE 802.11. Whenever you use wireless networking to access the Internet at your home or workplace or in a public location such as a cafe or library, you are using Wi-Fi.

Wi-Fi (Wireless Ethernet) A means of connecting computers and other devices wirelessly. Another name for it is IEEE 802.11, its technical standard.

NOTE

IEEE is the Institute of Electrical and Electronics Engineers. It publishes the standards for many different technologies. IEEE 802.11 is the standard that governs Wi-Fi, but there are also many other standards. For example, 1394 is the standard for FireWire, and 802.15 is the standard for Bluetooth (although nobody calls Bluetooth by its standard number).

There have been different versions of the Wi-Fi standard since its original development. The popular version today is 802.11n, which can carry up to 600 Mbps of data over a range of up to 230 feet indoors or 840 feet outdoors. An update to it called 802.11ac has recently been approved; it may already be incorporated into networking devices you can buy in stores by the time you read this. 802.11ac has a maximum throughput of 1.3 Gbps, more than doubling the capacity of 802.11n. Table 8.1 lists the different Wi-Fi standards and their speeds and distances.

Table 8.1 Wi-Fi Standards

Standard	Distance (indoors/outdoors)	Speed
802.11a	115 feet / 390 feet	54 Mbps
802.11b	115 feet / 390 feet	11 Mbps
802.11g	125 feet / 460 feet	54 Mbps
802.11n	230 feet / 860 feet	Up to 600 Mbps
802.11ac	230 feet / 860 feet	Up to 1.3 Gbps

Bluetooth

Bluetooth is a wireless technology used to connect individual devices to one another in close proximity. It is most commonly used to connect a computer to an input or output device. For example, you might have a Bluetooth headphone that you use with your smartphone, or you might have a Bluetooth-enabled printer that you can use with your notebook PC. A personal area network (PAN) forms when the devices are within range of each other and they are paired (by using software to authenticate them to one another). When the devices are no longer in range of one another, the PAN stops. Bluetooth is limited to about 20 feet in range, so it isn't a practical technology to use for wireless networking in general (such as to share an Internet connection with computers all over a home or office).

Bluetooth An inexpensive short-range networking technology used for computer-to-device connections such as computer-to-printer or phone-to-headset

pair To connect a Bluetooth input or output device to a computer.

Put It to Work

Pairing Bluetooth Devices

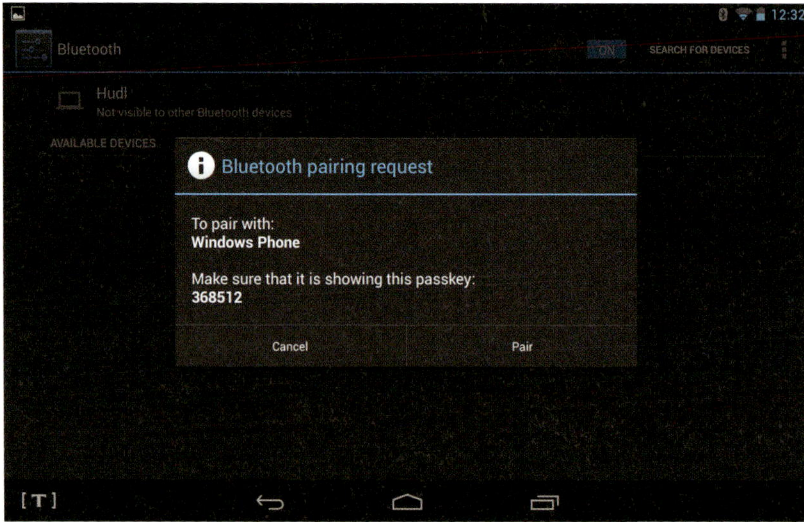

To connect devices via Bluetooth, you must pair them. Pairing can take several different forms, depending on the devices. For example, one device might generate a PIN code, and the other one might prompt you to type that PIN code to confirm. Obviously, that works only if both devices have a display screen on which a PIN code could display. For a device without a display, such as a Bluetooth mouse, the device will have a button you can press to make it temporarily discoverable. Press the button (you may have to hold it for a few seconds), following the directions in the device's documentation to make it discoverable, and then select it on the screen of the device with which you want to pair it. In Windows, you can access the Bluetooth controls via the Control Panel.

Infrared

infrared Older type of wireless communication that used light waves to pass simple information between nearby devices.

Infrared technology uses light waves to "beam" information from device to device. Infrared was the method of choice for connecting wireless peripherals a decade or so ago, but Bluetooth has mainly superseded it today. However, infrared is still used for most remote controls for TVs and other home theater components. The main drawback of infrared transmission is that it must have a clear line of sight between the two points. The standard for an infrared connection is IrDA (short for Infrared Data Association, the organization that created and manages the standard).

Microwave

microwave communication system A secure, point-to-point wireless networking technology that requires a line of sight between the two points.

Microwaves are high-frequency radio waves. A **microwave communication system** allows two locations to be wirelessly connected by using a high-frequency communication band, much higher than that used for Wi-Fi or Bluetooth. The points can be miles apart (up to about 25 miles), but as long as there are no visible obstructions between them, they can exchange data. Because line of sight is so critical for microwave communications, the transmitters are often placed high up on towers or buildings. Microwave technology is not as widely used today as it was prior to the development of satellite networking systems, but it still has some special uses; for example, military forces use it to quickly set up communications in areas where the terrain is too rugged to support wired connections and security is critical. (A point-to-point microwave connection is more secure than a connection that goes through a satellite.)

Quick Review

1. What is the difference between a LAN and a WAN?
2. Name three different wireless networking technologies.
3. What is a client/server network?

Network Hardware

Network connectivity requires both hardware and software. The software portion is handled by the operating system; all modern operating systems include network support. However, not all computers include networking hardware, and some network hardware is independent of any one computer, so you may at some point find yourself shopping for networking hardware. In the following sections, you will learn about several common network hardware devices.

Network Installer

Careers in IT

© iStockphoto.com/805promo

Technicians who install networks have an active work environment. Rather than sitting at a desk all day, as most IT professionals do, installers are out crawling around in the attics and basements of buildings, running cables and mounting satellite dishes. They set up closets with stacks of switches and routers in them, configure network security settings, and make sure all network hardware is installed correctly and functioning well. To install networks, you should have at least a high school diploma, plus a technical certification such as CompTIA Network+. To learn more about Network+ certification, see `http://certification.comptia.org/getCertified/certifications/network.aspx`.

Network Adapters

Each network client device (computer, tablet, printer, and so on) must have a network adapter. A **network adapter** enables the computer to participate in the local area network. Most desktop and notebook computers come with a wired Ethernet adapter built in, and notebook computers almost always include a built-in wireless adapter as well.

network adapter A hardware component that enables a computer to connect to a network.

When a network adapter is not built into the motherboard, but instead installed as an expansion board, it is called a **network interface card (NIC)**. Although it is not technically accurate, the term NIC (pronounced "nick") has come to refer to any network adapter, not just an add-on card. Most portable computers (notebooks, tablets, smartphones) have a Wi-Fi network adapter built in. A portable device may also have other built-in network adapters, such as a Bluetooth adapter.

network interface card (NIC) A network adapter that is on an expansion card, rather than built into the computer's motherboard. Sometimes used informally to refer to any network adapter.

You can configure a device's network adapter via the Settings or Control Panel in the operating system. You can turn the various wireless adapters on or off on a tablet or smartphone, for instance. Many people choose to keep Bluetooth and Wi-Fi turned off to save battery life when those adapters are not being used.

Step by Step

Checking Device Manager for Network Devices

Not sure what network adapters are installed on your PC? Follow these steps to find out:

1. In Windows, click Start and click Control Panel.
2. Click Hardware and Sound.
3. Click Device Manager. The Device Manager window opens.
4. Click the arrow to the left of Network Adapters to expand that category. The available network adapters appear. Four network adapters are shown here. You can deduce from their names what kind of networks they support.
5. Double-click the network adapter with Ethernet in its name. Its Properties dialog box appears.
6. Click each of the tabs in the dialog box to review its settings and then click Cancel.
7. Close the Device Manager window, and close the Control Panel window.

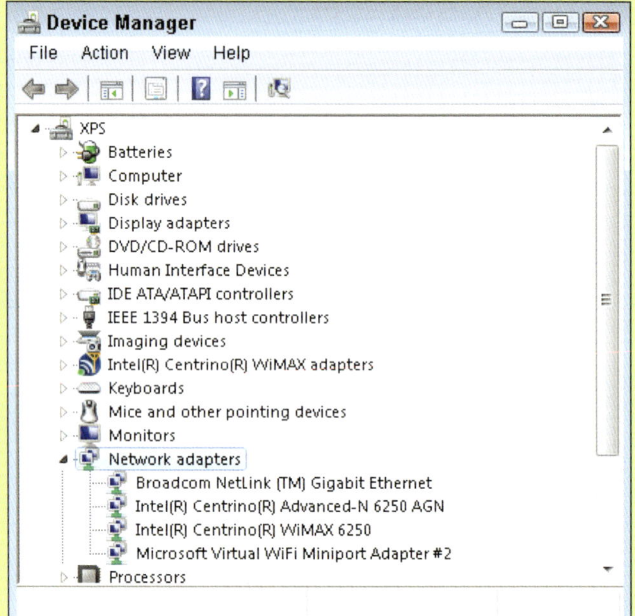

media access control (MAC) address A unique hardware address for a network adapter.

Each network adapter has a hardware address, called a media access control (MAC) address, that is unique in all the world. The MAC address is separate from the network-specific address, such as the IP address (covered in Chapter 10, "Web Basics").

Switches and Hubs

switch A gathering point for the computers in a LAN to connect with to participate in the network.

wireless access point (WAP) A wireless switch.

A switch is a box that provides a central gathering point for all the computers in an Ethernet LAN. Each computer's network adapter connects to the switch, either via a cable or wirelessly. (Bluetooth and infrared wireless networks don't use switches because they only connect individual devices to one another, not groups of devices.) The switch manages the data traffic between the devices. A wireless switch is called a wireless access point (WAP).

An earlier version of a switch, called a hub, was not so intelligent. Rather than sending the message only to the correct port, it would send all traffic to all ports and rely on each computer to ignore anything that wasn't addressed to it.

hub A primitive version of a switch that lacks the capability to read packet addresses and route them to the appropriate port.

Routers

A router performs all the same functions as a switch, but it also has an added bonus: It can direct traffic into and out of the LAN. For example, suppose you have two separate groups of computers, each group connected to its own switch, and you want their computers to be able to communicate with one another. If you use a router instead of a switch for each group, the routers will be able to transfer data packets that belong to the other group.

router A connection box for Ethernet networks that physically joins the devices in the network (wired) or provides wireless connectivity (wireless), and enables a connection to an outside network such as the Internet.

Routers serve an important role in home networks because they enable multiple computers to share a single Internet connection. The broadband modem connects to the router's output port, and the router directs all Internet requests from each of the computers to that port. When data comes in from the Internet, the router directs it to the computer that requested it. The type of router used for this purpose is sometimes called a broadband router. A broadband router can be wired or wireless.

Repeaters

A repeater does just what the name implies—it repeats a network signal. As network traffic travels a long distance, the signal weakens and errors may be introduced. A repeater reads the incoming data and then rebroadcasts it.

repeater A device that receives and retransmits a network signal.

Network Cables

Wired communication media consists mainly of various types of cables. Data can be carried efficiently and reliably through cables, and some cables can carry data at very high speeds. Here are the most common types of network cables you may encounter.

- Twisted-pair cable gets its name from the pairs of copper wires inside the cable. Most of the Ethernet cables in business and residential buildings are twisted-pair cable. The wires twisting around each other help reduce electromagnetic interference (EMI) caused by the magnetic field generated when electricity passes through the cable.
- Most twisted-pair cable is unshielded-twisted pair (UTP). Shielding is an optional copper mesh in the lining of a cable that cuts down on EMI getting through to the cable from external sources. Shielded-twisted pair (STP) contains this extra lining, and is used in environments where EMI is a problem, such as in cables run through ceilings with fluorescent light fixtures in them.

twisted-pair cable Cable that transfers data via pairs of copper wires that are twisted around each other to reduce electromagnetic interference.

electromagnetic interference (EMI) The corruption of data as it is passing through a cable due to the magnetic field generated by a nearby cable.

unshielded twisted pair (UTP) A type of twisted-pair cable that does not have an outer sheath that protects against external EMI.

shielded twisted pair (STP) A type of twisted-pair cable that has an outer sheath that protects against external EMI.

coaxial cable Cable that consists of a solid copper core with an insulated sleeve around it.

- **Coaxial cable** is the type of cable used for cable TV connections; if you have cable Internet, it's the cable that runs from the wall to your cable modem. Like twisted-pair cable, it carries data in electrical signals. It's a more expensive cable than twisted pair, but it can carry much more data and at faster speeds. Coaxial cable consists of a single copper wire in the center, surrounded by insulation, with a plastic jacket on the outside. See Figure 8.7. Coaxial cable is not normally used for networking within a building anymore, although some older, now-obsolete forms of networking used it.

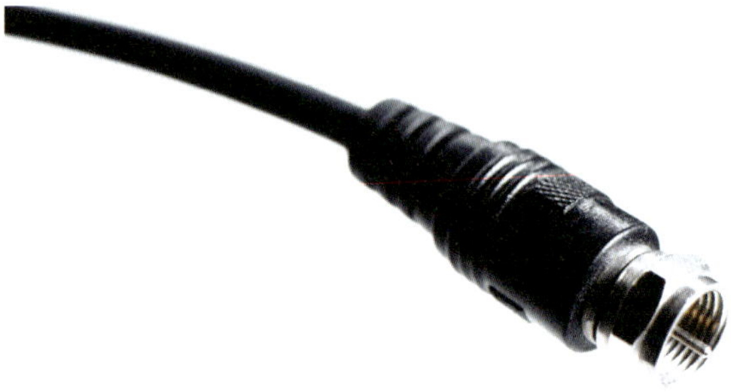

Figure 8.7 A coaxial cable has a solid copper core in the center, surrounded by insulation.

fiber optic cable Cable that carries data using light pulses through a bundle of glass fibers.

- **Fiber optic cable** carries data in pulses of light along a glass fiber (see Figure 8.8). Each fiber is very tiny—about the thickness of a human hair. Each cable contains hundreds of fibers, and can carry billions of bits per second. Fiber optic cable is often used as the backbone (the central part) of a network, to move large amounts of data between points on the Internet. It's reliable, fast, and very hard to snoop or hack into, making the connection very secure. Fiber optic cable isn't widely used at the consumer level, though, because it is expensive and difficult to install and maintain. It's also not compatible with most consumer-level networking equipment.

Figure 8.8 A fiber optic cable contains multiple thin strands of glass fiber.

Quick Review

1. How is a router different from a switch?
2. What kind of cable should you buy for an Ethernet network?
3. Name two advantages of fiber optic cable over other types.

Understanding and Connecting to the Internet

The Internet began as a way of enabling research institutions and the military to share information. Today, however, it is the largest and most-used network in the world, and it is used not only by schools and governments but by businesses, non-profit organizations, and individuals in every country and of every profession. You can use the Internet to look up information on the web, send and receive email, exchange instant messages, upload and download files, and much more. You will learn more about the uses of the Internet in Chapter 9, "Online Communication," and Chapter 10, "Web Basics."

Internet Structure

Structurally, the Internet is a mesh of routers and servers connected to one another at multiple points, as illustrated in Figure 8.9. This makes the Internet very fault-tolerant. If any single router or server goes down, network traffic is simply routed around the point of failure.

Figure 8.9 A mesh network does not rely on any one point being active; traffic can easily route around any blockages.

Internet Speed

The Internet itself does not have a fixed speed. Data travels through the Internet as fast as it can go on whatever cable it travels through, and a single data packet may travel at different speeds during different parts of its journey. At the heart of the Internet are high-capacity, high-speed data pathways that are like superhighways for data. These pathways form the Internet's **backbone**. The backbone is made up mainly of fiber optic cables that can carry data very fast—literally at the speed of light! Large ISPs have entire buildings full of servers that are connected directly to the Internet off of this main backbone. From the ISP's servers to the individual neighborhoods and individual homes and businesses, the connection speeds are lower because the cheaper copper-based cables used in those areas carry data at a lower rate. Some ISPs charge different prices

backbone The central connection pathways of a network, where connection speeds are high and the data pathway is wide.

for different speeds of Internet connection, and they throttle the connection speed (usually at the broadband modem) for customers who have signed up for a slower connection.

The Internet service that you subscribe to has two speeds, both measured in megabytes per second (Mbps). The first is its theoretical maximum speed, which is what your ISP tells you that it is delivering under optimal conditions. The second is your actual speed, which will be lower.

Put It to Work

Testing Your Internet Connection Speed

How fast is your connection? To find out, use an online speed test. Open your web browser and go to a site that offers free testing. You can search for a free testing site, or try one of these:

- `http://speedtest.comcast.net`
- `www.cnet.com/internet-speed-test`
- `www.dslreports.com/speedtest?flash=1`

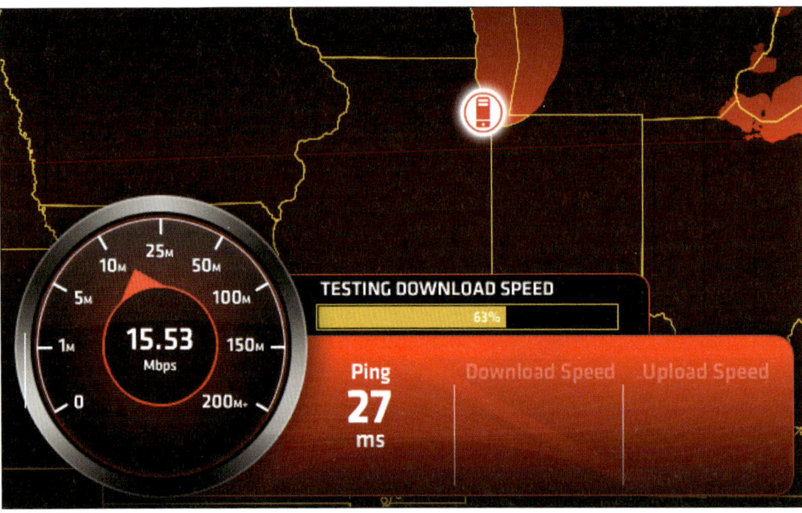

Types of Internet Connections

When choosing Internet service for your home or business, there are a variety of factors to consider. Speed is important, of course—faster is better. However, faster may also be more expensive. It's also important to look at availability, and evaluate any package deals you may be able to get with other services such as cable TV or phone service.

In the following sections, you'll learn about the major types of Internet connections available to consumers today. All of these types except dial-up are always-on **broadband** connections. The word broadband literally means *wide path*, but when referring to Internet connectivity it refers to a connection with a speed higher than 256 Kbps. Many of today's broadband Internet options are much faster than that.

broadband A fast, always-on network connection.

Dial-Up Internet

In the early days of the Internet, dial-up access was all that was available. A dial-up connection uses a telephone line to connect to an ISP at a maximum speed of around 44.8 Kbps. Dial-up connections have many drawbacks. You cannot use the phone line for telephone calls while you are connected to the Internet, and the Internet connection is not always on; you must connect to the Internet when you want to use it, and then disconnect when you are finished. The speed is very slow (less than 1/100th of a more modern connection, on the average), resulting in frustrating waits for every operation. A dial-up connection is established using a **dial-up modem**.

dial-up modem A device that converts between analog and digital data so computer data can be sent over analog phone lines.

Cable Internet

At the other end of the speed spectrum from dial-up is cable Internet access. Cable is currently the fastest type of commercially available Internet access for residential customers, theoretically delivering top speeds of up to 30 Mbps (although most connections top out at around 20 Mbps).

Cable Internet is delivered through the same coaxial cable as the cable TV programming. You connect a splitter to the cable coming in from the wall, to allow the cable to go to both your TV and to a **cable modem** (which may be provided by the cable company for a monthly lease fee).

cable modem A broadband modem designed to work with a cable Internet connection.

You can also optionally share the Internet connection with other computers in your home or office by using a broadband router. Some cable modems are dual-purpose units, with a router built in. If you have one of these, you do not need a separate router.

DSL Internet

Digital subscriber line (DSL) is a high-speed Internet connection from your local land-based telephone company. DSL uses the same twisted-pair cable to provide Internet that it does to provide voice service, with a splitter used to separate the data and voice signals so you can use them both at once. This type of DSL has a speed ranging from 256 Kbps to 20 Mbps depending on the distance between the service address and the phone company's connection box. It can also deliver high-definition TV and phone service, all on a single line.

digital subscriber line (DSL) A broadband Internet technology provided by the telephone company.

Satellite Internet

Satellite Internet service uses the same communication satellites that you learned about earlier in this chapter. Satellite Internet service involves using a satellite dish for receiving and a satellite transmitter for sending data.

satellite Internet A broadband Internet technology that uses satellites and a transmitter/receiver to provide Internet access.

Satellite service is not likely to be anyone's first choice as a broadband Internet connection. It is relatively slow (around 1 Mbps), and suffers from significant **latency** (delay) issues that make it unsuitable for performance-sensitive online activities like videoconferencing and playing action-based games. However, satellite is available just about anywhere. When faced with the choice of dial-up modem connection or satellite, people who need a broadband connection will go with satellite.

latency A period of waiting for another component to deliver data needed to proceed.

Internet over Cell Phone Networks

Modern cell phone network providers such as Verizon and AT&T not only offer telephone service, but also Internet service. This service is mainly offered to be used to access the Internet via smartphones, but it can also be used to connect other devices as well, such as tablets, notebooks, and even desktops to get Internet access in situations where Wi-Fi and other Internet connection methods are not available, such as when riding in an automobile.

3G Digital technology for moving data through a cell phone network at up to 14 Mbps.

4G Digital technology for moving data through a cell phone network at up to 100 Mbps.

Not all areas of cell phone networks worldwide have the appropriate technology and speed to access the Internet. There have been many different cell phone standards and technologies over the years, and it has only been recently, with the development of 3G, that cell phone networks have become fast enough to support Internet use. **3G**, which stands for 3rd Generation, supports download speeds of up to 14 Mbps. An even newer and faster technology, **4G**, can support up to 100 Mbps downloads. Cell phone companies provide coverage maps that show the areas in which they provide 3G or 4G service.

CAUTION If your cell phone data plan is not unlimited, be aware of how much you are using the Internet via your cell phone, to avoid extra charges for going over your data limit. Your cell phone provider may have a website or a phone utility that enables you to see how much data you have used on the current billing cycle.

Quick Review

1. What are the drawbacks of using a dial-up modem?
2. Name three factors that may potentially affect the actual performance of an Internet connection.
3. Which Internet connection technologies offer the fastest service?

Summary

Our Connected World: Communication Systems

Networking is everywhere. A computer network is a **packet-switched network**, which sends and receives data in packets that may take different routes to the destination.

The **Internet** is the world's largest network. It uses various standard **protocols**, so that services like the web and email work the same everywhere. Most companies don't connect directly to the Internet; instead they connect to an **Internet service provider (ISP)**.

The Internet is based on a **protocol stack** (a set of protocols) called **Transmission Control Protocol / Internet Protocol (TCP/IP)**. TCP/IP provides a common set of standards by which data can be sent and received. It is used not only on the Internet, but in most private networks today as well.

To tighten security when using the Internet as a conduit, many companies use a software technology called **virtual private networking (VPN)**. VPN technology creates a secure, tamper-resistant data tunnel between two points on the Internet.

A **satellite** is a transmitter/receiver unit that orbits the Earth, thousands of miles up. Satellite networks are used to deliver services such as TV and video broadcasts, satellite radio, and satellite Internet service. Cellular telephone companies have their own data networks, using a combination of satellites, cables, and on-ground towers with transmitters and receivers on them. Some cell phone networks can also be used to access the Internet. You can access the Internet on a **smartphone** (a cell phone that includes computer functionality), and you can **tether** (connect) a smartphone to a computer and use the phone as a modem to allow the computer Internet access.

Ways of Classifying Networks

There are several ways to classify computer networks. One way is according to the geographical range that they cover: **personal area network (PAN)**, **local area network (LAN), metropolitan area network (MAN),** or **wide area network (WAN)**. Another way is to look at whether or not a server is involved. In a **peer-to-peer network**, there is no server; in a **client/server network**, there is at least one server.

An **intranet** is a network accessible only from inside a company. An **extranet** is a network that is for the use of those outside the organization.

Ethernet is the most popular Internet technology, having outlived many competitors. Ethernet can be wired or wireless; the wireless version is also called **Wi-Fi**. Ethernet devices have a certain maximum speed.

A wired connection runs a cable between the points, whereas wireless connects the two points via radio frequency (RF) or infrared. **Wi-Fi** is short for wireless fidelity. It's the common name for the wireless networking technology that's used for almost all home and business networks today, often referred to by its standard number: IEEE 802.11. **Bluetooth** is a wireless technology used to connect individual devices to one another in close proximity. It is most commonly used to connect a computer to an input or output device. When the devices are within range, they are **paired**. **Infrared** technology uses light waves to "beam" information from device to device. Infrared was the method of choice for connecting wireless peripherals a decade or so ago, but Bluetooth has mainly superseded it today. A **microwave communication system** allows two locations to be wirelessly connected by using a high-frequency communication band, much higher than that used for Wi-Fi or Bluetooth.

Network Hardware

A **network adapter** enables a computer to participate in the local area network. When a network adapter is not built into the motherboard, but instead installed as an expansion board, it is called a **network interface card (NIC)**. Each network adapter has a hardware address, called a **media access control (MAC) address**, that is unique in all the world.

A **switch** is a box that provides a central gathering point for all the computers in an Ethernet LAN. A wireless switch is called a **wireless access point (WAP)**. An earlier version of a switch, called a **hub**, was not so intelligent. A **router** performs all the same functions as a switch, but it also has an added bonus: It can direct traffic into and out of the LAN.

A **repeater** does just what the name implies—it repeats a network signal to strengthen it on its way to its destination.

Most of the Ethernet cables in business and residential buildings are **twisted-pair cable**. Most twisted-pair cable is **unshielded twisted pair (UTP)**. **Shielded twisted pair (STP)** contains this extra lining. **Coaxial cable** is the type of cable used for cable TV connections. It is also used for some networking, such as delivering cable Internet to a home. **Fiber optic cable** carries data in pulses of light along a glass fiber.

Understanding and Connecting to the Internet

The Internet began as a way of enabling research institutions and the military to share information. Structurally, the Internet is a mesh of routers and servers connected to one another at multiple points.

At the heart of the Internet are high-capacity, high-speed data pathways that are like superhighways for data. These pathways form the Internet's **backbone**.

Types of Internet connections include dial-up and broadband. A dial-up connection is established using a **dial-up modem**. It is a very slow and inconvenient connection. Broadband connections are usually always on. Types of broadband connections include **cable modem**, **digital subscriber line (DSL)**, **satellite Internet**, and cell phone networks.

Key Terms

3G
4G
backbone
Bluetooth
broadband
cable modem
circuit-switched network
client
client/server network
coaxial cable
dial-up modem
digital subscriber line (DSL)
electromagnetic interference (EMI)
Ethernet
extranet
fiber optic cable
hub
infrared
Internet
Internet service provider (ISP)
intranet
latency
local area network (LAN)
media access control (MAC) address
metropolitan area network (MAN)
microwave communication system
network adapter
network interface card (NIC)
packet-switched network
pair
peer-to-peer network
personal area network (PAN)
protocol stack
protocol
repeater
router
satellite
satellite Internet

shielded twisted pair (STP)
smartphone
switch
tether
twisted-pair cable
unshielded twisted pair (UTP)
virtual private networking (VPN)
wide area network (WAN)
Wi-Fi
wireless access point (WAP)

Test Yourself

Fact Check

1. Which type of network would you use to copy a photo from your smartphone to your laptop?
   a. personal area network
   b. local area network
   c. wide area network
   d. metropolitan area network
2. The Internet is based on what protocol stack?
   a. UTP
   b. TCP/IP
   c. WPA
   d. HTML
3. What type of network creates a secure tunnel through the Internet?
   a. virtual private network
   b. Ethernet
   c. infrared
   d. Bluetooth
4. Which type of network has no servers?
   a. Ethernet
   b. P2P
   c. client/server
   d. VPN
5. What kind of network is only for the use of people within the company?
   a. P2P
   b. extranet
   c. intranet
   d. Ethernet
6. Which of these is *not* a type of wireless networking?
   a. 802.11
   b. microwave
   c. Bluetooth
   d. bridge

7. In what type of device would a wireless network adapter be found?
   a. notebook computer
   b. keyboard
   c. mouse
   d. monitor
8. Every NIC has a unique ______.
   a. router
   b. access point
   c. MAC address
   d. server name
9. Data packets travel on the Internet through a mesh of
   a. switches
   b. routers
   c. hubs
   d. modems
10. DSL Internet service is provided through
   a. telephone lines
   b. cable TV lines
   c. wireless Ethernet
   d. satellites

Matching

Match the term to its description.

a. modem
b. NIC
c. hub
d. repeater
e. router
f. switch

1. ________A gathering point for network connections that is unable to route any packets.
2. ________A gathering point for network connections that can route packets only to devices directly connected to it.
3. ________A gathering point for network connections that can route packets out of the local network, such as to the Internet.
4. ________A network device that strengthens and rebroadcasts a signal.
5. ________A device that connects to your ISP to provide Internet service.
6. ________The network adapter in an individual computer

Sum It Up

1. List three types of wireless connection.
2. How do a switch and a router differ?
3. Explain the difference between STP and UTP cable.
4. What is TCP/IP?
5. List four ways to connect to the Internet.
6. Why is satellite Internet not more popular?

Explore More

Finding a Fast Internet Connection

Suppose a neighbor wanted to know what the best Internet connection available in your neighborhood is. Use the Internet to research this topic, and find the fastest service available at your home address. Collect all the information you can about this service, including:

- What company is providing it?
- What is the advertised speed of the connection?
- What connection technology does it use?
- How much does it cost per month?
- Are there any start-up costs involved?

Think It Over

Virtual Private Networking

With a VPN, a company can use the Internet to establish a secure communication channel between two points without going to the expense of leasing a data line. There are some people who say that it's unfair, though, that large companies can use so much bandwidth, making the whole Internet run slower for everyone else, without paying for it. Do you agree? Do you think companies that transfer a large amount of data on an everyday basis should pay more, or should be forced to lease their own lines?

Metropolitan Area Networks

Suppose you are the mayor of a small town, and it has been suggested that the town install a metropolitan area network that will provide low-cost, high-speed Wi-Fi to all citizens who want it. Proponents say that it will encourage people to move to the town and will encourage highly educated young adults to stay in town instead of moving away. Opponents argue that the town will go into debt paying for such a system with no guarantee that enough people will sign up for the service to make it pay for itself. What questions would you want answered in order to help you make up your mind?

Chapter 9

Online Communication

Learning objectives

- Understand the channels available for Internet communications
- Recognize the features of the different communication types
- Choose the correct communication medium for a particular situation
- Understand appropriate etiquette for online communication
- Understand the basic features of email programs and how to use them

The way we communicate with friends and business associates has changed dramatically in the last decade, thanks to the Internet. Our communication channels are increasingly shifting toward computer-assisted technologies, many of which are not only more immediate but also less expensive to use than the non-computerized alternatives. For example, a business can save a great deal of money by sending its advertisements to customers by email rather than postal mail, and by meeting with clients through videoconferencing rather than having employees travel to the client site, and families can keep in touch using video chat services, as in Figure 9.1.

With all these new technologies for communication available, though, it can be a challenge to select the appropriate communication medium for a situation. In addition, each new form of communication comes with its own social conventions about the type of language to use, the format messages should take, and the appropriate level of formality. Whether or not you conform to these communication rules directly affects how well your message is received.

In this chapter, we will review the many different types of computer-assisted communication technologies available in today's world. You'll learn about their pros and cons and accepted uses, and you'll learn some of the etiquette rules and customs that will enable you to get your message across effectively.

© iStockphoto.com/arekmalang

Figure 9.1 The Internet has changed the way people communicate by offering technologies such as video chatting, email, and instant messaging.

Internet Communication Types

The Internet in its original form was for the transfer of data between computers over a network. Email was one of the first Internet applications and is one of the most popular means of communication. Many more ways of communicating online are now available, including:

- Instant messaging
- Social networking
- Blogs and microblogs
- Newsgroups
- Forums
- Voice over IP (VoIP)
- Video chat/videoconferencing

Many of these communication options require little more than a web connection and a username and password for the particular service. This chapter explains how some of these systems work and helps you choose appropriate communications tools.

Email

email A computer-based system for exchanging messages through mail servers.

Email (short for electronic mail) is the computer equivalent of postal mail. Billions of email messages are exchanged every day through a worldwide system of email servers.

store-and-forward A message delivery system in which messages are forwarded between servers and then stored on those servers until they are picked up.

mail server An online server that sends and/or receives email messages on behalf of the email addresses it supports.

Email is a store-and-forward system, as shown in Figure 9.2, not an instant communication medium. When you compose and send an email, your provider's outgoing mail server forwards it to the recipient's incoming mail server. The message is stored there until the recipient logs in and picks it up. Each ISP or organization that provides email service has its own mail servers that participate in this global network for mail delivery. To access your messages on your incoming mail server, you can use a mail client (email software installed on your computer) or you can log into a web-based interface maintained by your email provider.

mail client Software installed on a computer that is used to compose and manage email.

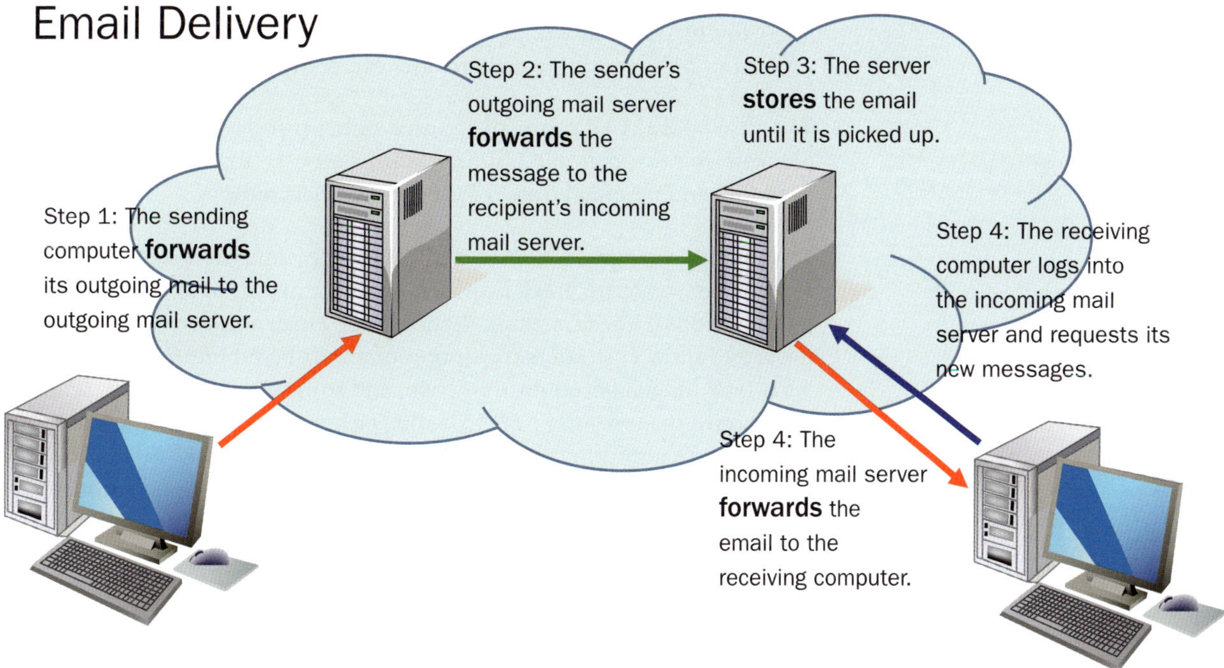

Figure 9.2 Email is a store-and-forward system involving mail servers on the Internet. Mail is forwarded from one mail server to another and then is stored until the recipient picks it up.

Most providers that offer free email services, like Google, Yahoo!, and AOL, are primarily web-based. These types of email accounts are sometimes referred to as HTTP email accounts. HTTP (Hypertext Transfer Protocol) is a protocol for web content transmission. You might be able to set up certain mail clients to work with those accounts, but it is generally expected that you will use the web interface.

HTTP email account An email account designed to be used with a web interface, and uses web technology for email management.

On the other hand, a mail client is customarily used for most email accounts that someone pays for, either directly or indirectly. For example, the email accounts at your workplace, the accounts that your ISP provides to you, and the accounts that you have through a web-hosting service (for example, if you own a domain name) are all designed to be used with a mail client.

Two kinds of email accounts are designed to be used with mail clients: a POP account and an IMAP account. Each uses a different protocol for receiving mail, and offers slightly different advantages.

POP account An email account designed to be used with an email client and uses POP protocol for receiving mail.

IMAP account An email account designed to be used with an email client and uses IMAP protocol for receiving mail.

Post Office Protocol (POP) A protocol for receiving email through a mail client.

- Post Office Protocol (POP) is a literal store-and-forward protocol. It holds the messages until you pick them up, but it doesn't maintain any direct communication with your email client. You can choose to leave the messages on the server or delete them from the server after you pick them up, but what you do with them after that point is of no concern to the server. For example, you could delete an email from your email client, and the message would continue to persist on the server. POP accounts work well for people who always work with their email from the same computer.
- Internet Mail Access Protocol (IMAP) is a modified version of store-and-forward. It continues to hold your messages even after you

Internet Mail Access Protocol (IMAP) A protocol for receiving email through a mail client.

pick them up, and anything you do in your email client is reflected on the server. For example, if you delete a message, or create a new folder for storing messages, that change is automatically reflected in the email clients of every device that you use. The drawbacks are that you may not be able to access old mail without an Internet connection and not every email provider offers IMAP accounts.

Simple Mail Transfer Protocol (SMTP) A protocol used for sending email for a POP3 email account.

The POP and IMAP protocol are used only for receiving email; a complementary protocol called **Simple Mail Transfer Protocol (SMTP)** is used for sending email from a POP or IMAP account.

The line between HTTP, POP, and IMAP accounts has become blurry in recent years, as more email providers have attempted to give customers more options without making them change email account types. Most providers allow customers the option of a web-based interface no matter what type of email account they have, and some email clients can send and receive mail from HTTP accounts, either natively or with some special setup. In addition, some free web-based email services offer customers the option of paying a small amount for an upgrade to an account that can be used as a POP or IMAP account.

Instant Messaging, Texting, and Chatting

instant messaging Sending and receiving short text messages in real-time over the Internet.

Instant messaging (IM) is another type of written message that is sent over the Internet. As its name suggests, the message is sent immediately rather than waiting for the recipient to log on to the service to retrieve his messages. In many cases, the recipient will be online at the same time as the sender and may respond immediately. The immediacy of IM makes it more like having an online chat.

push technology A technology that sends information to a recipient without the recipient asking for it each time.

pull technology A technology that sends information to a recipient only when the recipient requests it.

Instant messaging is a **push technology**. That means that the messages are pushed out to the recipient if he or she is logged in; it doesn't require the recipient to do anything to check for new messages. In contrast, email is a **pull technology**, because the recipient must actively check for messages in order to pull the new messages to his computer. (The email client can be set to automatically check for new messages at certain intervals, so the email messages may seem to be arriving on their own, but it is actually the client software pulling them.)

Instant messaging requires you to have IM client software installed for the service you are using. For example, Yahoo! Messenger's client software for Windows appears in Figure 9.3. Other instant messaging clients include AOL Instant Messenger (AIM) and Microsoft Lync (formerly known as Microsoft Office Communicator). IM client software is available for Mac, Windows, and Linux operating systems, plus several smartphone and tablet operating systems.

Some instant messaging services include voice and even video chat capabilities, as well as picture sharing. Including these features takes the applications beyond simple instant messaging, into the realm of Voice over IP (VoIP) and videoconferencing, both of which are covered later in this chapter.

Short Message Service (SMS) The text messaging technology used on cell phone networks.

texting Sending and receiving short text messages in real-time over a cell phone network.

You can also send and receive instant messages on smartphones using a technology called **Short Message Service (SMS)**, which goes through your cell phone provider's network. This type of messaging is called **texting**.

The differentiation between SMS and IM messages can get blurry because services are available that can cross the platforms. For example, some IM services offer clients for certain smartphone operating systems, and there are computer-based applications that can send and receive SMS messages. If you use one of these services, it may not be obvious how the message delivery will be billed (that is, whether the messages count as SMS messages toward your cell phone plan's text message allowance, or whether the messages use the phone's Internet data plan), so monitor your usage carefully until you are sure.

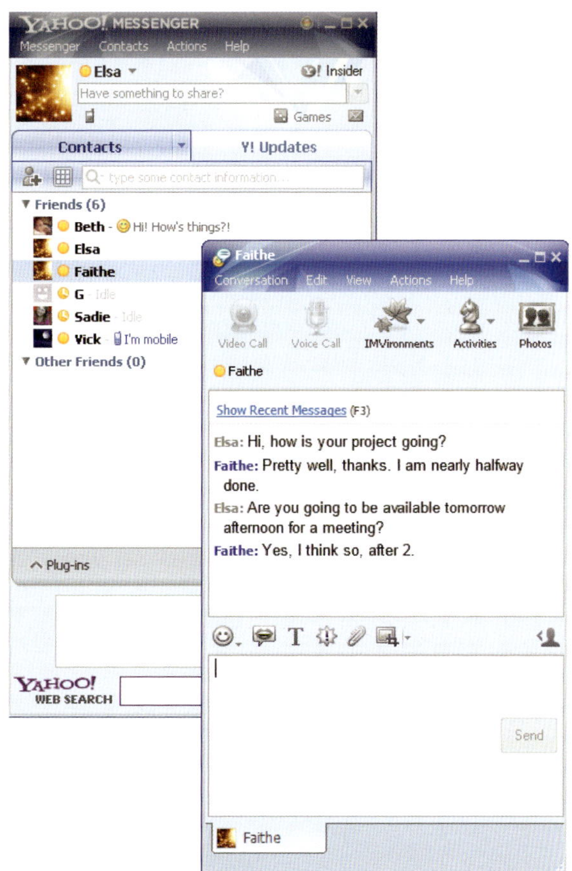

Figure 9.3 Yahoo! Messenger's client software for Windows enables you to have one-on-one text chats with others.

New Technologies

WhatsApp

Depending on your cell phone plan, you may only get a certain number of SMS text messages per month. If you find yourself running out of SMS messages each month, consider using WhatsApp Messenger, a cross-platform smartphone application that can send text messages using your phone's Internet data plan, bypassing the phone's SMS service. You are still sending text messages, but you're doing so through an Internet server, so you aren't charged per message, but only for the small amount of Internet data used. WhatsApp is available for iPhone, BlackBerry, Android, Windows Phone, and Nokia. WhatsApp was originally developed by a very small company, but was purchased by Facebook in February 2014, giving it a much broader audience and greater financial backing for future development.

Some IM clients allow group chats, but they are normally with people whom you specifically invite. In contrast, many public or semi-public **chat rooms** enable you to have group conversations with people you may not know. Many websites include chat room software on some of their web pages that anyone can log into to participate in a group chat. For example, a recovery support site for alcoholics might have a group chat every night at a certain time.

chat room An online virtual room in which you can meet and talk to other people.

The largest system of public chat rooms is **Internet Relay Chat (IRC)**, with about 400,000 users worldwide. IRC is a system of chat servers that users log into using IRC client software. The user can then select a **channel**, which is a chat room for a particular subject of discussion, and enter the channel to join the conversation.

Internet Relay Chat (IRC) An online system of public chat servers.

channel An individual chat room on a chat server such as IRC.

Social Networking

social network An Internet-based system that enables users to interact in real-time and by using messaging programs.

Social networking is an umbrella term for sites such as Facebook, Twitter, LinkedIn, and Google+, in which users can post information about themselves and create groups of people with shared interests with which to chat and exchange ideas and web links.

Each user creates a profile, which can include details about her location, job, family, and interests. Social networks grow organically by friends inviting friends who in turn invite or include their own friends. Users are able to post and comment on photos and videos published to the network, share links, send each other emails, and conduct web chats.

tag A topic or subject assigned to a social networking post. Also called a **hashtag.**

Some social networks make extensive use of **tags**. These are searchable labels that can be added to posted content allow other people to find like-minded users and join interest groups, fan pages, and more. However, these self-applied tags are also useful to marketers and enable them to target potential customers far more accurately. Information sharing and access to people's private information has thus become an important area of debate. On Twitter and some other services, tags are preceded by hash symbols (#) and are referred to as **hashtags**.

Instagram A social network for posting and sharing photos.

Vine A social network for posting and sharing video clips.

Reddit A social network for posting news snippets.

YouTube A social network for posting and sharing videos.

Facebook A social network for posting interesting updates, web links, and photos, and for chatting with friends.

Twitter A microblogging platform used to post frequent updates and to comment on events as they happen.

Some social networks are specialized. You might use **Instagram** to share photos, **Vine** for video clips, **Reddit** for news snippets, and **YouTube** for video-sharing. Other networks, such as **Facebook** and **Twitter**, are more general but allow you to cross-post updates to and from other social network sites.

One reason social networks are so successful is that they have accompanying mobile apps, so it's easy for users to post updates and read posts from their smartphones or tablets. Many apps let you log in using your existing Twitter or Facebook details. This makes for a convenient user experience and is also useful to the app developers and Facebook/Twitter as a mechanism for promotion.

Careers in IT

Social Media Marketer

A social media marketer specializes in helping companies promote themselves using social networking tools such as blogs, social networks, and microblogs, including Twitter. Their purpose is to increase public awareness of the company and its products. The role requires marketing expertise and a thorough understanding of how search tools work and how to call attention to the client companies. Using this knowledge, the social media marketing person adds keywords and hashtags to the content they create. This helps the client company's web pages appear more prominently and frequently in search results and rank higher in page rank indexes. The process of writing content in this way is known as **search engine optimization (SEO)**. Marketing and business skills and professional courses in SEO marketing are expected for such a role. A successful social media marketer will demonstrate her expertise by maintaining her own use of social networks.

search engine optimization (SEO) The process of writing web content so as to increase a page's ranking in online search results.

blog A web page containing the author's personal experiences and opinions.

post An article published on a blog.

Blogs and Microblogs

A **blog** (originally called *weblog*) is a web page where an individual or group publishes stories, essays, or articles that are generically referred to as **posts**. Blog posts differ from websites that contain news stories and marketing information in that they are personal and often opinionated in nature. Whereas a news story is objective, a blog post may put forth a point of view or an extended commentary. Some blogs are similar to personal diaries, but others are run by users with specialist knowledge of a topic they want to share with other people. A blog owner is likely to engage directly with readers who comment on the topic and follow the blog.

Popular blogs with lots of followers and comments can be highly influential in their sphere of expertise. Social media tools such as Twitter and Facebook (`www.facebook.com`) are used to promote posts and get more people to contribute to the commentary.

Companies often use blogs to share news about forthcoming product launches and ideas they are working on. A blog of this type may be part of a company's website. For example, Microsoft hosts several official blogs written by employees in various departments to let the public know informally about what its teams are working on for future products and services. Figure 9.4 shows the Extreme Windows blog, for example, found at `http://blogs.windows.com`, which highlights advanced-level technologies for Windows.

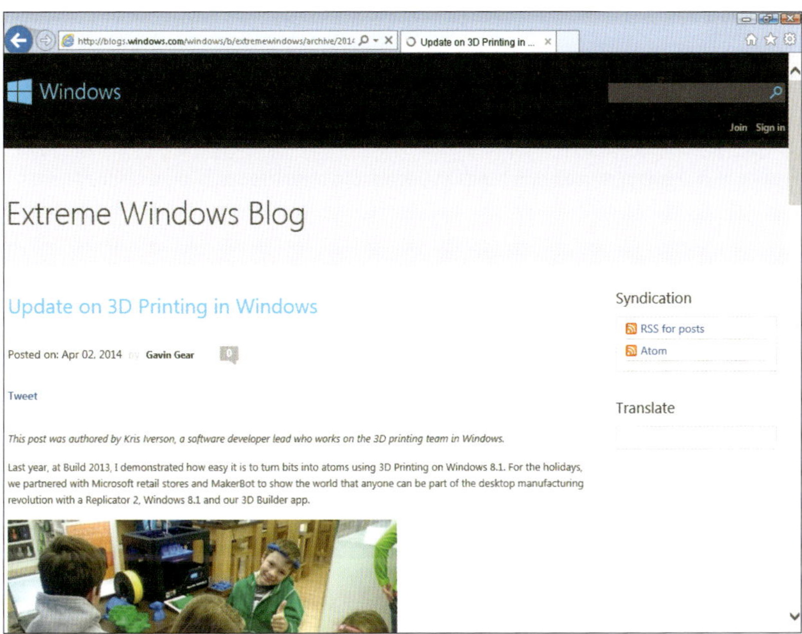

Figure 9.4 Although blogs are best known for containing individual writers' personal stories and opinions, some blogs are corporate-sponsored, like this one.

Many individual bloggers use a **blog platform**, which is a free or low-cost blog-hosting website. Some of the most widely used blog platforms are WordPress, Typepad, and Blogger. These platforms act as the web host and offer customizable design templates as part of the blog. For a small additional fee, extra features are available, such as the capability to use your own domain name.

blog platform A web server that hosts the blogs of individuals, either free or for a small fee.

Microblogging is a form of blogging that allows users to post brief text commentary or post photos and audio clips. On Twitter (the best-known microblogging platform), each post (called a "tweet") can be no longer than 140 characters. This restriction is intended to keep updates interesting and make people think about the essence of what they're trying to say. Some updates are used to link to blog posts the users have written or

microblog A service that allows the posting of short messages.

to online articles they've found interesting and want to share or discuss, as in Figure 9.5, while others serve as a means for people in the public eye to communicate with their fans.

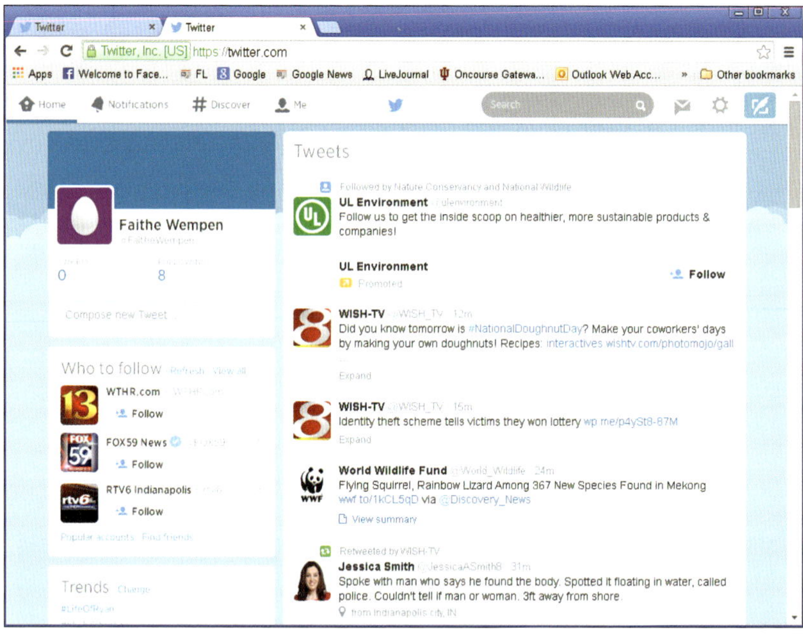

Figure 9.5 Twitter is used by all sorts of people and organizations to promote themselves and to comment on events.

Unlike email, microblogs can be seen by anyone and can be commented on by anyone, though people must usually register with the service to comment. To address a post to someone, put an @ sign in front of the username. To find a topic of interest, you can search within the blogging platform. To make a post more likely to be found, you can add a # (hashtag) indicating the topic. Figure 9.6 shows a search for items tagged "Wimbledon."

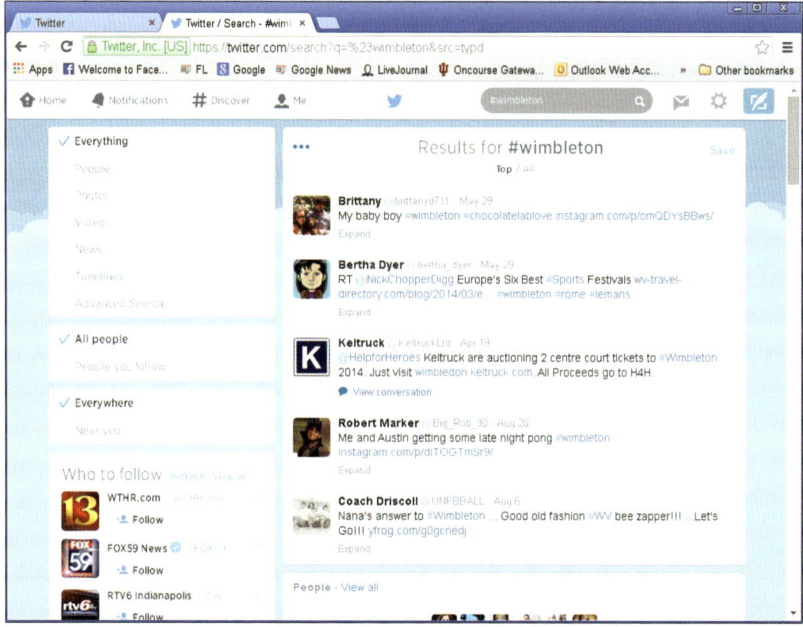

Figure 9.6 Adding a hashtag to a post ensures it's more likely to be found.

The best-known microblogging platforms are Twitter, Tumblr, and Google+. Video and photo-sharing sites Vine and Instagram can also be thought of as microblogs, because users generally post a photo or a video clip with a caption and then invite comments.

Smartphone and tablet apps for microblogging sites enable users and followers to view new posts and get notifications about them or about replies to their own posts. Relevant and interesting posts are reposted by followers to their own followers, thereby helping to promote the original post. A particularly significant tweet from a prominent public figure might be retweeted thousands of times.

Wikis

A **wiki** is an online database of information that any user can copy or amend using a web interface. Wikis are usually set up so users can collaborate and share information and knowledge. If someone has additional information related to the wiki's content, he can add it to the wiki. Wikipedia is the best-known example of a wiki; it is a form of online encyclopedia created by and edited by web users. Figure 9.7 shows the Wikipedia web page that describes a wiki.

wiki A web-based application that can be edited by anyone and that is usually informational or instructive in nature.

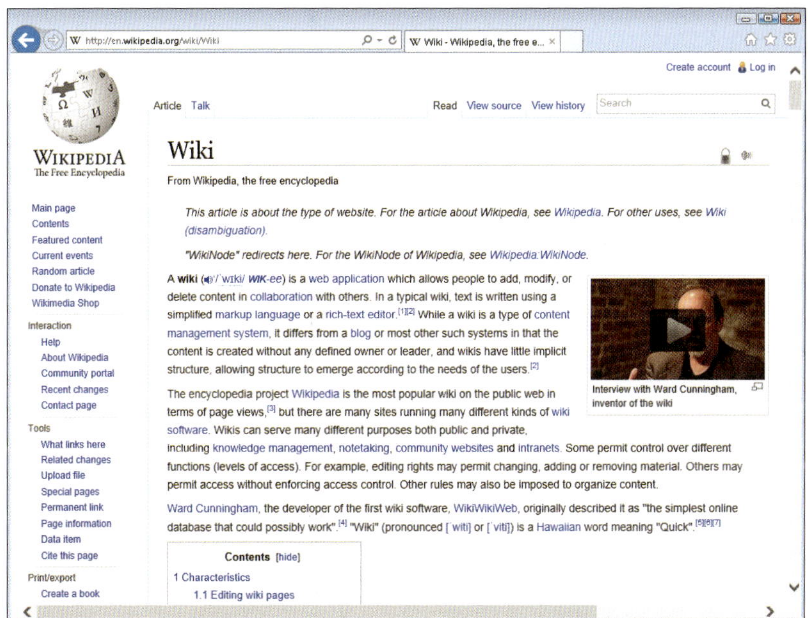

Figure 9.7 A wiki is an online database used for collaborative projects.

Newsgroups

Newsgroups were created long before the web and were the forerunners to the web-based forums we use today. These groups are part of a system called **Usenet**, which is a global distributed discussion system. Usenet users read and post messages to various categories known as newsgroups. Discussions are stored as threads, which follow a particular topic. Posts are not stored on individual servers; they are stored on a set of distributed servers that form part of the Usenet network. Newsgroup servers are connected to each other to form a network. Newsgroups have their own protocol for accessing the posts, called NNTP (network news

newsgroup An online discussion group.

Usenet A global distributed system of servers that host public newsgroups.

transport protocol), which transports news articles between news servers and clients reading and posting articles. The client computer needs an application called a newsreader to read Usenet articles, or needs to use an email client that supports news reading.

newsreader Software that organizes incoming messages from newsgroups and allows users to read and respond to them.

Newsgroups usually focus on a particular topic of interest, but some groups allow postings on any topic. Discussions are not held on the servers indefinitely and typically will disappear after a few months. Newsgroups have declined in popularity as other forms of online communication have come to prominence, but there are still more than 100,000 active groups.

Forums

forum A web-based discussion and advice-sharing site.

forum thread A post on a forum along with all the comments to it.

Web forums are a more sophisticated type of newsgroup. A forum is hosted on a standard website and can be accessed using any web browser. Many forums have a question-and-answer format in which members request advice from other forum members. Comments and replies to a post create a forum thread. Forum threads are saved and archived so that other users can easily find the answer to the same or similar question in future. You don't always need to become a forum member in order to find useful advice on a forum or to search its threads, but you must join in order to create a new post and ask a question or start a discussion.

If you're looking for advice on a brand or product, try typing that product name plus the word **forum** into a search engine. For example, if you wanted to buy a new digital SLR camera, you might use a search engine to find answers to the question *Which DSLR camera under $500 shall I buy?* Your search results may include a link to a forum thread covering this topic at `www.photography-forum.org` (see Figure 9.8). You could then read everyone's comments and advice on the matter, but you would need to join the forum to contribute to the discussion.

Figure 9.8 The home page of a photography forum.

Forums are often set up by interest groups and cover every aspect of life—from hobbies to transport, technology, health, and so on. Other forums are hosted on a company's website so customers can request help with support issues and get advice from other customers and from technicians within the company. On many forums, users can give a thumbs-up to a post to show appreciation for it and to increase the poster's forum rating.

VoIP

Voice over Internet Protocol (VoIP) is used to make voice calls via the Internet by turning the voice message into small packets of data. IP, short for Internet protocol, is used to identify individual devices that are connected to the Internet and to route calls between them. For more detail at how IP addresses work, refer to Chapter 10, "Web Basics."

Voice over Internet Protocol (VoIP) A means of providing web-based telephony. The best-known example is Skype.

Making VoIP calls requires a reliable web connection with plenty of bandwidth. This bandwidth is needed in order to translate your voice into bits of data, transmit it to your friend, and then reassemble it in the correct order so what you said makes sense. On slower web connections, this process may not work so smoothly and the caller's speech may sound garbled or have delays.

VoIP calls can be made from your computer using a SIP (session Internet protocol) client and a URI (unique resource indicator), but it's far easier—and much more common—to use a VoIP service such as Skype, FaceTime, or an IM client that also allows you to make voice calls, such as Yahoo! Messenger. VoIP calls can also be made from a tablet or smartphone using a VoIP app. Skype, Facebook Chat, and Truphone are popular VoIP apps. Google users in some countries can also make calls from their Google accounts just by clicking on the name of the person they want to call.

Skype A Microsoft-owned VoIP service used to make phone calls and sometimes video calls over a broadband, Wi-Fi, or cellular mobile web connection.

FaceTime An app installed on Apple iPhone and iPad devices that is used to make video calls between Apple device owners. VoIP was originally designed for making web-based phone calls, but the advent of much faster broadband and fixed-line Internet connections has made it possible for the web to carry video calls too. Not only has VoIP become so dependable that many offices have replaced their telephone systems with VoIP-based ones, but it is now also routinely used for corporate videoconferencing.

Skype is the most popular VoIP service in the world. Skype began as a VoIP service for making free computer-to-computer calls, but can also now be used to make cheaper international calls from a smartphone and for one-to-one video calls. Other VoIP services work in a similar way to Skype, but they don't all have video calling options.

To use Skype, download the software client from `www.skype.com`. Then use the software to create a user profile for inclusion in the Skype database so others who might want to call you can find you. You can also use your email contacts list and call anyone on it who also uses Skype. Skype is part of Microsoft, so if you already have an Outlook, Messenger, or Hotmail account, you can sign in with those credentials. You can also sign in with your Facebook account details. A commercial version of Skype enables you to add a Skype phone number that non-Skype subscribers can use to call you.

To use Skype for VoIP calls on a computer or laptop, you need built-in speakers and a microphone, or to use an external microphone and speakers or a headset. To make video calls using Skype, you also need a webcam. You can also make calls using a Skype app on your tablet or smartphone.

Videoconferencing

videoconferencing A means of conducting a video conversation remotely using an Internet connection and the webcam or camera on your laptop, phone, or tablet.

Most video calls you make using Skype or another video calling app involve one person at each end of the line. Videoconferencing is a multiparty version of the video call, as in Figure 9.9. An advantage of videoconferencing is that meetings can be held without the need for participants to travel, saving travel time and associated costs. Videoconferencing is also becoming prevalent in education: Online lectures can be delivered, backed up with video-call–based mentoring sessions.

Figure 9.9 Videoconferencing enables multiple people to video chat at the same time.

Videoconferencing uses the same underlying protocols as VoIP uses, but it requires much more bandwidth. Corporate videoconferencing facilities can cost many thousands of dollars to set up, but the costs are quickly recouped because hotel bills, travel expenses, and time out of the office are not required. Companies such as Cisco and Polycom provide videoconferencing telephony equipment. Microsoft Lync provides a phone and laptop-based videoconferencing service that companies can sign up their employees to use.

Videoconferencing can be far more effective than phone-based meetings because relevant graphics can be shown and because participants can see each other and interact in real-time.

Quick Review

1. Which protocols are used for sending and receiving email?
2. What distinguishes a microblog from other blogs?
3. Which type of communication uses hashtags (#)?
4. What is VoIP used for?

Communicating Appropriately

The way you express yourself online is just as important as choosing the best means of communicating. The language and tone you use can be chatty, friendly, respectful, or persuasive. You should always choose the appropriate medium and tone to fit the occasion and relationship with your intended recipient.

Professional versus Personal Communication

As the use of social media plays an increasingly larger role in our lives, it's easy to fall into the trap of being overly familiar in your communication. When corresponding with people you don't know well, or who are older or in a position of authority, address them formally and use polite language. Avoid jargon and slang. Emoticons such as smiley face characters are also inappropriate in professional communication.

When sending professional communications, use a sincere but not overly friendly tone and diplomatic language. Avoid unnecessary capitalization and exclamation marks. Read through what you've written before sending the document. Check spelling and grammar. Microsoft Word and other word processors have automatic spell-checkers and grammar checkers, but keep in mind they are not foolproof. If the document is a job application or a letter asking for a work experience placement, your written material will be scrutinized on these elements in addition to the content.

Personal communication also involves a measure of good judgment. Remember that jokes aren't always appreciated; something you think is funny and friendly may inadvertently upset someone else. Emails and text messages can come across more negative than the writer intended. Emoticons can help, but they can also be misinterpreted. If possible, talk to the person face-to-face or chat online. Verbal communication and IMs can be a lot friendlier and allow your tone of voice or, in the case of video calls or face-to-face chat, gestures and facial expressions, to help convey your meaning.

For any type of digital communication, avoid language that could offend on the basis of race, religion, disability, sexuality, or gender. A good rule for any form of communication is to ask yourself if you would be happy to see the message printed in a newspaper or another public outlet.

Verbal versus Written Communication

Online communication has become the standard contact method for many people, but a phone call or face-to-face conversation can sometimes be the better choice. When deciding between written and verbal communication, consider these factors:

- With whom am I communicating? If you know someone well and the two of you regularly chat face-to-face and by email, a less formal means of communicating, such as an instant message or a Facebook message, could be fine.

- What is the context or subject of the communication? If you want to discuss something serious or enlist someone's help and support, verbal communication is often the best approach.
- Am I likely to need a record of the communication? Written communications are generally best when you need a record of proof. An email may suffice, but a legal document or formal notification or application may require a typed letter sent by regular mail service. For business communication, address the recipient formally, using a courtesy title such as Mr., Mrs., or Ms., and use polite, respectful language.
- Is the speed of communication important? Some people check their email and social media messages frequently; other people do so much less often. Check whether the person you want to communicate with uses online communication regularly.

In any medium, stay calm and moderate your language, even if someone is criticizing you. Slang and profanities undermine any argument.

Choosing the Appropriate Online Medium

Using the right means of online communication shows you understand what message you want to get across and whom you are corresponding with.

The following checklist can help you choose the right medium for the particular occasion.

Email

- Suitable for most types of communication, especially if they are not time-sensitive.
- Good for formal messages and communication with strangers.
- Provides a permanent record of outgoing and incoming messages (unless, of course, you delete them).

Instant messaging

- Ideal to get a quick answer to a question or for passing small amounts of information between colleagues.
- Useful for quick updates with friends.

Social networking—personal

- Appropriate mainly for your personal world.
- Useful for informing your network of friends what is happening in your life, not necessarily work related.
- Good for posting photos and videos of recent events you've been involved in.

Social networking—business

- Increasingly used for advertising and business promotion.
- Many social networking sites are dedicated fully or in part to matching job-seekers with potential employers.

Blogs

- Ideal for expressing personal opinions and providing updates about yourself publicly as well as to your friends.

Microblogs

- Best for very short summary updates you want existing followers to see and that can also be found by anyone searching for you or for the topic you cover.

Forums

- Best for discussing topics of shared interest and communicating as part of a community.

VoIP calls

- Useful for chatting with friends or business associates. Requires a reliable, high-speed web connection and use of the same VoIP service. Works well for families keeping touch around the globe using phone or video.

Videoconferencing

- Appropriate mainly for the workplace or schools and colleges so groups can interact visually.

Choose your communication method carefully, understanding the benefits and drawbacks of each channel. Tailor your communication to what you need to accomplish and with whom you communicate.

Quick Review

1. What would be an appropriate medium for quickly checking with someone to confirm an appointment time?
2. Under what conditions is a forum the best method of communication?
3. In what ways should using social networks for personal use differ from using them for business communication?

Using and Managing Email

Email is the online communication method you will probably use the most in your daily work, school, and personal life. As you learned earlier in this chapter, you can access your email using a web interface or you can use an email client application. In the following sections, you'll learn how to use Microsoft Outlook 2010, the email client that comes with the Microsoft Office suite of applications that you have studied in earlier chapters. The general principles are the same no matter which email client you use, though, such as setting up accounts, sending and receiving mail, and organizing messages into folders.

Setting Up Email

When you install an email client, the Setup utility offers to set up your email account. You can add more email accounts later, though, in the same email client so that you receive messages from multiple accounts in a single Inbox folder. Each time you send an email, you can choose which account it will be sent from. If you are using a web-based email interface, you do not have to set up your account; logging in with your correct email address and password is all that's needed.

CAUTION When you sign up for an email account, you will be asked what password you want to use. Make sure you choose a **strong password**. A strong password is one that is difficult to guess; it may include a combination of uppercase letters, lowercase letters, numerals, and symbols. A strong password should be fairly long (at least eight characters) and should not match any word in the dictionary or any common phrase or number sequence.

strong password A password that includes a combination of uppercase letters, lowercase letters, numerals, and symbols, making it difficult to guess.

Some email clients can automatically configure some types of accounts without your having to enter the technical settings for them (such as the incoming and outgoing mail server names and the account type). When you set up an email account, Outlook attempts to determine the correct settings for that account automatically. It doesn't always succeed, so you may need to manually configure the account settings. The following Step by Step exercise shows the steps for setting up a new account in Outlook 2010.

Step by Step

Setting Up a New Account Automatically in Microsoft Outlook 2010

Follow this procedure to set up a new account in Outlook 2010 by allowing Outlook to automatically detect the correct settings to use. Try this method first:

1. Click File, and click Add Account. The Add New Account dialog box opens.
2. Fill in your name, email address, and password in the fields provided. Then click Next.

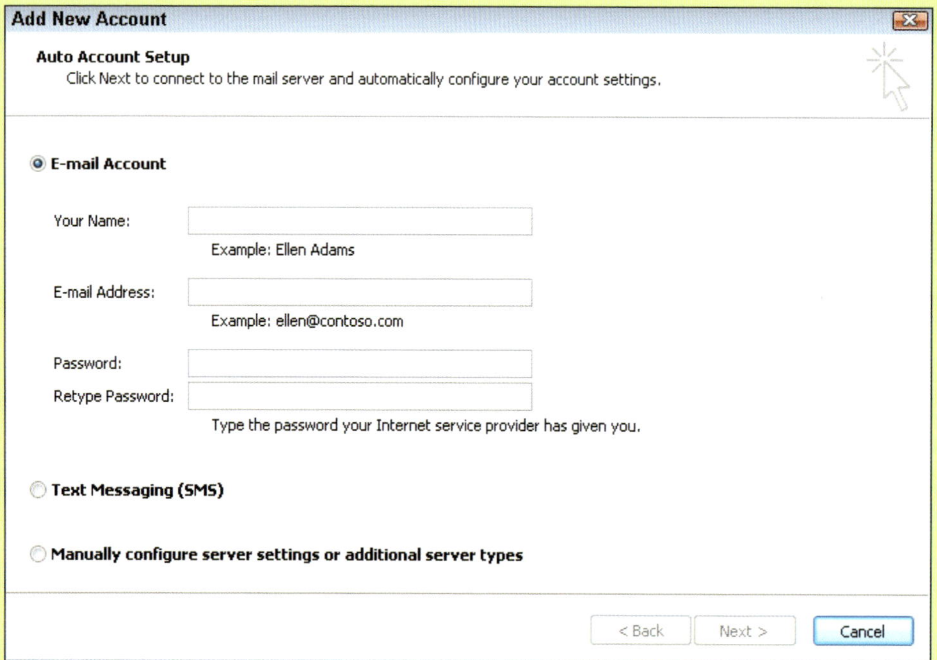

3. If you see a box asking whether to allow a website to confirm server settings, click Yes.

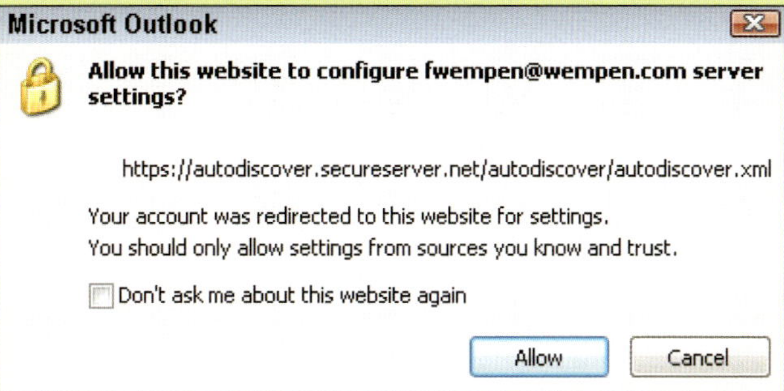

4. If a message appears that the account has been successfully configured, click Finish, and you're done. If, on the other hand, a message appears that the account cannot be automatically configured, click Cancel and then see the next section.

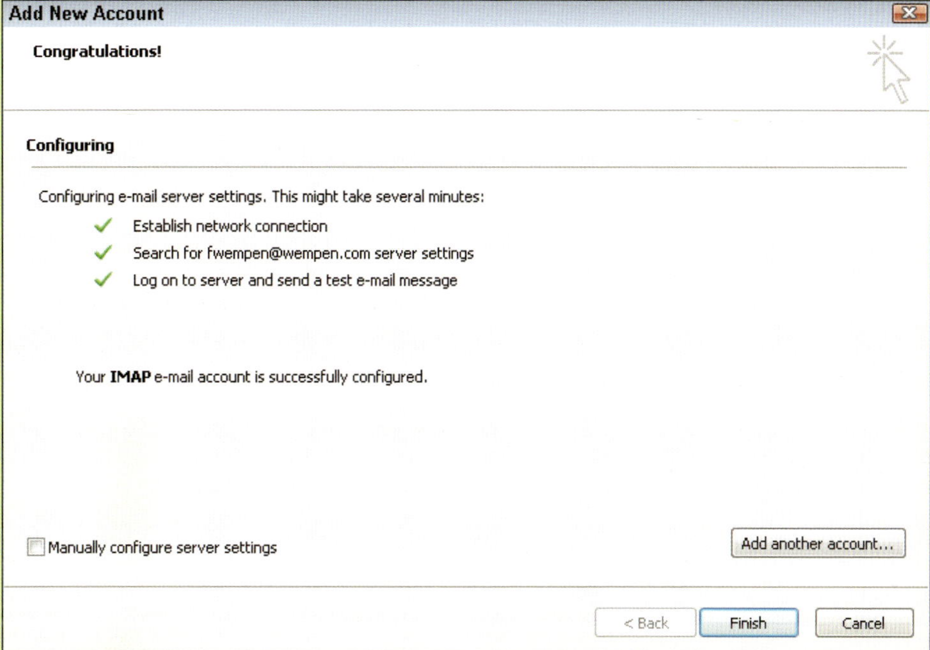

Setting Up a New Account Manually in Microsoft Outlook 2010

Follow this procedure to set up a new account in Outlook 2010 manually. Use this method if the previous method has failed, or if your account has some special settings that email clients in the past have failed to detect.

1. Click File, and click Add Account. The Add New Account dialog box opens.
2. Click Manually Configure Server Settings or Additional Server Types, and click Next.
3. On the Choose Service screen, accept the default of Internet Mail and click Next.

4. On the Internet Email Settings screen, fill in all the requested information. You will need to know the incoming and outgoing mail server names; if you don't know these, get that information from your email provider.

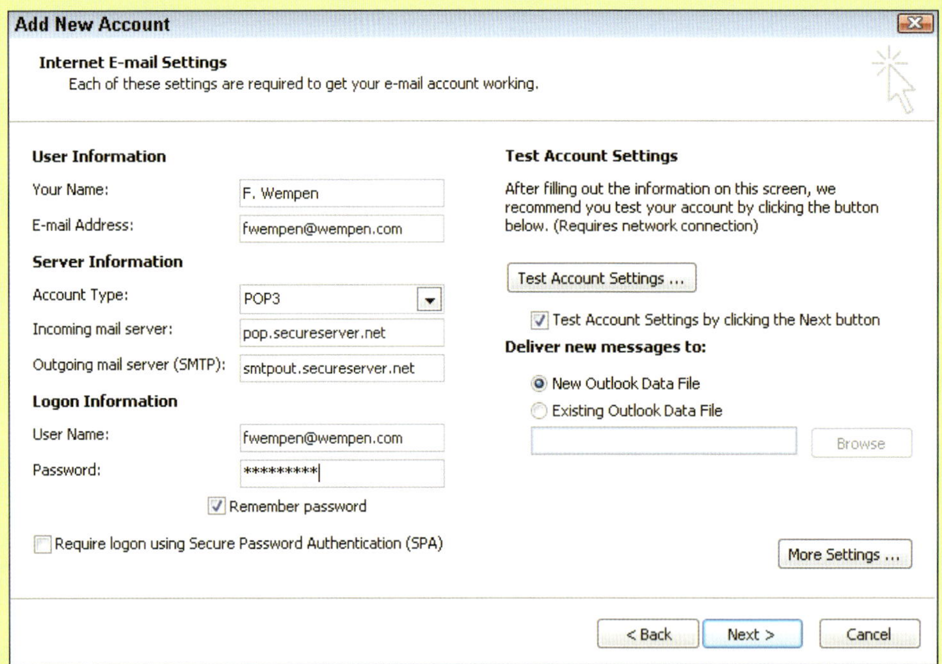

Note: By default Outlook creates a new data file for each email account you set up. If you want the new email account to use an existing data file (for example, outlook.pst), select the Existing Outlook Data File option button and then browse for the data file. This is an issue only for POP3 accounts, IMAP accounts store the mail on the server.

5. Click Next. Outlook tests the settings by sending and receiving a message. If both incoming and outgoing tests show Completed, click Close and then click Finish; your settings are correct.

   If, on the other hand, you see a message that Outlook cannot connect to either your incoming or outgoing mail server, click Close and then click More Settings to open the Internet Email Settings dialog box.

6. Use the options in the dialog box to configure your settings as directed by your email service provider. For example, here are some common settings you might need to change:

   - On the Outgoing Server tab, select the My Outgoing Server (SMTP) Requires Authentication check box.
   - If your email provider has told you that you need an SSL connection, on the Advanced tab, mark the This Server Requires an Encrypted Connection (SSL) check box.
   - On the Advanced tab, change the port numbers for the incoming and/or outgoing servers to the numbers that your email service provider has specified.

7. Click OK, and then return to Step 5 to recheck your settings.

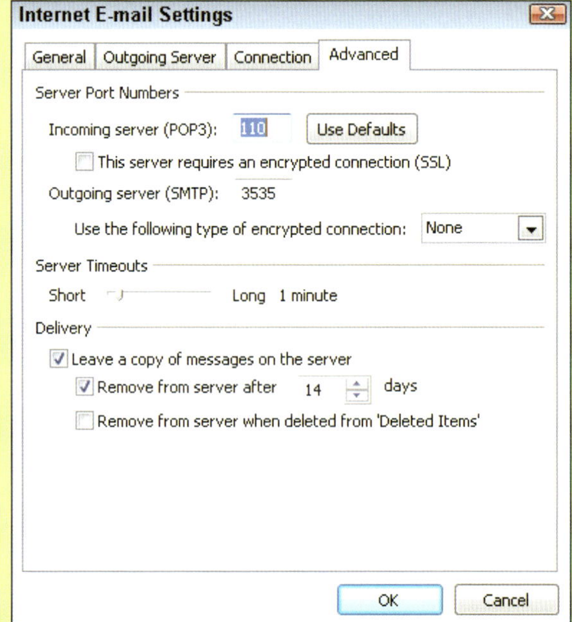

Receiving Email

Once the account is set up, your email client will automatically start using it. Your email address and password are stored, and you will not have to enter them again.

NOTE If you are using Outlook, and if you followed the Step by Step exercise in the preceding section to set up the account, the first message you will probably receive is the test message you sent yourself. You may also receive other messages too, and you can send yourself additional test messages for practice.

The navigation pane in an email client typically appears on the left and shows a list of mail folders, with one of them being Inbox. The Inbox folder is where incoming mail appears by default. Nearly all email clients work this same way, with a navigation pane at the left. There are also folders there for Outbox (where outgoing messages wait to be sent), Sent (where copies of the messages you send are stored), and Trash (where deleted messages are stored). There may also be a Junk Email folder, where incoming messages that the email client classifies as junk mail are placed. Figure 9.10 shows these in Outlook 2010. Note that unread messages appear in bold in the list of messages.

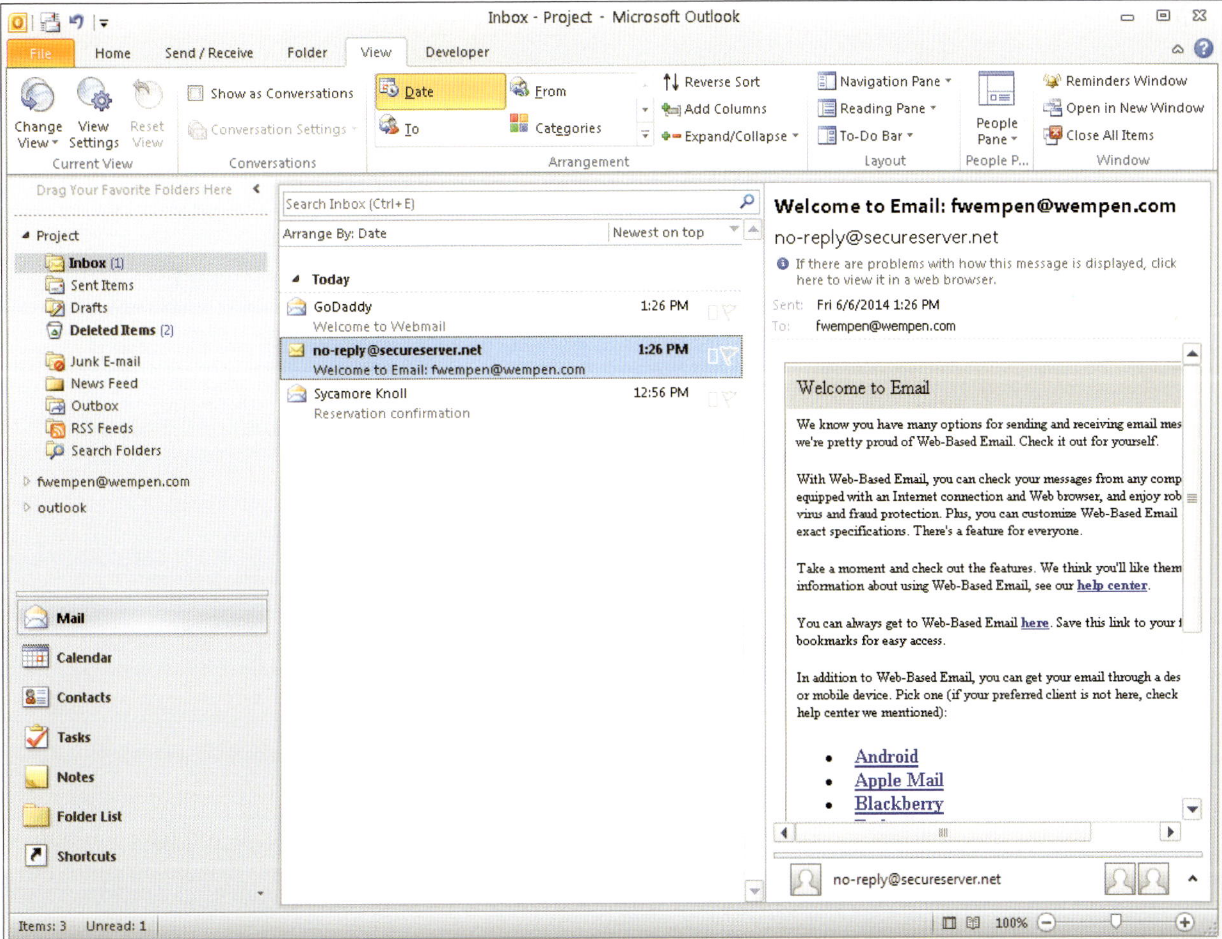

Figure 9.10 The Inbox in Outlook 2010 with received messages.

reading pane A pane in a mail client that previews the content of the selected message.

Also in Figure 9.10, notice that Outlook 2010 provides a **reading pane**, which shows the content of the selected message. When you use a reading pane, you do not have to open a message (by double-clicking it) to read its contents; you can preview that content just by selecting the message in the list. The Reading pane can appear either on the right or at the bottom of the window; you can control its setting on the View tab. Other email clients typically also have a reading pane. A web interface may or may not have one.

Your email client is probably set to send and receive message automatically at certain intervals, such as every ten minutes. If so, messages will appear in your Inbox throughout the day, as long as your email client is running. You can also manually initiate a send/receive operation. To do so in Outlook 2010, click the Send/Receive All Folders icon on the Quick Access Toolbar (above the File tab).

Sending Email

To send a message in Outlook 2010, click the Home tab and click New Email. Or, in another email client, click the equivalent button, which may have a slightly different name (like New or Compose). A message composition screen appears. Fill in the information as prompted, as shown in Figure 9.11, and then click the Send button.

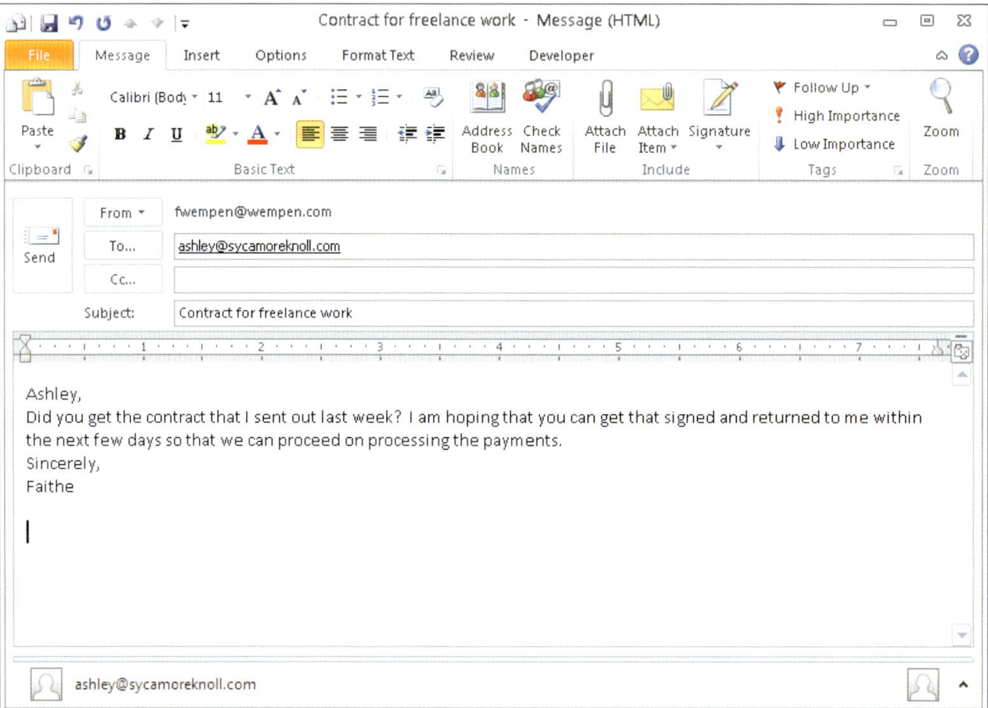

Figure 9.11 An email message being composed in Outlook 2010.

- **From:** This field might or might not appear. If you have multiple email accounts set up in your mail client, you may be prompted to choose which account the message will be sent from.
- **To:** Put the recipients' email addresses here. If there is more than one recipient, separate the names with semicolons. You can also look up recipients from a stored address book in your mail client; in Outlook, addresses are stored in the Contacts list.

- **Cc:** If you want to send an informational copy of the message to someone, put that person's email address in the **Cc** field.
- **Bcc:** This field might or might not appear. A **Bcc** is a blind copy—in other words, a copy that other recipients are not aware is being sent. In Outlook 2010, this field doesn't appear by default, but if you click the To or Cc button, a dialog box appears in which you can select or enter Bcc recipients along with To and Cc recipients.
- **Subject:** This is the title of the message, which will appear in the recipient's Inbox list. The subject should be short but descriptive; avoid general subject likes like "Hi" or "Info."
- **Body:** This is the area where you type the main part of the message.

Working with Attachments

Email you receive may have attachments, which are files that travel along with the text of the email. You can also send attachments with emails you send yourself.

When you receive a message with an **attachment**, a symbol may appear on the message in your Inbox to indicate its presence. In Outlook 2010, the symbol is a paperclip, as shown in Figure 9.12.

attachment A file that travels along with a text email to a recipient.

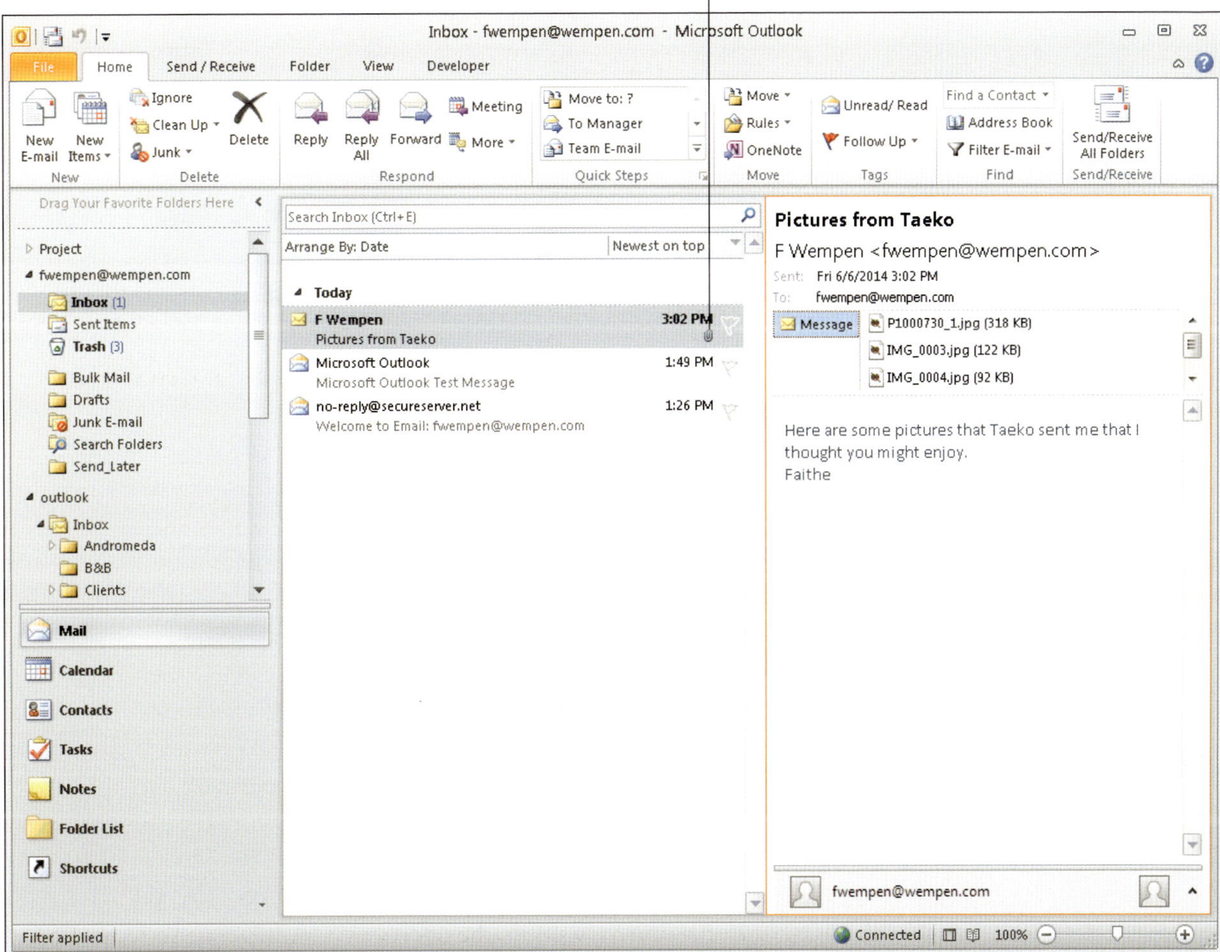

Figure 9.12 A received email with several attachments.

To open an attachment, double-click it. To save it to your hard drive, right-click it and choose Save As (for one) or Save All Attachments (for all).

To send an attachment yourself, as you are composing the message, look for an Attach button or command. In Outlook 2010, an Attach File button appears on the Ribbon. Click it and then follow the prompts to attach the file(s).

The following Step by Step explains how to compose and send a message in Outlook 2010 that contains an attachment.

Step by Step

Composing and Sending an Email that Contains an Attachment in Outlook 2010

Follow this procedure to use Outlook 2010 to send an email that contains an attachment:

1. Click the Home tab, and click New Email. A new message composition window appears.
2. Enter the recipient(s), the subject, and the message in the fields provided.
3. Click the Attach File button on the Ribbon. The Insert File dialog box opens.

Attach File

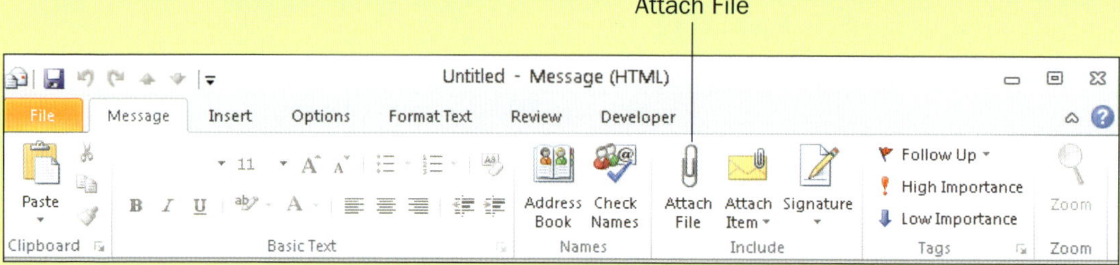

4. Select the file(s) to insert and then click the Insert button.

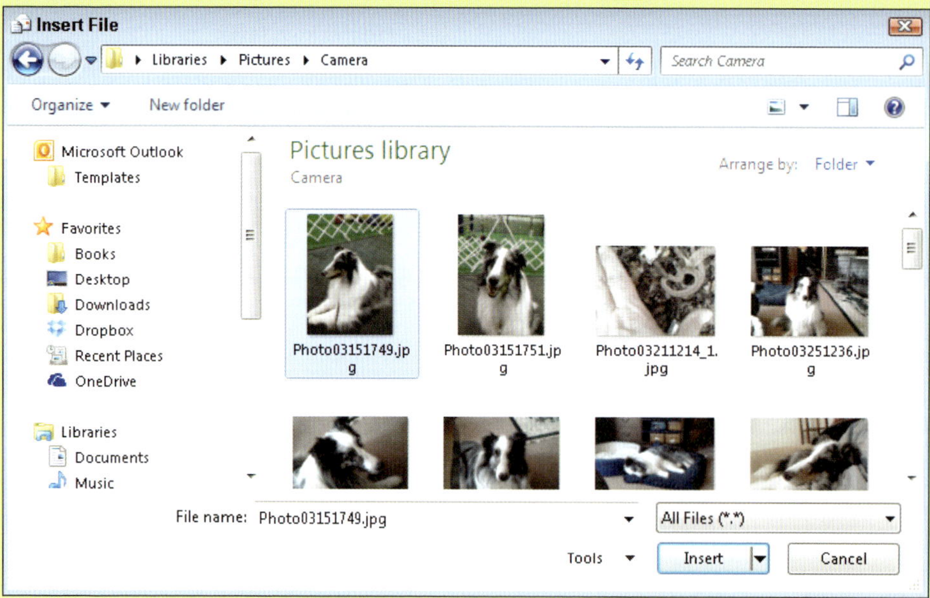

5. Click Send to send the message.

Working Around Attachment Size Limitations

Email providers have specific (but varying) limits to overall size of emails and their attachments. Larger files (such as video clips) will be rejected and prevent the email containing them from being delivered. If you want to send a large file, try compressing it first. You can do this by right-clicking the file in Windows Explorer and choosing Send To ⇨ Compressed folder. If it still exceeds your email provider's limit, it's better to send a link for your friend to download the item. You can use an FTP service or upload a file to OneDrive or Dropbox (online storage services you can use for free) and send your friend a link to download it. This can also be preferable because large emails take longer to send and use up a large chunk of the recipient's mailbox.

Troubleshooting

Working with Stored Contacts

Outlook 2010 is a full-featured contact management application, and it includes separate sections for email handling, contact management, and calendars. All these sections are connected, though, so you can use them together. The contact management section is called **Contacts**. To view it, click Contacts in the lower-left corner of the Outlook 2010 screen. Figure 9.13 shows the Outlook 2010 Contacts list with three contacts in it. When you first open the Contacts list, you may not have any contacts there. You can create some if you like by clicking the New Contact button and filling out the form that appears.

Contacts The section in Outlook that stores people's contact information.

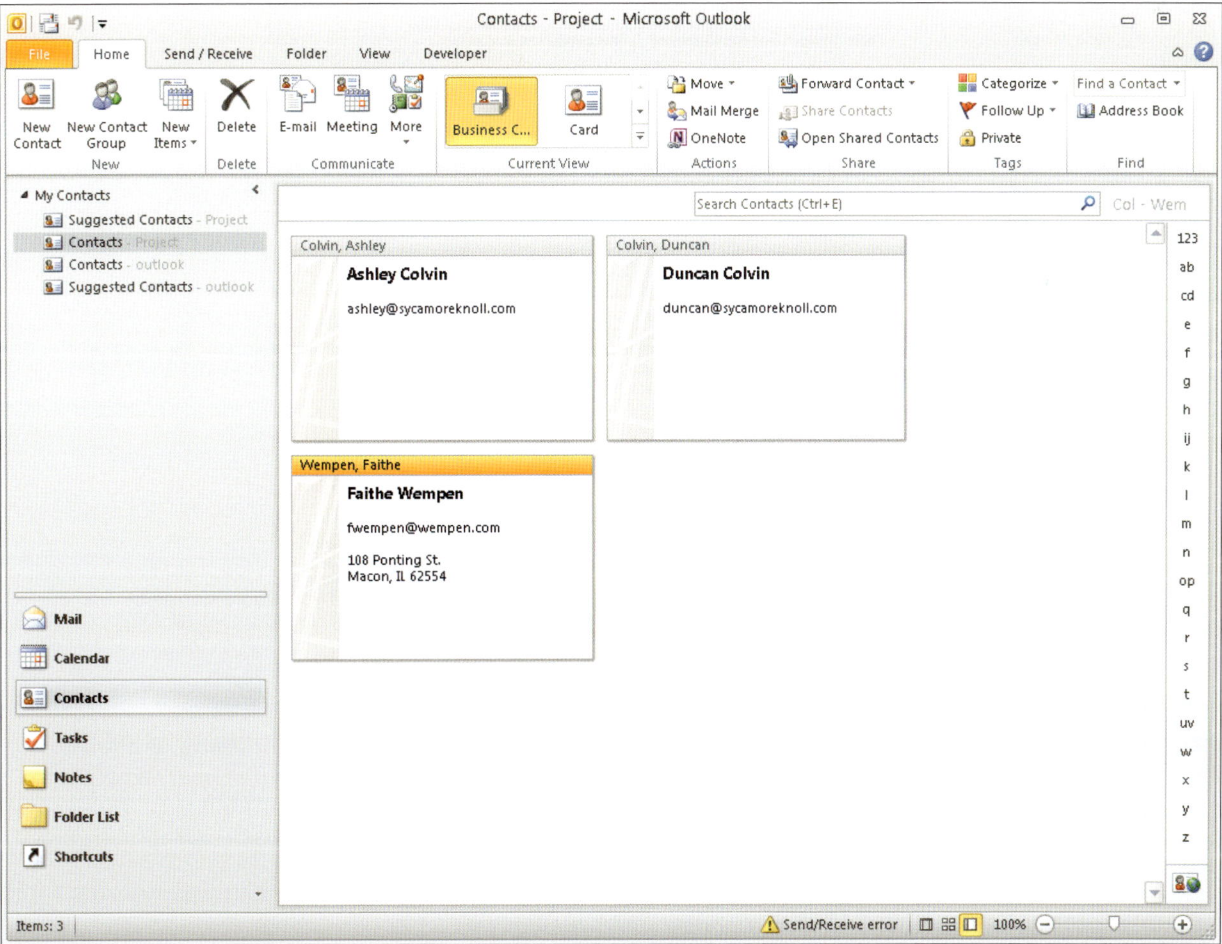

Figure 9.13 The Contacts list in Outlook 2010. You may have many more contacts, and they may be arranged differently. Use the View tab to change how the contacts appear.

When addressing an email message, if you know the person's email address, you can type it directly into the To, Cc, or Bcc field. As you start typing, the email client's autocomplete feature may offer to fill in the address for you. You can also select from your Contacts list, as shown in the following Step by Step.

Step by Step

Addressing an Email Message from the Contacts List in Outlook 2010

Follow this procedure to look up email addresses in the Contacts list as you are composing a new email in Outlook 2010:

1. Click the Home tab, and click New Email. A new message composition window appears.
2. Click the To button. The Select Names: Contacts dialog box opens.
3. Click the name of the person to whom you want to address the email.
4. Click one of the buttons at the bottom of the dialog box to indicate the appropriate field in which to place the person's email address: To, Cc, or Bcc.

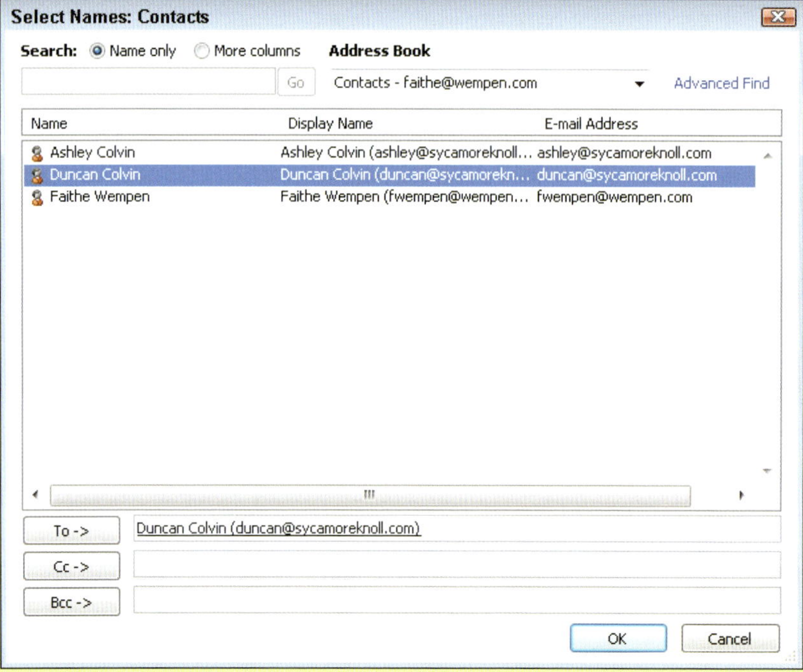

5. Repeat Step 4 to add more recipients if desired.
6. Click OK to return to the message composition window and complete the email as you would normally.

CAUTION

Make sure you don't share others' contact information without permission. If you're sending an email to multiple people, and you don't want them to see each other's addresses, put your own email address in the To field and then put all the recipients' addresses in the Bcc field.

Responding to and Forwarding Emails

When you receive an email, you can choose to reply to it by creating a new message, but it is often easier to use the Reply feature in your email client. When you select a message and then choose Reply, the mail client starts a new message for you that is pre-addressed to the original sender, with the original subject in the Subject line preceded by RE: and the original message quoted in the message body. This saves time because all you have to enter is your reply. Figure 9.14 shows a reply being composed in Outlook 2010.

Reply A message that is sent back to the original sender.

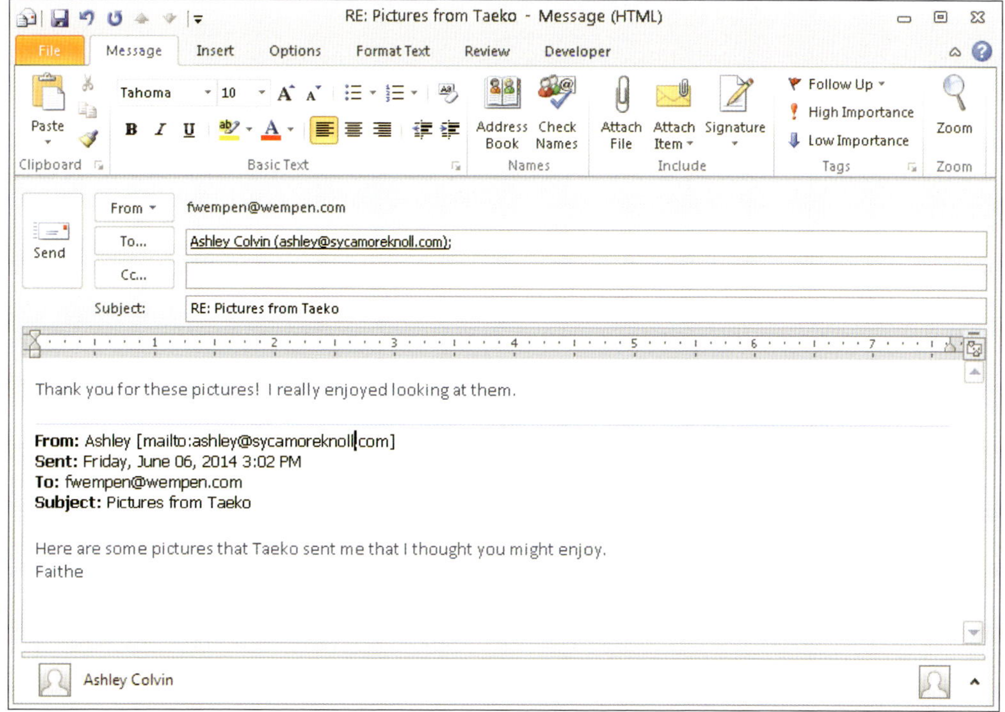

Figure 9.14 A reply includes the original subject and message body, and the original sender is set as the recipient.

The Reply All feature works just like Reply except it addresses the message not only to the original sender but also to any co-recipients on the original message. (It does not include recipients who got their copies through Bcc.)

Reply All A message that is sent back to the original sender plus to any other recipients.

To send a message you've received from one person to someone else, use the Forward feature. When you forward a message, the original subject appears in the Subject line, preceded by FWD:. The original message body appears in the body area, and if the original message contained any attachments, they are included as attachments in the forwarded email too. Everything is filled in for you except the new recipient. Fill in the new recipient in the To box and send the message.

Forward A copy of a message sent on to someone other than the original sender.

Out of Office/Automatic Replies

If you know you won't be responding to emails for a few days, it's polite to set up an out-of-office message. When people send you an email, they'll get an automatic response explaining that you are out of email contact at present but will attend to their messages as soon as you return.

out-of-office message A message that people receive when you are unable to personally answer your email for a certain time.

A good out-of-office message should include the dates that you will be gone and an alternative contact person who can be reached in case of an urgent matter.

For example, here is a typical message:

> I will be out of the office from March 1 to March 15 and will not be checking messages. If this is an urgent matter, please contact my supervisor, Mary Clark, at 317-555-2811 or mary@sycamoreknoll.com. Otherwise, I will respond to your message when I am back in the office.
>
> Sincerely,
> Ashley Colvin

automatic reply A feature on a mail server that automatically sends a message back to each one received when it is enabled.

Out-of-office messages are set up on your mail server, not in your email client. That's because when you are out of the office, your email client software won't be running, so you can't count on it to handle the **automatic reply**.

In some cases, you may be able to set up automatic replies through your email client. It depends on the incoming mail server. If you are using a Microsoft Exchange mail server (for example, through your company's network at work), you can use the Automatic Replies feature in Outlook 2010. Click File, and click Automatic Replies. If you don't see that command after clicking File, you can't use automatic replies in Outlook.

To set up an automatic reply on your mail server, log into your mail provider's website, or log into your hosting account if the email account you are working with is part of a domain you own. In the provider's configuration pages online, you will find a feature that will enable you to set up an out-of-office message. You may also be able to set up an automatic reply in the web-based interface for your account, as shown in Figure 9.15.

Signatures

signature Text that is automatically appended to outgoing messages.

Rather than typing your name at the end of each email you send, you can append a **signature** that is added automatically. This can include your Skype name, mobile phone number, Twitter handle, blog address, or other information. You set up a signature in your email client. The following Step by Step section shows how to set one up in Outlook 2010.

CAUTION

Be conservative with the information you put in a signature line if you are using the same email account for both business and personal email. You might write a formal email address to a business client, for example, and forget that you have something very informal and silly in your signature.

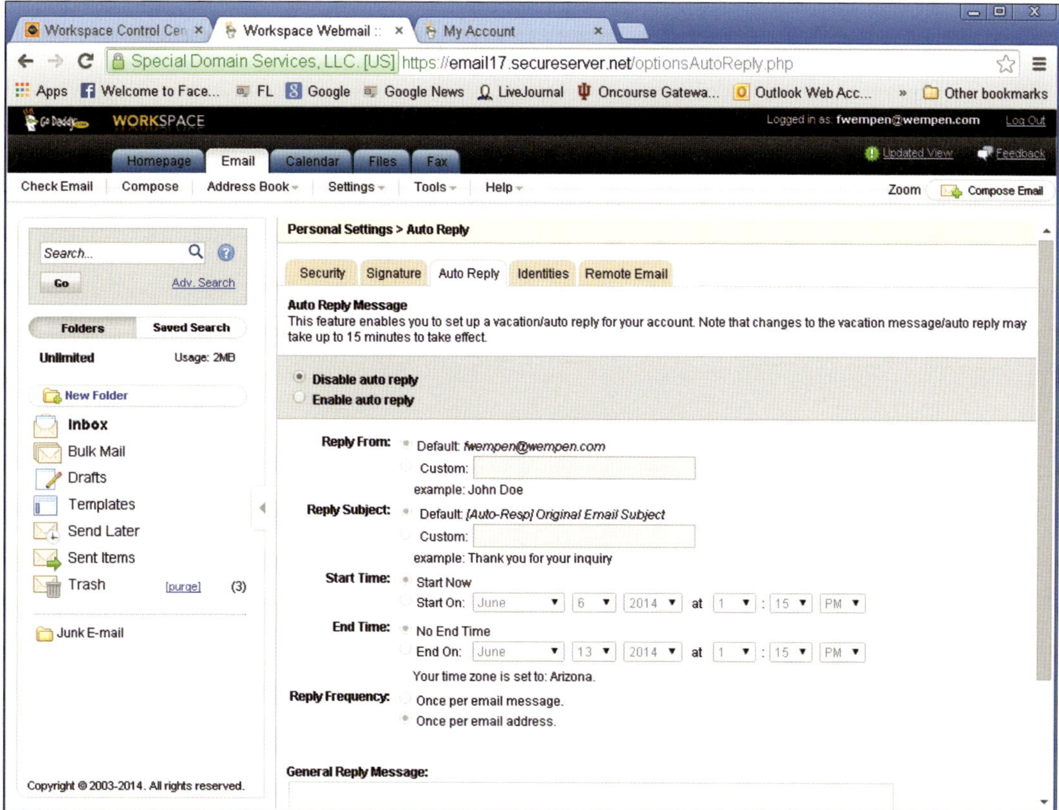

Figure 9.15 It may be possible to set up an automatic reply in the web interface for your email account.

Step by Step

Creating a Signature in Outlook

To create a signature in Outlook, follow these steps:

1. Select File ➪ Options ➪ Mail. Under Compose Messages, choose Signatures. A Signatures and Stationery menu appears.
2. Click New, type a name for a new signature, and click OK.
3. Type the text for the signature in the Edit Signature area. Use the formatting tools above the text entry area to format the text as desired.
4. Repeat Steps 2 and 3 as needed to create additional signatures if you want different signatures for different accounts or situations.
5. Open the E-mail Account drop-down list and choose an email account for which you want to set a signature.
6. Open the New Messages drop-down list and choose the signature you want to use for that email for new messages, or choose (none) to turn off signatures.

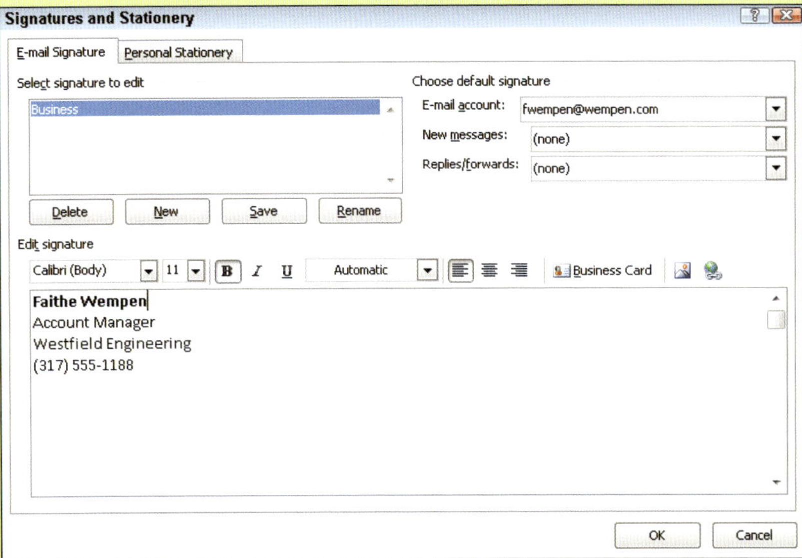

7. (Optional) If you want to use a signature for replies and forwards, open the Replies/Forwards drop-down list and choose the signature you want to use, or choose (none) to turn off signatures.
8. (Optional) Repeat Steps 5–7 to configure additional email accounts if desired.
9. Click OK.

Archiving Emails

Your email client keeps emails indefinitely, so over time the data file for your email client may become very large. The larger the data file, the longer it takes for the application to open, and the longer it takes for some operations, such as searching. A large data file also takes longer to back up.

One solution is to delete the old emails, and it's a good idea to do so if there are emails that you know you will never want to refer to again. However, there's another way to keep your email data file small: You can archive old messages to a separate data file. That way, you can open that archive any time you need to refer to older mail, but your old mail isn't in your mail client taking up space on a daily basis.

archive To move items from the current location to another for backup purposes; a useful way of storing old messages while freeing up space for new ones.

Some email clients have an Archive command that you can use to automatically archive items that meet certain criteria. Other clients require you to create archive files manually and move content into them manually by dragging and dropping content from existing folders to the archive folders. Outlook 2010 has a very good archiving feature, explained in the following Step by Step.

Step by Step

Setting Up AutoArchiving in Outlook

To set the defaults for automatic archiving, follow this procedure:

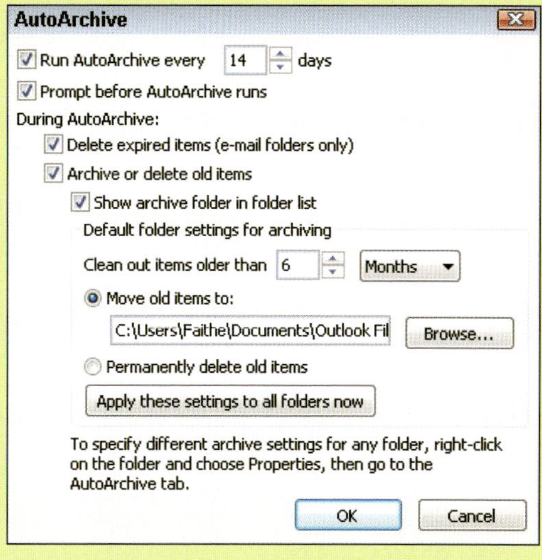

1. Click File, and click Options.
2. Click Advanced.
3. In the AutoArchive section, click the AutoArchive Settings button.
4. In the AutoArchive dialog box, adjust the default settings as desired. For example, you can choose where to move old items to, and how old an item must be before it is archived.
5. Click OK.

Opening an Archive

To review archived content, follow these steps:

1. Click File, click Account Settings, and click Account Settings.
2. Click the Data Files tab, and click Add.
3. Select the data file containing the archive, and click OK.
4. Click Close. Now the archive data file appears in the navigation pane at the left, below your main Outlook data file's folders.

Setting up AutoArchiving for specific folders

To set the AutoArchiving options for specific mail folders, follow these steps:

1. Right-click the folder in the navigation pane and choose Properties.
2. Click the AutoArchive tab.
3. Choose Archive the Items in This Folder Using the Default Settings.

   OR

   Choose Archive This Folder Using These Settings, and then adjust the settings as desired.
4. Click OK.

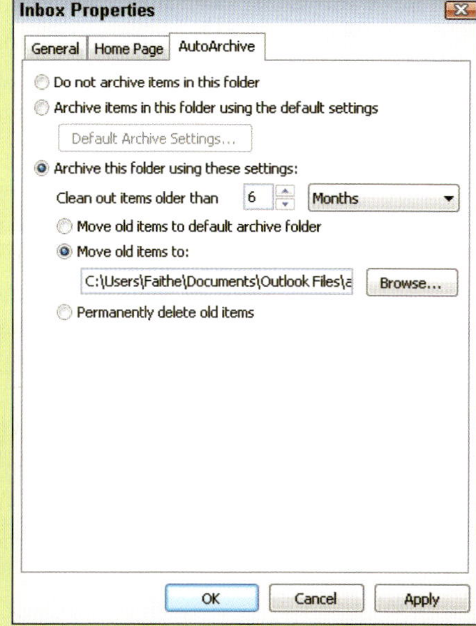

Manually Archive (One-Time Operation)

If you would prefer to retain control over archiving, do it manually, rather than setting up automatic archiving. Follow these steps:

1. Click File, click Cleanup Tools, and click Archive.
2. In the Archive dialog box, select a folder to archive, or to archive all folders, select the parent folder at the top of the list.
3. Choose a date from the Archive Items Older Than pop-up calendar.
4. Confirm the archive file name in the Archive File text box.
5. Click OK.

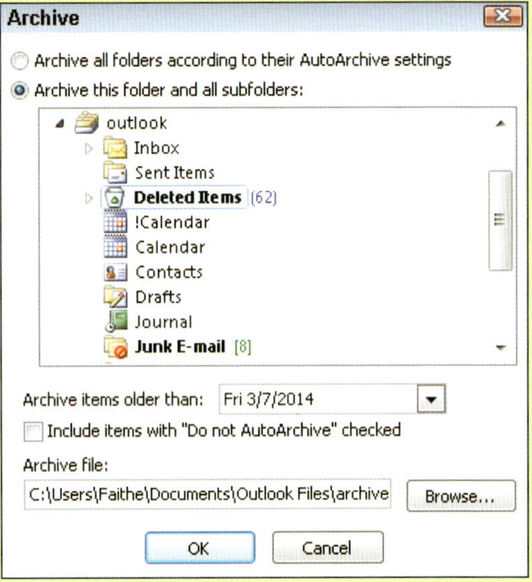

Managing Junk Mail

spam Unsolicited "junk" mail, typically containing offers (some legitimate, some not) of products or services to buy.

Junk email, also called spam, is sent out by the millions of messages every day on the Internet. By some estimates, it accounts for more than 80 percent of all email sent. Mail filtering software helps cut down on the number of unsolicited ads you receive by analyzing your incoming messages and applying message sorting rules and filtering to them to determine which ones are ads and which ones are legitimate correspondence. Using mail filtering software can save you lots of time because you don't have to go through large amounts of junk mail to find the important messages sent to you.

There are several ways to filter junk mail. Many email applications include a junk mail filter that automatically moves messages it suspects to be spam into a Junk Mail folder. You can periodically look through that folder to see if there is anything you want, and then delete the rest.

Many ISPs also offer junk mail filtering. This type of filtering is typically invisible to the end user; the mail that's filtered out never even reaches your email client software. Because of the danger of missing a legitimate message, this type of filtering is usually very conservative in its targeting of junk mail.

Third-party junk mail filtering programs can work with your email client and can be fine-tuned for the level of filtering you are most comfortable with. Some people prefer to get more junk mail in order to be assured they aren't missing any legitimate messages, whereas other people prefer to enable the most aggressive junk mail filtering settings. Some filtering software can even get better over time by learning from the choices you make.

When you identify a piece of junk mail, you can add its sender to a **blacklist**. Any further mail from that sender will be automatically discarded upon receipt. If you want to make sure that you always receive mail from a certain recipient, regardless of your junk mail settings, you can add that address to a **whitelist**, also called a *safe list*. Whitelisted senders will always have their mail delivered to your inbox.

blacklist A list of prohibited email senders.

whitelist A list of allowed email senders; also called a safe list.

In Outlook 2010, you can control your junk mail options by clicking the Junk button on the Home tab and then choosing Junk Email Options from the menu. In the dialog box that appears (see Figure 9.16), you can choose a level of filtering and choose whether junk mail will be deleted or stored in a Junk E-mail folder.

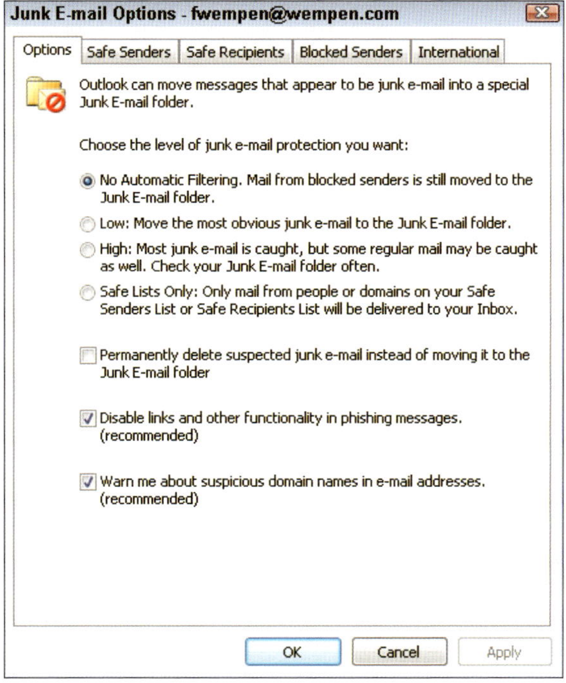

Figure 9.16 Manage junk email settings in Microsoft Outlook 2010.

Quick Review

1. What is the benefit of using a signature?
2. How do you include an attachment in an email?
3. How do you set up an automatic response when you are out of the office?
4. What is archiving, and what is its advantage over deleting messages?

Summary

Internet Communication Types

The Internet has fostered many means of communication, and it is important to choose the correct medium for a situation. **Email** is like postal mail for computers; it is not instantly delivered, using a **store-and-forward** system that employs **mail servers** to move the mail from place to place and a **mail client** to pick up one's mail.

Some email accounts are web-based, also called **HTTP email accounts**. Most people use them via web interfaces. There are also **Post Office Protocol (POP)** and **Internet Mail Access Protocol (IMAP)** accounts, which are both designed for use with mail clients. POP and IMAP protocols are only for receiving email; they are both paired with the **Simple Mail Transfer Protocol (SMTP)** for sending mail.

Instant messaging (IM) consists of instant text messages sent over the Internet. When instant messages are sent over phone systems, it is called **texting** or **Short Message Service (SMS)**. IM is a **push technology**, whereas email is a **pull technology**.

Chat rooms are like group instant messaging. You signal your willingness to participate by entering a chat room, such as a **channel** in an **Internet Relay Chat (IRC) server**.

Social networking is an umbrella term for sites such as Facebook, Twitter, LinkedIn, and Google+. Users can post their own text and pictures and express their opinions. **Tags** (hashtags) are used to identify topics. Some common social networks are **Instagram**, **Vine**, **Reddit**, **YouTube**, **Facebook**, and **Twitter**.

A **blog** is a web page where an individual or group publishes **posts,** which may contain news, opinions, photos, and essays. Blogs can be either personal or commercial. A **blog platform** is a service that enables people to create their own blogs and hosts the blogs on its server. **Microblogging** allows users to post brief text commentary, photos, and audio clips. Twitter is the best-known microblogging site.

A **wiki** is a collaboratively managed database of information. Wikipedia is the largest and most popular wiki. **Newsgroups** are no longer very popular, but used to be extremely so; they are public message forums exchanged through a service called **Usenet**. To read in newsgroups, you use **newsreader** software. A **forum** is a web-based public discussion area.

Voice over IP (VoIP) is a technology for making voice calls over the Internet. These calls can also include video, through services such as **Skype** and **FaceTime**, or an IM client that includes video chat capabilities. **Videoconferencing** is a multi-user version of video chat.

Communicating Appropriately

Because there are so many means of online communication, the appropriate tone and language need to be chosen for each. More formality is typically expected in business communication than in social networking. Poorly written communications send out the wrong message and can be misinterpreted, leading to conflict. Face-to-face communications and phone calls are preferable to online exchanges in some circumstances because non-verbal communications methods, including gestures and tone of voice, can be used to ensure the message is correctly conveyed.

Using and Managing Email

Email is sent and received through an email client or a web interface. Microsoft Outlook is one of the most popular email clients. When you set up a new email account, make sure you choose a **strong password**, which is a password that is not easy for someone to guess.

To get started with an email client, you set up your account(s) in that program. Your messages then appear in the Inbox, and you can compose your own messages from that program's interface. The Inbox may include a **reading pane**, which shows the content of the selected message.

When composing email, you must enter a recipient, a subject, and a message body. You may optionally include an attachment. When addressing email, the To box is for the main recipients, **Cc** is for those who will receive a copy, and **Bcc** is for those who will receive an undisclosed copy. You may optionally select recipients from the **Contacts** list in Outlook (or equivalent in your email application).

Most email clients enable you to save email addresses of people with whom you correspond and use them when addressing messages. In Outlook, this is the Contacts list.

You can reply to a received message by clicking the **Reply** button; other options include **Reply All** and **Forward**.

An **out-of-office message** sends an **automatic reply** to anyone who emails you while you are away. You can set this up in Outlook only if you use an Exchange server. Otherwise, you must set it up with your mail provider. You may be able to configure it from the web-based interface that the provider supplies for your email account.

A **signature** is text that is automatically appended to outgoing emails. You can set this up in your mail client.

To avoid having your mail file get too big, you can periodically **archive** messages, which means to transfer messages to an auxiliary storage folder based on criteria you specify.

Unsolicited junk mail, also known as **spam**, can be minimized using mail filtering software, which may include both **blacklists** and **whitelists**.

Key Terms

archive
attachment
automatic reply
Bcc
blacklist
blog
blog platform
Cc
channel
chat room
Contacts
email
Facebook
FaceTime
forum
forum thread
Forward
HTTP email account
IMAP account
Instagram
instant messaging (IM)
Internet Mail Access Protocol (IMAP)
Internet Relay Chat (IRC)
mail client
mail server
microblog
newsgroup
newsreader
out-of-office message
POP account
post
Post Office Protocol (POP)
pull technology
push technology
reading pane
Reddit
Reply
Reply All
search engine optimization (SEO)
Short Message Service (SMS)
signature
Simple Mail Transfer Protocol (SMTP)
Skype
social network
spam
store-and-forward
strong password
tag (also hashtag) (social media)
texting
Twitter

Usenet
videoconferencing
Vine
Voice over Internet Protocol (VoIP)
whitelist
wiki
YouTube

Test Yourself

Fact Check

1. Which of the following systems limits the size of any message you post?
   a. social networks
   b. blogs
   c. microblogs
   d. forums
2. What would be the most appropriate communication to use when submitting your resume?
   a. Post to a forum.
   b. Post onto your blog.
   c. Add it to your Facebook profile.
   d. Attach it to an email.
3. The ______________ system is used by newsgroups.
   a. Facebook
   b. Usenet
   c. FTP
   d. Twitter
4. Which would be an appropriate use of a forum?
   a. Check to see if there are known problems with a device.
   b. Request a refund for a purchase.
   c. Transfer a file.
   d. Communicate privately with a teacher.
5. Which of the following is a collaborative online information database?
   a. VoIP
   b. wiki
   c. IMP
   d. forum
6. You want to send a copy of an email to someone without the main recipient being aware you have sent that other copy. Which address field do you use when composing the mail in Outlook?
   a. Acc:
   b. Bcc:
   c. Cc:
   d. Dcc:

7. Which of the following communication systems is the best channel for you to publish your thoughts and feelings onto a website for all to see?

   a. forum

   b. blog

   c. Skype

   d. newsgroup

8. Which of these is a push technology?

   a. texting

   b. forums

   c. wikis

   d. email

9. Out-of-office messages can be set up in Outlook only if:

   a. you have Signatures enabled.

   b. you are using an Exchange server.

   c. you have a POP account.

   d. you have an IMAP account.

10. Where are archived messages sent?

   a. online storage area

   b. desktop

   c. Recycle Bin

   d. specified archive file

Matching

Match the term to its description.

a. microblog

b. post

c. forum

d. videoconferencing

e. FaccTimc

f. tags

1. ________An app installed on Apple iPhone and iPad devices that is used to make video calls between Apple device owners.

2. ________A web-based discussion and advice-sharing site.

3. ________A means of conducting a video conversation remotely using an Internet connection and the webcam or camera on your laptop, phone, or tablet.

4. ________An article published on a blog.

5. ________Labels that can be added to posted content on social networks to allow people to find content of interest to them.

6. ________A service that allows the posting of short messages.

Sum It Up

1. Name four online communication options available for talking with a friend who lives in another city.
2. Give two examples of situations where email should be used to communicate rather than texting or instant messaging.
3. Name two video chat clients.
4. Explain the purpose of an email signature.
5. What are the advantages of archiving your email?

Explore More

Following the Trail in Outlook

Try looking at the email headers in Outlook to get an idea of what happens to an email in transit.

1. Open Outlook and highlight an email in your Inbox.
2. Double-click the mail to open it in a new window.
3. Click the File tab, and under Info, select Properties at the bottom. The Properties box for the mail opens and at the bottom is a box titled Internet Headers. In that box, you can see the history of the mail.
4. From the information in the Properties box, can you work out how many mail servers the email went through and how long it took to arrive?

Think It Over

The Impact of Social Networking

Social networking has become a major player in Internet communication and is now moving into the workplace. Look at your environment, school, college, or workplace and consider the impact of allowing social networking on the internal network. Ask yourself the following questions:

- Would being able to use social networking during working hours affect productivity?
- Can social networking replace existing communications in the workplace?
- Are there disadvantages to using social networking in the workplace?

Discuss these questions with your colleagues, and compare their views with yours.

Chapter 10
Web Basics

Learning objectives

- Identify the components that make up the web
- Use the basic functions of a web browser
- Search the Internet
- Understand the need for security and recognize secure connections

In the span of a single generation, the Internet and World Wide Web have revolutionized our lives. Using these technologies, we can connect with others—whether they are next door or halfway around the globe—more easily than ever before. The Internet also makes it possible to engage in electronic commerce and expand our knowledge of topics far and wide.

But how does this technology work? What components and technologies are necessary to facilitate this communication? How does one find the information one needs online? These topics are the focus of this chapter.

How the Web Works

Internet A global packet-switched network created cooperatively by multiple companies, governments, and standards organizations.

World Wide Web (WWW) A network of interconnected pages of information stored on publicly accessible servers.

The Internet is a global network of millions of computers that can communicate with each other. Provided that two computers are connected to the Internet, they can share information between them. The World Wide Web (WWW), often referred to as "the web," is part of the Internet; it is a network of interconnected pages of information stored on publicly accessible servers using a consistent page layout and formatting language.

Web Browsing Components

Web browsing involves three components:

- **Web servers:** Store and provide access to websites
- **Web browsers:** Request and display information to individuals
- **Web pages:** The individual documents that web servers store and web browsers request.

Web Servers

When someone connects to the Internet, he typically uses a computer with a desktop operating system, such as Windows 7. The information accessed by that person, however, is stored on a different type of computer, called a web server. As you learned in Chapter 8, a server is a powerful computer that exists in order to provide data or services to other computers. A web server is a server on which web pages are stored and made available to the public.

web server A server that receives requests for web page data and supplies it by sending it over the Internet.

Careers in IT

Web Designer

A web designer creates websites for businesses, schools, organizations, and individuals. Web designers not only have a strong background in programming tools like HTML, Java, and ASP, but also an eye for what makes a page functional, attractive, and easy to use. If you are interested in being a web designer, you will want to study computer technology, programming, user interface design, and computer graphics.

web browser An application used to access websites and to retrieve or upload information. Often referred to as a **browser**.

Web Browsers

A web browser, often referred to simply as a browser, is an application used to access websites and to retrieve or upload information. The browser runs on an individual user's computer and provides a communication interface to web servers.

Many different browsers are available. The most popular ones include:

- Internet Explorer
- Firefox
- Chrome
- Safari

All these browsers work in a similar fashion. Typically, if you know how to use one, you'll be able to find your way around any of the others.

Internet Explorer comes preinstalled on computers that run the Windows 7 operating system. To use a different browser, simply download it from the manufacturer's website and install it. Note that certain web applications prefer certain browsers, so you may want more than one. You can have multiple browsers installed in Windows, and even have more than one open at a time. You'll learn more about using a browser later in this chapter.

Web Pages

A **web page** is a file that is formatted for use on the World Wide Web. The content of a web page is displayed in a browser. Web pages can contain a variety of content, including text, graphics, audio, and video.

web page A file formatted for use on the World Wide Web.

Most web pages are written in **HyperText Markup Language (HTML)**, which defines the layout of a web page by using a variety of tags and attributes. When a web page is downloaded into a browser, the browser uses the instructions in the markup language to display the page as the page author intended.

Hypertext Markup Language (HTML) A language for encoding data and graphics for display in a web browser.

Most web pages contain hyperlinks. A **hyperlink**, sometimes simply called a "link," is a clickable link to another page (or another spot on the same page). The hyperlink is the main mechanism for navigating through a website. Each page on a website might have any number of links to content stored elsewhere on the site or even on another site altogether. When the mouse cursor changes from an arrow symbol to a hand, that indicates the presence of a hyperlink.

hyperlink A pointer to another point on a web page, which you access by clicking the hyperlink.

Some web pages are static. That is, their content does not change until their owners update them manually. Other web pages are dynamic, frequently updating information such as a current stock price or weather report.

Understanding URLs and IP Addresses

You know what the main components of the Internet are. But users actually access the web pages they need online by using URLs and IP addresses.

URLs

A **uniform resource locator (URL)**, sometimes called a web address or a uniform resource identifier (URI), is the set of characters you enter into your web browser's address bar to navigate to a specific web page. An example of a URL is `http://www.microsoft.com`. If you type this URL in your browser's address bar, your browser will display the main page of Microsoft's website.

uniform resource locator (URL) A string of characters that identifies the location of a resource on a website.

What makes up a URL? The full string of a URL is composed of three components:

- **The protocol:** A protocol is a set of rules that govern the transmission of data between two devices. On the Internet, the **HyperText Transfer Protocol (HTTP)** is commonly used for this purpose—hence the presence of **http://** in most URLs. Another example of a protocol used on the Internet is the Internet Protocol (IP).

HyperText Transfer Protocol (HTTP) The protocol used to send and receive web pages on the Internet.

- **The destination server (domain name):** This is indicated by a domain name, such as **bbc.co.uk** (you'll learn more about domain names in a moment.). In most cases, this domain name is preceded with the letters **www** followed by a period.
- **The path:** This is the exact location of the file you are requesting on the server. For example, the document might be stored in a folder on the web server called **news**. A path might also include a specific filename, such as **news/story24871.htm**. If no filename is included in the path, a default page from the specified folder location loads.

A full URL would be `http://www.bbc.co.uk/news/story24871.htm`. Figure 10.1 identifies each portion of the URL.

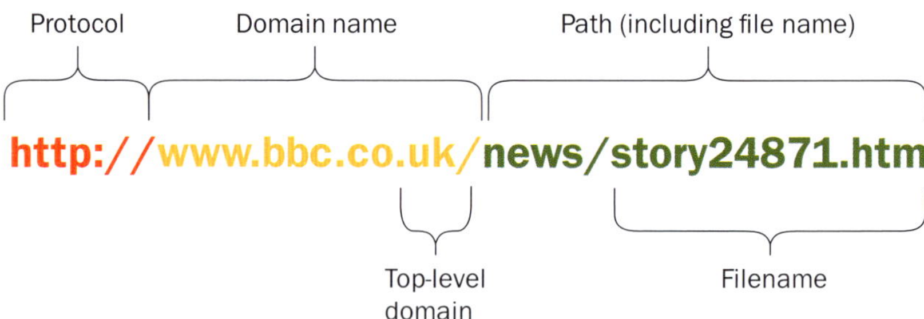

Figure 10. 1 The URL explained.

NOTE Notice the use of the forward slash as a separator. This is in contrast to the backslash used in Windows to describe a file path.

domain name A name that identifies an entity on the Internet.

A domain name is a name that identifies an entity on the Internet. It's a key part of a URL. A company or individual can register for a domain name. That name can then act as an identifier for that company or person.

top-level domain The code at the end of a URL that indicates the type of organization the name represents, such as COM for commercial businesses.

In its basic form, a domain name consists of an identifier followed by an extension, like **microsoft.com**. The extension, also called the top-level domain, is often used to identify the type of organization that the name represents. For example, the **.com** extension represents a commercial organization, whereas the **.edu** extension is reserved for educational institutions, like **harvard.edu**.

Some domain names also include a two-letter country code—for example, **.uk** for the United Kingdom, **.ca** for Canada, and **.sa** for Saudi Arabia. Domain names can also include sub-domains—for example, **training.microsoft.com** or **marketing.microsoft.com**.

TIP Companies that are global in nature should register their domains in multiple countries. For example, if you type **`www.microsoft.se`**, you receive Microsoft's home page in Swedish.

Registering a Domain Name

Put It to Work

For any company wanting to do business on the Internet or just have an online presence, choosing the right domain name is critical. Ideally, the domain name will match the company name as closely as possible. An exact match may not be possible, however, because the name may already be taken. If your company needs a specific name that is already taken, you may be able to buy the rights to that name from the current owner, or you may be able to register the name with a different top-level domain. For example, instead of a .com address, you might be able to get the .net or .biz version.

Anyone can register a domain name, as long as it doesn't belong to an existing company or organization. You can register a domain name with a domain registrar company such as GoDaddy.com or 1&1.com. The exact cost varies with the registrar, but is generally between US$10 and US$30 a year.

The name registration must be renewed on a yearly basis, but you can pay for multiple years at a time. When the owner of a domain name fails to renew it, it becomes available for someone else to claim and register.

IP Addresses

Every computer that connects directly to the Internet has its own unique numeric address, called its IP address. IP stands for Internet Protocol, one of the protocols in the TCP/IP suite of protocols. A protocol is an agreed-upon rule or standard; the Internet is based on TCP/IP rules. Most networks today, including the Internet itself, use IP addressing to identify computers. If you connect to the Internet through an Internet service provider (ISP), your ISP assigns you an IP address automatically. Depending on the ISP, that address may be a static IP address (that is, permanently assigned to your modem) or a dynamic IP address (that is, temporarily assigned to your modem as long as it is connected to the ISP).

IP address A numeric address by which a particular computer is known on a network.

static IP address An IP address that is permanently assigned to a device.

dynamic IP address An IP address that is temporarily assigned to a device.

Running the **ipconfig** command at a command prompt displays your computer's IP address, which is the private address assigned to it by your router. To display a command prompt, click the Start button, type cmd, and press Enter. Look for a line that includes "Local Area Connection." You should see the two addresses allocated to your computer—IPv6 first, followed by IPv4.

If you want to see your computer's public address—that is, the one it uses on the Internet—visit `http://whatismyipaddress.com`. The main page will display your computer's public IP address. There is also a map that shows the geographical location of your Internet service provider.

How Domain Names and IP Addresses Are Related

If you enter an IP address in your web browser, the browser goes directly to that site. If you enter a domain name, though, it goes to a Domain Name System (DNS) server on the Internet, which is a directory lookup that converts domain names into their corresponding IP addresses. Looking up a name and finding the IP address is known as name resolution, or resolving the address. Your browser does this for you automatically.

Domain Name System (DNS) The naming system employed to enable users to access websites using their domain names or URLs rather than their IP addresses.

name resolution The process of translating domain names to numerical IP addresses. A DNS server is used to resolve a name to an address.

Quick Review

1. What are the three main components of the Internet?
2. What are the three main components of a URL?
3. What are the two types of IP addresses?
4. What type of server is used to resolve (convert) domain names or URLs to IP addresses?

Accessing the Web with a Browser

As mentioned, you use a web browser to access content on the Internet. In this section, you'll learn how to start your browser, access websites, navigate those sites, bookmark your favorite sites, and more.

NOTE This section assumes you're using the Internet Explorer browser, which is included with the Windows 7 operating system. Browsers are constantly being updated. When Windows 7 was launched, it included Internet Explorer version 8. The latest version of Internet Explorer (IE) at the time of writing, however, is version 11. If you have Windows Updates enabled (refer to Chapter 11, "Network and Internet Privacy and Security"), your system likely has the latest version.

Starting Your Browser

You can open Internet Explorer in a few different ways:

- Click the Start button and select Internet Explorer from the list of programs (see Figure 10.2).
- Double-click the Internet Explorer shortcut icon on your desktop (if there is one).
- Click the Internet Explorer icon on your taskbar (assuming it's been pinned there; see Figure 10.2).
- Click the Start button, type **iexplore** into the Search Programs and Files box, and press Enter.

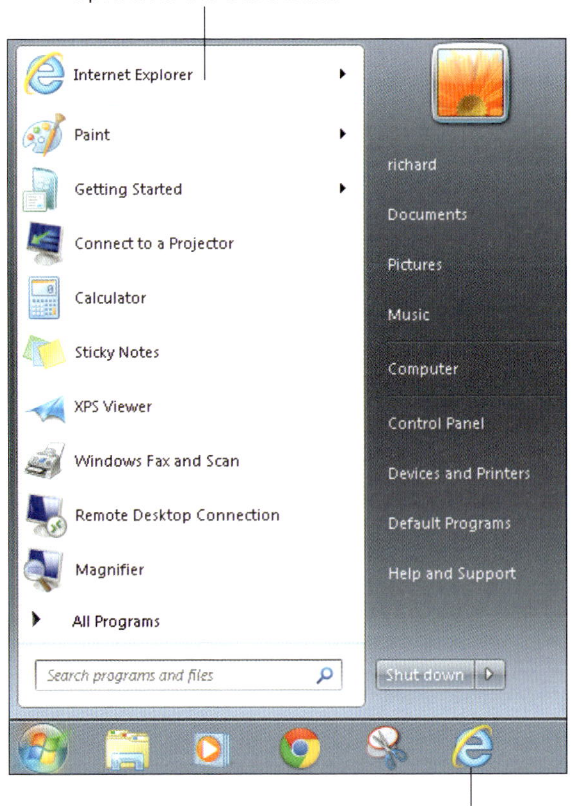

Figure 10.2 Opening Internet Explorer from the Start menu. You can also see the Internet Explorer icon pinned to the taskbar.

You can also start Internet Explorer (or your default browser, if not IE) by clicking a web hyperlink in an email address or document. In some programs, such as Microsoft Word, you have to hold down the Ctrl key as you click on a hyperlink to open it in a browser.

When Internet Explorer opens, it takes you to your home page. Your **home page** is the page that is presented every time you open the browser. By default, the browser's home page is **msn.com**. You can set your home page to the site of your choice, however. If you use a particular site all the time, you can set that site as your home page. This makes browsing more efficient.

home page The page that is displayed when you first launch your web browser.

Step by Step

Changing Your Internet Explorer Home Page

To change your Internet Explorer home page, follow these steps:

1. Open Internet Explorer using one of the methods listed previously.
2. Type the address of the website you want to set as your home page into the address bar and allow it to load.
3. Click the Tools button (the one that looks like a gear wheel in the upper-right corner of the browser screen). A menu appears.

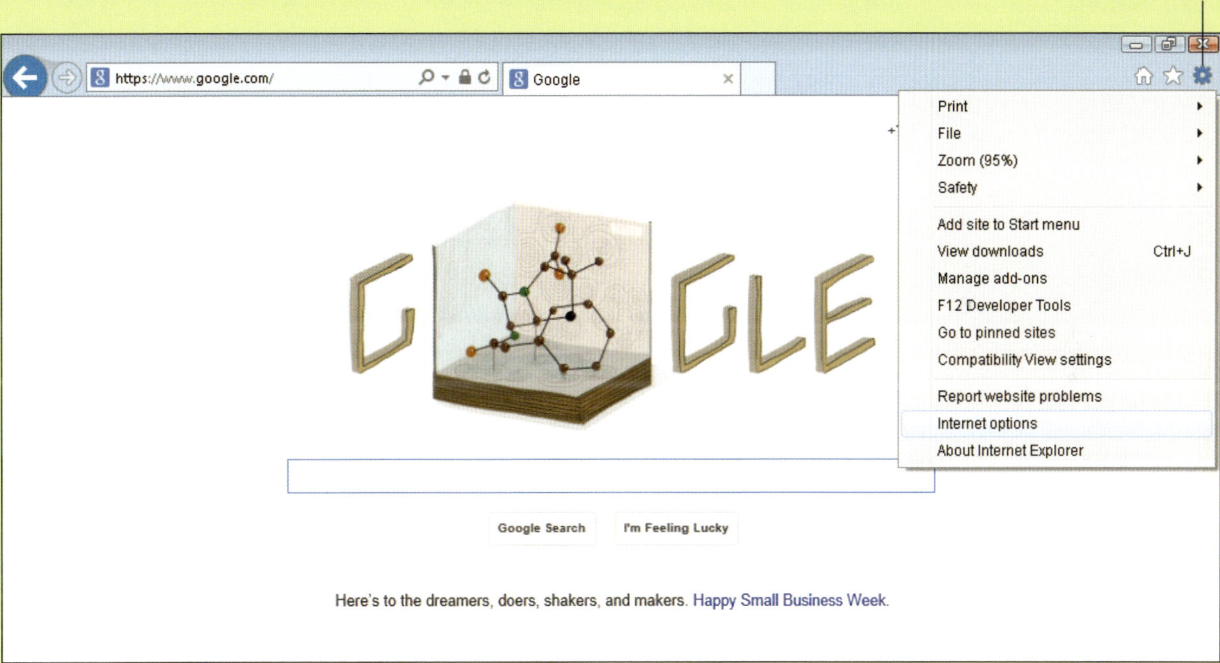

4. Select Internet Options. The Internet Options dialog box opens, with the General tab displayed.
5. In the Home Page section of the General tab, click the Use Current button. The box above it should now contain the URL of the current site.
6. Click the Apply button. The next time you launch the browser, the home page you selected will be displayed.

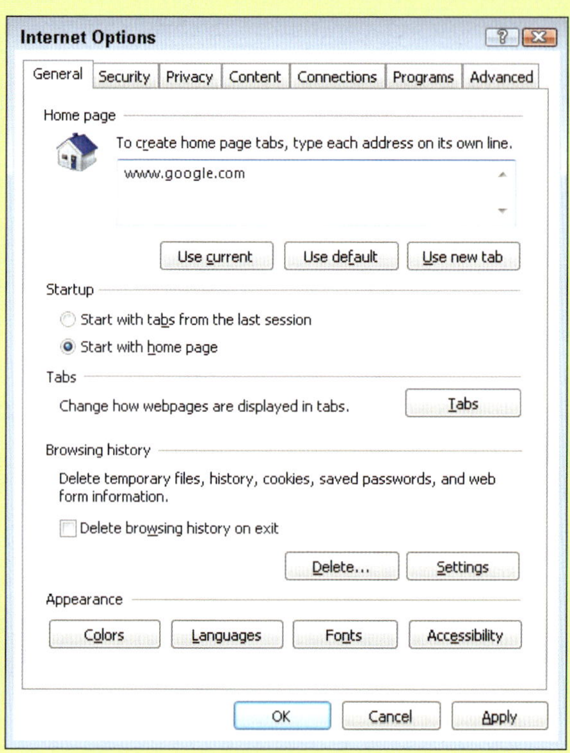

Accessing a Website

After you launch your web browser, you simply type a URL in the address field to visit the site associated with that URL. DNS will resolve the URL to an IP address, and you will be presented with the page you specified. You can then click on hyperlinks on that page to see additional pages and information, or to visit other sites.

Put It to Work

Identifying Secure Sites

When you browse a website that uses the HTTP protocol, everything is transmitted and received in clear text. That means someone using a packet sniffer (discussed in Chapter 11) could easily intercept the information. This is okay for normal browsing, but not when carrying out financial transactions that involve entering credit card information or other personal details.

To make it more difficult for criminals to acquire your information, a secure encrypted connection is required when you are sending sensitive data. HyperText Transfer Protocol Secure (HTTPS) provides an encrypted connection between the web browser and the web server. With HTTPS, the two endpoints exchange an encryption key, enabling the encryption of all future communication between them. When a connection uses HTTPS, the URL starts with `https://` rather than `http://`, as shown. In addition, a padlock appears in the browser's address bar, and in some browsers the address bar may appear with a green background. A secure connection happens automatically when you log into a secure site; you do not have to do anything special to initiate it.

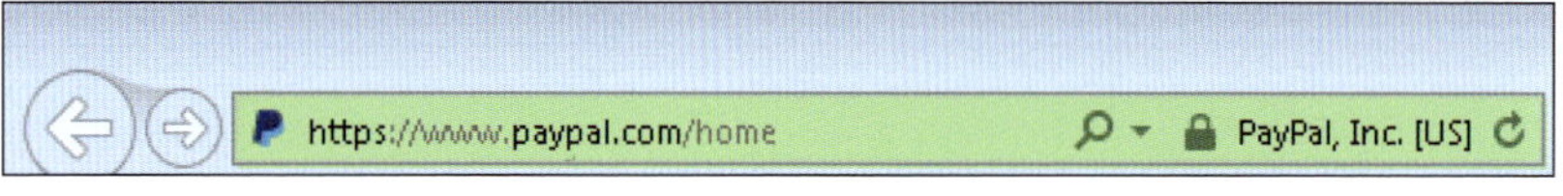

Going Back, Going Forward, and Refreshing

Suppose that while visiting a website, you've clicked several hyperlinks to view many different web pages. Or maybe you've viewed additional websites during the same browser session. Either way, it may be that you want to revisit a page that you viewed previously. To do so, simply click the Back button in the upper-left corner of the browser window. (It's the button with a left-pointing arrow on it.) This returns you to the page you viewed last. Click the button multiple times to cycle back to additional viewed pages.

When you click the Back button, the Forward button becomes active (that is, it turns blue). The Forward button is next to the Back button and features a right-pointing arrow. If, after clicking the Back button, you want to return to the original page, you can click the Forward button.

You can also refresh a web page. You might do so to make sure you are viewing the most current version of the page. (Sometimes, if you've visited a web page before, your browser saves it and reloads it the next time you visit. This helps to speed downloads but may result in an outdated page being displayed.) To do so, click the Refresh button. It's the clockwise circular arrow at the right end of the address bar. Figure 10.3 shows the Back, Forward, and Refresh buttons.

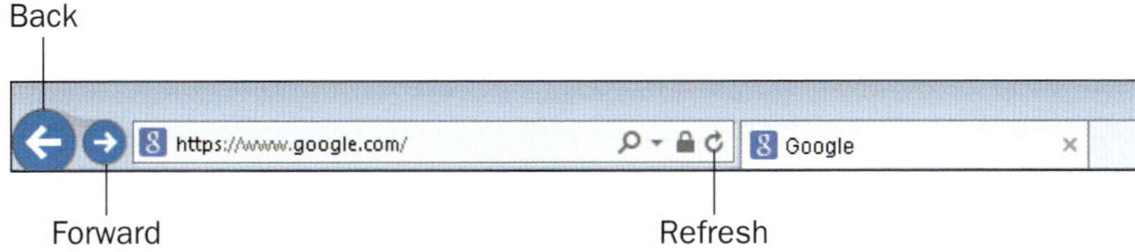

Figure 10.3 The Back, Forward, and Refresh buttons.

Engaging in e-Commerce

One of the most important and culture-changing uses for the web is as a means of conducting online financial business, also known as e-commerce. E-commerce can be business-to-business (B2B), business-to-consumer (B2C), or consumer-to-consumer (C2C). E-commerce can include a business ordering supplies or materials from another business, a consumer buying a book from an online bookstore, and a friend sending money to a friend.

From the consumer perspective, e-commerce is a win-win. Thanks to e-commerce, consumers have many more choices. Because e-commerce is global, people can buy from retailers all around the globe 24 hours a day, without leaving the comfort of their homes.

E-commerce makes economic sense for retailers as well. With e-commerce, there's no need to maintain a brick-and-mortar storefront. Online retailers can work from one or more large warehouses, selling and shipping a wide range of items.

With e-commerce, you aren't limited to purchasing goods online. E-commerce covers all aspects of business and life. For example, many governments now offer services online, enabling citizens to pay their taxes, sign up for government services, and license their vehicles online.

When engaging in e-commerce, be sure you buy from secure sites. You'll learn more about how to tell whether a site is secure in Chapter 11.

Put It to Work

Working with Tabs

tab A web browser feature that enables users to have multiple pages open at once within the same browser window.

A tab enables you to have multiple web pages open at once within the same browser window. When you launch Internet Explorer, it displays your home page on a tab. To open another tab—leaving the page on the first tab accessible—click the New Tab button (the grey box to the right of the existing tab). A second tab opens, again with your home page displayed. You can then type a URL in the address bar to visit a different page as normal.

Perhaps even more useful, Internet Explorer enables you to open pages via a hyperlink on a separate tab. To do so, right-click the hyperlink and choose Open in New Tab from the menu that appears. Internet Explorer opens a second tab and displays the linked page on it. Figure 10.4 shows a browser window with multiple tabs open.

Figure 10.4 Multiple tabs open, with the New Tab button highlighted.

Adding Favorites (Bookmarks)

favorite A website or page that you visit frequently, and to which you want easy access.

If you frequently visit a website, you might want to store it in your browser so you don't have to type its URL every time you visit it. To do so, you can save it as a Favorite (also called a Bookmark). A favorite is a website or page that you visit frequently, and to which you want easy access.

Step by Step

Adding a Website to Your Favorites List

To add a website to your Favorites list, follow these steps:

1. Click the View Favorites, Feed, and History button in the upper-right corner of the browser screen. (It's the one that looks like a star.) The Favorites Center pane opens. It has three tabs: Favorites, Feeds, and History. The Favorites Center pane also contains an Add to Favorites button.
2. Click the Add to Favorites button. The Add a Favorite dialog box opens.
3. Click the Add button to add the website to the Favorites tab.

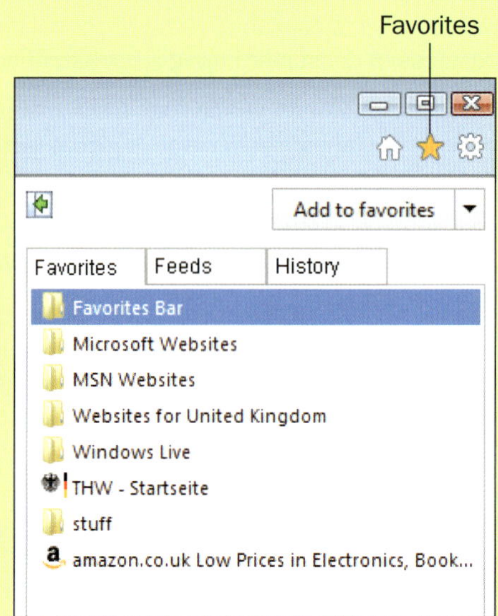

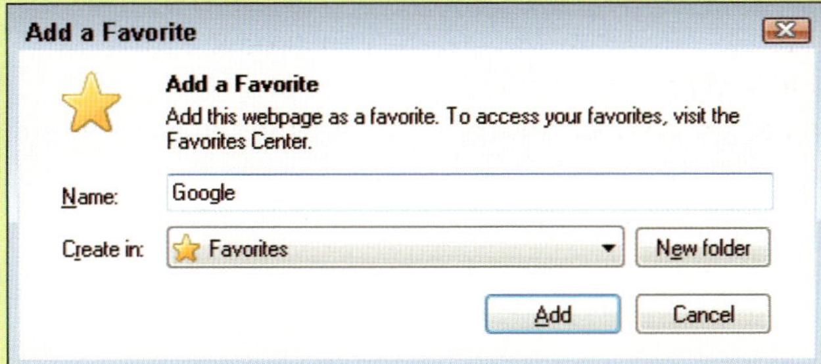

Accessing Your Favorites

To access a website on your Favorites list, follow these steps:

1. Click the View Favorites, Feed, and History button to open the Favorites Center pane.
2. If necessary, click the Favorites tab to view your Favorites list.
3. Click the link for the site you want to visit. Internet Explorer opens the site.

Organizing Your Favorites in Folders

If you collect a lot of favorites, you might like to organize them in the Favorites Center pane to make them easier to find. One approach is to place them into folders. For example, you could place all your news-related Favorites in one folder, all your cooking-related Favorites in another folder, and so on.

To create a folder for your favorites, follow these steps:

1. With a site you want to add to your new folder open, click the View Favorites, Feed, and History button to open the Favorites Center pane.
2. Click the Add to Favorites button. The Add a Favorite dialog box opens.
3. Click the New Folder button. The Create a Folder dialog box opens.
4. Type the name of your new folder and specify the folder's location. (You can nest folders—create them inside one another—if required.) Then click the Create button.
5. Click Add. The folder is created and includes a link to the website you have open.

Another option is to add frequently visited websites to the Favorites bar. If enabled, the Favorites bar appears along the top of your browser window, just below the address bar. To enable it, right-click the title bar and choose Favorites Bar.

You can click a site in the Favorites bar to access it. Every new site you add to the Favorites bar will appear on the far-left end. When the bar is full, two small chevrons will appear on the right side of the bar, as shown in Figure 10.5. Click the chevrons to display a menu containing additional Favorites not visible on the Favorites bar.

Figure 10.5 The Favorites bar.

Step by Step

Adding a Site to the Favorites Bar

To add a site to your Favorites bar, follow these steps:

1. Click the View Favorites, Feed, and History button to open the Favorites Center pane.
2. Click the down arrow to the right of the Add to Favorites button. A menu appears.

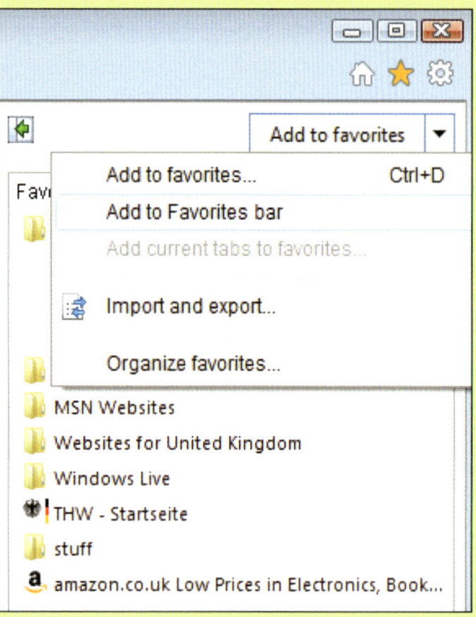

3. Choose Add to Favorites Bar. A link to the site appears on the Favorites bar.

TIP An even faster way to add a site to your Favorites bar is to click the Add to Favorites Bar button on the left side of the Favorites bar (see Figure 10.6).

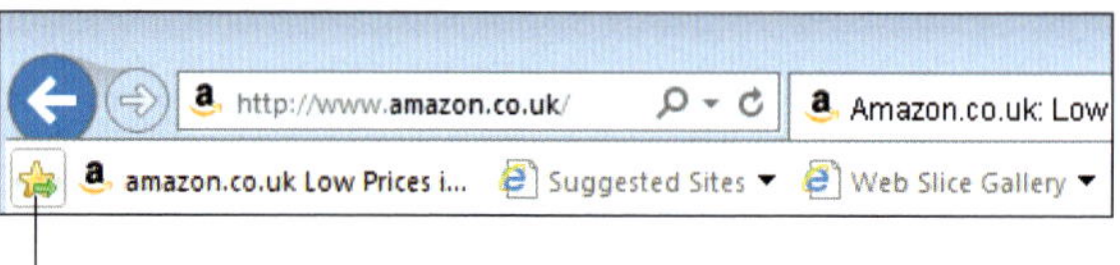

Add to Favorites button

Figure 10.6 Shortcut for adding favorite sites to the Favorites bar.

To remove a Favorites from your Favorites list, simply right-click it in the Favorites list or Favorites bar and choose Delete from the menu that appears.

Viewing Your Browser History

By default, Internet Explore stores a list of recently visited websites, called the **browser history**. If you forget the URL of a site you've visited recently, you may be able to access it from this list.

To view your browser history, click the down arrow on the right side of the address bar. A menu of previously visited sites appears. (See Figure 10.7.) Simply click the site you want to visit, and the browser will reload it.

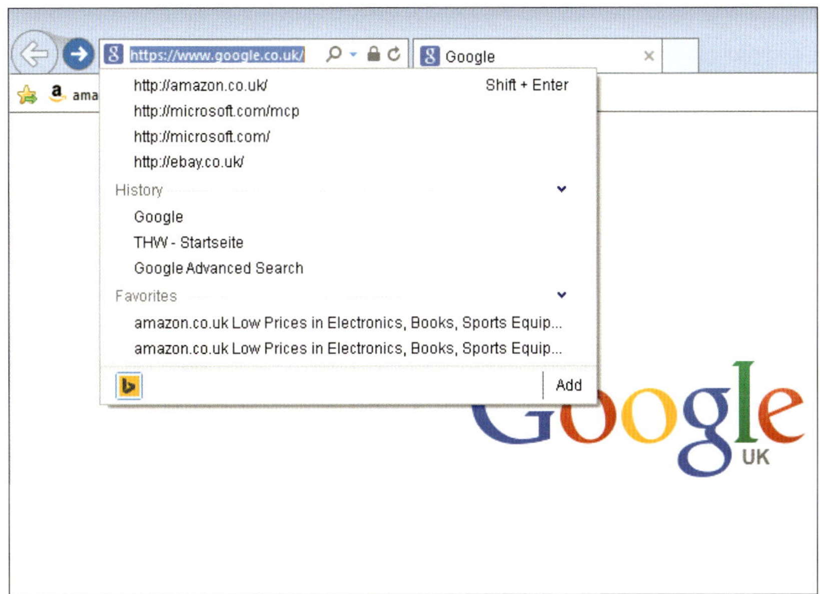

Figure 10.7 Using the Browser History feature.

To view even more sites visited, you can open the Favorites Center pane and click the History tab. There, you can choose to view sites by date—that is, from the current day, current week, one week ago, two weeks ago, or three weeks ago. (See Figure 10.8.) Or, you can open the drop-down menu at the top of the pane and choose to view sites in alphabetical order (choose View By Site), by frequency of visit (choose View Most Visited), or in the order they were visited today (choose View By Order Visited Today). You can also search your history list by choosing Search History from the drop-down list, typing a search term, and clicking the Search Now button.

Internet Explorer automatically saves your browsing history for 20 days. If you like, you can change this setting. The maximum is 999 days.

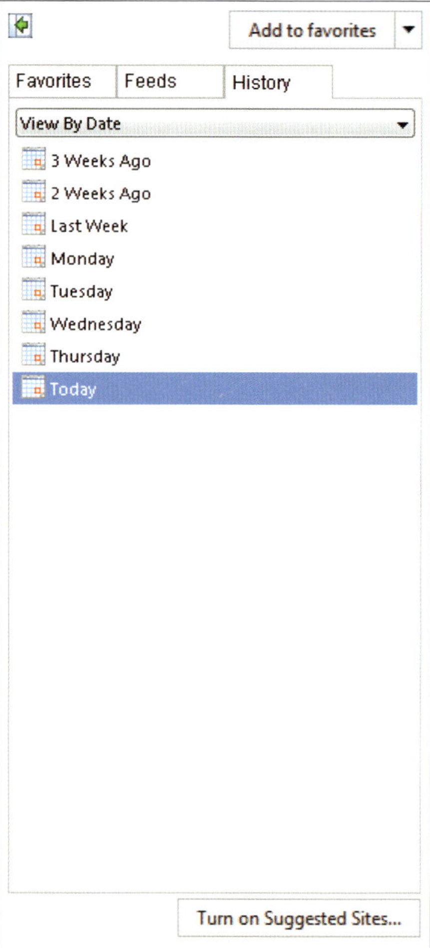

Figure 10.8 Using the Browser History feature to view by date.

Step by Step

To change the History settings, follow these steps:

1. Click the Tools button in the upper-right corner of the browser screen. A menu appears.
2. Select Internet Options. The Internet Options dialog box opens, with the General tab displayed.
3. Click the Settings button in the Browsing History section. The Website Data Settings dialog box opens.
4. Click the History tab.
5. Change the number of days the history is kept and click OK.

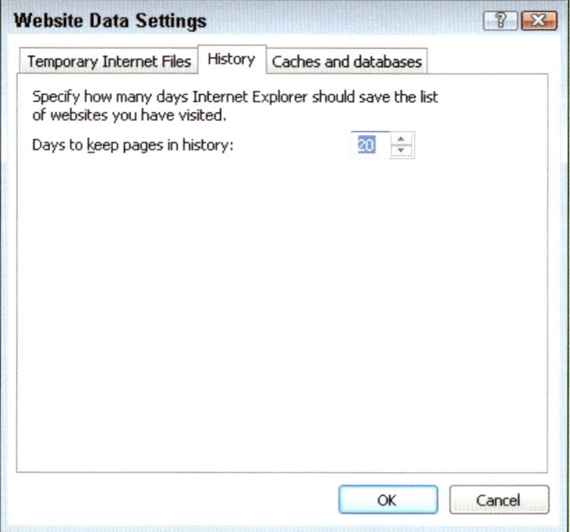

If you'd prefer not to store information about your browsing history, open the Internet Options dialog box as described. Then, in the Browsing History section of the General tab, select the Delete Browsing History on Exit check box. Finally, click OK. Every time you exit the browser, all history will be erased.

Downloading and Uploading Content

Internet is a vast repository of data in the same way that a library is full of books. Some data is for onscreen consumption only, but much of the data is also downloadable.

When you click a hyperlink that points to a downloadable file, a dialog box may appear automatically inviting you to specify a file name and location on your local computer in which to save the file. You can also right-click the hyperlink and choose Save Target As (or an equivalent command, depending on the browser you are using). Some browsers automatically download files to a default Downloads folder, using the file's default name, so you are not prompted for a name or location.

You can also upload content—that is, copy it from a desktop computer to a server on the Internet. You might do this to back up your data, storing it online on a personal storage site such as Microsoft OneDrive or Dropbox (also known as **cloud storage**). You can also use these sites to share data with others.

Another way to upload files for storage or sharing is to use the File Transfer Protocol (FTP). FTP is used solely for the transfer of files online. In the same way that there are web servers on the Internet, there are also FTP servers, maintained by businesses and individuals to enable users to upload and download files. Some of these are private, requiring a user ID and password; others are public, for distributing files that anyone may access.

You access an FTP site using a web browser in much the same way as a website; the main difference is that the address you enter into the browser starts with **ftp://** rather than **http://**. You can also access an FTP site using an FTP application. FileZilla (`www.filezilla-project.org`) is a free FTP client that anyone may download and use. It is shown in Figure 10.9.

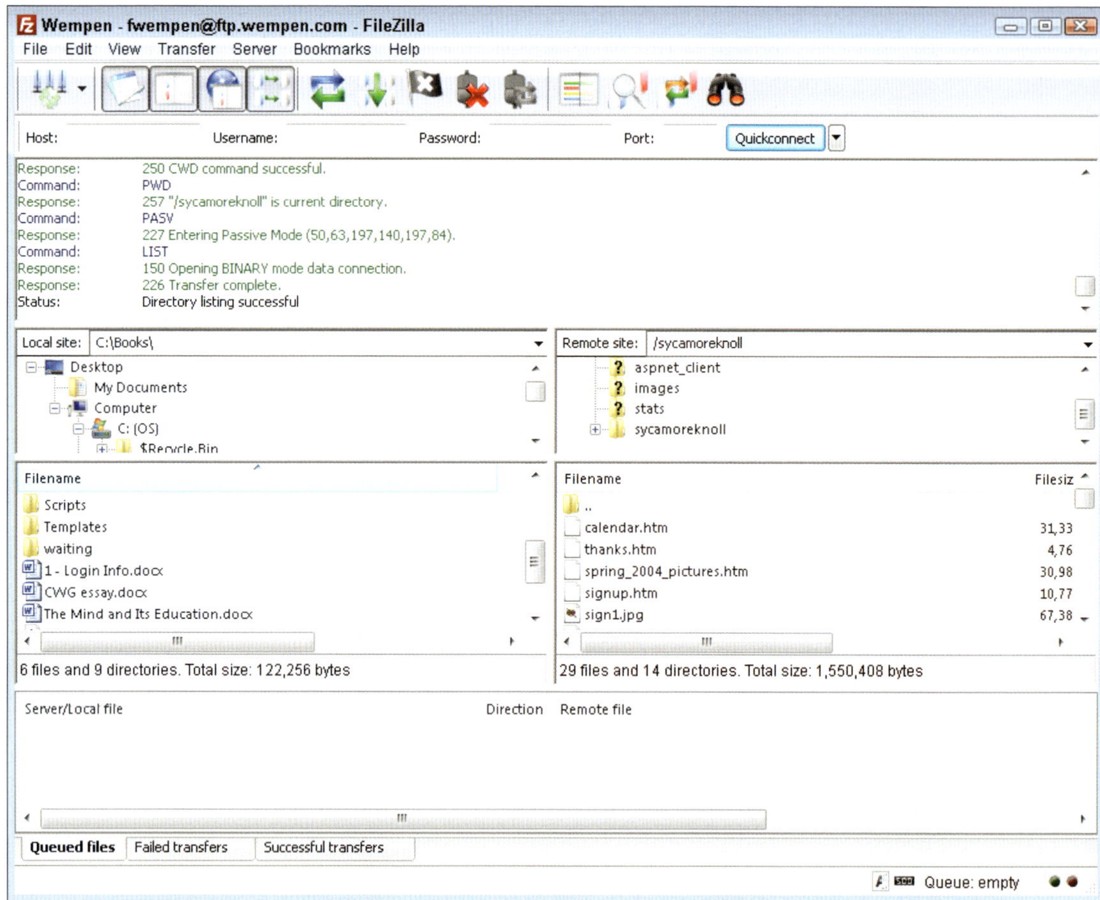

Figure 10.9 FileZilla is an FTP application, used for uploading and downloading files from an FTP server online.

Managing Plug-ins (Add-ons)

plug-in A piece of software added to a web browser to give it additional functionality.

A **plug-in**, also called an add-on, is a piece of software that can be added to a web browser to give it additional functionality, like the capability to view movies or Flash content. Two of the most common plug-ins are Adobe Shockwave Flash Object and Java.

In most cases, you do not have to search for or manually install plug-ins. If one is needed, your browser will display a message offering to find and install it for you, or will direct you to a web page where you can download and install it.

Step by Step

Managing Installed Add-ons

To view and manage currently installed add-ons, follow these steps:

1. Click the Tools button in the upper-right corner of the browser window. A menu appears.
2. Choose Manage Add-ons. The Managed Add-ons window appears, displaying currently installed add-ons, organized by type.

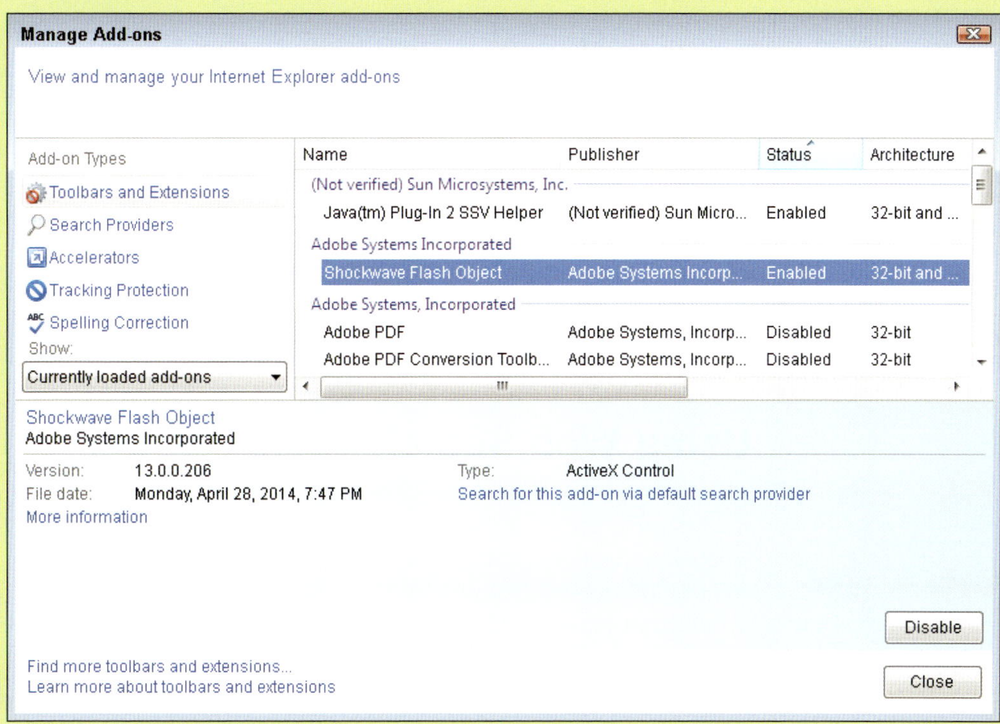

3. Click on any of the installed add-ons to view further details. When the add-on's details are displayed, you have the option of enabling or disabling that add-on.
4. Click Close to close the dialog box.

Using Web-Based Applications

These days, developers can use a number of programming languages to run web-based applications within a web browser. A **web-based application** is software that is downloaded and run within the web browser rather than being installed directly on the user's computer.

A good example of a web-based application Outlook.com (previously called Hotmail). You use this program to read and write email messages. All the messages are stored on the server, not on your computer.

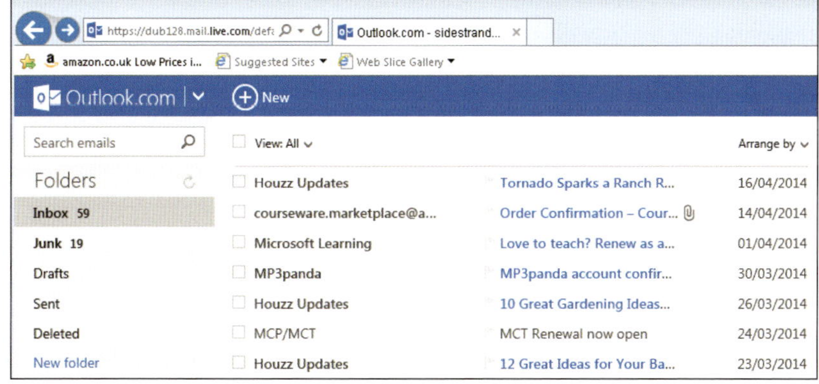

Web-based applications offer developers increased flexibility. Because they are browser-based, developers can build applications that work regardless of operating system. Web-based applications also alleviate concerns about local data storage. Finally, web-based applications are easier to update; there is no need to install and maintain applications on the local level. To capitalize on this new technology, many companies are moving to a subscription-based model, where users pay a monthly fee to use it rather than purchasing it outright.

web-based application Software that downloads to your computer and then runs within a web browser.

Quick Review

1. Why might you choose to change your browser's home page?
2. Why might you save a site as a Favorite?
3. By default, how long does Internet Explorer save your browsing history?
4. What is a plug-in?

Using Web Search Tools

search engine A software tool used to locate information on the web.

The answer to just about any question you may have is likely available on the Internet. The problem is knowing where to look to find it. This is where search engines come in. A **search engine** is an application that builds an index of sites on the Internet. Users can then search that database using keywords or phrases to find sites that contain the information they need.

Put It to Work

Top Search Engines

This book uses Google as the basis for its examples, but you are free to try out other search engines too. Here are some of the most popular search engines that provide English-language results. To try out one of these, type its name (followed by .com) in the Address bar of your browser.

1. Google
2. Bing
3. Yahoo!
4. Ask
5. AOL
6. Wow
7. WebCrawler
8. MyWebSearch
9. Infospace
10. Info

Conducting a Search

To conduct a search in Google, you type a keyword or phrase into the Search field and click the blue magnifying glass button on the right. Google returns a list of sites that contain information matching the word or phrase you typed. It also shows you how many matches Google found, and how long it took Google to conduct the search.

As shown in Figure 10.10, each entry in the list contains three pieces of information:

- **The title:** This indicates the source of the information.
- **The URL:** This is the web address for the page containing the information.
- **The text:** Google shows an excerpt of the information, with the search words highlighted in bold.

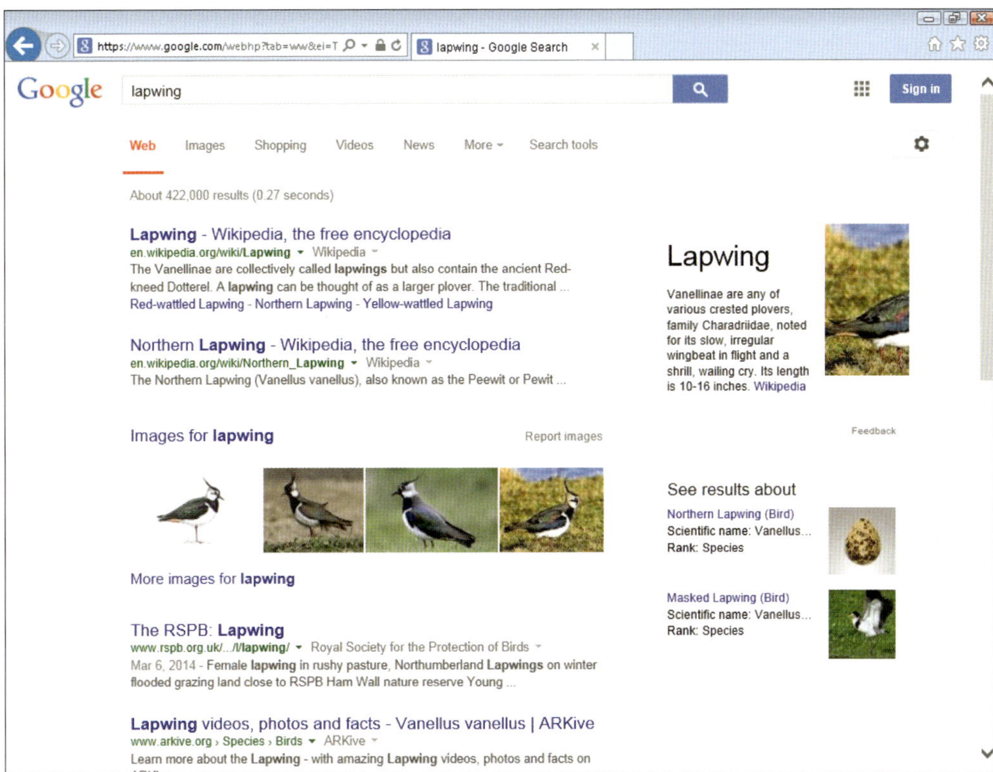

Figure 10.10 The results of a Google search for "lapwing."

To access a site that appears in the results, click it in the list.

Narrowing Your Search

Sometimes, you may find that a search yields too many results to be useful. To pare things down, try adding words to your search string. For example, if you type **lapwing**, Google finds more than 337,000 results. If you search instead for **lapwing nesting habits**, the number of results drops to 41,300. The longer the search phrase, the more likely it is to narrow down the results to a manageable number.

Advanced Search Options and Features

Some search engines offer advanced search features, and Google is no exception. To access these features, type **`http://www.google.com/advanced_search`** in the browser's address bar. You'll see a screen like the one shown in Figure 10.11. Fill in any of the relevant fields to narrow your search. For example, fill in the This Exact Word or Phrase field if you want to find pages that contain that text verbatim. Or, fill in the None of These Words field if you want Google to omit pages that contain that word from your search results. You can also narrow results by language, region, and more. After you enter all your search criteria, click the Advanced Search button to see a list of results.

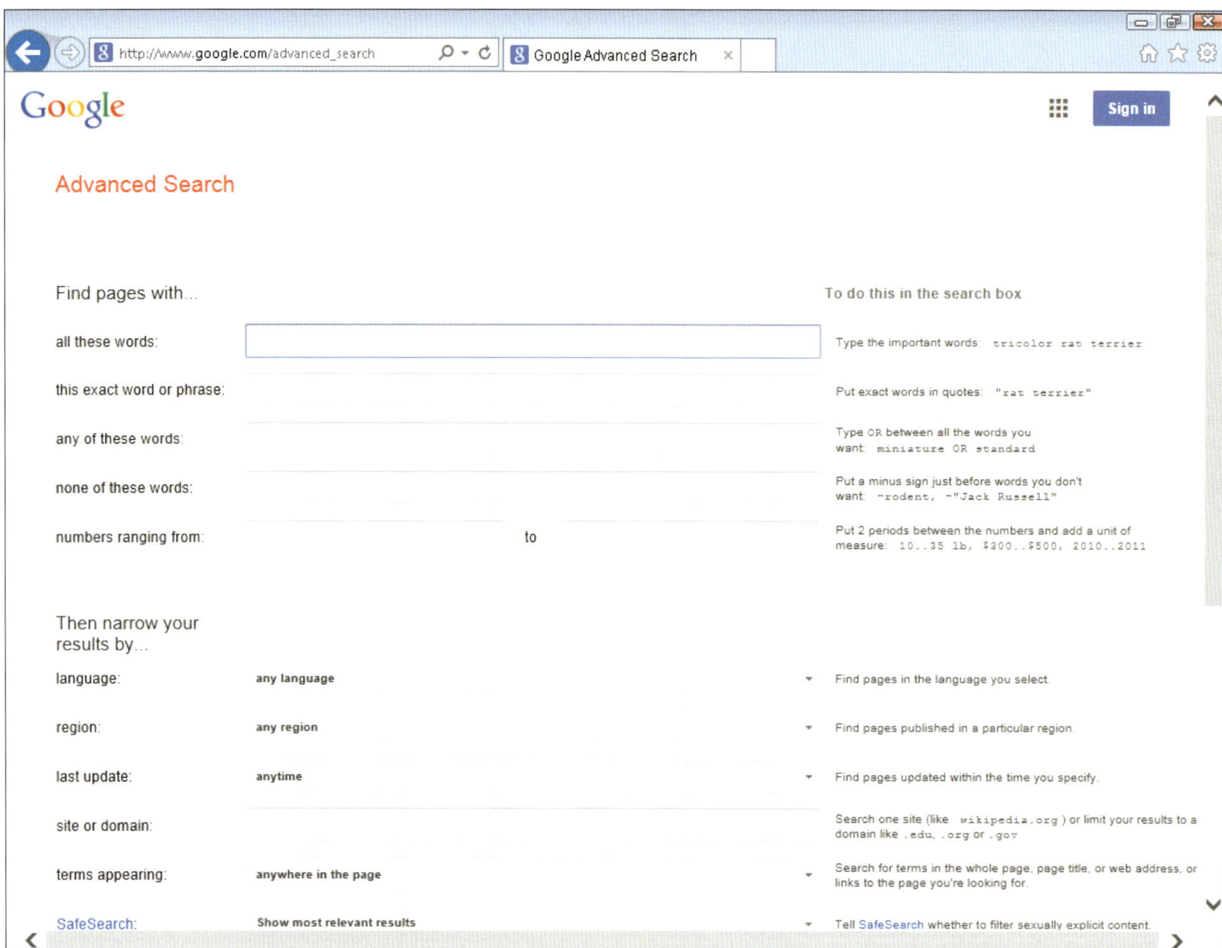

Figure 10. 11 The Google Advanced Search page.

Using Search Operators

search operator A word or symbol that has a specific function when carrying out a search.

Another way to narrow your search is to enter specific search operators in the Search field. A **search operator** is a word or symbol that has a specific function when carrying out a search. These operators tell the search engine to follow specific instructions when it carries out the search. Table 10.1 outlines the most commonly used search operators.

Table 10.1 Common Search Operators

Operator	***Result***
site:	Gets results from only the site or sites listed
inurl:	Limits the search to words contained in the URL string
allinurl:	Returns entries that contain all the words specified in the URL
intitle:	Returns entries that contain one of the specified words in the title
allintitle:	Returns entries that contain all the specified words in the title
author:	Returns entries or articles by a specific author
- (minus sign)	Excludes what follows from the query

To use a search operator, simply type the operator, including the colon, followed by the keyword or phrase, and then click the Search button. Figure 10.12 shows the results achieved by entering the following query: **site: microsoft.com accounting**. Notice that all the entries returned are from Microsoft, and either they contain the word "accounting" or pertain to finance and accounting.

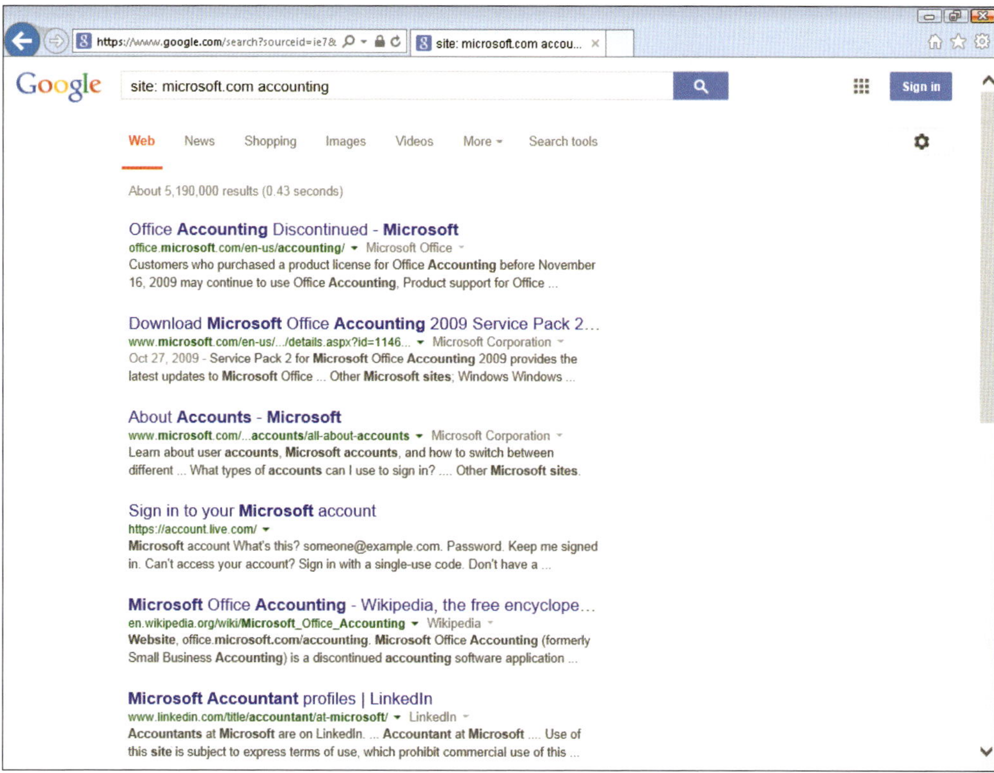

Figure 10.12 Using search operators.

You can enter more than one advanced search operator into a search query.

TIP

Evaluating the Accuracy of Web Information

The wonderful thing about the web is that anybody can create a website and publish her own information. The bad thing about the web is that anybody can create and publish her own information.

The web can provide answers to your questions, but how do you know how accurate or reliable this information is? To gauge this, consider the source of the information. If the information appears on a website hosted by a university, respected institution, or reputable company, it is likely that the information is accurate. If not, it's possible that the information is accurate, but there is no way of knowing for certain. The information is only as good as its source. Information on an individual's blog, for example, is not usually reliable information.

Keep in mind that many websites are created with an agenda in mind that may conflict with providing objective facts. For example, someone selling a product may exaggerate the product's benefits or post fictitious reviews, and someone promoting a certain political agenda may twist or intentionally misinterpret data to create an impression that supports his or her position.

sponsored link A hyperlink that is placed on a page because a payment has been made.

Many web pages contain ads, and the ads are not always sectioned off separately from the main text; they may appear between the paragraphs of an article and might trick you into thinking they are part of the article. An ad is never a reliable source of information. Similarly, sponsored link are mini-ads that contain hyperlinks to other websites. Do not assume that a sponsored link is relevant to the topic of the article or that the author of the article even knows that the sponsored link is placed there.

forum A web-based discussion and advice-sharing site.

Forums are public message boards that you access via websites. They may be sponsored by a particular company, such as a support forum for a certain kind of hardware or software, or they may be created and managed by an individual. Because the posts on a forum are made by the general public, not by known experts, you must be cautious about applying any advice you read in forums. For example, a forum post might recommend that you download and install a certain file, but that file might have a virus or might cause compatibility problems on your computer. Some forums are monitored by official or unofficial representatives of the hosting company.

knowledge base A set of articles provided and maintained by a company or government agency about its products.

A knowledge base is a more reliable source of information. It is a set of articles provided and maintained by a company or government agency about its products. For example, Microsoft has a knowledge base in which you can look up officially approved articles about various Microsoft products.

wiki A web-based application that can be edited by anyone and that is usually informational or instructive in nature.

Wikipedia A free, online encyclopedia. Wikipedia is an example of a wiki.

Encyclopedia sites vary in their accuracy and reliability. Well-known encyclopedias such as *Encyclopedia Britannica* and *World Book Encyclopedia* may generally be thought of as accurate. However, many sites that appear to be encyclopedias at first glance are actually wikis. A wiki is a knowledge base in which content is user-generated, so that anyone can post or edit entries, even someone who is not an expert on the topic or who has an agenda to promote. The best-known wiki is Wikipedia (`www.wikipedia.org/`). While Wikipedia is a good source of basic information on a topic, it cannot be trusted as a reliable source by itself, because of its nature; verify any information you learn from Wikipedia or any other wiki with other sources.

Virtual Private Networks

Suppose you work for a company that has a head office and several remote sites. The company wants to connect the sites to form one network, and also to allow staff to work from home using the company network. However, the company doesn't want to go to the expense of running secure dedicated network cables between each person's home and the company headquarters.

Virtual private networking (VPN) enables a user to create a secure connection to a remote server by going through the Internet. A VPN creates a secure tunnel, or pipeline, between a VPN-enabled web server and an individual computer. This tunnel is very difficult to hack, so the connection is safe enough to use for sensitive data.

To connect to a VPN using Microsoft Windows, open the Network and Sharing Center (right-click the network icon in the notification area and choose Network and Sharing Center, or go through the Control Panel). From there, click Set Up a New Connection or Network, and click Connect to a Workplace. Choose Use My Internet Connection (VPN), and then follow the prompts to set up the connection, using the settings provided to you by the owner of the VPN server (your employer or school, for example).

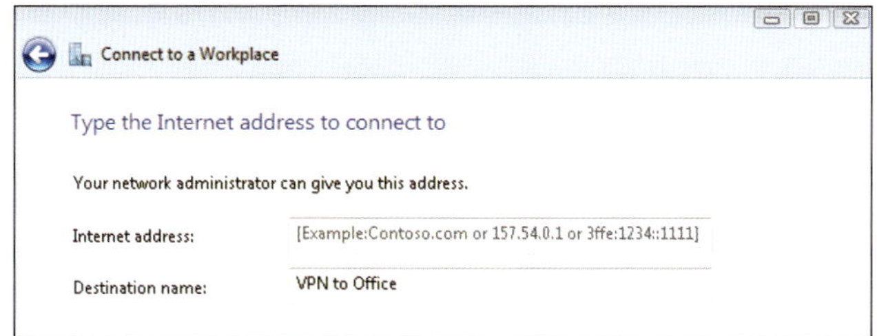

Security and Privacy

virtual private networking (VPN) A method of creating a secure, private communication tunnel using a public communications channel such as the Internet.

Quick Review

1. What is a search engine?
2. What are the three pieces of information contained in a result returned by a search engine?
3. Why is it a good idea to narrow your search results?
4. What is the purpose of a VPN?

Summary

How the Web Works

The **Internet** is a global network of millions of computers that can communicate with each other. The **World Wide Web (WWW,** or the **web)** is one part of the Internet; it is a network of interconnected pages of information stored on publicly accessible servers. Web pages are stored on web servers, and accessed by web browsers. A **web page** is a file that is formatted for use on the web. A **web server** is a server on which web pages are stored and made available to the public. A **web browser** is an application that can display web pages.

Most web pages are written in **HyperText Markup Language (HTML)**, a coding language that tells the browser how to display the content. A **hyperlink** is a clickable link to another page.

A **uniform resource locator (URL)** is the address you enter into your web browser's address bar to navigate to a specific web page. A URL consists of a protocol, a domain name, and, optionally, a path following the domain name.

A **domain name** is a name that identifies an entity on the Internet. It's a key part of a URL. In its basic form, a domain name consists of an identifier followed by an extension, like **microsoft.com**. The extension, also called the **top-level domain**, is often used to identify the type of organization that the name represents. Some domain names also include a two-letter country code.

Every computer that connects to the Internet has its own unique numeric address, called the **IP address**.

Domain Name System (DNS) is the naming system employed to enable users to access websites using their domain names or URLs rather than their IP addresses. The process of mapping domain names to IP addresses is called **name resolution** and is done by DNS servers.

Accessing the Web with a Browser

To open Internet Explorer, use the shortcut on the Start menu or the taskbar, or click a web hyperlink in a document. The page that opens by default is the **home page**. Click on a hyperlink to go to a web page. Use the Forward and Back buttons to navigate between pages you have recently visited. Use the Refresh button to reload a page, or use the Stop button to stop a page from completing its loading. Internet Explorer enables you to have multiple **tabs** open at once, each displaying a different page.

To store a URL so you can easily recall it later, save it as a **Favorite**. IE maintains a list of recently visited sites called **History**. To access both favorites and history, click the View Favorites, Feed, and History button (which look like a star).

When you click on the hyperlink for a downloadable file, your browser downloads it, or prompts you for a filename and location to download it. To upload a file to a server, you can use a web-based uploading interface, such as with Microsoft OneDrive, a type of **cloud storage**. You can also use the FTP protocol in your web browser (on some sites) or use a separate FTP application.

A **plug-in** (also called an add-on) is a piece of software that can be added to a web browser to give it additional functionality, like the capability to view movies or Flash content. If you need a plug-in to play a certain type of content, your browser will prompt you to install it.

Using Web Search Tools

A **search engine** is an application that builds an index of sites on the Internet. Users can then search that database using keywords or phrases to find sites that contain the information they need. Examples include Google, Bing, and Yahoo!.

Sometimes, you may find that a search yields too many results to be useful. Search using multiple keywords to narrow down a search, or use **search operators**. Different search engines support different operators.

To gauge the accuracy of information you find on the web, consider the source of the information. Forums, ads, sponsored links, and blogs are all unreliable sources. Knowledge bases and official company sites are generally more reliable. A **wiki** may contain accurate information or not; it is not reliable.

Key Terms

domain name
Domain Name System (DNS)
dynamic IP address
Favorite
home page
hyperlink
HyperText Markup Language (HTML)
HyperText Transfer Protocol (HTTP)
Internet
IP address
knowledge base
name resolution
plug-in
search engine
search operator
static IP address
tab
top-level domain
uniform resource locator (URL)
virtual private network (VPN)
web-based application
web browser
web server
wiki
Wikipedia
World Wide Web (WWW)

Test Yourself

Fact Check

1. What is the name of the process that changes the domain name into an IP address?
   a. name conversion
   b. name translation
   c. name changing
   d. name resolution
2. What would be the best domain extension to use for a fund-raising charity?
   a. com
   b. org
   c. ac
   d. edu
3. What do you call software that adds functionality to a browser such as Internet Explorer?
   a. extension
   b. plug-in
   c. browse tool
   d. socket

4. Which of the following indicate that a web browser connection is secure? (Select two.)
   a. padlock icon
   b. key icon
   c. `http://`
   d. `https://`
5. What kind of online server translates between IP addresses and domain names?
   a. DNS
   b. IPSec
   c. SSL
   d. PPTP
6. Which option would you select in Internet Explorer to remove any trace of previously visited websites?
   a. Refresh Browsing History on Exit.
   b. Delete Browsing History on Exit.
   c. Update Browsing History on Exit.
   d. Remove Browsing History on Exit.
7. The purpose of a VPN is to be able to
   a. Connect securely to a remote network
   b. Upload large files quickly
   c. Send and receive email from multiple addresses
   d. Protect your PC from viruses
8. If you wanted to visit a web page that you looked at last week, where would you look for a link to it?
   a. Favorites
   b. History
   c. Forums
   d. Feed
9. What is the name of the object on a web page that you can click to open another page?
   a. hyperlink
   b. hypertext
   c. hypervisor
   d. web connector
10. What is the name of the type of website where individuals can edit and delete content?
    a. wiki
    b. mapi
    c. miki
    d. diki

Matching

Match the following words to the correct phrase.

a. web server

b. home page

c. IP address

d. web-based application

e. search engine

f. domain name

1. _______________An application that runs within a web browser
2. _______________A name that identifies an entity on the Internet
3. _______________A unique numeric address for a computer on the Internet
4. _______________A software tool used to locate information on the web
5. _______________A computer that responds to requests for web content
6. _______________The page that is displayed when you first launch your web browser

Sum It Up

1. What is the relationship between the Internet and the World Wide Web?
2. What does a hyperlink do?
3. What type of server is used to resolve domain names and URLs to IP addresses?
4. What browser feature enables users to open multiple web pages in a single browser window?
5. What function does a search engine serve?
6. What is a VPN?

Explore More

Identifying the Path from Source to Destination

To see happens when you type a URL into a web browser to visit a web page, you can use the **tracert** command. It traces the path from the browser to the website, noting all the devices it goes through en route.

1. Click the Start button, type **cmd** into the Search Programs and Files box, and press Enter. A command prompt window opens.
2. At the command prompt, type **tracert** followed by a space and then the URL for the website of your choice (for example, **`www.bbc.co.uk`**) and press Enter. The command prompt window will list all the devices that your request travels through before it gets to the chosen destination. The program will also list the IP address of each device. When the process completes, the window will say "Trace Complete."

As you can see, when you send the request, it leaves your computer, goes through your router, and then passes through a series of other devices between your browser and the destination. Notice that your request can probably get from one side of the world to the other in about 15 stages or hops—sometimes fewer.

Try using **tracert** with `www.disney.com` as the target. As the request moves from device to device, see if you can identify the cities through which your request travels based on the names of the devices it passes.

Decoding URLs

When you visit a website, look at the complete path of the URL, including any folder names. Try different pages on the site and see if you can map how the site is laid out based on the different folder names you see.

Exploring DNS Name Resolution

DNS name resolution is a process that happens automatically whenever you type a URL into the web browser. This exercise enables you to see which DNS server you are using:

1. Click the Start button, type **cmd** into the Search Programs and Files box, and press Enter. A command prompt window opens.
2. At the command prompt, type **nslookup**, followed by a space and then the URL for the website you want to visit (for example, type **nslookup `www.google.com`**) and press Enter. The command prompt window lists the name and address of the DNS server you are using, followed by Google's IP address. If you see more than one address in this part of the results, it means the DNS knows about five different Google servers. Your browser usually will go to the first one in the list, but if it is not available, your browser will go to the second, and so on.

Think It Over

Evaluating Web Browsers

Imagine you are working for an organization that uses Windows computers and notebooks. Users have been allowed to download any software they like onto these computers, including different browsers. This creates a problem for the support department, so your supervisor has asked you to evaluate possible web browsers so that all computers can be standardized with one program. What browsers might you evaluate? What features might you consider most important?

Chapter 11

Network and Internet Privacy and Security

Learning objectives

- Understand the basic concepts of computer security
- Identify common threats when using a computer on a network
- Identify various malware programs
- Recognize the importance of securing personal data
- Develop strategies to make a computer more secure

You learned how computers are connected via networks and the Internet in Chapter 8, "Networking and Internet Basics." Computers connected in this way are vulnerable to a range of malicious activities. These machines are at risk for attacks that can cause poor performance or destroy data, or can cause users to become victims of fraud or identity theft.

In this chapter, you will learn about some of the threats that exist when using networks and the Internet, and about some of the precautions you can take to protect yourself and your computers from exposure.

Careers in IT

Security Specialist

Computer security is among the biggest growth areas in IT. With this comes a growing demand for engineers who have the skills to protect computers and networks. Security specialists are responsible for ensuring that all the security devices in a company are correctly configured. These specialists must also be able to spot different types of attacks and know how to respond to each one.

To work in this area, you will need to master skills such as understanding operating systems and networks. You will also need good computer qualifications from a college or university, plus industry certifications from companies like CompTIA and EC Council. Finally, you will need experience in other areas of IT, such as troubleshooting and support, before you can move into this role.

© iStockphoto.com/baranozdemir

Network and Internet Security Concerns

Computer crime is becoming increasingly common. It is relatively easy to attack computers to cause disruption or steal data. In fact, this can be carried out over a network or the Internet with low risk of the crime being traced back to the perpetrator.

Because of the ease with which attacks can be launched, it is essential that you remain aware of security and take the necessary steps to secure your data and online identity.

Computer security is built around upholding three basic goals:

- **Confidentiality.** Your data should be visible and accessible only to those whom you choose to see it.
- **Integrity.** The data you see and store should be reliable and accurate, and should not be tampered with. You need to be able to trust this data.
- **Availability.** Your data should be accessible when you want it, including after a mishap or disaster.

The threat assessment and security measures discussed in this chapter center around the need to uphold these three goals.

Security Threats Posed by Computer Criminals

Computer criminals engage in many types of activities that can compromise your computer system, your data, and your online identity.

Phishing

One of the common threats—and one that is also easy to carry out—is phishing. In a **phishing** attack, offenders send email messages to unsuspecting users in an attempt to trick them into giving away personal information such as login details or credit card information. The attackers then use this information to conduct fraudulent activity. This type of attack is often successful because the email messages appear to be from a trustworthy source, such as a bank or other reputable organization.

phishing The act of attempting to acquire information such as usernames, passwords, credit card information, and so forth, by pretending to be from a genuine, trustworthy source such as a bank.

CAUTION

Legitimate banks and other companies will ***never*** send an email asking you to submit sensitive personal information online. Never click on the links in such emails. As a good Internet citizen, you should report the emails to the bank or other company to make it aware of the phishing attempts.

Phishing emails are getting more sophisticated and harder to recognize, but here are some considerations that will help you identify them:

- Do you actually have an account with that bank or company? If not, then it's reasonable to assume the message is an attempt at phishing.
- Check the source of the email. Does the email address match the organization's standard email address? Check not only the address that appears as text in the message, but also the address that appears as a ScreenTip when you point the mouse at it.
- If you hover over the link to the company website with your mouse, it shows you the true URL. Is the address correct?
- Are there grammar and spelling mistakes? Does the message appear in the language you would expect? Even if the body text is in the expected language, are there buttons or other details with text in another language? These are all indications of a possible attempt at phishing.
- Check for the presence of the security padlock icon in the address bar. The presence of the security padlock icon is an indication that the message may be genuine—although it is not a guarantee.

Finally, remember that real companies and banks *never* ask for personal information in this way.

CAUTION

In April 2014, security experts discovered a security bug that affected Internet users worldwide. Called "Heartbleed," the bug placed around half a million of the world's secure servers—the ones indicated by the aforementioned security padlock icon—vulnerable to attack, placing the servers' private keys and users' session cookies and passwords at risk. Most sites quickly patched the problem, but sensitive data for many users was vulnerable in the interim.

Figure 11.1 shows an example of a phishing email. The message claims to be from Apple, telling a user that his Apple account has been suspended. Notice that the email is from `service@id-appactivate.com`. The address doesn't end in `@apple.com`.

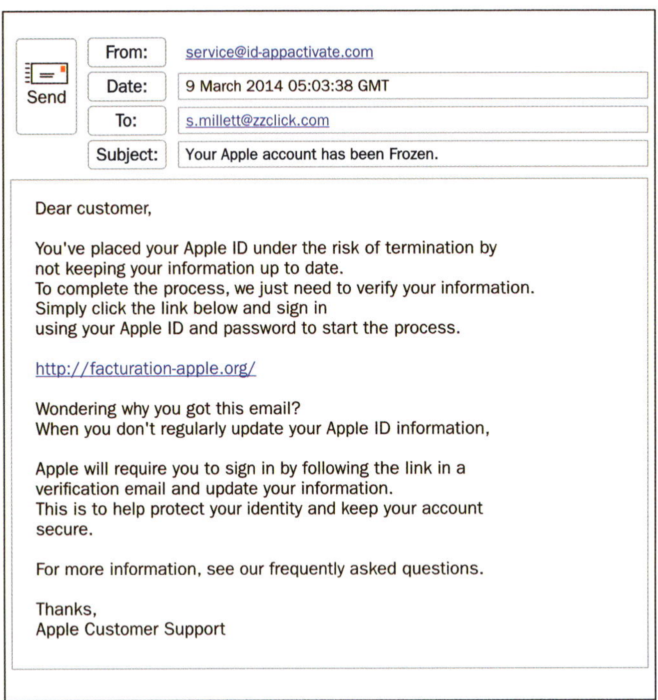

Send

From: service@id-appactivate.com

Date: 9 March 2014 05:03:38 GMT

To: s.millett@zzclick.com

Subject: Your Apple account has been Frozen.

Dear customer,

You've placed your Apple ID under the risk of termination by
not keeping your information up to date.
To complete the process, we just need to verify your information.
Simply click the link below and sign in
using your Apple ID and password to start the process.

http://facturation-apple.org/

Wondering why you got this email?
When you don't regularly update your Apple ID information,

Apple will require you to sign in by following the link in a
verification email and update your information.
This is to help protect your identity and keep your account
secure.

For more information, see our frequently asked questions.

Thanks,
Apple Customer Support

Figure 11.1 An example of a phishing email.

CAUTION Recipients of phishing emails should delete them without opening them. If they do open the mail, they should not click on the embedded link.

Password Cracking

When you log in to a computer or connect to an account on the Internet, you identify who you are with a username or number and you authenticate your identity, typically with a password. Passwords are the most common method of authentication because they are easy to use and maintain. Most systems and programs allow users to choose their own passwords, provided the passwords satisfy the system or program's security policy.

It may be relatively easy to determine someone's username. However, finding out someone's password is often much more difficult. People who want to break into a system or account often attempt password cracking—that is, they attempt to identify a user's password. Password cracking can be accomplished in several ways, for example, by guessing, using a keylogger (see Figure 11.2), engaging in social engineering, and using password-cracking tools.

Figure 11.2 A hardware keylogger. This model looks similar to a flash drive.

password cracking The act of attempting to identify a user's password in order to gain access to a system or program.

keylogger A piece of hardware or a software program that captures every keystroke a user types.

social engineering The art of obtaining someone's password either by befriending her or tricking her into sharing it.

Malicious Programs

As noted in the preceding section, computer criminals engage in a wide variety of activities to compromise your computer system, data, and online identity. They are aided in their efforts by various types of malicious software, grouped together under the title malware. This section outlines the main types of malware programs.

malware Harmful or maliciously created software, such as a virus or spyware.

Viruses

A virus is a piece of malicious software that is installed without the user's knowledge or consent. When executed, the virus program replicates and spreads to "infect" other computer programs, data files, or even the boot sector of the hard drive.

virus A type of malware that attaches itself to an executable file and spreads to other files when the program is run.

Viruses often carry a malicious payload. For example, a boot-sector virus might stop the computer from loading the operating system. Some viruses might delete all files of a certain type—for example, Word documents. Other viruses may simply have annoying consequences—perhaps opening and closing the CD drawer. Some viruses hide as long as they can so they can do as much damage as possible before being discovered. New viruses appear virtually every day, so it is vital that you take precautions and protect yourself from them.

The most common way for a virus to spread is for a user to open an infected email attachment or Internet link without having virus protection in place. This allows the malicious software to gain access to the system. If the infected file is sitting in RAM memory and you run another program, the virus attaches a copy of itself to the second program—and so on and so forth.

Worms

A worm is similar to a virus in that it may have a malicious payload. However, worms are designed to automatically spread from computer to computer over a network or the Internet. Like viruses, the consequences

worm A malicious computer program that spreads itself to other computers over a network or the Internet.

of worms range from destructive to annoying. A worm might delete files or direct users to a fake website, or it might just do something annoying like swapping left and right mouse button actions. At the very least, a worm will consume network bandwidth.

CAUTION Some worms are designed to compromise the user's email address book and send itself to all the user's contacts. If you receive an odd or unexpected message from one of your contacts, it could indicate that her address book has been infected by a worm. Before opening the email, contact the sender to determine whether the email is legitimate and to alert her to the possibility that her machine has been infected.

Trojans

According to Greek mythology, the Greeks conquered the city of Troy through trickery. They constructed a large wooden horse, which they presented to the Trojans as a gift. Unbeknownst to the Trojans, however, the Greeks had hidden a select team of soldiers inside the horse. After the Trojans dragged the horse inside the city walls, the Greek soldiers emerged from the horse and opened the city gates, enabling the rest of the Greek army to swarm the town.

Trojan A piece of malicious software that looks harmless but has a detrimental effect on a computer when it runs.

It is after this horse, called the Trojan horse, that Trojans are named. A **Trojan** is a piece of software, such as a game or utility, that may look innocent but has a malicious purpose. Typically, the user knowingly installs the game or utility, but doesn't realize there's a Trojan inside. When the user runs the program, the Trojan starts running in the background, often without the user's knowledge.

A Trojan can do nasty things to a computer, but more likely it is there to gather information. For example, many Trojan programs are keyloggers. As described, a keylogger records all the keys the user presses on the keyboard and saves them in a file. It then sends the file with the user's keystrokes to the person or group who sent the Trojan. In this way, whoever sent the Trojan can learn what the user does on the computer. More importantly, they can uncover the user's username and password, enabling them to log in themselves.

A common type of Trojan is one that displays a screen that recommends that you purchase and download some type of anti-malware software, as shown in Figure 11.3. In this case, however, the software is fake and will probably put more Trojans on your computer. Worse, if you buy it, the thieves will then have your credit card details.

spyware A type of malware that spies on the user's activities and reports them back to the spyware's developer.

Another type of Trojan runs spyware. **Spyware** is software that monitors what the user does on the computer without her knowledge. It then sends the information it gathers to a third party, which uses it to target the user with pop-up advertisements—often for fake products.

Figure 11.3 A Trojan advertising fake anti-virus software.

Ransomware

Some new, very nasty Trojans are called **ransomware**. These Trojans encrypt files on the system, such as photos, music, and documents. The Trojan then displays a message describing how to get the files back. Retrieval inevitably involves sending a payment over the Internet to an unknown destination with the promise that once the money is received, you will receive the key to unlock your files. The key doesn't exist and the damage is already done, however. You will not get your files unlocked. Your best protection against ransomware is to frequently back up your system on an external hard drive. That way, if you fall prey to this type of Trojan, you can simply copy the files from your backup drive. You'll learn more about backing up your system later in this chapter.

ransomware A type of Trojan that encrypts files on a user's system. It then displays a message describing how to decrypt the files—which inevitably involves sending payment over the Internet. Even after the money is sent, however, the files are not decrypted.

Protecting Yourself against Malware

The earliest anti-virus programs were designed to detect and protect against viruses, but have improved over the years into broader security solutions that can detect viruses, worms, Trojans, and sometimes more complex threats. A good anti-virus package provides a wide range of protective measures and may include firewall management (discussed later in this chapter) and anti-spyware as well.

Many good anti-virus products are in the marketplace: Symantec, Sophos, Kaspersky, and McAfee are among the most popular security solutions. They all work in a similar way and produce similar results. In addition, Microsoft has its own product, called Security Essentials. You can also find free anti-virus software, such as AVG (see Figure 11.4) or ClamWin. Free products usually have a more limited range of services than the commercial choices, but in some cases, you can upgrade to a paid version for expanded offerings.

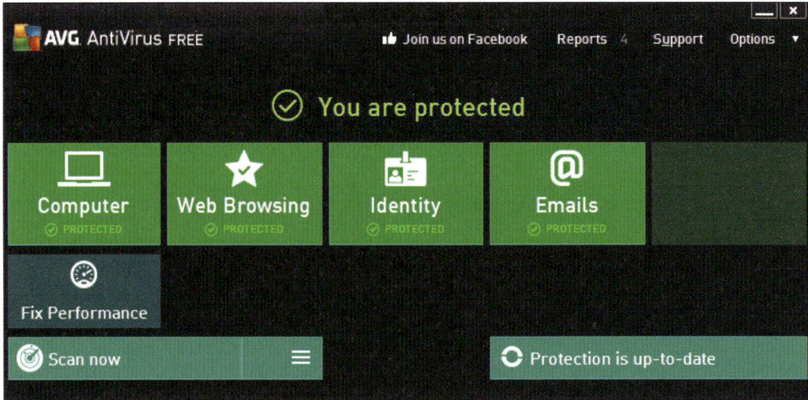

Figure 11.4 Free anti-virus soft-ware.

DoS Attacks and Zombies

denial of service (DoS) attack A coordinated attack in which the target website or service is flooded with requests for access, to the point that it is completely overwhelmed.

In a **denial of service (DoS) attack**, the attacker floods a website or service with thousands of requests for access—so many that it cannot deal with them all. As a result, legitimate users are prevented from accessing the site or service. DoS attacks often involve many thousands of computers from all over the world, all launching multiple requests against the target website or service, making them difficult to prevent. Once an attack is started, it can render the target site unavailable very quickly.

zombie A computer used to conduct a DoS attack.

bot A type of Trojan, used to infect a zombie computer to conduct a DoS attack.

botnet A network of zombie computers infected with bots, often numbering in the thousands. Computer criminals use botnets to conduct DoS attacks.

The computers that launch these attacks are called zombies. A **zombie** is a computer that has been infected with a particular type of Trojan called a **bot**. Initially, the bot runs in the background, doing very little beyond communicating with its master over the Internet every now and then, awaiting instructions. One day, it, along with thousands of other bots, receives instructions to bombard a particular website as part of a DoS attack. This is called a **botnet**. Millions of computers around the world are part of multiple botnets, all used for DoS attacks.

Wi-Fi Networks

Hackers frequently target Wi-Fi networks. When Wi-Fi networks are not properly secured, it is easy to steal data on them with little chance of being caught. Hackers don't even need any special equipment to penetrate such a Wi-Fi network.

When people use their devices to locate and connect to a wireless network, they see a list of available networks, as shown in Figure 11.5. Some of these networks may be open access, meaning you don't need a password to connect. Others may require a password and will provide users with a secure connection. Insecure networks are identified with a small exclamation mark; the other networks have encrypted connections.

Figure 11.5 Visible wireless networks.

Some wireless networks appear to be genuine, but in fact attempt to intercept your traffic. These types of Wi-Fi networks are called **rogue Wi-Fi**. These Wi-Fi networks usually seem authentic, often with a name that is similar or the same as a legitimate network. The difference? This network "sniffs" all your traffic, making a copy of everything you type—including any usernames, passwords, and credit card numbers.

rogue Wi-Fi A wireless network that "sniffs" traffic, making a copy of everything users type—including usernames, passwords, and credit card numbers.

Public places where many people are looking for Wi-Fi, such as coffee shops, restaurants, and airports, are common locations for rogue Wi-Fi connections. How can you tell whether a Wi-Fi network to which you want to connect is in fact rogue? It's not easy. If you are directed to a "Terms of Service" page after you connect, that's a good indication that the network is legitimate. A time limit is another sign that the network may be genuine. But your best bet is to simply ask someone who works at the location whether it offers Wi-Fi, and if so, the name of the network.

Quick Review

1. What are the three goals of computer security?
2. What are two ways to detect a phishing attack?
3. What are the three main types of malware?
4. What is the best protection against malware?

Network and Internet Privacy Concerns

The Internet has changed the way people live, learn, and communicate. While the Internet offers enormous power to communicate and to find information, it also makes us more vulnerable to invasions of privacy. The Internet consists of vast amounts of data spread globally across millions of websites; thanks to the sheer size and scope of the Internet, it's impossible to know how all this information is stored and how private it is!

Here are just a few of the ways in which using networks and the Internet can put your privacy at risk:

- When you use a search engine, the search engine site can gather information about you based on the terms you search for and the questions you ask.
- When you provide personal information on the Internet—such as your name, address, email, and so forth—to a website, that website can store the information and perhaps use it for purposes other than those you intended.

CAUTION Be aware of the personal information you make available online. That information may spread far beyond the sites you contact directly!

- Your computer has a unique identity. Someone who knows this unique identity can access your computer via a network and view, change, or delete your personal data.

Data Storage

When you store data on your computer, you store it as files. As the number of files grows, it becomes harder to locate the data you want. This is where databases come in. A **database** stores data in a way that enables you to search for and locate it quickly.

database A collection of data stored in a structured format, with the same facts stored about each instance. A database stores data in a way that enables you to search and locate it quickly.

There are millions of databases worldwide that, together, store billions of files. Often, these files contain information about individuals. For example, large companies have databases that contain information about their customers. Similarly, social networks like Facebook have huge databases to store the information about their users. If these networks are vulnerable to unauthorized access, sensitive data for many people may be compromised.

Most of this data is stored by private companies, and we rely upon them to handle personal data with care. Everything should be based on the principle of least privilege—that is, you give people minimum access for the jobs they have to do. If you request data about yourself, that is all you should see—no one else's details.

Privacy Laws

To protect people's privacy, there are rules to govern how personal information is handled. Most countries have data protection and privacy laws to control the access and distribution of this personal information. These laws are needed to regulate the companies that hold our personal information and to ensure that all our information is properly protected.

Different countries have different rules, but most require that any personal information stored is:

- Used only for the intended purpose
- Accurate
- Sufficient for the purpose, with no unnecessary information held
- Accessible by the owner
- Obtained legally
- Kept secure from unauthorized access
- Deleted when no longer needed

Understanding Social Networking Risks

A **social network** is an Internet-based system that enables users to interact in real time and by using messaging programs. With a social network, users can share every aspect of their lives with others. Examples of social networks include Facebook, Twitter, and Instagram.

social network An Internet-based system that enables users to interact in real-time and by using messaging programs.

While sharing information via social networks can be wonderful, it is not without its risks. It is easy to get carried away on social networks and publish information about yourself that would be better kept private. Before you publish too much information about yourself, you must consider just who can see that data. After you have published it, it is very difficult—if not impossible—to remove it from the Internet.

CAUTION Never leave a computer or laptop without logging out of any social network sites you have open. If you remain logged in, someone else could post information while pretending to be you.

Social networks pose another risk—namely, that some of the "friends" you make online may not be who they say they are. Be careful how much you reveal about yourself to such people. Remember: A social network is global, your new "friends" could be anywhere, and some of them may ask you to do things you shouldn't.

CAUTION Never agree to meet in person someone you've met online unless you bring a friend with you for protection and meet in a very public place, like a coffee shop.

Cyberbullying

Social networks have become part of our everyday lives—particularly among young people. Indeed, millions of young people spend time on sites such as Facebook, Twitter, Instagram, and other social network sites, often to stay in touch with friends.

Sometimes, however, what starts as a fun activity—interacting with friends online—turns ugly. Someone makes unpleasant comments about you online. Others join the conversation. People might even post rumors or altered images of you in an attempt to harass you. This is called **cyberbullying**—and it's a growing problem.

What should you do if you are being cyberbullied? The most important thing is to tell someone who can help. If you are being bullied at school or in the workplace, then your instructor or employer needs to know about it. He or she may be able to take action to stop it. Of course, telling others about the cyberbullying may be difficult because some of the comments may be hurtful or embarrassing. But it is important to let people know it is happening. You can't just ignore it and hope it will go away. All that does is empower the bullies.

cyberbullying Using computers and the Internet to deliberately harass or harm others by making malicious statements.

cookie A small file placed by a website on a computer that stores information about the user's interaction with the website.

Deleting Cookies

When you visit some websites, they place a cookie on your computer. A **cookie** is a small file that stores information about your interaction with the website. When you revisit the site, the site reads the cookie on your computer to identify you. Figure 11.6 shows where cookies reside in a Windows 7 system, while Figure 11.7 shows examples of actual cookies. Just one visit to a website can result in the installation of several cookies on your computer.

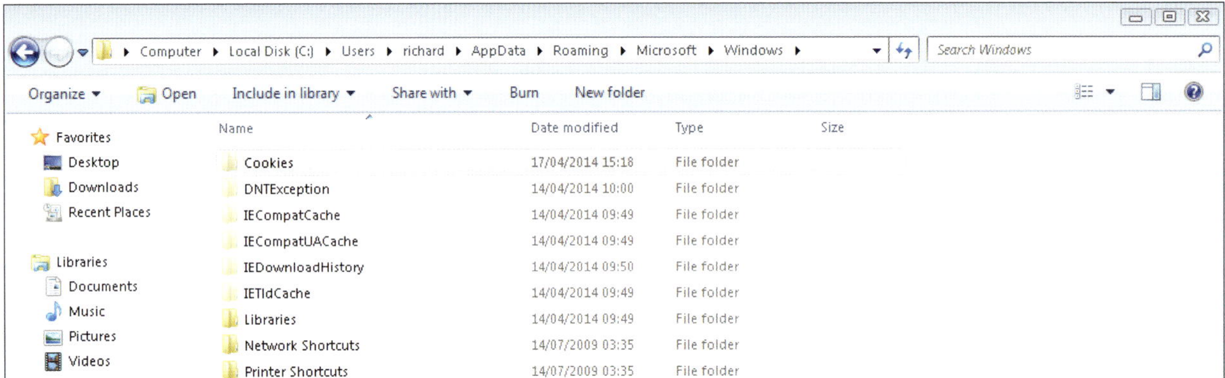

Figure 11.6 Where to find cookies in Windows Explorer.

Name	Date modified	Type	Size
26F578OI.txt	03/05/2014 15:52	Text Document	1 KB
LQ7FVZS7.txt	03/05/2014 15:52	Text Document	2 KB
Z4EY9C8R.txt	03/05/2014 15:52	Text Document	1 KB
Z6JGH5BV.txt	03/05/2014 15:51	Text Document	1 KB
2SVOWK5X.txt	03/05/2014 15:51	Text Document	1 KB
6S1MA63S.txt	03/05/2014 15:51	Text Document	1 KB
7V6NX5VV.txt	03/05/2014 15:51	Text Document	1 KB
D0LCUQUF.txt	03/05/2014 15:51	Text Document	1 KB
DZ0NYBS8.txt	03/05/2014 15:51	Text Document	1 KB
LV72GE74.txt	03/05/2014 15:51	Text Document	1 KB
5F2TNWR8.txt	03/05/2014 07:11	Text Document	1 KB
7I16NCIZ.txt	03/05/2014 07:11	Text Document	1 KB
79NNQZO3.txt	03/05/2014 07:11	Text Document	1 KB

Figure 11.7 The cookies generated by visiting two websites.

While this can sometimes be handy—for example, for sites that you've personalized—it's not always a good thing. For example, some cookies contain personal information that a hacker could use to gain access to a website while pretending to be you. The hacker could then use your PayPal or credit card information in a fraudulent manner, for example. Or, a hacker could trick you into downloading a Trojan that steals your cookies and sends them to the hacker's computer, enabling him to use them at will.

To prevent this, you can delete cookies, and prevent your computer from storing them in the future. If you do so, the next time you go to a website, it will not be able to identify you because there will be no cookies on your computer. While this may be frustrating on occasion—you may have to input information all over again—it can be a safer way to use the Internet. When you delete or disable cookies, you no longer leave a trail of information that others could use for malicious purposes.

Step by Step

Deleting and Disabling Cookies in Internet Explorer

To delete and disable cookies in Internet Explorer, follow these steps:

1. Open Internet Explorer.
2. Click the Tools button (the one with a cog wheel icon, located in the upper-right corner of the window) and choose Internet Options from the menu that appears.
3. The Internet Options dialog box opens with the General tab displayed. Under Browsing History, click the Delete button.
4. The Delete Browsing History dialog box opens. Ensure that the Cookies and Website Data check box is checked and then click the Delete button. This deletes all cookies currently stored on your system.
5. To prevent your system from storing additional cookies, select the Delete Browsing History on Exit check box in the Internet Options dialog box.
6. Click the Apply button. Then click OK.

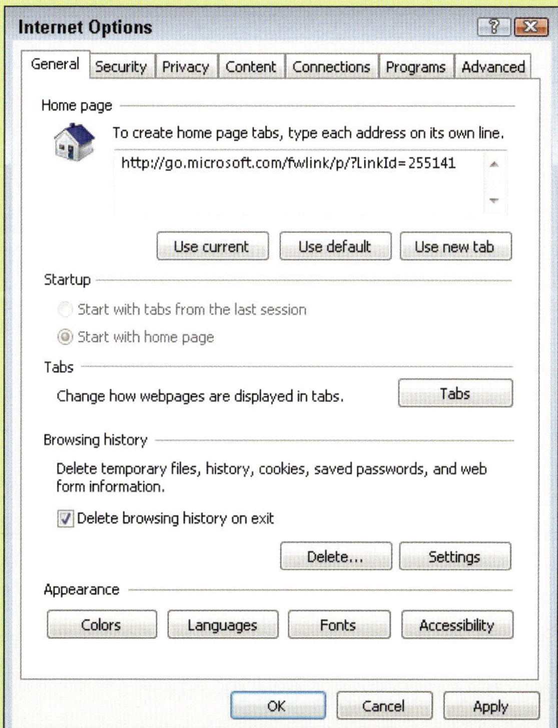

If you do not use Internet Explorer as your web browser, search your browser's Help files for the phrase "delete cookies."

Quick Review

1. What is a social network?
2. What should you do if you are being cyberbullied?
3. What is a cookie?
4. What happens if you delete a cookie from your system?

Strategies for Improving Security

How can you improve security? Some of the work is done for you by operating system vendors, who typically add security features when they produce new versions of an operating system. For example, Microsoft Windows now has a built-in firewall, and Microsoft offers its own anti-virus security products. The operating system is also more secure thanks to better login mechanisms and fewer vulnerabilities. There is still some work you can do, however. For example, you can restrict access to data, use encryption, protect against data loss, update your operating system, and more.

Restricting Access

Perhaps the easiest and most effective security measure you can take is to restrict access to the data on your computer. You can do this by using passwords, applying permissions, and enabling firewalls.

Using Passwords

When Windows is installed on a computer with only one user account, it does not require the use of a password to log in to the operating system. When you start the computer, it takes you straight to the desktop. That means anybody could start the computer and see what is stored on it as well as run programs without permission. This is not a good practice.

It's critical to create a strong password for your computer. That way, no one who does not know the password can log in. A strong password should contain a mix of uppercase and lowercase letters, numbers, and special characters such as @ or #, and be difficult or impossible for other people to guess. An example of a weak password might be "manchester." You could easily strengthen the password, however, by changing out some of the letters for other characters, like this: "M@nch35Ter." You should, of course, create a password that you can remember, and also change the password on a regular basis.

Step by Step

Creating or Changing Your Password

To create or change a password on a Windows computer, follow these steps:

1. Click the Windows Start button and choose Control Panel.
2. In the Control Panel, click User Accounts and Family Safety.
3. Under User Accounts, click Change Your Windows Password.
4. The Make Changes to Your User Account screen appears. Click Change Your Password.

5. If you are changing your password, type your current password in the Current Password field. Then type your new password in the New Password field, and type it again in the Confirm Password field. If you are creating a password for the first time, type it in the New Password and Confirm Password fields.
6. If you want, type a password hint in the Password Hint field.
7. Click the Change Password button.

You should create similarly strong passwords for any accounts you create on the Internet. That way, you ensure no one "cracks" your password and accesses your online accounts.

Locking the Computer

If you're logged in to a computer, you should never leave it unattended, even for a few minutes. If you do, someone could easily access your files, install a Trojan, or send an improper email as if it was from you. One simple security measure you can take to prevent this is to lock your computer when you are away from the machine.

You can lock your computer in one of two ways. One is to press the Ctrl+Alt+Del keys at the same time. You will be presented with an options screen; select the Lock This Computer option to lock the computer. Alternatively, press the Windows+L keys at the same time. To unlock the computer, simply enter your system password, as shown here.

A locked screen requires a password to open

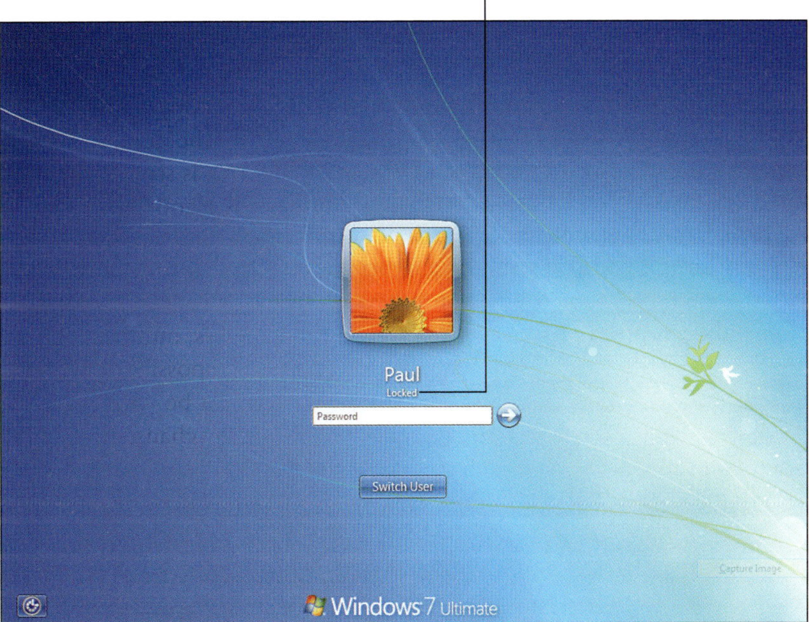

Privacy and Security

Sharing Folders with Permissions

If your Windows computer will have more than one regular user, you can create a user account for each person. Each user can choose to share some of his folders with other users on the computer, without granting access to all the data in his account. You can also share folders and files with other users over a network. This is done through the use of *permissions*.

Before you start assigning permissions to share data with others, you should consider what you wish to share and how much access to allow. For example, you can set a folder's or file's permissions to give others access to its contents, but not allow them to change the contents. Or, you could set a folder's or file's permissions such that others can add, change, and/or delete items.

Be cautious when sharing folders and files with others. Give people only the level of access they need—and no more.

Using a Firewall

firewall A security barrier on your computer or network that controls what traffic is allowed to pass through.

A **firewall** is a security barrier on your computer or network that controls what traffic is allowed into and out of your computer or network. The barrier is designed to separate your computer or network, which you trust, from an external network, which you might not.

Computers that run later versions of the Windows operating system include a firewall application by default, called Windows Firewall.

CAUTION Do not disable the firewall unless you have another form of protection in place. If you don't have an active firewall, your computer or network will be exposed to all sorts of threats that could damage your computer or cause you to lose files or data.

Encrypting Data

encrypt To scramble the contents of a file so it cannot be read without the required permission to decrypt it.

decrypt To reverse the encryption of a file so that the file appears in its original form again.

When you store data on a hard drive, the data is written such that it can be read by anyone who has access to the drive, which means that your data is vulnerable. Fortunately, there are ways to protect your data so that only you can access it. One method is to use encryption. **Encryption** involves using a mathematical process to scramble data to such an extent it is impossible to read . . . unless you have the key. The key unscrambles or **decrypts** the data so that it is readable again. When you use encryption on your computer, you work as normal; the encryption and decryption processes take place in the background.

CAUTION Don't save the recovery key on the hard drive you have just encrypted. You won't be able to read it if you lose the password!

Encrypting Internet Communications

In addition to encrypting your hard drive and the individual files on it, some websites enable you to encrypt your Internet communications. To determine whether an Internet connection is secure, check to see whether the URL starts with https rather than http or look for a padlock icon in the web browser's address bar. (The padlock icon appears to the right of the URL in Internet Explorer and to the left in Firefox, as shown here.) Both indicate a secure connection between your computer and the website; data captured between these two points will be unreadable. (That said, see the Caution about the Heartbleed virus earlier in this chapter.)

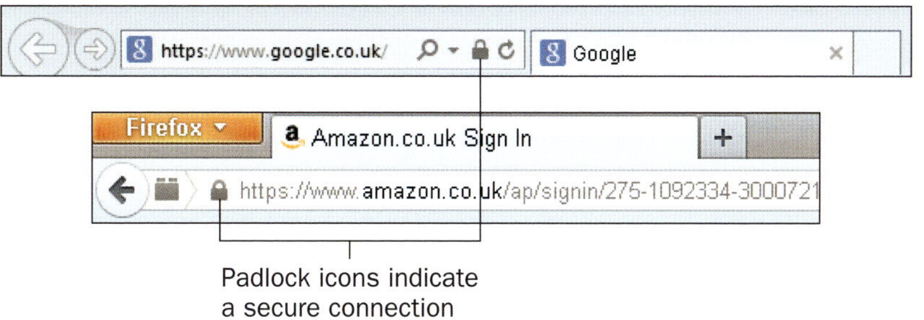

Preventing Data Loss

Security is not just about preventing unauthorized access to your data. It's also about protecting your data from damage or loss. To facilitate this level of security, you must be sure to store at least one copy of your data somewhere safe. One approach is to connect an external hard drive to your computer and copy all your important files onto it. This is called "making a backup," or "backing up." After you have backed up the data, you must store the drive somewhere safe. You should back up your system on a regular basis. That way, you know you have copies if something goes wrong.

Windows comes with a built-in backup utility, Windows Backup, that you can use to back up your files and also restore them in the event of damage or loss.

Step by Step

Setting Up Windows Backup to Perform Automatic Backups

To set up Windows Backup to back up your files automatically on a regular basis, follow these steps:

1. Click the Windows Start button and choose Control Panel.
2. In the Control Panel window, click the System and Security option.
3. In the System and Security window, click Backup and Restore.
4. The first time you run Windows Backup, you must set it up. To begin, click the Set Up Backup link.
5. Specify the drive on which you want to save your backup (usually an external drive for safekeeping). Then click Next.

   If you prefer, you can save the backup to a network location rather than a hard drive. To do so, click Save on a Network. Then enter the network location's file path in the Network Location field. (If you don't know the path, click Browse, locate and select the folder on the network in which you want to save your backup, and click OK.) Finally, enter the appropriate username and password to access the network in the Username and Password fields and click OK.

6. Specify what files you want to back up. Note that you can let Windows choose (recommended) or choose yourself. Then click Next.

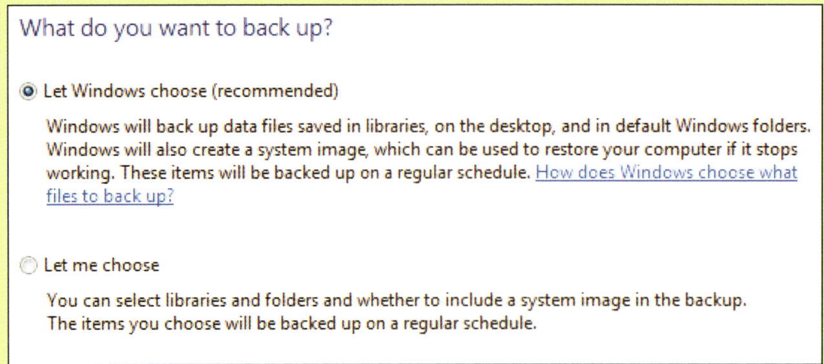

7. The Review Your Backup Settings screen summarizes your settings, including when and how often backups will occur. To change the backup schedule, click the Change Schedule link.

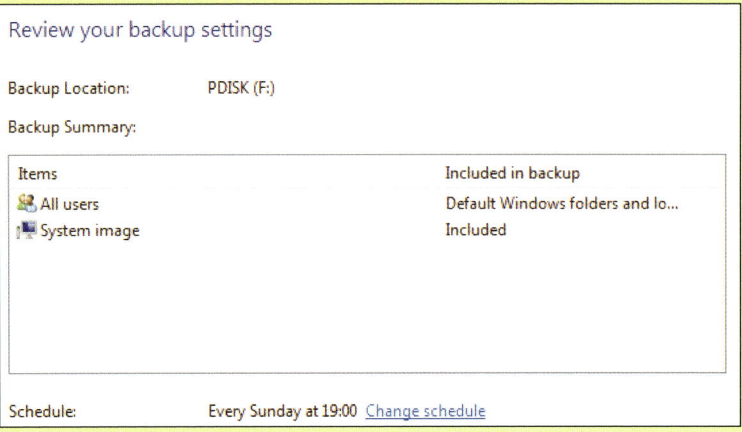

8. The How Often Do You Want to Back Up screen appears. Make sure the Run Backup on a Schedule check box is selected.
9. Click the How Often drop-down list and choose Daily, Weekly, or Monthly. If you chose Weekly or Monthly, also click the What Day drop-down list and choose the day on which backups should occur.
10. Click the What Time drop-down list and specify the hour on which backups should occur.
11. Click OK to close the How Often Do You Want to Back Up? screen. Then click Save Settings and Run Backup in the Review Your Backup Settings screen. Windows launches the backup operation; subsequent backups will occur on the schedule you specified.

Performing a Manual Backup with Windows Backup

You don't have to wait for your system to back up automatically. You can also perform a manual backup. You might do so if you're about to make a system change, or if your computer was turned off when the automatic backup was scheduled to occur. To perform a manual backup, follow these steps:

1. Click the Windows Start button and choose Control Panel.
2. In the Control Panel window, select the System and Security option.
3. In the System and Security window, click Backup and Restore. The Backup or Restore Your Files screen appears.
4. Click Back Up Now to launch the backup operation.

Restoring Files with Windows Backup

If you've used Windows Backup to back up the files and folders on your computer, you can restore the backed-up files and folders in the event of system failure or some other disaster. To restore the files, first connect the medium on which the backed-up files are stored. For example, if you stored the backed-up files and folders on an external hard drive, you must connect it to your PC. Then follow these steps:

1. Click the Windows Start button and choose Control Panel.
2. In the Control Panel window, select the System and Security option.
3. In the System and Security window, click Backup and Restore. The Backup or Restore Your Files screen appears.
4. Click Restore My Files. Windows launches the Restore Files Wizard.
5. To restore all folders and files in your system, click Browse for Folders. A Browse dialog box appears.
6. Click the folder containing the backup of your hard drive and click Add Folder. The folder is added to the Restore Files Wizard's list of items to restore; click Next.

   If you need to restore only certain files, click Browse for Files instead of Browse for Folders. Then locate and select the files you want to restore.
7. Select the In the Original Location radio button to restore the folder to its original location on your hard drive.
8. Click Restore. Windows restores the files, notifying you when the restore operation is complete. Click Finish.

Backing Up to "the Cloud"

In addition to backing up data to an external hard drive or network location, you can also back it up to "the cloud"—that is, to a data storage site on the Internet. When you back up your files to the Internet, you can access them from anywhere. Microsoft OneDrive (formerly SkyDrive) is an example of one such site. After you set it up, it appears as a local folder on your computer. (Chapter 3 provides more information about Microsoft OneDrive.) Other examples of data storage sites in the cloud are Google Drive and Dropbox. All these storage providers offer users a certain amount of free storage with the option to buy additional capacity as needed. You could even be extra cautious and back up to both a hard drive and to a storage site in the cloud. That way, if something happens to one of your backups, you still have another copy of the data.

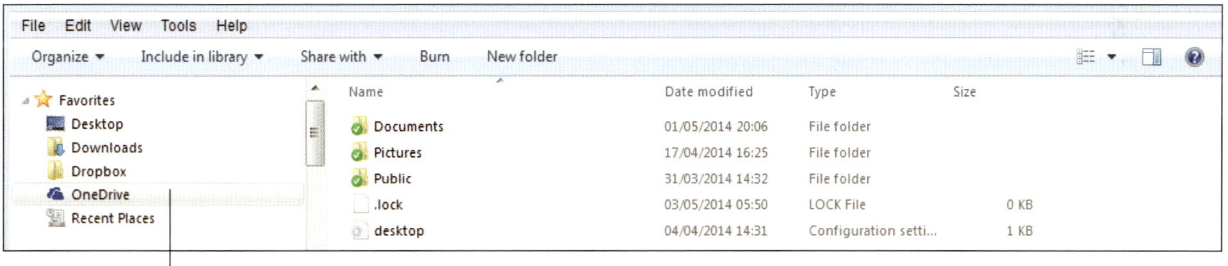

A OneDrive folder is added to your computer and appears in Windows Explorer

New Technologies

Installing Operating System Updates

When you buy a computer, it usually comes with an operating system preinstalled so you can start work straightaway. The version of the operating system that is installed is typically the version that was available when the computer was manufactured. Operating systems are constantly being updated, however. Many of the improvements made to operating systems after their initial release pertain to fixing bugs and patching security holes—hence, the use of the word "patches" to describe these fixes.

It's critical that you install updates to your computer's operating system (and to the programs that run on it) to ensure that all the most recent patches are applied.

service pack A collection of patches, released in a single package.

Software manufacturers can distribute a patch as a single update to a program or as a group of updates to several programs. Periodically, Microsoft groups several patches together and produces a package called a **service pack**. A service pack contains all the patches released either since the product was launched or since the last service pack was released. To determine whether any service packs have been installed on your Windows computer, open the Control Panel and select the System and Security option. Then click System to see the current status of your operating system. (See Figure 11.8.)

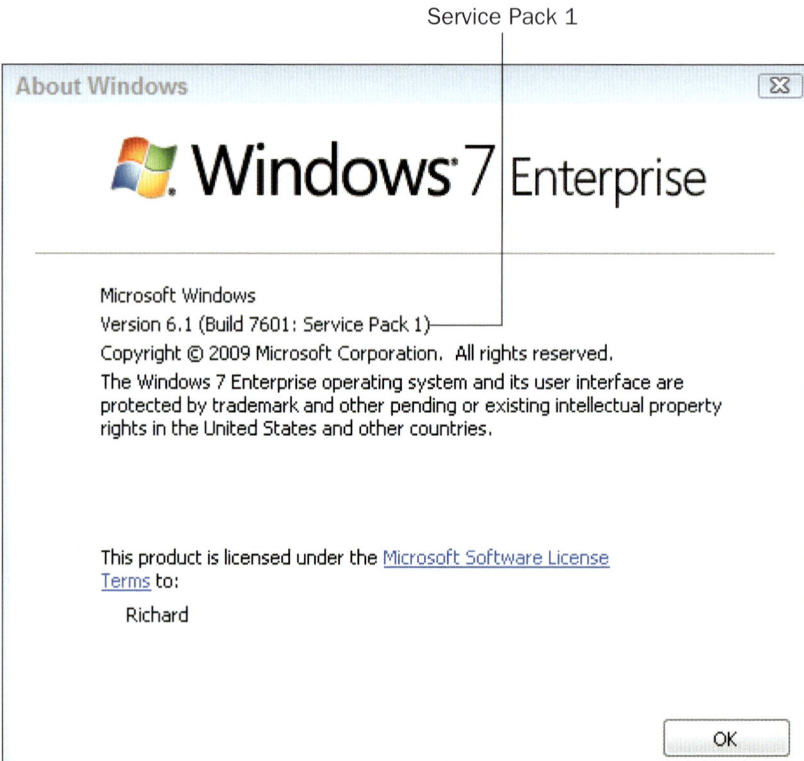

Figure 11.8 Windows 7 running with Service Pack 1.

Windows Update A feature in Windows that automatically downloads and installs updates to Windows and optionally to some Microsoft applications.

To make it easier for you to keep your system up to date, Microsoft offers the **Windows Update** tool. To access it, open the Control Panel, click System and Security, and choose Windows Update. As shown in Figure 11.9, you can click on the links to choose from the following options:

- **Check for Updates:** Select this option to perform an immediate check for new updates.
- **Change Settings:** Choose this option to specify how and when updates are installed.
- **View Update History:** To see when updates were installed, select this option.
- **Restore Hidden Updates:** This option enables you to install updates that you have chosen not to install previously.

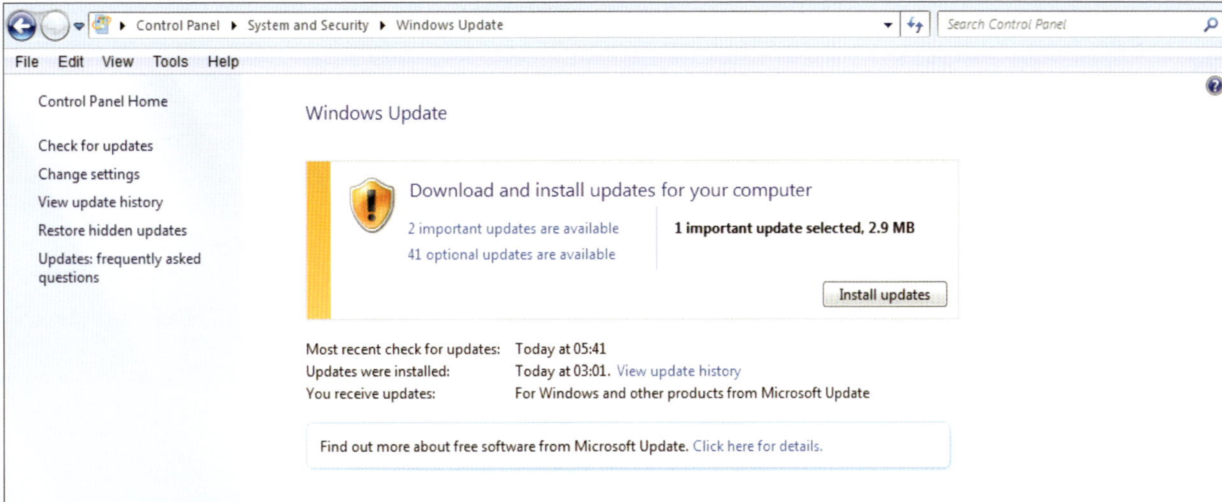

Figure 11.9 Using Windows Update to keep your system up to date.

The simplest way to manage updates is to allow your system to install them automatically; you can select that option by choosing Change Settings in the navigation bar at the left and then adjusting the settings on the Choose How Windows Can Install Updates screen that appears. If your system has not installed an available update, you will see a message in the notification area at the bottom-right corner of the screen, indicating that updates are available.

Wiping Old Drives

In Chapter 5, "Introduction to Windows 7," you learned how to delete files. You may not have realized, however, that when you delete files from a computer, you do not delete the data in those files. Instead, you delete the information about where to find the data on the hard drive. Many software programs can recover files that have been deleted. That's good news if the files were deleted by mistake. But it's bad news if someone in possession of your hard drive—for example, someone who obtains it after you have disposed of it—uses one of these programs to recover files you deleted on purpose.

To permanently remove files from your hard drive, you must use a software program that erases the hard drive permanently and securely. These programs work by writing a series of patterns over the entire disk so that all existing data is overwritten and cannot be recovered. Several good programs perform this task. Some are even available free of charge, such as Active@ KillDisk for Windows (see Figure 11.10) and Eraser.

If you want to dispose of a hard drive, even if only to give it to a friend, it's important to remove all traces of personal information from the drive by running one of these programs on it beforehand. That way, you can be sure that the hard drive is blank, and there is no chance that anyone else could recover your data.

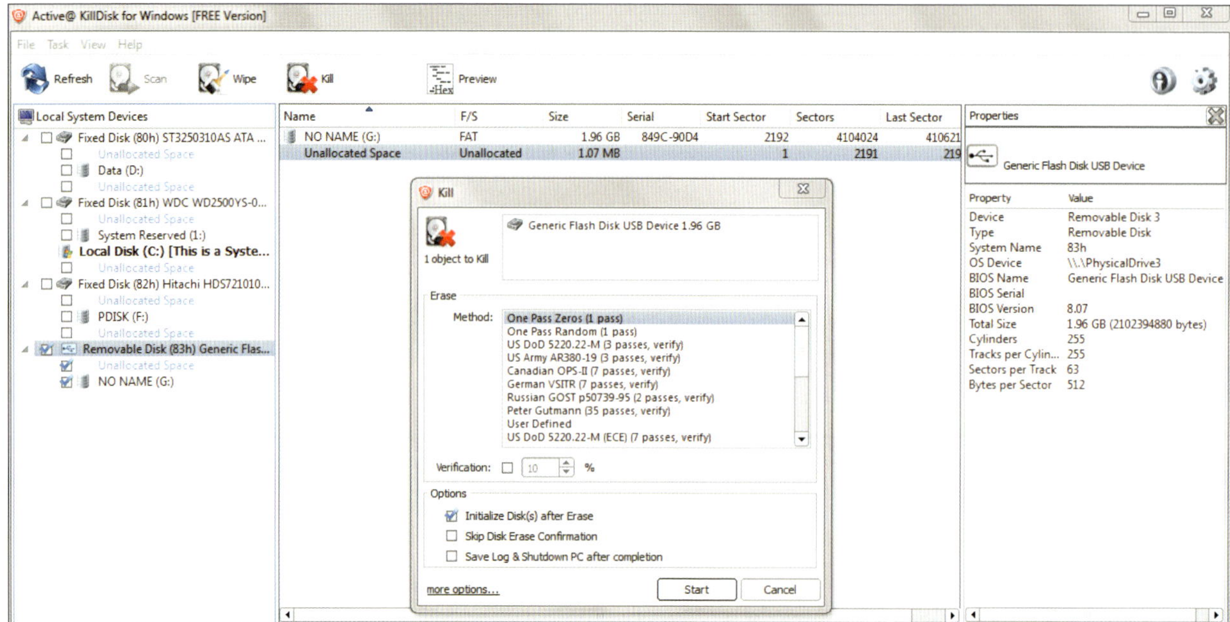

Figure 11.10 Using a disk eraser program.

CAUTION Before you erase your hard disk, copy all the data on it to a new hard drive unless you are sure you no longer want this data. Once you start the overwriting process, you can't retrieve the data.

Quick Review

1. What are the characteristics of a strong password?
2. What level of access should you give others to your files and folders?
3. What does a firewall do?
4. What is needed to decrypt encrypted data?

Summary

Network and Internet Security Concerns

Computer crime is becoming increasingly common. It is essential that you be aware of computer security and take the necessary steps to secure your data and online identity.

Computer criminals engage in many types of activities that can compromise your computer system, your data, and your online identity. One of the common threats is **phishing**. In this type of attack, nefarious users try to trick unsuspecting users into giving away personal information such as login details or credit card information.

Often, the goal of hackers or crackers is to obtain a user's password. To do so, they often attempt **password cracking**—that is, they attempt to identify a user's password. Password cracking can be accomplished in several ways, including guessing, using a **keylogger** to record the user's keystrokes, **social engineering**, sniffing, or using any one of a variety of password-cracking tools.

Many computer criminals employ **malware**—that is, malicious software—in their efforts to compromise a user's computer system, data, and online identity. There are several types of malware, including **viruses**, **worms**, **Trojans**, **spyware**, and **ransomware**. To protect yourself against malware, you must run a security program. Although these programs are often called "anti-virus programs," they have evolved over the years into a broader security solution that can detect and protect against viruses, worms, Trojans, and sometimes more complex threats. A good anti-virus package provides a wide range of protective measures and may include firewall management and anti-spyware. Many good anti-virus products are in the marketplace, including Symantec, Sophos, Kaspersky, and McAfee.

Anti-virus programs are less effective against **denial of service (DoS) attacks**. In this type of attack, the attacker floods a website or service with thousands of requests for access—so many that the site or service cannot deal with them all. As a result, legitimate users are prevented from accessing the site or service. The computers that launch these attacks are called zombies. A **zombie** is a computer that has been infected with a particular type of Trojan called a **bot**.

Users should also be wary of Wi-Fi networks. When Wi-Fi networks are not properly secured, it is easy to steal data on them with little chance of being caught. It's not just un-secure networks that pose a risk, however. Some wireless networks *appear* to be genuine, but in fact attempt to intercept your traffic. These types of Wi-Fi networks are called **rogue Wi-Fi**. Public places where many people are looking for Wi-Fi, such as coffee shops, restaurants, and airports, are common locations for rogue Wi-Fi connections.

Network and Internet Privacy Concerns

Using networks and the Internet can put your privacy at risk in a number of ways. For example, search engine sites can gather information about you based on the terms you search for and the questions you ask. In addition, websites for which you provide personal information, such as your name, address, email, and so forth, can store that information and perhaps use it for purposes other than those you intended. Finally, someone who ascertains the unique identity of your computer can use this information to access your computer via a network and view, change, or delete your personal data.

To protect people's privacy, most countries have data protection and privacy laws to control the access and distribution of this personal information. These laws regulate the companies that hold our personal information and ensure that all our information is properly protected.

Of course, just because there are laws designed to protect your privacy online does not mean that you should not take additional steps to keep yourself safe. As a first step, you should determine what personal information is available online by conducting a search for your name. You should also take care when using **social media** to avoid sharing information about yourself that would be better kept private. Another strategy is to delete **cookies** from your computer. That way, no one can use your cookies in a malicious way.

Strategies for Improving Security

You can take many steps to improve security. One step is to restrict access to your computer and data by using strong passwords, applying permissions, and enabling **firewalls**. You can also use **encryption** to scramble the data on your hard drive, thereby preventing others from being able to read it.

Security is not just about preventing unauthorized access to your data, however. It's also about protecting your data from damage or loss by storing copies of your data somewhere safe. This process is called "making a backup," or "backing up." You should back up your system on a regular basis. To do so, you can use the Windows built-in backup utility, called Windows Backup. If you used Windows Backup to back up the files and folders on your computer, you can restore the backed-up files and folders in the event of system failure or some other disaster.

It's important that you run the most up-to-date version of your operating system. That way, as manufacturers fix bugs and patch security holes, you ensure that all the most recent patches are applied. To make it easier for you to keep your system up to date, Microsoft offers the Windows Update tool, which performs automatic updates to the operating system. Using this tool, you can check for new updates, change the automatic update settings, view your update history, and more.

If you want to dispose of data you have on a hard drive, even if only to give your computer to a friend, you must remove all traces of personal information from the drive. To do so, simply run a special software program that is designed to permanently erase the contents of your hard drive. These programs work by writing a series of patterns over the entire disk so that all existing data is overwritten and cannot be recovered.

Key Terms

bot
botnet
cookie
cyberbullying
database
decryption
denial of service (DoS) attack
encryption
firewall
keylogger
malware
password cracking
phishing
ransomware
rogue Wi-Fi
service pack
social engineering
social network
spyware
Trojan
virus
Windows Update
worm
zombie

Test Yourself

Fact Check

1. What type of program would a hacker use to capture the password someone has typed?

    a. keylooker

    b. keylogger

    c. keyloader

    d. keyblocker

2. Which of the following types of malware are designed to infect multiple files on your computer?

    a. worm

    b. virus

    c. Trojan

    d. rogue

3. Which of the following types of malware is likely to use your address book to spread itself to other computers?

    a. virus

    b. Trojan

    c. spam

    d. worm

4. Which of the following would be the strongest password?

    a. August23

    b. birmingham

    c. NewYork

    d. M3rl1n@t

5. What is the name of a single piece of software that looks innocent but carries out malicious activity on your computer?

    a. virus

    b. worm

    c. router

    d. Trojan

6. What is the name used for a computer that launches denial of service (DoS) attacks over the Internet?

    a. rogue

    b. evil twin

    c. spam bot

    d. zombie

7. An email that requests you provide personal information but is not from the company it represents itself to be from is an example of _______.

    a. phishing

    b. hacking

    c. logging

    d. sniffing

8. Which of the following is the best approach to controlling access to data?

    a. Give users as much access as they need.

    b. Only give users the minimum access they need.

    c. Allow users to decide how much access they need.

    d. Don't give users any access.

9. A _______ attack is an attempt to prevent users from accessing a website.

    a. denial of service

    b. social engineering

    c. phishing

    d. hacking

10. What should you do if you receive an email telling you that you have won a competition you did not enter?

    a. Open the message and claim the prize.

    b. Open the message to see if the prize is worth claiming.

    c. Contact the sender of the email and tell him he has made a mistake.

    d. Delete the mail immediately.

Matching

Match the security threat to its definition.

a. phishing

b. password cracking

c. virus

d. Trojan

e. worm

f. rogue Wi-Fi network

1. ________The act of attempting to acquire information such as usernames, passwords, credit card information, and so forth, by pretending to be from a genuine, trustworthy source such as a bank.

2. ________A malicious computer program that spreads itself to other computers over a network or the Internet.

3. ________A wireless network that "sniffs" traffic, making a copy of everything users type—including usernames, passwords, and credit card numbers.

4. ________The act of attempting to identify a user's password in order to gain access to a system or program.

5. ________A piece of malicious software that looks harmless but has a detrimental effect on a computer when it runs.

6. ________Malicious software that copies itself (replicates) to other programs on the same computer to "infect" them.

Sum It Up

1. List four types of activities that computer criminals engage in.
2. Why is it important to have an active firewall either on your computer or at the edge of your network (or both)?
3. How many different types of threats can be detected by security solution software products?
4. Why do you need to be careful when using Wi-Fi in public places?
5. What are the effects of a denial of service attack?

Explore More

Backing Up Your Data

Have a look at the files on your computer and make a list of those that contain personal data. Compare the different methods and devices you could use to make a copy of this data and identify the best way of making a backup copy. If you have the means, make a backup copy and identify a safe place to keep it.

Keeping Your System Up to Date

Explore your computer to check how up-to-date it is. Does it have a service pack installed? Run the Windows Update process to see if there are any uninstalled updates. Is there a reason why you have not installed them?

Protecting Yourself against Malware

Identify what type of anti-virus solution you have in place. Every package has its own control panel for administration. Open this panel and see how often the software checks the Internet for updates. Carry out a manual scan of your computer.

What Are the Latest Threats?

Visit the website of one of the anti-virus software providers and look at what the latest threats are and how recent they are. Identify how many pieces of malware have been discovered in the last seven days.

Think It Over

Planning for Security

Imagine that you are going to purchase a new computer running a Windows operating system. Thinking of security, what steps would you take to ensure that the computer is secure from unauthorized users and that your data is protected against loss or damage? Think of any software programs you may install to provide additional protection and compare the features of the different products to identify which would be best for your situation.

Chapter 12

Legal, Ethical, Health, and Environmental Issues in Computing

Learning objectives

- Be aware of the legal issues that arise from using computers and the Internet
- Understand how to use the Internet in an ethical manner
- Understand the potential impact on health when using a computer
- Be aware of what to consider when disposing of a computer

This chapter moves beyond the technical aspects of working with computers and software to examine the legal and ethical issues related to computer use. These issues range from the legal ownership of online content to the ethical options for acquiring and using software, as well as what is appropriate (and inappropriate) online activity. This chapter also covers various health risks posed by computer use and the appropriate methods for disposing of computer hardware.

Legal Issues in Computing

Nearly everything we do in life is governed by laws of one sort or another. Not surprisingly, these laws extend to cover our use of computers and the Internet. Legal issues in computing are complex, however. Whereas we are usually governed by the laws of the country in which we reside, the Internet is global, and different countries have different laws. That means you might access Internet content in your web browser that is regulated by local law, but the content itself is hosted on a server in another jurisdiction, and as such is governed by another set of rules. What is legal in one country is not necessarily legal in another, so you could end up unwittingly being guilty of an offense. For example, in some countries, online gambling is legal, and citizens may both participate in online gambling and host their own gambling sites. In other countries, not only is it illegal to host an online gambling site, but it is also illegal for citizens of that country to use an online gambling site hosted in a country where it is legal.

Intellectual Property

intellectual property (IP) The exclusive rights to the ownership of something that has been created or produced.

Intellectual property (IP), also called intellectual property rights (IPR), is a legal term that grants people the exclusive rights to the ownership of content that they have created. "Created" is the important word here. This can apply to tangible items, such a book, as well as to ideas that have been documented, such as patents, artistic works, photographs, and music.

IP has evolved over many years and can now be applied to certain aspects of computing and the Internet. For example, suppose you design a web page or produce some written material for a website. Depending on the nature of the material (and on any agreements you have in place with others), you may have the exclusive rights to use it because you created it. In effect, it belongs to you. Intellectual property provides protection for the owner of the material.

Copyright Laws

copyright The granting of exclusive rights to the creator of a work for a limited period of time.

Copyright is a subset of intellectual property but differs in interpretation and use. Copyright is a legal protection that usually gives the creator of a work—be it written or artistic—exclusive rights to its use and distribution for a limited time period. For example, when an author writes a book, he might choose to obtain the copyright for that book. Then, the author (and his descendants) will be entitled to royalties from the sale of the book until the copyright expires. In many countries, a work's copyright lasts for the duration of the creator's lifetime plus an additional 50 years after his death. (Note that in some cases, a book's publisher might hold the copyright on the work, depending on the agreement struck by the author. Note, too, that copyright can be limited to geographical boundaries unless there is some form of international agreement between the parties.)

There is no symbol to identify IP, but when something is copyrighted, you will usually see the © symbol along with the copyright owner's name and sometimes a year. For example, if you look inside the front cover of this book, you will see the following copyright: ©2014 John Wiley & Sons, Ltd. Copyright has become difficult to enforce with the advent of digital media and the Internet, which make it easy to download and redistribute material. Unless some form of digital rights management (DRM) is in use, it is impossible to enforce copyright law over so many jurisdictions. (You'll learn more about DRM in the next section.)

Digital Rights Management

digital rights management (DRM) The use of technology to control access to copyrighted material.

Digital rights management (DRM) involves the use of technology to control access to copyrighted material. It is a practical attempt to address the growing problem of the unauthorized copying and distribution of material. The practice of distributing digital content over the Internet via file-sharing networks has made the enforcement of traditional copyright laws difficult.

DRM helps to prevent illegal downloads by requiring access verification to protected material. To access DRM-protected material, the user needs a username and password, which are stored in a database. DRM also helps to prevent already downloaded files from being widely shared with others. For example, iTunes downloads can be burned to an audio CD a limited number of times, can be placed only on portable devices that are registered to the signed-in user, and will not play if manually copied to another computer.

Some software vendors use DRM to allow document authors to protect content created with the software. Access to a document may be restricted by requiring anyone who opens the file to log into a DRM server online.

Opponents of DRM

DRM is not without controversy. Indeed, many organizations and computer scientists are opposed to the practice. Some argue that the use of DRM restricts users' access from using content they have rightfully purchased as they see fit. For example, DRM prevents legitimate users from making personal copies of materials, lending copies to friends, and so on. In addition, DRM may on occasion prevent legitimate users from accessing their content. Finally, many argue that the use of DRM is pointless, as more often than not, users are able to crack the codes used to secure content.

Software Licensing

When you install an operating system or software program, one of the first stages of the process is to agree to its terms and conditions. These terms and conditions are presented in a legal document called an End User License Agreement (EULA), the end user being you. The EULA defines what you as a user can and cannot do with the product you are about to install.

End User License Agreement (EULA) A legal document that grants you permission to use a piece of software.

You will not be able to proceed to the next stage of the install until you accept the agreement (see Figure 12.1). If you choose not to accept the terms and conditions, you won't be permitted to install the software. It may take a few minutes to read through the terms and conditions, but it's a good idea to do so, so you will know what you can and cannot legally do with the software.

NOTE

For most vendors, licensing is a way of ensuring that they collect revenue for the products they offer. Vendors also use licensing to ensure that if people use the software to break any laws, it is the user who is in trouble, not the vendor.

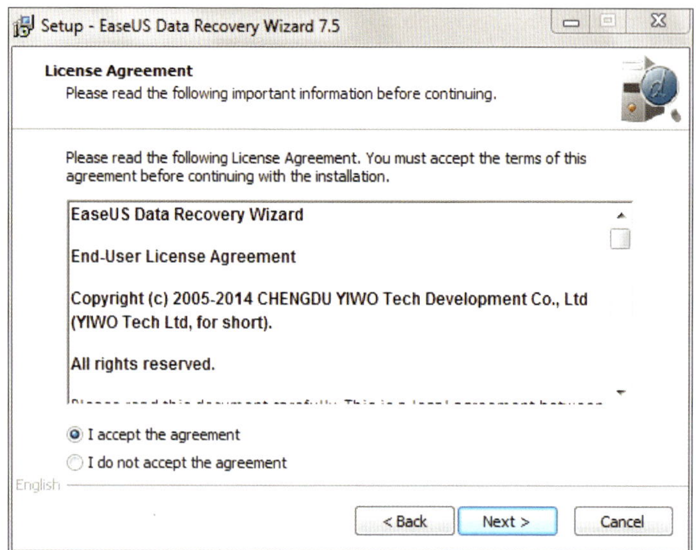

Figure 12.1 A typical End User License Agreement (EULA).

Privacy and Security

Product Activation

During installation, some products require you not only to agree to the terms and conditions, but also to enter a license code or key to activate the product. This key can be sent by email as part of the registration process. Alternatively, it could be provided on a printed card as part of a physical software package.

Many products, particularly the more expensive ones like Microsoft Office, also require online activation. This calls for an active Internet connection. Online activation adds the license key to a database of active licenses, maintained by the software vendor. This prevents someone from using the same code again to license the software more than once, thus breaking the terms of the single user license. This figure shows the result of an online activation.

Types of Software and Licensing

proprietary software Software to which the vendor retains ownership rights. Users merely have usage rights.

Software may be released either as proprietary software or as open-source software. Proprietary software is software you can use but do not own. The vendor retains ownership; you simply have the right to use one or more copies of the software after purchasing it and agreeing to the EULA. The source code used in this type of software is kept private. That is, users are not permitted to access and/or change the code.

Trial Software

Some vendors enable users to download a free trial version of a proprietary software program. When you do, you still have to agree to the terms and conditions, and you only get to use the software for a short period of time—typically from 7 to 30 days. You may also find that the trial version is a scaled-down version of the full program, without all the features. In other words, certain aspects of the full-version software don't function. The idea behind the trial software is for you to evaluate the software and see if it is the right product for you. At the end of the trial period, if you want to continue using the software, you will be asked to purchase a license. If so, you will be sent a code to activate the product.

Put It to Work

Open-source software is software that is not only free to use, but also whose source code is accessible to users to modify and redistribute. You may be wondering, why is it free? What's in it for the software developers? The answer is simple: The open-source movement is all about promoting freedoms and removing licensing restrictions. The theory is that by allowing the free distribution of software that can be enhanced by others, the computer world benefits from having consistently improved products—and from that, we *all* benefit.

open-source software Free access to a software program and the source code that produced the program.

Although open-source software is about removing licensing restrictions, many types of open-source software do carry a license, called the **General Public License (GPL)**. The GPL—developed by an organization called the Free Software Foundation, that exists to support the creation and distribution of free software—is a simply worded license that enables individuals and companies to legally copy and modify software. This gives users much greater freedom with the product, allowing them to make as many copies as they like, installing it on all their computers, distributing it to friends, and, of course, making changes to the source code if they so desire.

General Public License (GPL) A license used for many types of open-source software, allowing the software to be legally copied and modified.

Software Piracy

Software piracy is the unauthorized copying of software programs. There are various types of software piracy:

software piracy The unauthorized copying and distribution of software.

- **Counterfeit software.** Counterfeit software is a copy of a legitimate product that is made and marketed as an original. With counterfeit software, the media and packaging may look genuine, but only because the software has been copied and packaged to look like the original. It is sometimes difficult to tell the difference between the genuine article and a fake. Counterfeit software is even easier to sell over the Internet—particularly software that is downloadable rather than distributed on a physical disc. This type of software is often sold on sites that appear to be authorized, but if you look closely, you can usually spot clues that the site is not legitimate, such as a slightly different spelling in the URL, grammar or usage errors that indicate a non-native speaker may have created the page, or blurry or incorrect logos.
- **Corporate piracy.** Often, a company or organization will purchase software in a legitimate way, but install the software on more machines than it is supposed to. For example, a company might buy software with 50 licenses but install it on 100 computers. This practice, which can save corporations many thousands or even millions of dollars, is called "corporate piracy." It may seem benign, but it is in fact a form of theft.

- **Unbundling packages.** When you purchase a computer or notebook, it frequently comes as an original equipment manufacturer (OEM) bundle. For example, the operating system comes preloaded on the computer and is licensed to that particular computer. If the bundle comes with a backup copy of the operating system on DVD and the owner sells that copy to someone else, this breaks the terms of the license and is a form of piracy.
- **Internet piracy.** There are many Internet sites where copyrighted software can be illegally downloaded free or at low cost. These sites even give users guidance on where to obtain the license key information necessary to use the program, or produce fake keys themselves. This is Internet piracy. With so many sites and so much software available, Internet piracy is virtually unstoppable. Much of the illegal software is published in countries where the necessary laws are not strongly enforced. Sites that offer these illegal activities sometimes contain malware that can infect your computer when you download from them.

CAUTION

Next time you accept an offer of some software from a friend, ask yourself these questions:

- Has it come from a genuine source?
- Is it okay to share this software with others?
- Is it licensed for more than one computer?

You could quite easily break the law by accepting the software and using it. Remember, though, that ignorance is not a legal defense.

Quick Review

1. What is the difference between intellectual property and copyright?
2. When you have purchased proprietary software, who owns the software?
3. What is the advantage of using open-source software?

Ethical Issues in Computing

With computing comes several ethical issues—particularly with regard to the Internet. These range from plagiarism to censorship, libel, slander, and beyond.

Plagiarism

plagiarism The act of copying someone else's work and pretending that it is your own.

Plagiarism is the practice of copying someone else's work and pretending that it is your own. Thanks to the Internet, it is all too easy to download a document from an obscure website and submit or republish it as yours.

Plagiarism comes in several forms:

- Copying work produced by someone else word for word and presenting it as your own.
- Inserting portions of someone else's work into your own and claiming full credit
- Changing a few words and phrases of a piece of work so it looks different but is based on someone else's work
- Taking material from multiple sources and putting it all together as your own work

Plagiarism has become a big problem in colleges and universities. Often, when students receive assignments, they simply research on the Internet, copy large blocks of text from various sources, stitch them together into a single document, and pass the result off as their own work. Even worse, some students patronize any one of several Internet-based companies that write assignments for them.

Using Citations

It is not always wrong to use someone else's work. In many cases, you can quote or paraphrase (discussed next) someone else's work in your own piece—provided you include a reference to the source (in other words, to the author and name of the work). This is called a **citation**. Including a citation to give credit to the original author of a piece of work is the only way to avoid plagiarism.

citation A reference to a source—that is, to the author and name of a published or unpublished work—following a quotation from said source.

Paraphrasing

In addition to quoting an author directly, you can paraphrase what he or she writes. When you **paraphrase**, you use different words to convey the same idea. Even so, you still must include a citation to acknowledge that the original idea came from someone else.

paraphrase To use different words to convey the same idea.

Combating Plagiarism

New Technologies

Recent years have seen the development of a range of anti-plagiarism software products, such as turnitin (`www.turnitin.com`). These programs compare a submitted document against a large database of quotes and texts. Mathematical processes check not only for actual word-for-word plagiarism, but also for paraphrased text where it can identify the original source. The results then highlight any suspect or copied areas in text and state where citations should be applied.

Using software like this, it takes only a few seconds to examine a document. Some educational institutions use this type of software as standard practice for all work handed in by students. Students can also use this type of software before turning in an assignment to ensure they have not inadvertently plagiarized.

Censorship and Filtering

censorship The act of suppressing speech or not allowing certain communications to be made public.

Censorship is the act of preventing something from being printed or heard. Historically, censorship has been used to prevent important information from reaching the population at large by controlling what can be printed or broadcast. Censorship is sometimes implemented by governments so they can control the flow of information for political or military reasons. For example, writing that is deemed to be obscene or advocates that citizens break the country's existing laws might be censored. Individuals or companies can also apply forms of censorship by not allowing certain types of information to be published. For example, if you post a negative review of a product on the manufacturer's website, your view may be deleted; this is an example of corporate censorship.

filtering Preventing something from getting through—in this case, content.

Filtering is a form of censorship performed by software. **Filtering** means to prevent something from getting through. For example, when you filter water, you remove all the impurities, making it safe to drink. Similarly, when you filter the Internet, you exclude certain categories of content from general access. For example, a parent might install web filtering software on a child's computer to prevent the child from accessing websites with graphic violent content, or a coffee shop might use filtering to prevent its patrons from accessing adult-themed sites when using the store's Internet connection. Companies also may filter their employees' web usage at work, such as blocking social networking sites like Facebook to improve productivity.

proxy server A server that sits between the user's web browser and the Internet that intercepts all requests for web pages and processes those requests.

Web filtering is accomplished by using a **proxy server**—that is, a server that sits between the user's web browser and the Internet and manages all requests for content.

When users attempt to access a filtered site, a message is displayed in their browser, notifying them that the request is denied. Figure 12.2 shows a list of blocked site categories on a proxy server.

Search URL blacklist

☑ ads	☑ adult	☑ aggressive	☑ antispyware	☑ artnudes	☑ astrology	☑ audio-video	☑ banking
☑ beerliquorinfo	☑ beerliquorsale	☑ blog	☑ cellphones	☑ chat	☑ childcare	☑ cleaning	☑ clothing
☑ culinary	☑ dating	☑ desktopsillies	☑ dialers	☑ drugs	☑ ecommerce	☑ entertainment	☑ filehosting
☑ financial	☑ frencheducation	☑ gambling	☑ games	☑ gardening	☑ government	☑ hacking	☑ homerepair
☑ hygiene	☑ instantmessaging	☑ jewelry	☑ jobsearch	☑ kidstimewasting	☑ mail	☑ marketingware	☑ medical
☑ mixed_adult	☑ mobile-phone	☑ naturism	☑ news	☑ onlineauctions	☑ onlinegames	☑ onlinepayment	☑ personalfinance
☑ pets	☑ phishing	☑ porn	☑ proxy	☑ radio	☑ reaffected	☑ religion	☑ ringtones
☑ searchengines	☑ sexual_education	☑ sexuality	☑ shopping	☑ socialnetworking	☑ sportnews	☑ sports	☑ spyware
☑ test	☑ updatesites	☑ vacation	☑ verisign	☑ violence	☑ virusinfected	☑ warez	☑ weapons
☑ weather	☑ webmail	☑ whitelist					

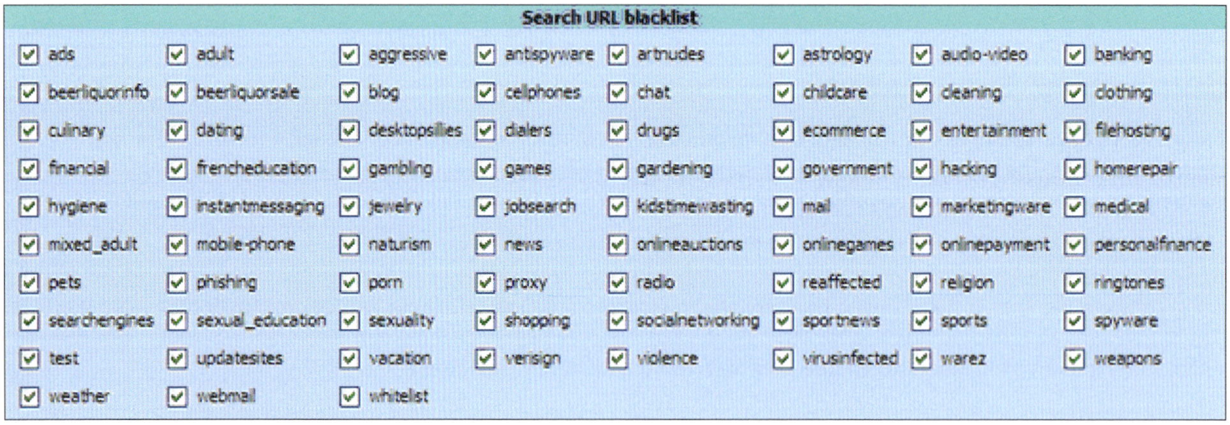

Figure 12.2 A list of blocked categories on a proxy server.

Flaming

Most likely, when you use chat rooms or social networks or comment on websites, you interact quite happily with other users. Occasionally, however, you may find that some users become quite hostile. This happens frequently on sites like YouTube, which gives users the option to post comments, and on social networking sites like Facebook. Some of the comments become negative and personal, complete with insults and swear words. This is called flaming. When the negativity escalates as more comments are posted, it is known as a flame war.

flaming Where Internet users interact in a hostile way with each other.

Libel and Slander

Libel and slander are similar in that both are statements that can cause damage to someone's reputation.

Libel is the act of putting a false and defamatory statement in writing. Any false statement that could damage the reputation of an individual or organization could be considered to be libel. Because it is written, it can have a lasting effect on the individual or company being libeled. For example, a libelous comment published on Twitter and then retweeted to others could spread quickly. It would be difficult to control the spread and to undo the damage caused. In most countries, libel is a civil offense. That means the person or organization being libeled would have to take legal action to obtain any form of compensation or redress. For libel to be upheld, it must be proved that the statement is untrue.

libel Putting in writing a defamatory statement that could damage a person's or organization's reputation.

Slander is the verbal version of libel. Slander might consist of negative comments about an individual or group that are made as part of a phone or face-to-face conversation; in the digital world, it may include slanderous comments made on an online-published video or in a group video conference. The effect is just as damaging to the reputation of the target individual.

slander Making a defamatory verbal statement that could damage a person's or organization's reputation.

Spamming

Spam—that is, unsolicited or "junk" email, typically containing offers (some legitimate, some not) for electronic goods, drugs, software, and so on—is a major problem on the Internet. These emails are sent in bulk, bombarding thousands if not millions of users at a time. There are varying estimates of how much email is spam, but most put the number at 80% or more. Although most email programs include a junk email filter, many of these emails still slip through to fill users' inboxes, as shown in Figure 12.3. As a result, users waste valuable time reading and deleting unwanted messages.

spam Unsolicited "junk" mail, typically containing offers (some legitimate, some not) of products or services to buy.

SpeedDate	View pics of singles - chat with ... ↓	27/04/2014
Prime Scrat...	Your account has been credited ...	25/04/2014
Prime Scratch Cards	Your account has been credited ...	22/04/2014
Jenna	Hello Shelagh, I have some mor... !	21/04/2014
Match.com	See Who's on Match.com - It's ... ↓	20/04/2014
First PREMIER Bank	First PREMIER Bank MasterCard ... ↓	18/04/2014
Houzz Updates	Elements of Contemporary Bathr...	16/03/2014
Paul Asadoorian	Webcasts: Expose the monsters I...	27/02/2014
Houzz Updates	Kitchen Backsplash 101 | Create...	16/02/2014

Figure 12.3 Examples of spam.

Not all email received from a business is spam. Businesses with whom you have a previous relationship, such as a store where you have ordered before, might send you promotional emails because you have given them your email address. You can unsubscribe from such emails with the Unsubscribe link provided in the email. Beware, however, of using the Unsubscribe link in a generic mass email that you get from a company that you have no relationship with. Sometimes unscrupulous spammers use the Unsubscribe link to confirm that their message has reached an active email address, and trying to unsubscribe will only get you added to more spammers' lists.

Is spamming legal? It depends on what country you are in. In the United States, spam is legal, provided the message conforms to certain formats. What is most definitely *not* legal is when spam encourages recipients to visit fake websites and share personal information. That's when spam becomes phishing.

Quick Review

1. Why do people use citations?
2. What is the difference between libel and slander?
3. What role does a proxy server play?

Health Issues in Computing

Using computers brings with it a host of health issues, from eyestrain to back and limb problems. The stress and strain placed on a human body while using a computer can cause discomfort and pain and can lead to long-term medical conditions if not addressed. To confront these problems, users can pay special attention to their work environment, using good posture, ergonomic furniture, and appropriate lighting.

Combating Eyestrain

When you use your computer, your eyes focus at a fixed distance on a small area (your screen) for a considerable period of time. They were not designed to do this, however. As a result, many computer users end up with eyestrain, which can lead to blurring or headaches.

Here are a few tips for combating eyestrain:

- Have regular eye examinations. If you have corrective eyewear, use it while working at the computer.
- Situate your computer monitor such that it is 20 to 40 inches (50 to 100 centimeters) from your face, with your eyes just above the center of the screen. If necessary, adjust the angle of the screen. (Adjusting the height and angle of your monitor will also help to protect your neck and shoulders.)
- Use incandescent rather than fluorescent lighting in your work area, because fluorescent lighting tends to flicker more. If you cannot avoid fluorescent lighting, avoid working directly underneath the light fixture if possible.
- Position your monitor so that bright light does not shine directly on it, to reduce glare.
- Use a flat-screen LCD monitor instead of the older CRT type. If you cannot avoid using a CRT, set its refresh rate to at least 100 Hz in the display settings in your operating system.
- Take frequent breaks. Avoid sitting in front of your monitor for more than an hour at a time.
- When you take a break, exercise your eyes. That is, look at items at different distances so your eyes get used to focusing normally again. Another way to exercise your eyes is to follow the 20-20-20 rule. That is, every 20 minutes, look away from the screen at something 20 feet away for 20 seconds. This prevents the eye muscles from being in the same position for too long.

In addition, to prevent eyestrain, opt for as large a screen as possible (19 inches, or 48 centimeters, is a good bet), and decrease the screen resolution so that icons and text appear larger. That way, you won't have to strain to see them. A lower resolution may make the display on an LCD monitor appear fuzzy, so you may have to balance between resolution and sharpness. (However, in Windows 7 and higher, you can increase the size of icons and text without decreasing the display resolution.) You can also adjust the brightness and contrast of your display to reduce eyestrain.

Step by Step

Changing Your Screen Resolution

To change your screen's resolution, follow these steps:

1. Right-click the desktop in Windows and choose Screen Resolution.
2. Click the Resolution drop-down list. Then, drag the slider that appears to adjust the resolution.

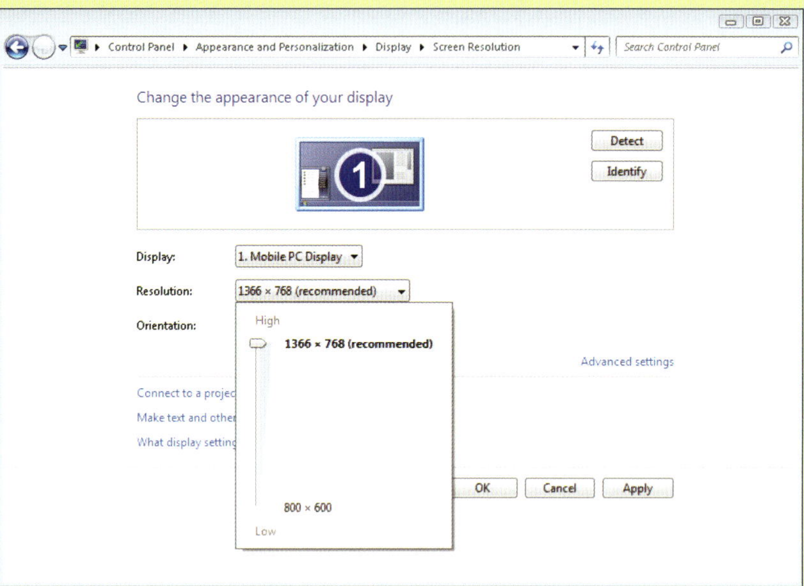

3. To see how the selected resolution looks, click the Apply button.
4. If you like the change, click the Keep Changes button in the dialog box that appears. Otherwise, click Revert, and repeat Steps 1–3 as needed.
5. When you are satisfied with the resolution, click the OK button to close the Screen Resolution screen.

Changing the Size of Icons and Text

To change the size of icons and text without changing your screen's resolution, do the following:

1. Right-click the desktop and choose Screen Resolution.
2. Click the Make Text and Other Items Larger or Smaller hyperlink.
3. Click one of the available option buttons to change the size of text and other items. (Here, Smaller is chosen.) Then click the Apply button. You'll be prompted to log off your computer and log back on to implement the change.

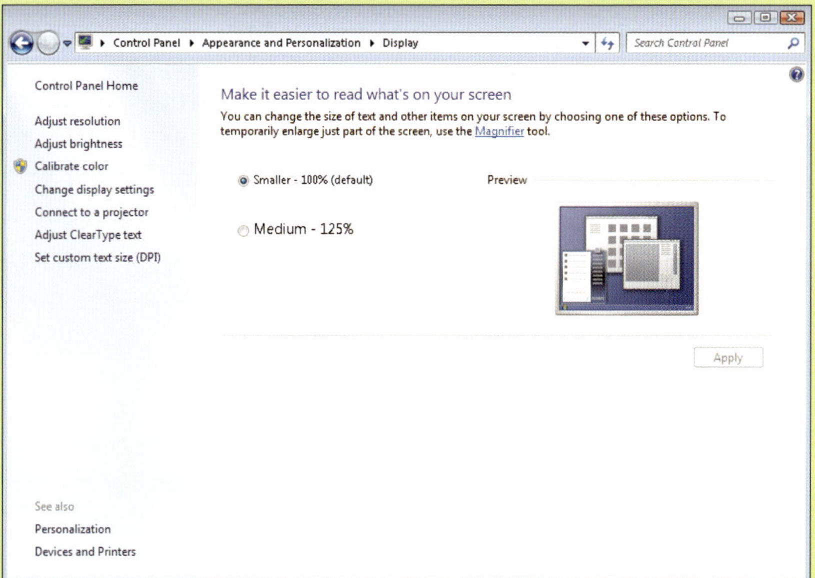

Adjusting the Screen Brightness

To adjust the screen's brightness, follow these steps:

1. Click the Start button and choose Control Panel to open the Control Panel window.
2. In the Control Panel window, click the Hardware and Sound heading.
3. Click the Power Options heading.
4. Drag the Screen Brightness slider, located at the bottom of the window, to adjust the brightness.

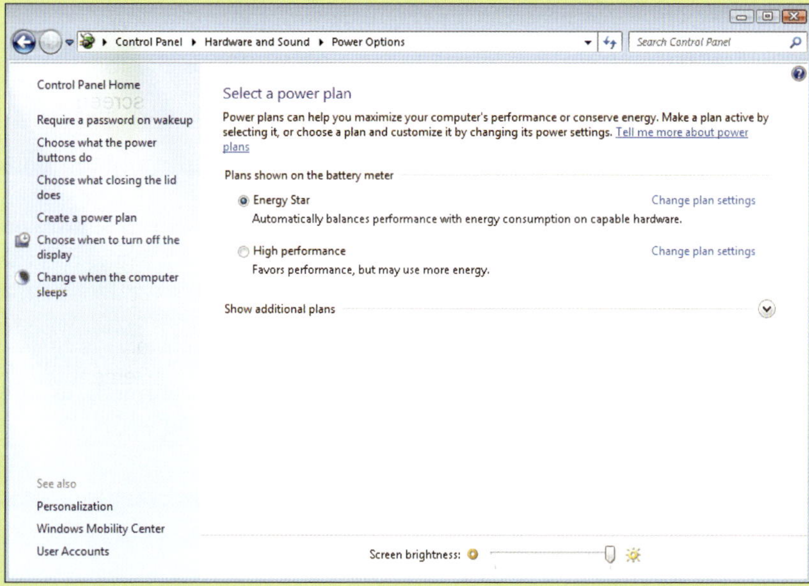

Easing Your Back and Upper Limbs

Everything we do depends on our back. If our back is injured or out of alignment, it affects our ability to perform even the most mundane tasks. And yet, the back is arguably the most abused part of the body. This is because we fail to adopt the correct position when we perform certain activities, such as lifting heavy items. Even sitting down must be done correctly to ensure back health.

Unfortunately, too many computer users suffer from back problems because they fail to care for their back while they work. Computer users are also subject to sore fingers, aching shoulders, tired arms, and injured elbows. Often, permanent damage is done. For help preventing this, read on.

Using Good Posture

posture How a person sits or stands. When someone has good posture, the body is straight and the spine is correctly aligned.

Posture refers to how we sit or stand. When using your computer (or doing anything else), it's critical that you use good posture. Otherwise, you put too much strain on your body.

A good working posture is one in which the body's position can be maintained with minimal physical effort. Your body should be relaxed. This allows you to maintain your position for longer, without putting strain on the body. Here are some hallmarks of good posture:

- The lower back is supported by the shape of the chair.
- The head is up and level.
- The upper arms are relaxed.
- The forearms are at a right angle with the upper arms.
- The wrists are in a straight line with the hands and forearms.
- The knees are level with the hips and the thighs are horizontal.
- The feet are flat on the floor (or resting on a platform or footrest).

For best results, obtain an adjustable chair. Then use it to adjust your position while seated—leaning slightly backward for a while, and then slightly forward. Moving around in this way will help reduce strain on your body. (Regardless of how good your posture is, it is not wise to sit in the same position for too long!) An adjustable table or monitor stand can also help, enabling you to position the monitor correctly, as well as promote the correct placement for your forearms and wrists.

TIP To prevent neck strain, position your monitor directly in front of you on the desk, not at an angle off to one side.

Compare Figure 12.4 with Figure 12.5. The person in Figure 12.4 is leaning forward, with his feet dangling in an unnatural position. This puts strain on the rest of his body. In contrast, the person in Figure 12.5 is more upright, and his feet are resting on the floor. His spine is in correct alignment.

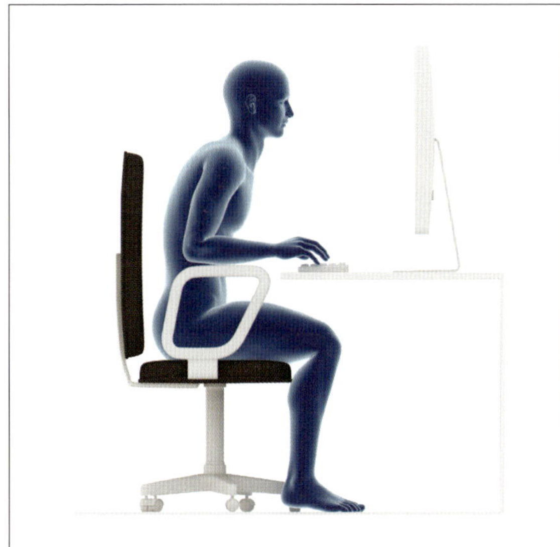

© iStockphoto.com/angelhell

Figure 12.4 Poor posture.

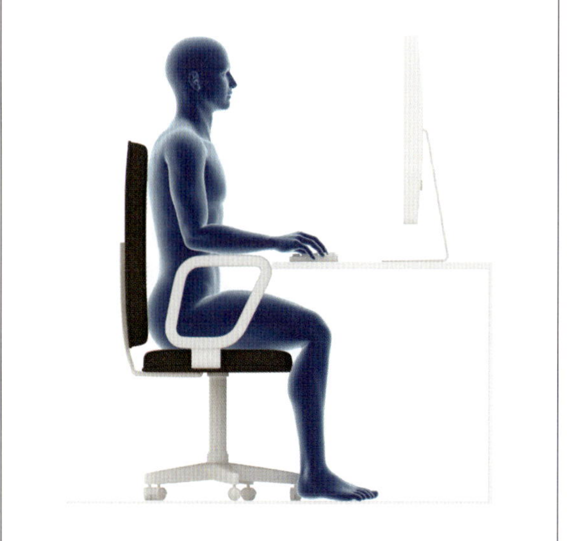

© iStockphoto.com/angelhell

Figure 12.5 Correct posture.

TIP

Even if you use perfect posture, you should take frequent breaks to maintain back health. Get up and stretch every 1 to 2 hours, at a minimum. Taking frequent breaks will also help you minimize stress and fatigue.

Positioning Your Desk and Chair

Desk and chair height can make a big difference in your body's comfort. For best results, think parallel lines. Adjust the desk and chair height so that when you sit up straight at the desk, your thighs are parallel to the floor and both feet are flat on the floor. Adjust the keyboard and mouse heights so that your forearms are parallel to the floor when you are using them. You may need to install a keyboard tray below the desk's main surface to achieve this.

Ergonomic Input Devices

Even with the proper vertical positioning of your keyboard and mouse, you may still experience some wrist strain when you use them for a long time. Repetitive stress injuries such as Carpal Tunnel Syndrome can make the tendons in your hands and wrists swollen and painful and cause burning or tingling.

One way to further protect your hands and wrists is to use ergonomically designed input devices. These special keyboards, mice, and trackballs are designed to reduce the strain placed on your body when you use them.

For example, the keyboard shown in Figure 12.6 has a split design, so that your hands extend straight from your wrists when typing, rather than curving inward. This keyboard also has a built-in wrist rest in front. Figure 12.7 shows an ergonomically designed mouse; notice how the hand and thumb fit naturally on it at rest.

© iStockphoto.com/webphotographeer

Figure 12.6 An ergonomic keyboard.

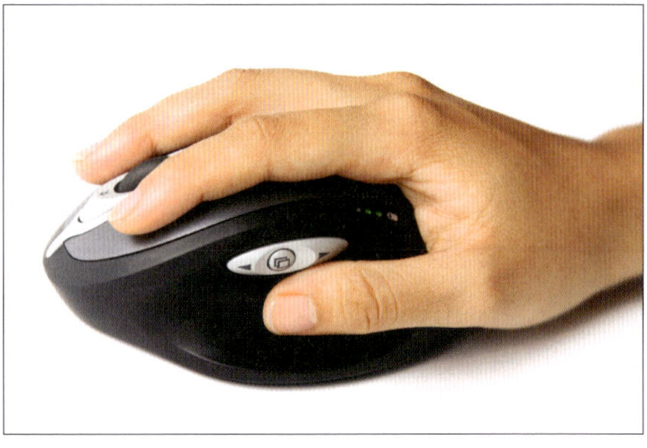

© iStockphoto.com/photosoup

Figure 12.7 An ergonomic mouse.

Quick Review

1. What can you do to prevent eyestrain?
2. Why is it important to adopt a correct posture when sitting at a computer?
3. What are two ways to reduce your risk of hand and wrist pain when using a mouse and keyboard?

Environmental Issues in Computer Disposal

Computers are made of more than just their metal or plastic case. They contain components such as a motherboard, hard drive, display, and peripherals. These components contain all sorts of different materials, some of which may be toxic to the environment.

To avoid damaging the environment, it's imperative that you dispose of your computer properly when you no longer want it. Dumping a computer in a landfill could cause heavy metals and poisons such as arsenic from the components to enter the area's water supply, putting the population at risk. Similarly, incinerating a computer could release elements such as mercury and cadmium into the atmosphere, which could be harmful to those nearby.

Many countries now have regulations that govern the disposal process. In some cases, these regulations require computer retailers and manufacturers to contribute toward having the computer recycled. This makes the disposal process much safer and easier.

Rather than disposing of an old computer, consider harvesting the components and using them elsewhere. Here are a few ideas:

- **Hard drive:** Consider reusing the hard drive in another computer, as an additional drive for yourself or someone else. Or, keep it as a spare. If you opt to give the drive away, be sure to wipe your data from it using a program such as Active@KillDisk (discussed in Chapter 11, "Network and Internet Privacy and Security").
- **Memory:** If the RAM is still usable and of a suitable capacity and speed, you could use it in another computer.
- **Keyboard and mouse:** These are pretty universal and could be used with any computer. It's always worth keeping old keyboards and mice as spares!
- **Display:** If the monitor is of the CRT variety, it is probably at the end of its life and should be disposed of. If it's a more modern, flat-screen monitor, you may be able to use it with another computer. Alternatively, you could use it as a second monitor on your primary computer, running dual displays.
- **Removable components:** A desktop computer may contain removable components such as a display adapter, sound card, or network interface card that could be saved for use in another computer.
- **Notebooks:** There is not much you can remove and reuse from a notebook computer other than the hard drive and possibly the RAM, so this is likely to be disposed of intact.

Alternative Uses for an Older Computer

Put It to Work

Before you dispose of your old computer, consider whether there is an alternative, environmentally friendly way of dealing with it—especially if the computer still has some life left in it. Here are a few ideas:

- **Sell it:** If there's nothing wrong with the computer, why not see if you can sell it—for example, on eBay or some other market place? (If you go this route, again, be sure you wipe the hard drive clean. See Chapter 11 for details.)
- **Give it away:** It may be that some deserving person or organization could make good use of your old computer. Why not donate it?
- **Assign it a new role:** Even if your old computer is a bit slow running newer versions of Windows, it's probably fast enough to run an alternative operating system, such as Linux. Try installing such an operating system on your old computer if you want an extra computer to play with!
- **Keep it as a spare:** It's not a bad idea to keep the old computer as a spare, just in case you have a problem with your new one. That way, if your main computer needs repairs, you'll still have a computer to use in the interim.

Quick Review

1. What are two environmental problems associated with disposing of a computer improperly?
2. What should you do with a hard drive before giving it to someone else to use?
3. What are two alternative uses for an old computer when you have a new one?

Summary

Legal Issues in Computing

Intellectual property (IP) is a legal term that grants people the exclusive rights to the ownership of content that they have created, such as books, artistic works, photographs, music, software, and patents. **Copyright** is a legal protection that usually gives the creator of a work exclusive rights for a specified time period.

Digital rights management (DRM) involves the use of technology to control access to copyrighted material in an attempt to prevent the unauthorized copying and distribution of material. When you install an operating system or software program, you must agree to legal document called an **End User License Agreement (EULA)**. The EULA defines what a user can and cannot do with a product.

Open-source software is software that is not only free to use, but whose source code is accessible to users to modify and redistribute. Although open-source software is about removing licensing restrictions, many types of open-source software do carry a license, called the **General Public License (GPL)**. The GPL enables individuals and companies to legally copy and modify software.

Software piracy is the unauthorized copying of software programs. There are various types of software piracy, including counterfeit software, corporate piracy, unbundling packages, and Internet piracy.

Ethical Issues in Computing

Plagiarism is the practice of copying someone else's work and pretending that it is your own. To avoid plagiarism, use **citations** when referencing the work of others. You must cite not only the source of exact wording, but the source of **paraphrased** ideas.

Censorship is the act of preventing something from being printed or heard. Governments, companies, or individuals can apply forms of censorship by not allowing certain types of information to be published or distributed.

Filtering means to prevent something from getting through. When you filter the Internet, you exclude certain categories of content from general access. A **proxy server**—that is, a server that sits between the user's web browser and the Internet—is used to filter web content.

Sometimes, online communications become hostile, with personal attacks and insults. This is called **flaming**. **Libel** is the act of putting a false, defamatory statement in writing. **Slander** is the verbal version of libel. Slander might consist of negative comments about an individual or group that are made as part of a conversation.

Spam is unsolicited junk email. Although most email programs include a junk email filter, many of these emails still slip through to fill users' inboxes, wasting users' valuable time.

Health Issues in Computing

To combat eyestrain, situate your computer so it is 20 to 40 inches (50 to 100 centimeters) from your face, with your eyes just above the center of the screen. If necessary, adjust the angle of the screen. Work in incandescent lighting rather than fluorescent when possible, and position your monitor so that light does not shine directly on it. Use an LCD monitor if possible rather than a CRT; if you must use a CRT, set its refresh rate to at least 100 Hz. Use as large a monitor as possible, and take frequent breaks from looking at it.

A good working **posture** is one in which the body is relaxed and can maintain its position with minimal physical effort. Even if you use perfect posture, you should take frequent breaks to maintain back health. Position your desk and chair so that your thighs and forearms are parallel to the floor as you work.

Repetitive use of the mouse and keyboard can strain on the hand and wrist muscles, causing them to become swollen and painful. To help prevent this, ensure that your arms and wrists are correctly positioned. Use ergonomic input devices if they are available to further reduce strain.

Environmental Issues in Computer Disposal

To avoid damaging the environment, it's important to dispose of your computer properly. Many countries now have regulations that govern the disposal process.

Rather than disposing of an old computer, consider harvesting the components and using them elsewhere. You could also sell the computer, donate it to a deserving person or charity, repurpose it, or keep it as a spare.

Key Terms

censorship
citation
copyright
digital rights management (DRM)
End User License Agreement (EULA)
filtering
flaming
General Public License (GPL)
intellectual property (IP)
libel
open-source software
paraphrase
plagiarism
posture
proprietary software
proxy server
slander
software piracy
spam

Test Yourself

Fact Check

1. Is it legal to send spam?

   a. Yes, you can send spam in any country.

   b. No, it is illegal to send spam from anywhere.

   c. It depends on what country you are in.

   d. Yes, provided you only send it to your friends.

2. ____________________ is the practice of insulting users during a conversation on the Internet.

   a. spamming

   b. phishing

   c. flaming

   d. filtering

3. What is it called when someone posts untrue written statements about you on a website?

   a. flaming

   b. bullying

   c. slander

   d. libel

4. What is the purpose of copyright?
   a. It gives you the right to copy material regardless of owner.
   b. It is a software tool that ensures copies are accurate.
   c. It protects the rights of the author of a piece of work.
   d. It allows for material to be distributed freely to others.
5. What is the purpose of a citation?
   a. It ensures credit is given to the author.
   b. It acknowledges you as the author of a piece of work.
   c. It prevents software piracy.
   d. It prevents the author from being credited for the work.
6. Which type of software license allows you to modify a program and republish it?
   a. proprietary license
   b. trial license
   c. modification license
   d. General Public License (GPL)
7. What is the purpose of a proxy server?
   a. To allow unlimited access to websites.
   b. To restrict access to undesirable content.
   c. To check documents for plagiarism.
   d. To act as a spam filter.
8. How far away from your face should your monitor be positioned?
   a. 20 to 40 inches
   b. 12 to 14 inches
   c. 6 to 10 inches
   d. 30 to 60 inches
9. A split keyboard is an example of a(n) __________ design.
   a. space-saving
   b. ergonomic
   c. high-efficiency
   d. wireless
10. What should you do before disposing of a computer?
   a. Make sure the computer is completely intact.
   b. Ensure all personal data has been removed and the hard drive erased.
   c. Replace all the original components.
   d. Ensure you have the original packaging.

Matching

Match the following words to the correct phrase:

a. flaming

b. paraphrase

c. citation

d. filtering

e. spamming

f. plagiarism

1. ______________The act of passing off someone else's work as your own.
2. ______________Acknowledging the source of your work.
3. ______________The process of controlling access to websites.
4. ______________Using different words to describe something.
5. ______________The act of interacting in a hostile way online.
6. ______________The process of sending bulk unsolicited emails.

Sum It Up

1. What non-technical issues must be considered when using computers and the Internet?
2. How is software protected from illegal copying and piracy?
3. What steps must Internet users take to behave ethically when it comes to using work that has been published by others?
4. In what ways can using computers be bad for your health?
5. What steps must be taken to ensure that computers are disposed of properly?

Explore More

Assessing Your Work Environment

Examine the physical environment where you use computers at home, at school, and at work. Look at the furniture you are using—the tables, chairs, and so forth—and see what improvements you can make to provide a healthier work environment. Are there any cost-free measures you can take? Or do you need to purchase new items to create a better environment?

Think It Over

Studying Software Licenses

Software licensing is an important issue for computer software vendors. Look at some of the license agreements for some of the software you have installed, or install some trial software so you can view the terms and conditions. Can you understand the terms being using? If not, where could you get help? Is the license agreement too complex and difficult to understand? Could you reword a license agreement so that it is understandable to nearly anyone and is only as long as it needs to be?

Answers to Chapter Questions

Chapter 1

Fact Check

1. d
2. b
3. a
4. d
5. operating system
6. a
7. processing
8. b
9. d
10. b

Matching

1. a
2. e
3. c
4. b
5. d

Chapter 2

Fact Check

1. b
2. b
3. a
4. b
5. c
6. a
7. d
8. c
9. a
10. power supply

Matching

1. e
2. c
3. b
4. f
5. a
6. d

Chapter 3

Fact Check

1. b
2. d
3. a
4. b
5. a
6. c
7. a
8. c
9. b
10. b

Matching

1. c
2. d
3. a
4. b
5. f
6. e

Chapter 4

Fact Check

1. a
2. b
3. a
4. d
5. d
6. c
7. b
8. a
9. d
10. a

Matching

1. a
2. b
3. c
4. e
5. d
6. f

Chapter 5

Fact Check

1. b
2. c
3. c
4. d
5. b
6. b
7. a
8. c
9. c
10. d

Matching

1. f
2. a
3. e
4. c
5. d
6. b
7. g

Chapter 6

Fact Check

1. a
2. b
3. d
4. c
5. b
6. a
7. b
8. c
9. b
10. b

Matching

1. a
2. e
3. b
4. d
5. f
6. c
7. g

Chapter 7

Fact Check

1. b
2. d
3. c
4. a
5. c
6. d
7. a
8. b
9. c
10. c

Matching

1. c
2. f
3. a
4. b
5. d
6. g
7. e

Chapter 8

Fact Check

1. a
2. b
3. a
4. b
5. c
6. d
7. a
8. c
9. b
10. a

Matching

1. c
2. f
3. e
4. d
5. a
6. b

Chapter 9

Fact Check

1. c
2. d
3. b
4. a
5. b
6. b
7. b
8. a
9. b
10. d

Matching

1. e
2. c
3. d
4. b
5. f
6. a

Chapter 10

Fact Check

1. d
2. b
3. b
4. a and d
5. a
6. b
7. a
8. b
9. a
10. a

Matching

1. d
2. f
3. c
4. e
5. a
6. b

Chapter 11

Fact Check

1. b
2. b
3. d
4. d
5. d
6. d
7. a
8. b
9. a
10. d

Matching

1. b
2. d
3. g
4. c
5. e
6. f
7. a

Chapter 12

Fact Check

1. c
2. c
3. d
4. c
5. a
6. d
7. b
8. a
9. b
10. b

Matching

1. f
2. c
3. d
4. b
5. a
6. e

Glossary

3G Digital technology for moving data through a cell phone network at up to 14 Mbps.

4G Digital technology for moving data through a cell phone network at up to 100 Mbps.

accounting software Software that enables a small business to manage and track its financial health and transactions.

active matrix An LCD type in which each pixel is actively maintained by a separate transistor.

address bar The field above the menu bar in Windows Explorer that shows the current path.

adware A type of malware that pops up unwanted ads on the screen.

All Programs The command at the bottom of the Start menu that opens up a hierarchical menu system of all the installed applications on the computer.

Android An open-source operating system used on a variety of portable devices, including tablets and smartphones.

anti-spam software Software that rejects junk email messages.

app An application, such as for a personal computer, tablet, or smartphone.

application software Software that helps a human perform a useful task for work or play.

archive To move items from the current location to another for backup purposes; a useful way of storing old messages while freeing up space for new ones.

archive attribute A file attribute that indicates whether or not a file has changed since its last backup.

aspect ratio The ratio of width to height on a display screen, such as 4:3 (standard) or 16:9 (wide).

ATA Short for AT Attachment. The IBM PC AT was an early type of computer (1984) that was among the first to support modern hard drive technology.

attachment A file that travels along with a text email to a recipient.

audio adapter Also called a **sound card**. A component of a computer system that accepts and processes audio input and delivers audio output.

automatic reply A feature on a mail server that automatically sends a message back to each one received when it is enabled.

backbone The central connection pathways of a network, where connection speeds are high and the data pathway is wide.

Backstage view The area of an Office application where you select commands that affect the entire active document or the application itself. Access it by clicking the File tab on the Ribbon.

backup set A set of backup files created during a single backup operation.

backup software Software that enables and automates the process of backing up files to external media.

bar code reader A scanner that reads and interprets bar codes such as UPC symbols.

benchmark A consistent measurement of performance.

BIOS The software that initializes and tests the system at startup.

bit A single binary digit, with a value of either 1 (on) or 0 (off).

blacklist A list of prohibited email senders.

blog A web page containing the author's personal experiences and opinions.

blog platform A web server that hosts the blogs of individuals, either free or for a small fee.

Bluetooth An inexpensive short-range networking technology used for computer-to-device connections such as computer-to-printer or phone-to-headset

Blu-ray disc (BD) An optical disc used for storing high-definition movies and data, holding up to 25 GB per layer.

bot A type of Trojan, used to infect a zombie computer to conduct a DoS attack.

botnet A network of zombie computers infected with bots, often numbering in the thousands. Computer criminals use botnets to conduct DoS attacks.

broadband A fast, always-on network connection.

bus A conductive pathway built into a circuit board, used to move data.

byte An 8-digit binary number, composed of eight bits.

cable modem A broadband modem designed to work with a cable Internet connection.

cache A small amount of fast memory located near or within the CPU.

cathode ray tube (CRT) An older type of monitor technology that uses a vacuum tube and electron guns to create a display image.

cell The intersection of a row and a column in a worksheet.

cell cursor The thick line around the active cell in Excel, indicating that this is where typed text will appear.

censorship The act of suppressing speech or not allowing certain communications to be made public.

central processing unit (CPU) The main processor in a computer.

channel An individual chat room on a chat server such as IRC.

charge-coupled device (CCD) The light-sensitive sensor in a scanner that records the amount of light bounced back from the image.

chat room An online virtual room in which you can meet and talk to other people.

chipset The controller chip on a circuit board.

Chrome OS A thin client operating system created by Google for small notebook computers (netbooks).

circuit-switched network A network that creates a point-to-point connection between locations that remains open for the duration of the communication.

citation A reference to a source—that is, to the author and name of a published or unpublished work—following a quotation from said source.

client A computer used by an individual to run applications.

client/server network A network that contains one or more servers.

Clipboard A reserved area in memory for temporarily holding content that has been cut or copied from an application or from Windows Explorer.

clock cycle One tick of the system clock.

cloud A secure computing environment accessed via the Internet.

cloud storage Storage that is accessed from a cloud environment.

cluster A grouping of sectors. The number of sectors in a cluster depends on the file system and the disk size.

coaxial cable Cable that consists of a solid copper core with an insulated sleeve around it.

codec A translation file used to play back a certain audio or video format. An abbreviation of coder/decoder.

cold boot To start up a computer from a power-off state.

color depth The number of bits needed to describe the color of each pixel in a certain display mode, such as 16-bit or 32-bit.

color palette A grid of color choices that opens when you click a button for a feature that is color-related.

command bar In Windows 7, the bar in Windows Explorer that contains an Organize button that opens a menu, and also other commands, which change depending on what location you are viewing. In Windows 8, a bar that appears at the top or bottom of a Windows 8 app when you right-click, offering buttons you can click to issue commands.

command-line interface A user interface based on typing text at a command prompt.

compact disc (CD) An optical disc used for storing music and data, holding up to 900 MB.

compression The process of reducing the size of a data file by encoding information using fewer bits than the original file.

computer-aided design (CAD) The process of using computer software to produce technical drawings that include the product's precise scale, simulate its textures, and show it in full three-dimensional detail.

consumables Printing supplies that must be replaced with use, such as paper and ink.

Contacts The section in Outlook that stores people's contact information.

contiguous Physically adjacent to one another.

cookie A small file placed by a website on a computer that stores information about the user's interaction with the website.

copyright The granting of exclusive rights to the creator of a work for a limited period of time.

core A set of the essential processor components that work together (control unit, ALU, and registers). A CPU may have multiple cores.

cyberbullying Using computers and the Internet to deliberately harass or harm others by making malicious statements.

cylinder All the tracks at a single position of the read/write heads' actuator arm.

data mining Extracting information from a database to zero in on certain facts or summarize a large amount of data.

database A collection of data stored in a structured format, with the same facts stored about each instance. A database stores data in a way that enables you to search and locate it quickly.

database management system (DBMS) An application that helps users create and manage databases.

decrypt To reverse the encryption of a file so that the file appears in its original form again.

denial of service (DoS) attack A coordinated attack in which the target website or service is flooded with requests for access, to the point that it is completely overwhelmed.

desktop The Windows 7 interface on which windows open containing applications. Can also refer specifically to the background image.

desktop PC A computer designed to be set up at a desk and not often moved, with input and output devices separate from the system unit.

desktop publishing software Software that helps create page layouts with text and graphics.

dialog box A window that appears in response to selecting a command, prompting for more information about how the user wants the command to be executed.

dialog box launcher An icon in the lower-right corner of a group on the Ribbon; when clicked, it opens a dialog box or task pane.

dial-up modem A device that converts between analog and digital data so computer data can be sent over analog phone lines.

differential backup A backup operation that backs up all files that have the archive attribute set to On but does not change that attribute.

digital camera A camera that captures and stores still images in digital form.

digital rights management (DRM) The use of technology to control access to copyrighted material.

digital subscriber line (DSL) A broadband Internet technology provided by the telephone company.

digital versatile disc (DVD) An optical disc used for storing standard-definition movies and data, holding up to 4.17 GB per side per layer.

digital video camera A video camera that captures and stores motion video in digital form.

Digital Visual Interface (DVI) A digital port for connecting a monitor to a PC.

digital whiteboard A whiteboard that is connected to a computer, so that whatever is written on the board is saved on the computer.

digitize To convert something from hard-copy to digital (computerized) form.

direct thermal printer A printer that heats certain areas of specially coated paper so that it turns black and forms the image.

direct-attached storage (DAS) Storage that is directly connected to the computer that accesses it.

disk One or more platters on which data is stored. Spelled *disc* when referring to the optical type (DVDs, CDs).

disk checking program Software that finds and fixes errors in the disk storage system.

display adapter The computer component that communicates instructions from the operating system to the display.

display screen A video screen that a computer uses to provide output to a human user.

distro Short for **distribution**, a packaged collection of an open-source kernel such as Linux along with helpful add-ons and utilities.

dithering Placing different colored dots side by side in an image so that from a distance they appear to be a third color.

document feeder A mechanical feature of some scanners that enables multiple pages to be scanned consecutively without user intervention.

domain name A name that identifies an entity on the Internet.

Domain Name System (DNS) The naming system employed to enable users to access websites using their domain names or URLs rather than their IP addresses.

dots per inch (dpi) A measurement of printed image quality, the number of individually colored dots in one row (or column) of one inch of the printed file. A printout can have a different horizontal and vertical dpi, although this is not common.

double data rate SDRAM (DDR SDRAM) SDRAM that performs two actions per clock tick.

drawing tablet A flat rectangular touch-sensitive surface on which a user can draw with a stylus to create onscreen artwork.

drive The mechanical components that read and write the data on a disk.

drum The rotating cylinder inside a laser printer, on which the page image is formed with electrical charges.

dual inline memory module (DIMM) A small rectangular circuit board that holds DRAM, fitting into a memory slot on a motherboard.

duplexing To print on both sides of the paper.

dynamic IP address An IP address that is temporarily assigned to a device.

dynamic memory Memory that does not retain its data unless it is constantly electrically refreshed.

educational software Software that teaches or trains an individual in a particular type of knowledge or skill.

Electrically Erasable Programmable ROM (EEPROM) ROM that can be erased and reprogrammed with electricity.

electromagnetic interference (EMI) The corruption of data as it is passing through a cable due to the magnetic field generated by a nearby cable.

email A computer-based system for exchanging messages through mail servers.

email application Software that assists in sending and receiving email.

encrypt To scramble the contents of a file so it cannot be read without the required permission to decrypt it.

End User License Agreement (EULA) The legal agreement between the owner of an application and the user who wants to install and use it.

e-paper A monitor technology used in book readers in which the screen retains its image but is unpowered except when the display changes.

ergonomic keyboard A keyboard that is designed with features that help reduce stress on the user's hands and wrists.

Ethernet The current dominant standard for local area networking devices.

expansion card A small circuit board that fits into a slot on the motherboard to add functionality.

expansion slot A slot in the motherboard into which an expansion card (a small circuit board) can be installed.

ExpressCard A metal cartridge inserted into an externally accessible slot in a notebook PC that adds a capability to the system, such as wireless networking.

extranet A special network set up by a business for its customers, staff and business partners to access from outside the office network; may be used to share marketing assets and other non-sensitive items.

Facebook A social network for posting interesting updates, web links, and photos, and for chatting with friends.

FaceTime An app installed on Apple iPhone and iPad devices that is used to make video calls between Apple device owners.

FAT32 A file system used in Windows 95, Windows 98, and Windows Millennium Edition. FAT stands for File Allocation Table.

favorite A website or page that you visit frequently, and to which you want easy access.

fiber optic cable Cable that carries data using light pulses through a bundle of glass fibers.

field A column in a table, storing one particular kind of information, such as Phone or Name.

file A group of related bits stored together under a single name.

file extension A code at the end of a filename that indicates the file's type.

file system A set of rules for storing and managing the files on a volume, such as NTFS or FAT32.

filtering Preventing something from getting through—in this case, content.

firewall A security barrier on your computer or network that controls what traffic is allowed to pass through.

firewall software Software that blocks hackers from accessing a computer by closing unnecessary services and ports.

flaming Where Internet users interact in a hostile way with each other.

flatbed scanner A scanner that has a large flat glass surface on which the page to be scanned is placed.

folder A logical organizing unit for grouping related files together.

folder tree A graphical representation of a volume's storage hierarchy, with subordinate branches for folders and subfolders.

form factor The size and shape of a circuit board, such as a motherboard.

format To create the file system on a volume.

formula A mathematical calculation to be performed in an Excel cell. It may refer to other cells for its values.

forum A web-based discussion and advice-sharing site.

forum thread A post on a forum along with all the comments to it.

Forward A copy of a message sent on to someone other than the original sender.

frame A still image that makes up part of a digital video clip.

full backup A backup operation that backs up all files and sets their archive attribute to Off.

fuser The heating element in a laser printer that melts the toner, fusing it to the paper.

General Public License (GPL) A license used for many types of open-source software, allowing the software to be legally copied and modified.

gigahertz One billion hertz.

global positioning system (GPS) A device that determines your current position by communicating with an orbiting satellite and provides maps and driving directions.

graphical user interface (GUI) A user interface based on a graphical environment, in which users interact with it using a pointing device or touch screen as the primary input device.

graphics software Software that enables you to create and manipulate visual images.

group A named section of a Ribbon tab.

groupware Software that helps people collaborate on business projects and work together in a team environment when they are not physically together.

hard copy Physically printed pages of a document or a printed photo; the opposite of soft (electronic) copy.

hard disk drive (HDD) A mechanical drive with an integrated set of disk platters that store data in patterns of magnetic polarity.

hard drive A sealed metal box that stores computer data using either mechanical or solid-state technology.

hardware The physical parts of the computer system.

hertz One cycle per second, a measurement of activity speed.

Hibernate mode A power-saving mode that saves the contents of RAM to the hard drive and then shuts down all power. When the computer wakes up, it reads the saved data back into RAM so the computer does not have to restart completely.

hierarchical database A way of organizing data from a single starting point or premise in a treelike parent and child relationship format. All records are shown in terms of how they relate to the originating point at the top of the tree.

Hierarchical File System Plus (HFS+) The file system used with Mac OS X.

high-definition multimedia interface (HDMI) A type of connector used to connect an HDTV to another device, such as a computer or a home theater system.

high-definition TV (HDTV) A television that displays at least 1920 × 1080 resolution (also known as 1080p).

home page The page that is displayed when you first launch your web browser.

homegroup A small group of mutually trusted computers on a peer-to-peer network such as in a home or small office.

HTTP email account An email account that is designed to be used with a web interface and uses web technology for email management.

hub A primitive version of a switch that lacks the capability to read packet addresses and route them to the appropriate port.

hyperlink A pointer to another point on a web page, which you access by clicking the hyperlink.

Hypertext Markup Language (HTML) A language for encoding data and graphics for display in a web browser.

HyperText Transfer Protocol (HTTP) The protocol used to send and receive web pages on the Internet.

icon A small picture representing a file, folder, application, or other object.

IEEE 1394A A connector used to connect certain types of devices to a computer that require high-speed connection, such as some external hard drives and video cameras. A competitor to USB. Also called FireWire.

IMAP account An email account that is designed to be used with an email client and that uses IMAP protocol for receiving mail.

incremental backup A backup operation that backs up all files that have the archive attribute set to On and then sets the attribute to Off.

information processing cycle The four-step process that data moves through as it is processed by a computer. Consists of input, processing, output, and storage.

information system An interconnected environment for managing and processing data using a computer.

infrared Older type of wireless communication that used light waves to pass simple information between nearby devices.

inkjet printer A printer that squirts ink onto paper with small nozzles (jets) to form the page image.

input device Hardware that enables the computer to accept commands or data from a human user.

insertion point The flashing vertical line that indicates where typed text will appear.

Instagram A social network for posting and sharing photos.

instant messaging (IM) Sending and receiving short text messages in real-time over the Internet.

Instructions per second A measurement of a CPU's throughput capability, taking into consideration factors such as number of cores and latency.

intellectual property (IP) The exclusive rights to the ownership of something that has been created or produced.

Internet A global packet-switched network created cooperatively by multiple companies, governments, and standards organizations.

Internet Mail Access Protocol (IMAP) A protocol for receiving email through a mail client.

Internet Relay Chat (IRC) An online system of public chat servers.

Internet service provider (ISP) A company that maintains a direct connection to the Internet and leases access to it to individuals and companies.

intranet A special network that only staff within the company network can access. For security reasons an intranet can only be accessed onsite and not remotely.

iOS The Apple-created operating system for Apple tablets and phones.

IP address A numeric address by which a particular computer is known on a network.

ISO 9660 A file system used on optical media such as CDs; also called CD File System, or CDFS.

joystick A pointing device consisting of a vertically mounted stick that can be tilted in any direction.

keyboard An input device that allows users to type data into a computer using a standard set of typing keys.

keyboard shortcut Two or more keys that, when pressed in combination, issue a command.

keylogger A piece of hardware or a software program that captures every keystroke a user types.

knowledge base A set of articles provided and maintained by a company or government agency about its products.

laser printer A printer that forms the page image by transferring toner to the paper via a rotating drum with electrical charges.

latency A period of waiting for another component to deliver data needed to proceed.

legal software Software that guides the user in creating legally binding contracts and forms.

libel Putting in writing a defamatory statement that could damage a person's or organization's reputation.

library A virtual folder that combines the contents of one or more specified folders into a single view.

Linux An open-source, cross-platform operating system that runs on desktops, notebooks, tablets, and smartphones.

liquid crystal display (LCD) A flat-screen display technology that passes electricity through liquid crystals to create a display image.

local area network (LAN) A network that connects devices housed in the same physical location.

lock To prevent unauthorized users from using a computer by displaying a password prompt.

log off To close a user account's session, closing all open programs and data files and unloading all of that user's personal settings.

Mac OS X The graphical operating system designed for Apple's desktop and notebook computers. Newer versions now run on the Intel platform.

magnetic card reader A scanner that reads and deciphers the information on the magnetic strip on a credit card or other ID card.

magnetic-ink character recognition (MICR) The scanning system used in the banking industry to read routing and account numbers on checks and deposit slips.

mail client Software installed on a computer that is used to compose and manage email.

mail server An online server that sends and/or receives email messages on behalf of the email addresses it supports.

mainframe A large and powerful computer capable of serving many users and processing large amounts of data at once.

malware Malicious software that consists of programs designed to disrupt the normal operation of computer systems.

Mavericks The code name for Mac OS X 10.9.

maximize To enlarge the window to fill the entire screen.

maximum resolution The highest display mode (the greatest number of pixels) a display can support.

mechanical mouse A mouse that operates by rolling a rubber ball inside a chamber containing sensors.

media access control (MAC) address A unique hardware address for a network adapter.

memory Temporary electronic storage that holds the values of data bits using transistors.

menu bar A horizontal bar near the top of a window containing the names of menus that can be opened by clicking on the names.

metropolitan area network (MAN) A network that connects devices within the area of a city or town.

microblog A service that allows the posting of short messages.

Microsoft Office A productivity suite of applications commonly used in businesses for word processing, spreadsheets, databases, presentation, and email.

Microsoft Windows The graphical Microsoft operating system designed for Intel-platform desktop and notebook computers.

microwave communication system A secure, point-to-point wireless networking technology that requires a line of sight between the two points.

minimize To shrink the window to a button on the taskbar.

monitor A display screen on which a computer's output appears.

motherboard A large circuit board inside a computer that controls the operations of all other components.

mouse A pointing device that the user moves with his or her hand across a flat surface to move an onscreen pointer.

multi-boot The ability to have more than one OS installed and to choose at startup which one to run.

multi-function device (MFD) A device that combines the functions of a printer, a copier, and a scanner into one unit, and also a fax in some models.

name resolution The process of translating domain names to numerical IP addresses. A DNS server is used to resolve a name to an address.

NAS appliance A specialized device that provides storage space to network users.

netbook A small notebook PC designed primarily for accessing the Internet.

network Two or more computers connected to share data and resources.

network adapter A hardware component that enables a computer to connect to a network.

network interface card (NIC) A network adapter that is on an expansion card, rather than built into the computer's motherboard. Sometimes used informally to refer to any network adapter.

network-attached storage (NAS) Storage that is accessed via a network.

New Technology File System (NTFS) The proprietary Microsoft file system used in modern versions of Windows.

newsgroup An online discussion group.

newsreader Software that organizes incoming messages from newsgroups and allows users to read and respond to them.

node (database) The point of intersection in a diagram or in a database; where several items share a node, the node itself becomes important.

non-contiguous Not adjacent.

notebook PC A portable PC where the screen and keyboard fold up against one another for storage and transport; also known as a laptop.

notification area The area to the left of the clock on the taskbar, containing icons for programs running in the background. Also called the **system tray**.

object An item that is separate from the rest of the document, with its own movable and resizable frame.

Office Clipboard The enhanced version of the Windows Clipboard that appears in Office applications. It can hold up to 24 items at once.

open-source software Free access to a software program and the source code that produced the program.

operating system Software that maintains the computer's interface, manages files, runs applications, and communicates with hardware.

optical drive A drive that reads discs that are stored in patterns of greater and lesser reflectivity, such as a DVD or CD.

optical mark recognition A scanner that detects the presence of a pencil or ink mark on certain areas of a standardized form.

optical mouse A mouse that operates by bouncing light off a flat surface and measuring the reflection.

organic light-emitting diode (OLED) A flat-screen technology that uses organic matter that lights up in response to electrical current to create a display image.

out-of-office message A message that people receive when you are unable to personally answer your email for a certain time.

packet-switched network A network that transfers data by breaking it up into separately transferred packets.

paging file The area of the hard drive set aside for use as virtual memory. Also called a swap file.

pair To connect a Bluetooth input or output device to a computer.

Parallel ATA (PATA) A type of connector used for older disk drives and optical drives such as CD and DVD drives.

parallel port A port used to connect some older printers to a computer. It is sometimes called an LPT port, which stands for Line Printer.

paraphrase To use different words to convey the same idea.

partition To create logical divisions of the available space on a storage medium such as an HDD; or, a logical division of space on a storage medium.

passive matrix An LCD type in which each pixel maintains its state on its own until it decays or is refreshed.

password cracking The act of attempting to identify a user's password in order to gain access to a system or program.

path The complete descriptor of a file's location, including the volume and folders.

PCI Express (PCIe) A new and updated version of the PCI motherboard slot. Different numbers of channels are used in different sized PCIe slots, such as 16, 4, or 1.

PCI Express Mini Card A small circuit board that can be installed in a notebook PC's PCI Express Mini expansion bay to add a capability to the computer, such as wireless networking.

peer-to-peer (P2P) network A network that consists only of clients (no servers).

Peripheral Component Interface (PCI) A motherboard slot that accepts PCI expansion boards. PCI is considered a legacy interface (mostly obsolete).

personal area network (PAN) A network formed when devices are connected to an individual computer.

personal computer A computer designed to be used by only one person at a time.

personal finance software Software that enables individuals to track and manage their bank accounts and investments.

phishing The act of attempting to acquire information such as usernames, passwords, credit card information, and so forth, by pretending to be from a genuine, trustworthy source such as a bank.

pinned Attached to a fixed feature onscreen, such as to the taskbar or the Start menu.

pixel An individual colored dot in a raster graphic or on a display screen.

pixilated The effect of seeing the jagged edges of individual pixels that occurs when a raster image is enlarged.

plagiarism The act of copying someone else's work and pretending that it is your own.

platform A type of computer hardware that is compatible with certain operating systems.

plotter A large-format printer that creates high-precision documents such as maps and engineering drawings.

plug-in A piece of software added to a web browser to give it additional functionality.

pointing device An input device such as a mouse or touchpad that enables users to move an onscreen pointer to select content and issue commands.

POP account An email account that is designed to be used with an email client and that uses POP protocol for receiving mail.

post An article published on a blog.

Post Office Protocol (POP) A protocol for receiving email through a mail client.

posture How a person sits or stands. When someone has good posture, the body is straight and the spine is correctly aligned.

power supply A component that converts AC power from a wall outlet to DC power and decreases the voltage to the level needed for the computer to operate.

presentation graphics software A program that combines charts, graphics, and bulleted lists of information as a series of slides that summarize a report or verbal presentation. Microsoft PowerPoint is the most widely used program.

primary storage System RAM in a computer, where processed data is first stored after it exits the CPU.

processor The chip in the computer that performs math calculations, processing data. Also called the Central Processing Unit (CPU).

productivity software Software that helps a human perform one or more business or personal enrichment tasks.

proprietary software Software to which the vendor retains ownership rights. Users merely have usage rights.

protocol A rule or custom that governs how something is done. In a computer context, it refers to a standard for transferring data.

protocol stack A related group of protocols—for example, TCP/IP.

proxy server A server that sits between the user's web browser and the Internet that intercepts all requests for web pages and processes those requests.

PS/2 A connector used to connect some older keyboards and mice to a computer. PS stands for Personal System. This connector was first introduced with the IBM PS/2 computer in 1987.

public switched telephone network (PSTN) The worldwide network of circuit-switched telephone lines.

pull technology A technology that sends information to a recipient only when the recipient requests it.

push technology A technology that sends information to a recipient without the recipient asking for it each time.

QR code A two-dimensional variant of a bar code, containing more information than a traditional bar code.

Quick Access Toolbar (QAT) The small, customizable toolbar above the Ribbon tabs in an Office application's interface.

QWERTY The standard layout for English-language keyboards.

radio frequency identification (RFID) chip A computer chip that communicates wirelessly with a device to authenticate a user.

Random Access Memory (RAM) Memory that can have its values changed freely, an unlimited number of times.

ransomware A type of Trojan that encrypts files on a user's system. It then displays a message describing how to decrypt the files—which inevitably involves sending payment over the Internet. Even after the money is sent, however, the files are not decrypted.

raster graphic A graphic that consists of a grid of colored pixels that collectively form an image.

read/write head A component in a disk drive that reads and writes to the disk(s).

reading pane A pane in a mail client that previews the content of the selected message.

Read-Only Memory (ROM) In general, memory that cannot be rewritten. However, there are exceptions to that in newer types of ROM.

record A row in a table, storing information about a specific person, place, or thing.

Reddit A social network for posting news snippets.

redundant array of inexpensive disks (RAID) A multi-disk storage system that optimizes performance, data safety, or both, depending on the type.

reference software Software that provides access to established facts and information on a variety of topics.

refresh rate The number of times each pixel in a display is refreshed per second.

registry The main system configuration database for Microsoft Windows.

registry cleanup program Software that analyzes the Windows registry and deletes unneeded entries.

relational database A spreadsheetlike database that shows how items in a database are connected or have attributes in common.

render To apply a surface texture and fill to a wireframe image to give it a solid appearance.

repeater A device that receives and retransmits a network signal.

Reply A message that is sent back to the original sender.

Reply All A message that is sent back to the original sender plus to any other recipients.

resolution The number of pixels that comprise a display, horizontally and vertically.

restore To shrink a window from its maximized state to the size it was before it was maximized.

Ribbon The main toolbar in Office applications and some other Windows applications, consisting of multiple tabbed pages of commands.

rogue Wi-Fi A wireless network that "sniffs" traffic, making a copy of everything users type—including usernames, passwords, and credit card numbers.

root directory The top level folder on a storage volume.

router A connection box for Ethernet networks that physically joins the devices in the network (wired) or provides wireless connectivity (wireless), and enables a connection to an outside network such as the Internet.

satellite A data transmitter/receiver in geosynchronous orbit with the Earth.

satellite Internet A broadband Internet technology that uses satellites and a transmitter/receiver to provide Internet access.

save location The location where files are saved when a user saves them to a library.

ScreenTip The information that appears about a command or button when you hover the mouse pointer over it.

scroll To page through the document so that a different part of it becomes visible.

scroll bar The horizontal or vertical bar to the bottom or right of the document, containing scroll arrows and a scroll box, which you can use to scroll.

scroll box The box in the scroll bar that you can drag to scroll the display. You can also click above or below the scroll bar to scroll one screenful at a time.

Search box The box at the bottom of the Start menu that enables you to type the name of a program or feature you are looking for to narrow down the Start menu's listing.

search engine A software tool used to locate information on the web.

search engine optimization (SEO) The process of writing web content so as to increase a page's ranking in online search results.

search operator A word or symbol that has a specific function when carrying out a search.

secondary storage Storage that retains data after the computer is turned off, such as a hard disk drive, DVD, or USB flash drive.

sector The smallest addressable unit of storage on a disk drive, at 512 bytes.

selection handles The markers on the border of an object that allow the object to be resized.

semiconductor Material that is electricity-neutral, neither a good conductor nor a flow preventer.

Serial ATA (SATA) A type of connector used for newer disk drives.

serial port A port used to connect some very old external devices to a computer. It is sometimes called a COM port, which stands for Communications (although actually many types of ports operate serially, not just this one).

server A computer that is dedicated to performing network tasks such as managing files, printers, or email for multiple users.

server farm A group of servers located in the same physical area.

service pack A collection of patches, released in a single package.

shell The user interface for an operating system. Some operating systems, like Windows, do not separate the shell from the kernel; others, like Linux, give you a choice of shells.

shielded twisted pair (STP) A type of twisted-pair cable that has an outer sheath that protects against external EMI.

Short Message Service (SMS) The text messaging technology used on cell phone networks.

shortcut A pointer to a file or folder.

shortcut menu A context-sensitive menu that appears when you right-click an object onscreen.

signature Text that is automatically appended to outgoing messages.

Simple Mail Transfer Protocol (SMTP) A protocol used for sending email for a POP3 email account.

single data rate SDRAM (SDR SDRAM) SDRAM that performs one action per clock tick.

Skype A Microsoft-owned VoIP service used to make phone calls and sometimes video calls over a broadband, Wi-Fi, or cellular mobile web connection.

slander Making a defamatory verbal statement that could damage a person's or organization's reputation.

Sleep mode A power-saving mode that keeps RAM powered but turns off everything else to save power.

slide A screen of information that is displayed in a static fashion while a presenter elaborates on its contents. Often, the slide will be part of an electronic presentation file and the presenter can move through successive files on demand.

smartphone A cellular phone that includes computer applications and Internet access capability.

social engineering The art of obtaining someone's password either by befriending her or tricking her into sharing it.

social network An Internet-based system that enables users to interact in real-time and by using messaging programs.

software The programs that tell the computer what to do.

Software as a Service (SaaS) A model of software sales that leases access to the software rather than selling a copy outright to the user.

software piracy The unauthorized copying and distribution of software.

solid-state hard drive (SSHD) A high-capacity solid state storage device that substitutes for an HDD as the main storage drive in a computer.

spam Unsolicited "junk" mail, typically containing offers (some legitimate, some not) of products or services to buy.

speech recognition software Software that can learn an individual's pronunciation and vocal inflection and translate it into digitized text.

sponsored link A hyperlink that is placed on a page because a payment has been made.

spreadsheet A program that presents rows and columns of figures and other items against which time and other variables can be plotted.

spyware A type of malware that spies on the user's activities and reports them back to the spyware's developer.

standard colors Fixed colors that are not affected by the theme in use.

Start button The button that opens the Start menu.

Start menu The menu that opens when you click the Start button, containing shortcuts to applications, storage locations, and settings.

static IP address An IP address that is permanently assigned to a device.

static memory Memory that retains its data without electricity being constantly applied.

status bar The bar at the bottom of an application's window that reports status information.

storage-area network (SAN) A distributed storage system that appears to each individual computer as a local volume on that computer.

store-and-forward A message delivery system in which messages are forwarded between servers and then stored on those servers until they are picked up.

striping Spreading the data across multiple drives to improve performance or protect the data.

strong password A password that includes a combination of uppercase letters, lowercase letters, numerals, and symbols, making it difficult to guess.

stylus A pen-shaped pointer used to drag across the surface of a touch-sensitive screen.

subfolder A folder within another folder.

suite A group of applications designed to complement each other's capabilities and work together closely, often with a consistent interface between the applications.

supercomputer The largest and most powerful type of computer, surpassing the capability of a mainframe, typically used in research and academics.

switch A gathering point for the computers in a LAN to connect with to participate in the network.

Switch User A Windows feature that enables another user to log in without the original user logging off first.

synchronous dynamic RAM (SDRAM) DRAM that operates at the speed of the system clock.

system memory The main pool of dynamic RAM (DRAM) on the motherboard.

system requirements The minimum hardware required to install and run an application.

system software Software that starts the computer and keeps it running, performing basic system tasks such as running applications, managing files, and correcting errors.

system unit The main part of the computer, containing the essential components.

system volume The volume on which the operating system files are stored.

system-on-chip (SoC) An operating system that comes preinstalled on a chip on a portable device such as a smartphone.

tab (Ribbon) A tabbed page of a Ribbon, or the name of a particular tabbed page.

tab (browser) A web browser feature that enables users to have multiple pages open at once within the same browser window.

table A collection of records, arranged in a row-and-column format.

tablet PC A lightweight slate-style computer with a touch screen, designed for easy portability.

tag A topic or subject assigned to a social networking post. Also called a **hashtag.**

taskbar The bar along the bottom of the Windows desktop, from which you can start programs and manage running programs.

tax software Software that enables individuals and small businesses to calculate the taxes they owe and file the needed forms with the government.

TCP/IP The protocol suite (set of rules) that defines how data will move on the Internet and on most other modern networks.

tether To connect a smartphone to a computer so that the computer can use the smartphone's Internet access.

texting Sending and receiving short text messages in real-time over a cell phone network.

theme A named set of formatting presets, governing font, color, and object effect choices.

theme colors The colors assigned to the color placeholders in a theme.

thermal dye transfer printer A printer that heats ribbons containing dye and then diffuses the dye onto specially coated paper.

thermal printer A printer that transfers images to paper using heat.

thermal wax transfer printer A printer that melts a wax-based ink onto paper in tiny dots.

thin client A computer with minimal hardware, designed for a specific task. For example, a thin web client is designed for using the Internet.

thin-film transistor An improved type of active matrix common in modern monitors and display screens.

title bar The bar across the top of a window that shows the window's name; you can move the window by dragging it.

toner The powdered mixture of plastic and iron used to form the image on a laser printer.

toolbar A group of graphical buttons representing commands.

top-level domain The code at the end of a URL that indicates the type of organization the name represents, such as COM for commercial businesses.

touch screen A touch-sensitive display monitor that functions both as an input and an output device.

touchpad A pointing device consisting of a touch-sensitive pad on which the user drags a finger to move the pointer.

track One of the concentric rings in a disk's organizational system.

trackball A pointing device in which the user moves the pointer by rolling a ball with his or her fingers.

transceiver A unit that provides the wireless transmission for a cordless device like keyboard or mouse, usually plugged in to a USB port.

transformer block A thick block built into a power cable for a device that handles the conversion of AC power to DC and decreases the voltage to the level needed.

triad A cluster of three phosphors: one red, one green, and one blue.

Trojan A piece of malicious software that looks harmless but has a detrimental effect on a computer when it runs.

twisted-pair cable Cable that transfers data via pairs of copper wires that are twisted around each other to reduce electromagnetic interference.

Twitter A microblogging platform used to post frequent updates and to comment on events as they happen.

uniform resource locator (URL) A string of characters that identifies the location of a resource on a website.

uninstaller utility Software that removes installed software along with its associated files and registry entries.

Universal Disc Format (UDF) An extension of the ISO 9660 file system, a file system used on optical media such as CDs and DVDs.

Universal Product Code (UPC) A bar code system used for identifying products for sale.

Universal Serial Bus (USB) A general-purpose port for connecting external devices to a PC.

unshielded twisted pair (UTP) A type of twisted-pair cable that does not have an outer sheath that protects against external EMI.

Usenet A global distributed system of servers that host public newsgroups.

utility software Software that performs some useful service to the operating system, such as optimizing or correcting the file storage system, backing up files, or ensuring security or privacy.

vector-based illustration A drawing that is constructed of mathematically created lines.

video chat Having an online conversation that includes both audio and video.

Video Graphics Adapter An analog port for connecting a monitor to a PC.

videoconferencing A means of conducting a video conversation remotely using an Internet connection and the webcam or camera on your laptop, phone, or tablet.

Vine A social network for posting and sharing video clips.

virtual folder A view that resembles a folder but has no direct equivalent in the computer's file system.

virtual machine An operating system running within another operating system.

virtual memory Memory that is simulated by swapping data out of memory and storing it temporarily on the hard drive.

virtual or onscreen keyboard A replica of a keyboard on the screen that users can tap or click to simulate typing.

virtual private networking (VPN) A method of creating a secure, private communication tunnel using a public communications channel such as the Internet.

virtualization Running a different operating system in a windowed environment within another operating system.

virus A type of malware that attaches itself to an executable file and spreads to other files when the program is run.

Voice over Internet Protocol (VoIP) A means of providing web-based telephony. The best-known example is Skype.

voice recognition software Software that recognizes spoken words that match words in its database to digitize spoken language.

volume A physical storage device, or a portion of one, that is assigned an identifying letter. Sometimes used interchangeably with *drive*, but a physical drive may actually contain multiple volumes.

warm boot To restart a computer that is already powered on.

web authoring software Software that helps create website designs and content.

web browser An application used to access websites and to retrieve or upload information. Often referred to as a **browser**.

web page A file formatted for use on the World Wide Web.

web server A server that receives requests for web page data and supplies it by sending it over the Internet.

web-based application Software that downloads to your computer and then runs within a web browser.

webcam A digital video camera that must remain connected to a computer as it operates.

what you see is what you get (WYSIWYG) A feature in an application that allows users to see their work exactly as it will be when it is distributed to others, such as in print or online.

whitelist A list of allowed email senders; also called a safe list.

wide area network (WAN) A network that spans at least two geographical locations; a business with two or more offices may have a LAN at each site but use a WAN to connect them all to the same network.

Wi-Fi Wireless Ethernet. A means of connecting computers and other devices wirelessly. Another name for it is IEEE 802.11, its technical standard.

wiki A web-based application that can be edited by anyone and that is usually informational or instructive in nature.

Wikipedia A free, online encyclopedia. Wikipedia is an example of a wiki.

window A movable rectangular block in which content appears.

Windows Phone The Windows version designed for smartphones.

Windows RT The Windows version designed for SoC tablet computers.

Windows Update A feature in Windows that automatically downloads and installs updates to Windows and optionally to some Microsoft applications.

wireframe A 3D vector drawing that consists only of drawn lines, without any surface textures applied.

wireless access point (WAP) A wireless switch.

wireless keyboard A keyboard that connects to the computer wirelessly rather than with a cable.

wireless mouse A mouse that communicates wirelessly with a transceiver connected to the computer, so it does not need a cord.

word processor A program used to create or view text-based documents.

word size The number of bits that the CPU can accept as input simultaneously.

World Wide Web (WWW) A network of interconnected pages of information stored on publicly accessible servers.

worm A malicious computer program that spreads itself to other computers over a network or the Internet.

YouTube A social network for posting and sharing videos.

zombie A computer used to conduct a DoS attack.

Zoom controls Controls at the right end of the status bar that adjust the magnification at which the data is displayed.

Index

SYMBOLS AND NUMERICS

A

B

C

F

G

H

I

N

O

P

Q

R

S

W

X

Y

Z